Why is it so hard to come out as a feminist? In this innovative deployment of feminist curiosity Penny Griffin links together the supposedly disparate realms of international political economy and popular culture, showing how they work hard to make 'anti-feminism' the new normal.

Terrell Carver, *University of Bristol, UK*

Violence and male heroes are omnipresent in popular culture. In this innovative and important new book Penny Griffin reveals how they are part of much deeper entrenched and highly problematic gender stereotypes that shape both our identities and our politics.

Roland Bleiker, *Professor of International Relations, University of Queensland*

This is a book brimming with curiosity about the intricate connections between feminism, popular culture and IPE. Griffin has taken the time to weave an accessible and lively path between the 'popular' and the 'academic'. Highly illuminating and energising.

Marysia Zalewski, *School of Social Science, University of Aberdeen, Scotland*

POPULAR CULTURE, POLITICAL ECONOMY AND THE DEATH OF FEMINISM

A number of scholars have examined the marginalization of feminist concerns in contemporary Western societies. They have articulated how representations matter to people's ideas, assumptions, perceptions and beliefs about the world, carefully connecting the world of 'make-believe' with the serious business of world politics. They have sought to understand how images and cultural constructions are connected to patterns of inequality, domination and oppression and have revealed how feminist concerns have been appropriated and absorbed by institutions that contribute to the perpetuation of gender inequalities. Some have argued that we live in a 'postfeminist' era that renders feminism irrelevant to people's contemporary lives.

This book takes 'feminism', the source of eternal debate, contestation and ambivalence, and situates the term within the popular, cultural practices of everyday life. It explores the intimate connections between the politics of feminism and the representational practices of contemporary popular culture, examining how feminism is 'made sensible' through visual imagery and popular culture representations. It investigates how popular culture is produced, represented and consumed to reproduce the conditions in which feminism is valued or dismissed, and asks whether antifeminism exists in commodity form and is commercially viable.

Written in an accessible style and analysing a broad range of popular culture artefacts (including commercial advertising, printed and digital news-related journalism and commentary, music, film, television programming, websites and social media), this book will be of use to students, researchers and practitioners of International Relations, International Political Economy and gender, cultural and media studies.

Penny Griffin is Senior Lecturer in International Relations in the School of Social Sciences, UNSW Australia.

Popular Culture and World Politics

Edited by Matt Davies (Newcastle University),
Kyle Grayson (Newcastle University),
Simon Philpott (Newcastle University),
Christina Rowley (University of Bristol), and
Jutta Weldes (University of Bristol)

The Popular Culture World Politics (PCWP) book series is the forum for leading interdisciplinary research that explores the profound and diverse interconnections between popular culture and world politics. It aims to bring further innovation, rigor, and recognition to this emerging sub-field of international relations.

To these ends, the PCWP series is interested in various themes, from the juxtaposition of cultural artefacts that are increasingly global in scope and regional, local and domestic forms of production, distribution and consumption; to the confrontations between cultural life and global political, social, and economic forces; to the new or emergent forms of politics that result from the rescaling or internationalization of popular culture.

Similarly, the series provides a venue for work that explores the effects of new technologies and new media on established practices of representation and the making of political meaning. It encourages engagement with popular culture as a means for contesting powerful narratives of particular events and political settlements as well as explorations of the ways that popular culture informs mainstream political discourse. The series promotes investigation into how popular culture contributes to changing perceptions of time, space, scale, identity, and participation while establishing the outer limits of what is popularly understood as "political" or "cultural."

In addition to film, television, literature, and art, the series actively encourages research into diverse artefacts including sound, music, food cultures, gaming, design, architecture, programming, leisure, sport, fandom and celebrity. The series is fiercely pluralist in its approaches to the study of popular culture and world politics and is interested in the past, present, and future cultural dimensions of hegemony, resistance, and power.

Gender, Violence and Popular Culture
Telling stories
Laura J. Shepherd

Aesthetic Modernism and Masculinity in Fascist Italy
John Champagne

Genre, Gender and the Effects of Neoliberalism
The new millennium Hollywood rom com
Betty Kaklamanidou

***Battlestar Galactica* and International Relations**
Edited by Iver B. Neumann and Nicholas J. Kiersey

Popular Culture, Political Economy and the Death of Feminism
Why women are in refrigerators and other stories
Penny Griffin

The Politics of HBO's *The Wire*
Everything is connected
Edited by Shirin Deylami and Jonathan Havercroft

Sexing War/Policing Gender
Motherhood, myth and women's political violence
Linda Ahall

Documenting World Politics
A critical companion to IR and non-fiction film
Edited by Rens van Munster and Casper Sylvest

POPULAR CULTURE, POLITICAL ECONOMY AND THE DEATH OF FEMINISM

Why women are in refrigerators and other stories

Penny Griffin

LONDON AND NEW YORK

First published 2015
by Routledge
2 Park Square, Milton Park, Abingdon, Oxon OX14 4RN

and by Routledge
711 Third Avenue, New York, NY 10017

Routledge is an imprint of the Taylor & Francis Group, an informa business

© 2015 Penny Griffin

The right of Penny Griffin to be identified as author of this work has been asserted by her in accordance with the Copyright, Designs and Patent
Act 1988.

All rights reserved. No part of this book may be reprinted or reproduced or utilised in any form or by any electronic, mechanical, or other means, now known or hereafter invented, including photocopying and recording, or in any information storage or retrieval system, without permission in writing from the publishers.

Trademark notice: Product or corporate names may be trademarks or registered trademarks, and are used only for identification and explanation without intent to infringe.

British Library Cataloguing in Publication Data
A catalogue record for this book is available from the British Library

Library of Congress Cataloging in Publication Data
A catalog record is available for this book

ISBN: 978-0-415-52226-7 (hbk)
ISBN: 978-0-415-71938-4 (pbk)
ISBN: 978-1-315-74053-9 (ebk)

Typeset in Bembo
by Book Now Ltd, London
Printed in Great Britain by Ashford Colour Press Ltd.

For Edie

CONTENTS

List of illustrations	*xiii*
Preface	*xv*
Series editor's preface	*xix*
Acknowledgements	*xxi*
List of abbreviations	*xxiii*

1	Introductions	1
	Background 3	
	Strategy(ies) of research 5	
	Notes 18	
2	Analysing popular culture	21
	Popular culture and the importance of visual language in studying global politics 22	
	'Culture', popular culture and (erroneous) high/low binaries 27	
	Popular culture and political economy 31	
	Commercial viability and (cultural) popularity 44	
	Notes 53	
3	Popular culture, produced, represented and consumed	55
	Production 56	
	Representation 60	
	Consumption 70	
	Notes 88	
4	Feminism(s), feminists and the (enduring) 'popularity gap'	89
	Feminist 'successes': How feminists have changed things 90	
	The (premature) burial of feminism 96	

xii Contents

Australia and 'men in blue ties' 106
The sexualization of popular culture and the recentralization of feminist concerns 109
Notes 116

5   In popular form (feminism and antifeminism in popular culture)   119
Overt antifeminism (1): Why the development of decent female movie
  characters is not encouraged 120
Overt antifeminism (2): Why women are in refrigerators 125
Overt antifeminism (3): Why games with female characters don't sell 129
Overt antifeminism (4): Why men are entitled to sex but (independent)
  female sexuality is unacceptable 132
Overt antifeminism (5): Why stupid girls are more profitable 134
Overt antifeminism (6): Why feminists can only be characterized negatively
  in popular culture 139
Tacit antifeminism (1): Why 'strong female characters' have become boring 141
Tacit antifeminism (2): Why Hollywood is not good at 'girl power' 144
Tacit antifeminism (3): Why women shouldn't read The Economist *148*
Tacit antifeminism (4): Why men's lifestyle magazines reflect sexual paranoia 151
Tacit antifeminism (5): Why the media promotes 'enlightened sexism' 154
Overt feminism (1): Young women are *interested in and* actually
  practice feminism 156
Overt feminism (2): The enduring strength(s) of liberal feminism(s) 162
Overt feminism (3): The (increasing) popularity of celebrity feminism 165
Overt feminism (4): 'Riot grrrl', sextremism and guerilla feminisms 169
Tacit feminism: Supportive but not self-professed 172
Notes 175

6   Conclusions   177
The trouble with IPE 177
Feminism, gender tropes and popular culture 178
Is antifeminism more commercially viable than feminism? 180
Note 183

Appendix A: Survey questions   185
Appendix B: Dolce and Gabbana   189
Glossary   197
Bibliography   211
Index   233

ILLUSTRATIONS

Figures

1.1	Demographics of survey respondents	14–16
2.1	Attendance at cultural venues and events, by region	30
2.2	Advertisement on Facebook	50
2.3	Author's Facebook newsfeed, 8:14am, October 2013	50
2.4	'Airbag by Porsche'	51
2.5	'Sydney Riders' Facebook Page, 17 July 2013	52
3.1	*Newsweek* cover, 23 November 2009	69
3.2	Average hours per week spent consuming media by online Australians aged 16 and over, 2007–10	75
3.3	'How to Synergize'	85
3.4	Advertisement for Cif Cream cleaner	86
4.1	'The Big Feminist But'	105
4.2	Mouse pad with wrist support	116
5.1	Searches related to 'feminists are' at www.google.com.au	140
5.2	'Rush Vs Feminism'	141
5.3	*The Economist*, slip-cover	149
5.4	'What is Feminism?'	162
5.5	Examples of guerrilla feminism	171
6.1	The Facebook page of *Zoo Weekly* magazine (Australia), 2012	182
B.1	D&G *Esquire* campaign images	191
B.2	D&G 'knives' campaign images	192
B.3	D&G 'objectifying men' campaign images	194

xiv Illustrations

Tables

4.1	Do you think women face more or less pressure over their behaviour and appearance than they did 20 years ago?	108
5.1	*The Dark Knight* trilogy	127
5.2	Survey Question 16, 'Feminism is Accessible to Young Women in the 21st Century' (age)	158
5.3	Survey Question 16, 'Feminism is Accessible to Young Women in the 21st Century' (education)	159

Boxes

3.1	How do adverts get made?	86
5.1	'My Feminism'	163

PREFACE

In 2009, as I began writing this book, I was struck that, in popular terms, feminism appeared very much in decline, its actual popularity seemingly at odds with conservative critiques that chastised it for its lingering and baneful power. At this point, it seemed that the status of feminism and the increasing sexualization of popular culture in Western societies more generally were related, and related inversely. Sexually explicit content and demeaning representations abounded, yet feminism seemed submerged by popular rhetoric and representations that questioned its relevance and obscured its incisiveness. Feminists appeared on television, when they appeared on television, as shrieking harpies devoid of humour, even across cultural sources I otherwise admired and enjoyed. If feminism was suffering from an image problem, how, I wondered, had the representational practices embedded in our everyday cultural lives come to constitute and shape feminism and our responses to it? Were cultures of production and consumption in the West contributing to derogatory attitudes to women and, particularly, to feminism? To what extent were negative representations of the women's movement in the popular media depoliticizing feminism as a form of collective politics in a world where young women were being taught that discrimination had been eliminated and individual efforts, self-definition and choice were key to women's advancement? Why was sexism so prevalent across popular culture? Why could popular culture produce at best only uninspiring, and uninspired, representations of women, while sexism was *all* that consumer culture seemed to be selling?

Like feminists such as McRobbie, Whelehan and Levy, I was convinced that popular culture was indeed reproducing the conditions in which feminism was being dismissed and the sexualization of market products valorized. I found myself irritated, as I started this book, that a leading fashion house would be patronizing enough to claim that the images it used to sell its products were not 'real life' and that, as 'artists', well known and widely publicized designers had no social

xvi Preface

responsibility (see Appendix B). During days spent teaching, it seemed that I only ever encountered students who insisted that they were not 'feminist', although, yes, they supported the projects espoused and achievements gained by the feminist movement and, no, they did not much care for the idea that they would earn more or less as graduates depending on their sex. When I began this book, I felt despondent; for the prospects of feminism in Australia, and for a future teaching apparently uninterested, desensitized, neoliberalized youth. Feminism did, indeed, appear 'undone' in the contemporary West, dismissible and irrelevant to young women's (and men's) lives and incompatible with a cultural landscape in which the sexualization of market products and objectification of the human body was valued above all else.

This book began, then, as a catalogue of sorts of the prevalence of discrimination, sexual violence, prejudice and asymmetry in the relations of power and authority that drive popular culture representations of women, men and children. Although I have long noted sexist and discriminatory practice across sources of popular culture (such as television, the internet, movies, music, books, and so on), it has only been relatively recently that I have come fully to appreciate the various levels of hostility generated by the 'f' word, both academically and across sites of popular practice. Some of the most vitriolic comments on feminism (and feminists), made so readily available now through the internet, have truly shocked, disgusted and disturbed me. I do not repeat the most profane in the pages that follow out of the fear that to reinscribe them is somehow to justify their presence.

When, in October 2012, Julia Gillard gave her now famous, if obviously crafted, 'misogyny' speech, and it seemed that, actually, not that many Australians were jeering, I was, then, quite surprised. This was not because women in Australia have not experienced sexism and would therefore not be encouraged by anything Gillard said in this regard, since Australia is undoubtedly sexist, and quite horribly so in some ways. I was surprised because I had begun to expect only disdain and sarcasm at the mention of feminism. I was well versed in student disinterest and celebrity denials ('I'm a humanist, not a feminist'), but, and it seemed almost sudden this change although on reflection it cannot have come from nowhere, people began publicly to admit that they might identify with the f word. Even my students started expressing an unprovoked (or possibly slightly provoked by me, but not consciously) interest in gender issues.

While my research has taught me that support for feminism appears cyclical, and thus potentially unstable, from something of an itinerary of failure, this book has evolved into a far more optimistic labour. This has surprised me. I have been even more surprised to find that there is little actual evidence (anecdotal or survey-based) to support any claim that young women, today, are less likely to support feminism or the women's movement than previous generations. Where only a couple of years ago I would likely have argued that young women were not as concerned with feminism as past generations, and that the, now rather clichéd, 'I'm not a feminist, but . . .' refrain was undoing feminism among my student cohort, examining in greater depth popular engagements with feminism has taught me that people are rarely as naïve in their appreciations of relations of power as I might once have worried. Positive representations certainly jostle for space with disappointing caricatures and unflattering stereotypes, but, for every derogatory portrayal of girls, women, feminism or feminists, a genuine and affirming engagement emerges to lift the spirits. What I have found that seems more significant to feminism's future, today, is that young women learn, unsurprisingly perhaps, to fear and reject negative media representations of feminism and the women's movement. Such representations need only be relatively common: the power of stereotype threat and the considerable complexity in what women say about feminism is such that better attention is probably paid to considering feminist practice rather than what (young) women say about feminism, per se. While popular culture represents feminism, and feminists, in various and ambiguous ways, the contradictions involved in understanding contemporary popular culture's representational practices make conclusive statements on feminism's future impossible.

This research has invariably found it easier to uncover examples of antifeminism, both tacit and overt, filtered through multiple popular culture channels, than examples of patent support for feminism. Yet such examples are rarely enough to support definitively any claim that feminism is 'in decline'. Rather, writing this book has taught me that the so-called 'death of feminism' is entirely irrelevant to understanding either the complexity of social relations in capitalist, liberal societies such as Australia, or the significance of feminist imaginings within popular culture and popular culture imaginings of feminism. The important question today is not 'where has feminism gone?' but 'where is feminism embodied?' and the answer to this, I suggest, lies in understanding feminism as simultaneously vibrant and fragmented. It is this that makes feminism both vulnerable and enduring. While feminism's very fragmentation is ambivalent, rendering feminism incomplete to some and vital to others, to argue that feminism has many and various definitions, to different people, is not to vacate feminism of meaning; it is not, as per Kalb's analysis, to argue that the meaning of feminism is so scattered that, really, feminism means nothing at all. Often stigmatized and, sometimes, celebrated, however many times popular media have heralded, and will continue to herald, the death of feminism, feminism continues to relate in multiple ways to the different challenges people pose to sexist, hierarchical and restrictive practices, structures and institutions. People arrive at feminism, or they do not, for all sorts of reasons. Refusing to police the boundaries of the political and defining feminism according to its multiplicity constitutes part of the strength, not the weakness, of our engagements with the term.

I did not know, when I began this book, that I would fall pregnant and would have a baby girl. While the discriminatory and derogatory possibilities that my daughter will face alarm me, I am also, however, more confident than I once was that alternative possibilities exist and will be available to her. I comfort myself with the knowledge that, empirically, feminist leanings have been linked to self-esteem, self-efficacy, gender perceptiveness and academic achievement and I hope that she

xviii Preface

learns as much from feminist practice as I have. Writing this book, I have learned (unconsciously, perhaps) to be less horrified by the shock tactics deployed by antifeminists, to expend much less emotional energy on the detractors and the hate speech, to feel sorry for the people that spend their time writing vitriolic nonsense and to be encouraged by those that seek to be a little different. Writing this book, I have been surprised by the diversity and prevalence of feminist messages across popular culture sites and I am, now, more sanguine about feminism's future, and more confident in the options my daughter will face as she grows up.

I am biased, of course, because I have always been inspired by feminist work. It has been feminist scholarship that has proved most instructive across my experiences of adult learning, from early engagements with Julia Kristeva and Simone de Beauvoir, to my current work on gender and the global political economy. I never felt as an undergraduate student that feminism might be considered a marginal, embarrassing even, subject area or mode of enquiry, a (now I discover) slightly unusual state of being that I perhaps owe to exceptional pedagogy during my studies. Feminists have, for me, always been the most astute commentators on social life, privilege, power and the production of (discriminatory) common sense. I have never really understood how people can claim to have made sense of the world, social relations or foreign affairs without thinking about the gendered restraints by which people everywhere are shackled.

Arguing that we ignore the significance of visual language in global politics at our peril, this book makes a case for centralizing analysis of popular culture in studies of international relations and political economy. Asking whether popular culture is contributing to a dismissal of feminism is a question worth thinking about because, more than simply being interesting, it is a question of the politics of power and the circulation (and regulation) of knowledge, exclusion and appropriate behaviour. Representations matter and the representational practices of contemporary popular culture help define our codes of conduct and horizons of possibility. While mainstream (conventional) International Relations and Political Economy frequently offer a picture of the world as a sequence of isolated events unrelated to everyday practices of social and cultural reproduction, this book instead proceeds on the assumption that we cannot understand the processes and forms of our social, economic and political activity without engaging the properties, biases and effects of the cultural systems in which we are located and that make 'real life' possible. Images and cultural constructions are intimately connected to patterns of inequality, domination and oppression: to understand their power is to begin to unravel the exclusive and discriminatory hierarchies that sustain them.

SERIES EDITOR'S PREFACE

Within international political economy, there has been a longstanding concern with examining the dynamics that conjoin popular culture and world politics. The focus has often been on how popular culture serves as a vehicle for the dissemination of dominant ideologies and/or how the structures of capitalism determine cultural forms. Thus, representations within artefacts themselves were understood as derivative of deeper underlying socio-economic structures. Popular culture simply reflected some other politics that was situated in some other place.

In this volume, Penny Griffin takes a different approach. She uses popular culture as a means of analysing contemporary feminisms from a perspective informed by international political economy. Her goal is to understand an important contemporary political paradox: how is it possible that as popular culture has become more overtly sexualisFed, popular rhetoric and representations have questioned the contemporary relevance of feminisms, portraying them as anachronistic vestiges from a bygone era of gender inequality that has passed? From this paradox, the analysis seeks to understand how cultural production is gendered so that particular understandings, meanings, and subjectivities that are hostile to feminisms emerge and circulate. The aim then is not to provide readings of popular culture that are read through feminisms but rather to see what popular culture tells us about contemporary feminisms, the politics of gender, and cultural political economy. Thus, throughout the book, we are confronted with the representational practices of popular culture that have made anti-feminisms more appealing, acceptable, and marketable for cultural producers and consumers. And we are introduced to new political subjectivities like the 'feminazi' and 'straw feminist' that emerge from these processes.

Griffin's focus is primarily on visual culture with an emphasis on those quotidian aspects that can be easily overlooked despite their ubiquity: advertizing, digital ephemera, and social media. But where the analysis becomes particularly innovative

xx Series editor's preface

is in its pursuit of the commercial logics underpinning their production. And what her analysis makes clear is that in the current historical period, market discourses and sexist discourses reinforce one another; producers point to the existence of objective market forces to justify decisions that contribute to the subordination of women while proponents of anti-feminism note that the popularity of sexist forms of representation demonstrates their broader acceptance. After all, as empirical work in the book demonstrates, often the most overt forms of misogynist sexualization are publicly justified on the basis of variants of the 'we're just having a laugh' defence. Thus, the book provides new insight into the politics of 'taste' and raises a troubling set of questions about the mores of neoliberalism.

By taking feminisms, political economy and popular culture seriously while also challenging traditional understandings of the spaces, processes, and relationships that produce them, Griffin makes a significant contribution to the study of popular culture and world politics. What this volume shares with others in this series is the firm conviction that popular culture matters politically. While it may be entertaining (and therein lies part of its appeal), if we are interested in how power and production contribute to forms of inequality – as well as forms of resistance to them – that are infused across the micro, meso, and macro levels of world politics, we must take popular culture seriously. This necessarily requires moving beyond an accounting of the allegorical properties of artefacts that can be mapped onto our preconceived notions of what world politics 'is'. Being serious means seeking to analyse how the popular culture-world politics continuum itself produces popular culture through practices of world politics and world politics through the practices of popular culture. In doing so, it is also a call to problematize the dividing lines that are assumed practically and analytically in contemporary IR scholarship between disciplines, locations of politics, methodological approaches, structure/agency, and production/consumption. In embracing the challenges of taking popular culture seriously and challenging arbitrary boundaries along the way, this volume is emblematic of the ethos of the series to better understand the relations of power that are productive of the popular, cultures, worlds, and their politics. Thus, for this reader, Griffin does partake in the forging of an international political economy more attentive to popular culture and more engaged with the ways in which markets, identities, and culture produce the relations of power that shape the private and public spaces of politics.

Kyle Grayson
March 2015

ACKNOWLEDGEMENTS

Many people have enabled and encouraged this research, which began in response to the questions raised at the Popular Culture and World Politics conference, at the University of Bristol in July 2009. I am particularly indebted to Christina Rowley and Jutta Weldes for supporting the initial development of this research and, especially, for having the unwavering faith that it would take shape as a monograph. I would like to thank all the Popular Culture and World Politics Series Editors' and editorial staff at Routledge, not least Kyle Grayson, Nicola Parkin and Peter Harris, who have each been unflappably cheery throughout the (somewhat extended) writing process.

Thanks are due to the Faculty of Arts and Social Sciences and the School of Social Sciences at the University of New South Wales for their financial and individual support of the research required to complete this project. I will be forever grateful to Ian Zucker, Julian Trofimovs and Charles Gregory for their enthusiasm, care and industry as research assistants. Conversations at the 2009 (BISA) IPEG conference at the University of York and with staff and students at the School of Political Science and International Studies, University of Queensland, in October 2012, were a great spur in the process of writing up this research. Thank you to all who attended, to Heloise Weber for inviting me and, especially, to Kath Gelber.

Many people completed an extended survey from which this research draws and to which it refers. Their time, attention and careful comments were inspiring and provoking. Thank you.

This book relies on various examples of popular culture sources and artefacts. Many of these are in the public domain but thanks are due to those who have granted permission for their images and work to be used here.

xxii Acknowledgements

On a personal note, I would particularly like to thank Jo Skinner for patiently listening to my various anxieties over this project for at least two years (and introducing me to 'Feminist Ryan Gosling', who holds a particularly dear place in my heart), Laura Shepherd for her constancy and kindness, Adam Thompson for his (eternal) enthusiasm and positivity, and for always being certain of me, even when I really was not, and, last but not least, Edie Isabelle Thompson, for waiting until I had sent this manuscript to the publishers before making her world debut.

ABBREVIATIONS

ABS	Australian Bureau of Statistics
ALP	Australian Labor Party
ASA	(British) Advertising Standards Authority
BBC	British Broadcasting Corporation
CBS	Columbia Broadcasting System (an American commercial broadcast television network)
CEDAW	United Nations Convention to Eliminate Discrimination Against Women
D&G	Dolce and Gabbana
EU	European Union
GPG	Gender pay gap
ICC	International Criminal Court
IMDb	The Internet Movie Database
IPE	International Political Economy
IR	International Relations
MPAA	Motion Picture Association of America
MRW	Media Report to Women
NGO	Non-governmental organization
OECD	Organisation for Economic Cooperation and Development
PC	Personal computer
UK	United Kingdom
UN	United Nations
UN-Habitat	United Nations Human Settlement Programme
US, USA	United States of America
WEF	World Economic Forum

Source: *The Hoopla* (2013)

1

INTRODUCTIONS

The use of sexual, sexually derogatory and sexually violent imagery across Western popular culture does not appear to be waning. Network-television crime dramas arrange silent female corpses across our screens while social media users are invited to consider cosmetic surgery on every Facebook page they open. Hollywood continues to produce movies in which women are noteworthy celluloid presences only for the speed with which they can undress, receive violence or await rescue. Advertising campaigns in fashion magazines glamorize gang rape, but fashion designers protest that those (feminists and others) who complain fail to see the point that fashion is about aesthetics. Aesthetically butchering women is, it seems, quite desirable.

This book explores the intimate connections between representation, the politics of feminism and the cultural practices of modern, Western, consumer society. It explores feminism 'made sensible' through visual imagery and popular culture representations, examining feminism's popular and commercial value. It investigates how popular culture is produced, represented and consumed to reproduce the conditions in which feminism is valued or dismissed. It asks where and how the sexualization of cultural products is maintained and to what effects. It asks, finally, whether sufficient evidence can be marshalled to argue that antifeminism exists in commodity form and is commercially viable.

This book argues, as many scholars have done, that representations matter. There are no 'facts' that speak for themselves, nor 'objects' that exist apart from (that is, separate to) our knowledge of them. 'Material objects' constitute reality only through our knowledge of them, and this is necessarily partial, contingent and fluctuating. This means also that our 'knowledge' of the world organizes us, and not that we are necessarily in control of it. We do not just learn to speak, 'we learn to construct utterances' and we learn more than language, we learn the system, which speaks through us (Bakhtin 2004, quoted in Griffin 2009: 28). Popular

2 Introductions

culture offers us pictures, stories, fantasies and imaginings about the world, and we recognize and respond to these strongly because they create *meaning* for us. If what exists in the world is made real to us only by virtue of our knowledge of it, and if we possess 'knowledge' only partially and inconsistently, according to the political, social, economic and cultural discourses in which we are located and that are available to us, it would be naïve, I think, to dismiss the power that popular culture, and thus storytelling, bring to our knowledge of the world. This book is based on the assumption that the processes and practices of Western popular culture are, as Weldes articulates, intricate and extensive and help 'to create and sustain the conditions for contemporary world politics' (2003: 6). The representative practices of contemporary popular culture are more than simply an aside to feminism's waning or ascending influence, they have come to constitute and shape feminism and our responses to feminism.

When I began the research for this book, it seemed to me that the status of feminism in Western societies and the increasing sexualization of popular culture in Western societies more generally were related, and related inversely. Sexually explicit content and demeaning representations abounded, yet feminism appeared submerged by popular rhetoric and representations that questioned its relevance and obscured its incisiveness. Feminists appeared on television, when they appeared on television, as shrieking harpies devoid of humour, even across sources I otherwise admired and enjoyed. Tina Fey and Amy Poehler had not yet made feminism on TV 'acceptable' and any criticism of a male public figure behaving like a lecherous old pervert was immediately decried as conspiracy. Thus I wanted to know why sexism was so prevalent across popular culture, since it seemed to me as if popular culture could reproduce at best only uninspiring, and uninspired, representations of women, while sexism was *all* that consumer culture was selling. I wondered if, in the West at least, antifeminism was more viable in popular and commercial form than feminism and whether there were in fact links to be made between the development and maintenance of commercialized antifeminism and the sexualization of popular culture artefacts. Like feminists such as McRobbie, Whelehan and Levy, I was convinced that popular culture was indeed reproducing the conditions in which feminism was being dismissed and the sexualization of market products valorized.

McRobbie argues that feminist work is often dismissed as irrelevant to people's contemporary lives, particularly the lives of young women, and that antifeminism is channelled routinely in and through the popular to disseminate aggressively 'modern' ideas about women 'so as to ensure that a new women's movement will not re-emerge' (2009: 1). Despite initially being convinced of this, I wanted with this book to fashion an enquiry into popular culture and feminism that took seriously that there were other possibilities. I was reluctant to simply assume that there is a case for arguing that feminism is being dismissed in and through popular culture. I designed this book, then, to investigate the relationship between feminism and popular culture without (hopefully) starting from my unproven assumption in 2009 that popular culture and feminism are antithetical.

Rather, I use this book to ask how the representative practices found in popular culture that have come to constitute and shape feminism (and our responses to feminism) might, or might not, make antifeminism a more appealing option, both for cultural producers and consumers.

To answer this question, however, I have found it increasingly important to expand my ideas about 'feminism'. As a category subjectively created and sustained across cultural sites, negotiating feminism (as it is understood and practised) has proved a much more challenging prospect than I anticipated. Feminisms and antifeminisms are sometimes overtly identifiable and sometimes far more tacitly located, contradictory and difficult to describe within and across popular culture. This book represents an effort to identify and categorize feminism as it is created and sustained in the popular, but such an endeavour will always be constrained by the limitlessness of popular imaginings. Whether the representations deployed by contemporary capitalist societies relate to any definable erosion of political engagement, activism and support for feminism is exceedingly difficult to ascertain. Scholars, such as McRobbie, have argued that 'postfeminism' represents the 'rewarding' of young women, with the promise of freedom and independence, for abandoning feminism, yet the 'truth' of this argument depends in large part on knowing exactly (and being able to assert) what 'activism' means today to young people, what young women actually think about feminist ideas and how feminism is perceived. The production of such knowledge is entirely fraught with peril. What diverse groups and generations believe to be and define as activism and feminism might not be recognizably activist or feminist to other groups, people or generations. Whether this is celebrated or dismissed involves judgements and claims to authenticity that are highly problematic.

Background

I found, like Shepherd, and as she so evocatively conveys in *Gender, Violence and Popular Culture: Telling Stories* (2013), that this book was easy to research but difficult to write. Finding sources to support analysis of popular culture artefacts and interpreting the artefacts themselves were 'relatively straightforward tasks to undertake' (ibid.: 2). Yet actually convincing oneself that the writing should be done (in the sense that the writing *mattered*) was much harder. My feminism is an intimate and constituent part of me, formed in waves of excitement for various literary, cultural and political theories. My earliest experiences of feminism were formed both within the academic *and* the popular (one might think that endless deconstructions of *Moderato Cantabile, Güten Morgen, Die Schöne, Fight Club* or *Boys Don't Cry* would kill my love of popular culture sources, but no) and I have rarely separated my feminism from my experiences of popular culture. This, for me, is what made this research so important, and yet so impossible to describe in a wider, 'so what?', 'who cares?' sense. The point that has always made this book so important, personally, for me, and so difficult to come to terms with, is that feminism is not an objective category and cannot be written about as if it is. Just

4 Introductions

as my feminism was formed entirely from the specifics of my own, subjective, experiences of reading, listening and watching, so the feminisms of others develop and coalesce around the wider world of their various experiences. Feminism is very much about the promulgation of certain principles, ideas and assumptions, and yet there is no uniform project and no 'authentic' feminism.

In terms of where my research comes from, I define myself as a scholar of International Political Economy (IPE), which some argue is a sub-discipline of International Relations (IR), while others assert exists as a discipline in its own right (I shall not attempt to negotiate this debate here). IR has frequently (and rather consistently) offered a picture of the world as a sequence of isolated events unrelated to everyday practices of social and cultural reproduction. Yet, if IR has struggled to take (frivolous and insubstantial) popular culture seriously (Weldes 2003: 4–5), IPE has not even got close. Popular culture is, in all its dimensions, a core part of the global political economy, its successful globalization, the enduringness of its corporate capitalist content, its legitimations, dominant narratives, practices, and sources of support and subversion, and yet IPE scholarship rarely considers it a worthy subject of analysis in and of itself.

It is thus a large hope of this book to generate an IPE that is more attentive to popular culture. This book argues that IR and IPE scholars need desperately to do more than investigate a variety of texts, sites and performances of meaning, they need, as Rowley notes, to put on their gendered lenses to see how world politics really works (2009: 322). I proceed here on the assumption that we cannot understand the processes and forms of our economic activity without being fully aware of the socio-cultural properties, biases and effects of the structures that govern us. Understanding the representational practices of contemporary popular culture requires a particular form of insight into world politics not elsewhere available and requires that we 'employ the full register of human perception and intelligence', both to understand 'the phenomena of world politics' and, then, to engage with 'the dilemmas that emanate from them' (Bleiker 2001: 519). Crucially, popular visual language is 'increasingly circulated through wireless networks onto the digital screens of our daily lives (computers, telephones, and televisions)', is experienced 'as much if not more by amateurs than it is by experts' and 'is increasingly the language that amateurs and experts rely upon in order to claim contemporary literacy' (Weber 2008: 137–8).

As Bleiker notes, many social scientists remain sceptical about approaches 'whose nature and understanding of evidence do not correspond to established scientific criteria' (2009: 44). Boundaries are, however, what have kept feminist international relations in place (Zalewski 2013: 127). Boundaries, though they offer comfort, exist to be violated. Cultural theorists have often discussed political economy in their considerations of culture and identity, but political economists (in their incarnation as a discipline in IPE, at least) have not often ruminated on the world of popular culture. I cannot say for certain that many IPE scholars would care what the relationship was between feminism, popular culture and political economy. The possibility that popular culture might undo some of IPE's

Introductions **5**

constructions of 'legitimate' knowledge remains, however, too tantalizing a prospect to ignore.

Strategy(ies) of research

As a political economist, my focus is often on showing how questions of economics are relevant to finding answers to problems that, superficially, appear unrelated to economics. These are not questions that mainstream economists would necessarily ask or be interested in and my concern is not to promote economism and economic determinism in analysing social life.[1] I do not suggest that there is a predetermined economic base to society, reproduced through a fixed mode of production. Where I look for the economics in questions that might not seem economically motivated, I try simply to find where we might ask questions about how, for example, the economic choices people face constrain their life chances, or how certain economic discourses reward particular behaviours that only a privileged few bodies have the resources to embody. The theoretical framework that underpins this research is relatively mixed, and this book draws from feminist theory, poststructural discourse analysis, cultural and communications studies, IR and IPE enquiry. As far as I know, there has been no sustained IPE scholarship that has, as yet, centred on the importance of analysing the meanings circulating in and though popular culture in order to answer questions relevant both to political economy and analysis of social life more generally.

As a feminist analysis of popular culture, this book takes seriously that feminism is important in and to understanding contemporary social life and the politics of social identity. By looking for representations of feminism in popular culture, this book, however, heeds Hollows and Moseley's advice to examine feminism *in* popular culture (rather than, say, as a political project standing outside popular culture and passing judgement on popular culture). Feminism here, therefore, is taken to be something shaped and understood through the popular. This book does not assume that there exists a 'real' or 'authentic' feminism somewhere outside popular culture, offering 'a position from which to judge and measure feminism's success or failure in making it into the mainstream' (Hollows and Moseley 2006: 1). As such, this book is less an examination of what feminism, or the feminist, can tell us about popular culture, than one of what popular culture can tell us about feminism (ibid.).

Feminist analyses of the media have so far, as Gill articulates, been drawn primarily from five key approaches. First, feminist approaches have examined representations and textual practices in some detail. They have, second, emphasized the active, creative negotiations that audiences make with their texts. Third, they have sometimes foregrounded the 'pleasures' offered by the media or, fourth, foregrounded the ideological impact of the media. Lastly, they have sought to go 'behind-the-scenes' and examine the production of particular media or the political economy of media industries. Feminist analyses of the media have, in particular, 'been animated by the desire to understand how images and cultural

6 Introductions

constructions are connected to patterns of inequality, domination and oppression' (Gill 2007: 7).

This book deploys a combination, of sorts, of some of these approaches, examining in detail examples of contemporary popular culture, including particular cultural products, representations and textual practices, their constitution, symbolism and impact (through and on an active audience) and of the media that (re)produce them. Through the survey, research here also examines audience experiences of and opinions around popular culture. To a certain extent, this book seeks to go 'behind-the-scenes' to investigate the political economy of contemporary popular culture industries, asking questions about the gendered nature of cultural production to sustain a critical investigation of the processes through which cultural industries and their products create and sustain prevailing ideas, subjectivities, representations and meanings.

In terms of understanding the *ideological impact* of the media, as a discourse analyst and poststructuralist, I understand the impact of the media less in ideological terms than through an understanding of the discursive relationship between gendered meaning, representation and authority in human encounters with cultural industries and their products. These industries (producing commodities that include commercial advertising, printed media, news-related journalism and commentary, film, television and radio programming) are central to Western commercial success and are thus highly significant in and to the contemporary global political economy. I do not suggest, however, that we should necessarily choose to understand these industries in ideological form. I take Storey's point that ideologies are discursive constructs that 'attempt to impose closure on meaning in the interests of power' and 'to make what is cultural (i.e. made) appear as nature' (2003: x). As such, they may produce, express and legitimate, at certain points in time, particular ideas and suppositions that may be defined as sexist, or racist, for example. Sexist and racist ideologies are, however, the products of wider social discourses, structures and practices and their coherence and apparent uniformity must be investigated and not assumed. Discursive structures and practices, as human products, are subject to change and renegotiation and will necessarily vary over time. The intonations, syntaxes and images they deploy are creative of many aspects of meaning and tell various stories about contemporary social life. They might, for example, provide the particular discursive parameters through which cultural products repudiate feminism. Or they may enable people to articulate responses to cultural products that exhibit a particular care to hold on to feminist categories and arguments.

Discourse, power and popular culture

Although methodologically, this work is closest to deconstructive, poststructuralist accounts of politics and, in particular, global politics, I share Derrida's scepticism of describing deconstruction as either a 'method' or 'tool' of analysis. Derrida himself was careful to reject the claims to objectivity, certainty, accuracy and truth

Introductions **7**

that characterize traditional approaches to human behaviour (or international affairs, state action, organizational process, etc.) (Griffin 2013a: 208–9). Derrida saw no separation in 'text' (which he defined broadly) and exterior application of method, advocating, rather, that deconstruction be considered always internal to the text (ibid.). Deconstruction, for Derrida, was less a method than a 'critical sharpness' applied to contextualizing, historicizing and seeking out the ambiguities and ambivalences in a given source.

> The point, for a deconstructive approach, is that the text always carries within itself its own undoing: the task of the analyst is simply to highlight the incoherencies, inconsistencies and problematic assumptions the text has otherwise rendered indiscernible. Thus, it might be more in keeping with Derrida's own thinking to see deconstruction as a form of critical sharpness rather than a method in and of itself.
>
> (Griffin 2013a: 209)

As Carver argues, the methodology of the discourse analyst is inherently internal to the world of political contingency and conceptualization: the discourse analyst is unlikely to claim any kind of position of objectivity and neutrality (the territory of scientific and empiricist philosophies) and they are unlikely to detail the descriptive case and offer causal rationalizations for it. Instead, they are far more likely 'to situate themselves politically, and to tell you contingently and conceptually where they think the power-relations are and how they are deployed' (Carver 2002: 51).

With this is mind, Andersen's conclusion that the 'method' of the discourse analyst is actually more of an 'analytical strategy' is pertinent (2003: xiv). As Andersen points out, discourse 'methodology' is less concerned with the observation of 'objects', but with observation of 'observations as observations' (ibid.: xii). Discourse analysis presents the reader with a theoretical framework based upon *interpretation*. Interpretive methodologies 'remind practitioners that social science is conducted through the medium of *language*, and that language is not a transparent "window" on "fact"' (Carver and Hyvärinen 1997: 2. Emphasis added). The driving force of my research does indeed lie in an analysis of language, which is argued to structure human relations at every level, but 'language' here should be broadly understood: verbal and visual, language might also be the language of behaviour, practice and institution, or the language of power and social pressures that forces the internal functioning of relationships, that is, people's personal drive, obedience, creativity and understanding.

As Shapiro (1986) contends, all research employs grammatical, rhetorical and narrative structures that bestow meaning, create value and constitute knowledge, intentionally or not. 'Raw data' never speaks for itself and meaning is applied, never implicit (although some forms of research seek to conceal their own political agendas by professing objectivity). As a researcher, I 'see' things in popular culture because of my history, context, training and personal tastes and I miss things for the same reasons. I ask questions, for example, about sexism, economy

8 Introductions

and sexuality, where I might miss important questions about race, disability or security, for example. I am thankful that both feminists and poststructuralists are more forgiving of the limitations of an individual's research agenda, since both these traditions are more likely to combine a sense of reflexivity with the knowledge that we are all bounded beings (in the sense that we live amidst multiple and various structural limitations). Deconstructing gendered relations of power does not, of course, tell us anything necessarily about the cultural and disciplinary racisms that discipline bodies and minds, but a project sensitive to the relations of power that enable certain behaviours, assumptions and representations to appear to gain mastery over reality opens possibilities for considering widely the constitution and effects of dominant, heteronormative, discursive structures. Discriminations rarely fit neatly into easily labelled boxes ('race', 'disability', 'gender', 'sexuality', and so on) and the intersectionality of 'isms' should be on the mind of all careful, committed and reflexive discourse analysts.

'Discourse', in this book, denotes a system of signification (meaning) infused by power as both productive and repressive. Beyond simply language, discourses are powerful purveyors of meaning, social practice and social reality: they 'are social configurations of political space, including at their core not only languages but material conditions and effects, institutions, texts (visual and written), imparted wisdoms, linguistic and cultural contexts, ideologies, processes of social production and reproduction, interactions and relationships' (Griffin 2009: 24). Dominant discourses provide the limits of intelligibility to our practices and knowledges, by, for example, configuring and prescribing human identity through certain sexuality and gender binaries, or successful economic behaviour according to stories about capitalist ingenuity, technological innovation and human progress through economic growth. Discourses are sign systems, systems of meaning-making, and they configure social, political, cultural and economic spaces. 'Bodies' in discourse (organic and inorganic, textual, visual, material and immaterial) exist as 'objects' of discourse and are surfaces and scenes of discursive inscription and although discourses exude language, they are more than language alone.

As a discourse analyst and employer of poststructural 'discourse theory', I analyse political life in terms of discourse, which means that my work understands 'power' as more complex and diffuse than a question of something having power over something else. The power of a photographic image, for example, is understood in this book less in terms of the extent of broadcasters' efforts to 'get their message across', than the ways in which the image produces meaning, and the effects of this. Images in popular culture are not dependent upon their makers: their importance lies in the effects they produce, the relationships that they create between representations of reality and our experiences of it. How we make sense of the world, and our ability to act within it, is regulated both overtly and tacitly, through institutions and mechanisms of governance, but also the formal and informal rules and conventions of our cultures, the patterns of authority and influence at play in any given form of communication and the social relations in which our cultural rules 'work'.

Introductions **9**

The world is much more than simply as we find it, and the structures and practices that mediate our realities, our knowledges and our experiences condition us through multiple channels. As Weldes describes, of course some of the power that defines and sustains world politics resides at a level far out of the reach of most, in what has been labelled the realm of 'high politics', or the arena of diplomacy, (inter)national security, war and peace (2003: 5). 'High politics' is not separate in any sense from the 'low' politics of, for example, gender, race, class and culture, and it is the mundane practices of the classroom, our family and working lives, bedroom politics, and so on, that constitute our exclusion from and ability to know and act in certain arenas. The artificial boundaries between 'high' and 'low' are discursively (and powerfully) useful when the public are to be kept out of 'official' decision-making processes, but the constitution of these boundaries is both contingent, on dominant forms of 'common sense' at any given time, and contestable and they remain permeable.

We might consider, for example, their permeability in relation to the ways in which official discourses draw upon popular culture sources to make plausible their representations. Tony Blair's now-cringeworthy (and much mocked) 1997 'Cool Britannia' reception at Downing Street, attended by Oasis guitarist Noel Gallagher, and Blair's other appearances with Britpop illuminati were, at the time, both a fuel to his popularity and considered symbolic of his closeness to 'normal'. Similarly, US President Obama has made frequent recourse to popular culture sources to sediment his authenticity as a 'man of the people', claiming to catch up on TV shows like *Mad Men* and *Homeland* as he flies to Afghanistan on Air Force One (CBS News 2012), engaging in witty putdowns of Zach Galifianakis on YouTube and, with his wife Michelle, making a combined 195 television and movie appearances since 2004, according to the Internet Movie Database (IMDB) (Rothman 2012).[2]

We might also consider the ways in which the permeability of the high/low political binary works to constitute sources of popular culture as credibly accurate in their representations. Trademark applications, for example, received by the US Patent and Trademark Office increased dramatically for exclusive use of the term 'shock and awe' following the 2003 US invasion of Iraq. The same term is also the tenth campaign mission in the video game *Call of Duty 4: Modern Warfare*. Increasingly not even those in the arena of 'high politics' are naïve enough to assume that their legitimacy is not sustained in the realm of the low.

(Mainstream) popular culture has often, as Shapiro has argued, tended to reinforce prevailing power structures 'by helping to reproduce the beliefs and allegiances necessary for their uncontested functioning' (1992: 1), but resistant forms of popular culture do frequently and subversively contradict convention and orthodoxy through more complicated narrative discourses. The modern culture industry is variegated and we can no longer assume (as per Adorno and Horkheimer's (1999) famous thesis) that popular culture only works conservatively and in the interests of those in power to produce safe, standardized products geared to the larger demands of the capitalist economy (Milestone and Meyer

10 Introductions

2012: 5). The codes and representations deployed in popular culture will most likely be contested and, as Hall has described, 'contradictory forms of 'common sense'' take root in and help shape popular life and culture (1986: 26).

Gender and popular culture

The stories that popular culture tells us and the images through and with which popular culture artefacts represent their narratives work in several, powerful, ways, including our vicarious experience of them and their role as fantasy:

> When we watch a story, we relate emotionally to the goals and obstacles of the main character. We temporarily give up our own subjecthoods to live the story through the point of view of the protagonist, who we relate to. Conversely, we also take pleasure in seeing particular circumstances played out, separate from ourselves ('fantasy'). In TV and film, women are traditionally not the protagonist (the subject of narrative), but the object of the protagonist's desire (the subject of fantasy). [...] [T]his relationship makes it difficult for women to claim the subject position in their own lives, as we learn how to desire and how to construct identities from the world around us, which has become entirely constituted by the world of images generated by media. If TV is always defining a woman in terms of the man in her life, that's how little girls will learn to define themselves.
>
> (Callot 2009)

Not only little girls, I would add. The constant repetition of gendered tropes through popular culture affects also how society more generally forms expectations of female (and male) behaviour.

This book deploys an understanding of 'gender' as a form of cultural meaning assumed by the human body, produced through discourse, language, culture, practice and history. As such, gender is discursive, a 'norm governing reality' (Griffin 2009: 31) that makes sense of our ideas about 'sex', 'gender identity', 'sexuality' and 'sexual practice' and thus appropriate and acceptable human behaviour. Gender, or discourses of gender, of course vary between social location, time and context, and are produced through language, culture, practice, history and circumstance: as such, they are inherently subject to change and the potential for transformation. The 'truth' about people, our very sense of personhood, are, as Butler has articulated so clearly, the results of matrices of power and discursive relations that regulate and make sense of concepts such as a 'person', a 'sex' or a 'sexuality' (1990: 42).

Taking gender seriously in analysing popular culture necessitates taking seriously that each of us are surrounded by overt and tacit sexual norms, which impact on our lives in various and important ways. As Milestone and Meyer argue (2012), gender and popular culture are connected in inextricable, pervasive and complex ways. Popular culture often and broadly depends on certain hierarchies of human

Introductions **11**

behaviour that are gendered: it represents women, men and children in certain ways (for example, as white, able-bodied, middle class, heterosexual), and it reproduces versions of the world that create and sustain certain ideas about what people can, or should, do according to a variety of (physical and psychological) attributes.

Understanding gender as constructed, and always possibly mutable, necessitates considering the ways in which popular culture convincingly represents certain 'truths', 'facts' and social 'realities'. Popular culture is not a uniform, fixed or determinable entity and its representations are dynamic. 'Popular culture' as a term also encompasses 'an enormous range of cultural texts and practices, from cinema films to newspaper articles, from designing computer games to playing music' and mass media such as the internet or email (Milestone and Meyer 2012: 1). Much, but not all, popular culture is media culture (TV, the press, radio, cinema) and relates to, but is not ultimately equatable with, mass media, corporate media and consumer culture. Popular culture is also, of course, a term that embodies both quantitative and qualitative dimensions. It is liked, practised and consumed by many, although this need not be the case, but it also imbued with many different meanings and is a more powerful concept than something we simply produce.

Challenging the gendered foundations on which hierarchies, 'truths', codes of sexual conduct, and so on, are built is an important part of many feminisms. Feminism's position within popular culture, and popular culture's creation of feminism within the popular, is more than simply an interesting question, it is a question of the politics of power and the circulation (and regulation) of knowledge, exclusion and appropriate behaviour. This book attempts to trace a picture of the links between the production, representational practices and consumption of Western popular culture and the nature (and successes) of feminism as it is constituted within the popular today. It argues that the ways in which feminism is treated and/or dismissed is central to understanding contemporary Western popular culture and hopes to contribute to ongoing (and productive) engagements between studies of popular culture, gender, IR and IPE.

Sources

Research findings and data were collected from my research of general discussions around and analysis of popular culture artefacts. The popular culture sources included in this book emanate largely, although not solely, from Australasia, the UK and USA. Television and film products are, however, often dominated by US-produced artefacts and research on US sources tends to monopolize reports in this regard. There was no categorized approach to the popular culture artefacts chosen; I elected simply to focus on and highlight as wide a range of discussions and analysis as I could. Needless to say, this gave my research a certain quality of potential infinity, and it was with some effort that I forced myself to stop writing.

I began this book reading two pieces of scholarship, both of which proved rather inspirational. The first was Angela McRobbie's impassioned *The Aftermath of Feminism* (2009), the second, Janet Halley's provocative and frustrating *Split*

12 Introductions

Decisions: How and Why to Take a Break from Feminism (2006). In *The Aftermath of Feminism*, McRobbie is convinced that popular appropriations of (and misengagements with) feminism have been achieved by aggressively disseminating 'modern' ideas about women 'so as to ensure that a new women's movement will not re-emerge' (McRobbie 2009: 1). Contemporary (Western) popular culture, she argues, helps not only to define our 'codes of sexual conduct', but, moreover, has deployed its 'many channels of communication' to routinely disparage and disencourage feminism (2009: 15). In each of its aspects (including textual, visual and survey-respondent analysis), research here examines the links between representations of feminism across popular culture (print, television, film and digitally based) and popular accounts of, attitudes to and support for feminism.

McRobbie's strength of argument has been particularly instructive. Feminist work, because it threatens important and powerful socio-cultural status quos, has often been dismissed as irrelevant to people's contemporary lives, particularly the lives of young women, while 'postfeminism' can, I believe, be argued to reward young women with the promise of freedom and independence for abandoning feminism. For McRobbie, 'an array of machinations', including crucial elements of contemporary popular culture, are perniciously effective in 'undoing' feminism, 'while simultaneously appearing to be engaging in a well-informed and even well-intended response to feminism' (2009: 11).

Halley suggests that feminism 'is running things' and that feminists themselves 'walk the halls of power' (2006: 20–1). Resoundingly critical of what she perceives as the irresponsibilities of governance feminism, Halley focuses her analysis on feminism's weaknesses and excesses. Feminism, or more specifically 'governance feminism', has become particularly problematic for Halley because it has failed to take responsibility for its pernicious effects, closing its eyes to the effects of its power on neighbouring but different theoretical and political projects and failing to acknowledge its costs (ibid.: 33).

For Halley, feminism has become most powerful in its 'governance' forms, which she finds evident in the domestic (US-based) governance of areas such as child sexual abuse, pornography, sexual harassment, sexual violence, family law, and so on. As Halley (among others, see also Hawkesworth 2004 and Prügl 2011) notes, feminism is also thoroughly institutionalized in the human rights establishment and in international organizations such as the EU and World Bank, achieving great and widespread success in national governments, international governance and through inter- and non-governmental organizations. This has been in large part, Halley suggests, because of the successes of family law, sexual harassment, domestic violence victories and highly effective feminist activism aimed at the ad hoc criminal courts in Rwanda and the former Yugoslavia. For Halley, 'governance' issues not only from the formal mechanisms of state and legislature, but from everyday processes and practices, including from employers, 'schools, healthcare institutions, and a whole range of entities, often formally 'private' (2006: 21). Feminism, she argues, 'has substantial parts' of these entities 'under its control' (ibid.). 'By positing themselves as *experts* on women, sexuality, motherhood, and so on', argues Halley, 'feminists walk the halls of power' (ibid., emphasis in the original).

It is this claim that, initially, proved a catalyst for this research. It is also a claim that is made in the midst of the prevalence of (often violent) sexually explicit imagery and highly derogatory innuendo in the advertising, marketing and selling of otherwise mundane commercial items. On first reading Halley's work, in 2008, I was annoyed that a prominent North American feminist scholar would seek to take aim at what I considered something of a sitting duck. I had already examined an extensive back catalogue of sexually derogatory and violent advertising campaigns and had had the misfortune of sifting through what felt like endless pages of antifeminist hate speech on various blogs and internet sites. Halley's suggestion that we reconsider our allegiance to 'feminism' struck me as ignorant and culturally blinkered, the protestations of a successful scholar spoiled by her North American, Ivy League privilege.

At the same time, at the earliest stages of putting together this project, I found myself often faced with a student cohort who seemed highly ambivalent about feminism and who, worryingly frequently it seemed to me, displayed outright hostility towards feminism. Faced with their obligatory 'week on gender' in a course on International Political Economy and asked about what gender might mean in the context of the machinations of the global political economy, young female students felt obliged to lead off with the much opined cliché 'I'm not a feminist, but . . .', while proceeding to catalogue a list of feminist concerns. Their male peers felt no need to qualify their sentiments, since how could a man possibly be a feminist? A few actively adhered to the school of 'women should sort out women's stuff', some paid lip service to feminist theory and others, more interested in diverse ideas about gender, also seemed uncomfortable that they might be seen to be treading on feminists' toes. Yet these students really did care about the human lives that capitalist development impinges on. When faced with what a gender pay gap might mean for their and their friends' futures, they were, often forcefully, angry. They felt keenly the dangers of assuming anything about a person based on a set of imposed attributes. What then was so embarrassing about admitting that one might be publicly identifiable as a feminist thus eluded me, but also inspired me to pursue this question more fully throughout this research.

Research findings were also collected from research participants and respondents, whose completion of an online survey generated analysis both of statistical relationships and descriptive analysis of respondents' longer-length written replies. Statistical relationships were analysed using SPSS software and respondents' comments were analysed and deployed qualitatively and are provided throughout this book, together with the age, gender and residency of the respondent cited. The survey is reproduced here in full in Appendix A. Respondents to the survey were questioned specifically and in some depth on their opinions, thoughts on and understandings of feminism and contemporary popular culture, and attitudes to and experiences of prevailing gender norms. Open from 12 April to 31 July 2012, the survey involved responses to a total of 45 questions, arranged in five parts, and received in total 169 responses.

The image used for Question 38 is not reproduced here,[3] but was circulating on Facebook in early 2012 through the Facebook page 'Meanwhile in Australia', which is dedicated to 'taking the piss out of all things Australian as well as debating news topics and showing everyday Aussies and the world what's happening in Australia' (https://www.facebook.com/MeanwhileInAustralia). The image details three, clearly intoxicated, young women squatting to urinate outside an office building, under the Facebook page's leading caption, 'Meanwhile in Australia'. The picture was removed from Facebook after a complaint was made to the social networking site, but not before several hundred comments had been made on the picture, many of which criticized young Australian women, 'ladette' culture, drinking culture in Australia (and elsewhere, particularly women's drinking) and the poverty of etiquette among young Australian women.

The survey itself was advertised to students (through my teaching and any relevant student organizations), via email to interested parties (academic and community-based), through organizational affiliations and professional associations and in a public post on the author's Facebook page. Students, academics and professionals constituted the biggest percentage of respondents, although education levels varied more evenly from high-school education to doctoral degrees. More women (79 per cent) responded than men, and most respondents classified themselves as Australian residents (72 per cent). In age ranges, the 25- to 34-year-old category represented 35 per cent of respondents, with age range varying from young to more established adult. Demographic data were generated using the survey report, self-generated by the survey site (https://www.surveys.unsw.edu.au) and computer software (SPSS) and are summarized in Figure 1.1.

Part One of the survey investigated respondents' demographic details, asking them their age, gender, ethnic/cultural background, residency, highest level of education and present occupation. Parts Two, Three, Four and Five of the survey asked respondents for their opinions in four areas in particular: the relevance of

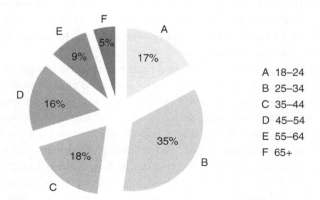

FIGURE 1.1 Demographics of survey respondents.

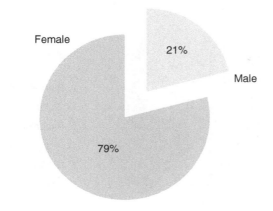
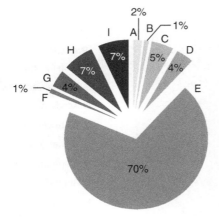
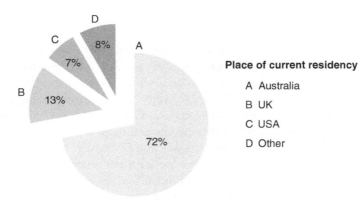

FIGURE 1.1 (*Continued*)

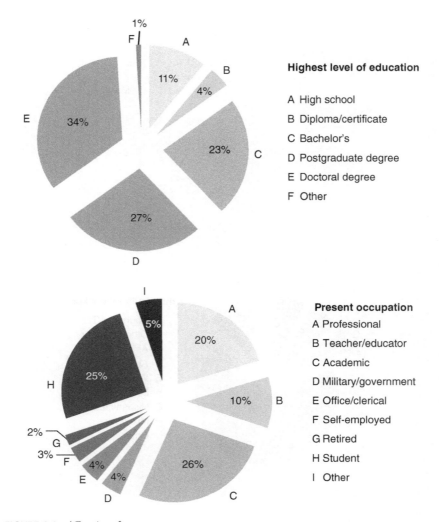

FIGURE 1.1 (*Continued*)

feminism today; the popularity and accessibility of feminism today; how feminism is practised today; and the relationship between popular culture and feminism.

The purpose of the survey was to generate an understanding of whether feminism can be described as a relevant, accessible and popularly practised category in the minds and lives of people across various walks of life. I wanted to know if people had experienced sexism and discrimination based on their sex, including how they would describe the impacts of this. Given my own discomfort, I wondered also how comfortable others are with the sexualization of popular culture. 'Feminism' in the survey was not intended to be considered an objective category (respondents were asked to define their own thoughts on what constituted,

Introductions **17**

for them, 'feminism'), although one respondent considered that it was being treated as such. I tried deliberately to avoid a situation where respondents were asked to define themselves either 'for' or 'against' feminism, since, as Aronson argues, a study that does so is unlikely 'to tap into the highly complex and contested meanings of feminism today', including 'the ways these diverse meanings influence people's reactions to the term itself' (2003: 906).

As Aronson notes, existing surveys of feminism have often looked exclusively at young women and tried to establish their feminist credentials. They have observed how, for example, young women view their own opportunities and obstacles, particularly when compared with those faced by women of their mothers' generation, how they perceive and experience gender discrimination, how they identify themselves with respect to feminism, how we can make sense of their seemingly contradictory perspectives and what the impacts are of racial and class background and life experience on attitudes toward feminism (Aronson 2003: 904). Such surveys have been particularly useful in outlining various types of attitude to feminism, which survey analysts have generally articulated according to five possible descriptions, 'I'm a feminist', 'I'm a feminist, but …', 'I'm not a feminist, but …', 'I'm a fence-sitter' and 'I never thought about feminism' (ibid.: 913–18; see also O'Leary and Reilly 2012).

These surveys have also, however, been criticized for tending to operate with uniform definitions of feminism and for ignoring generational differences. While I wanted to share previous surveys' focus on how people identify themselves with respect to feminism, and how we might begin to make sense of their seemingly contradictory perspectives, I did not wish with the survey conducted here to isolate young women, or indeed women, but to interrogate wider social and popular perceptions of feminism. Surveys on young women have, Aronson notes, offered study groups that are too homogeneous to provide conclusions about the full diversity of today's young women (2003). With a relatively small sample of respondents, this survey can make no claim to speak widely to a general population's perceptions of feminism, but I would challenge any claim that it necessarily constitutes a 'homogeneous' sample.

Several statistically viable relationships did emerge from the data collected that are worth detailing and the strongest relationships and statistical associations that emerged are summarized below (where I refer to a relationship or association as 'significant', this refers to the relationship having met the criteria of statistical significance). Short answer responses to longer questions also received some interesting, and unexpected, responses and showed a wealth of engagement with, and knowledge about, feminism and popular culture that I had not quite expected.

1   Data analysis revealed a relationship between gender and whether individuals describe themselves as feminist (Q7). A strongly negative statistical relationship exists here, with male survey respondents less likely to self-describe as feminist compared with female respondents.

18 Introductions

2   The relationship between education level and whether individuals describe themselves as feminist (Q7) is significant. A moderately strong negative relationship exists here, with lower levels of education resulting in the decreased likelihood of individuals describing themselves as feminist.

3   Data analysis revealed a significant difference in the responses of male and female respondents to Q39 ('The feminist movement, like the civil rights movement, is one that almost everyone is afraid to criticise. [...] Do you agree?'). Male respondents were, on average, more likely to agree with the statement, while female respondents, on average, were less likely to agree.

4   There was no statistical difference between men and women in rating feminism 'being as relevant to men today as it is to women' (Q12). On a seven-point scale, where 1 is disagree, 7 is agree, men averaged 5.94, women 5.96, indicating both were more inclined to agree that feminism is relevant to both genders.

5   Male respondents viewed feminism's representation on television (Q29) more positively than female respondents.

6   Male respondents viewed feminism's representation in film (Q31) more positively than female respondents.

7   Male respondents agreed more frequently than female respondents with the assertion that 'feminists largely see men as the enemy' (Q13).

8   Post-hoc testing of Q10 ('Feminism is professionally relevant to me') revealed that individuals with a postgraduate or doctoral degree rated the professional relevance of feminism higher than other groups.

Notes

1   These ideas refer to the simplistic belief that society is defined entirely in economic terms or that anything interesting socially, culturally or politically might be explained only in relation to economic factors.

2   According to Rothman (2012), Obama overtook Ronald Reagan as the most televised President in US history in early 2012.

3   A complaint specifying that the position of the women in the picture might be considered 'compromising' was received. I removed the picture to avoid further antagonizing the complainant, who perhaps is not as aware as I am of the depth of freely available but potentially troubling representations of women across the Internet. I suspect that an image detailing three drunken men urinating in public would have been largely ignored and this double standard (including the use of women 'misbehaving' as symbolic of social decline) was one of the key reasons I used the image. No offence was intended.

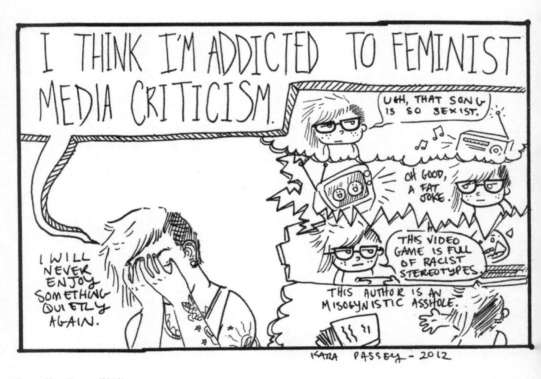

Source: Kara Passey (2012)

2

ANALYSING POPULAR CULTURE

As noted in the previous chapter, and as many scholars have articulated, 'representations matter' (Gill 2007: 7). They 'are not "only" words and images, but reflect and encourage certain ways of thinking about and acting in relation' to human bodies (Milestone and Meyer 2012: 112). When we ask how much impact popular culture can have on people's ideas, assumptions, perceptions and/or beliefs about the world, we need to ask what kinds of 'common sense' about what people can, ought to or will do is reproduced through contemporary popular culture. This is why, I argue, it is important to examine, for example, popular culture if we are interested in feminism, or to ask what fictive scenarios and representations have to do with the serious business of world politics. The ways in which feminism is treated and/or dismissed, and how this is related to the successes of Western popular culture, is more than simply an interesting question. It is a question of the politics of power and the circulation (and regulation) of knowledge, exclusion and appropriate behaviour. Feminist analyses of the media have, in particular, 'been animated by the desire to understand how images and cultural constructions are connected to patterns of inequality, domination and oppression' (Gill 2007: 7). As Rowley articulates, 'our understandings of gender, like our understandings of world politics, are to such a large extent constituted through our interactions in popular culture and in our everyday lives' (2009: 310).

In Australia, watching or listening to television remains the activity that absorbs the most amount of people's leisure time, according to the Australian Bureau of Statistics (2011a). Australian children, of ages 5–17, spend an average of over two-and-a-half hours a day watching television. According to the 2012 documentary, *Miss Representation*, in the USA a teenager will, over the course of one week, watch 31 hours of television, listen to music for 17 hours, watch movies for 3 hours, read magazines for 4 hours and spend 10 hours online. This 'adds

22 Analysing popular culture

up to *10 hours and 45 minutes of media consumption a day'* (*Miss Representation*, 2012, emphasis in the original).

> Teenagers are constantly bombarded with media, and the quality of what they consume will shape their sense of self. After watching hours and hours of Nickelodeon, even I would want to be iCarly.
>
> (Miss Representation 2012)

As *The Feminist Wire* notes, 'popular children's channels such as Disney and Nickelodeon have the power to dictate and even create teen and tween culture in the United States' (Sánchez 2012).

> According to Nielsen data provided by Horizon Media, over the past year, Nickelodeon averaged 1.1 million daily viewers between the ages of 2 and 11. Disney averaged 978,000. This is especially troubling because teenagers are currently the hottest consumer demographic in America. At 33 million, they make up the largest generation of teens in American history, even larger than the Baby Boom generation. Last year, America's teens spent $100 billion, while influencing their parents' spending by $50 billion. *This huge cultural and economic influence allows media to manufacture anti-feminist ideologies that are targeted to young girls.* In *JESSIE*, for instance, a show about a small town Texas girl who moves to New York City and becomes a nanny to a celebrity couple's four children, the children are depicted as much smarter than their bumbling 18-year-old nanny. *Shake it Up*, which revolves around two best friends who become professional dancers on a local show, depicts teenage girls as shallow, vain, and ditsy, perpetuating the notion that young women can be little more than cute or pretty.
>
> (Sánchez 2012, my emphasis)

Popular culture and the importance of visual language in studying global politics

> [T]he mechanically or electronically reproduced image is the semantic and technical unit of the modern mass media and at the heart of post-war popular culture. However, while this is acknowledged widely within the discipline of media and cultural studies, normally via ritual reference to the seminal work of Walter Benjamin, *the visual image or photograph seems only of interest as the origin*, as the technological dawn, of a great process of development in which, in an era of mass communication and the commodification of information, messages can be transmitted in principle to a plurality of recipients and audiences.
>
> (Evans and Hall 1999: 2, my emphasis)

In the introduction to their visual culture reader, Evans and Hall argue that visual culture has been neglected by the 'linguistic' (or 'cultural') turn in the social and human sciences. Enquiry has instead privileged the linguistic model in the study of representation, which has led to an 'assumption that visual artefacts are fundamentally the same, and function in just the same way, as any other cultural text' (Evans and Hall 1999: 2). Accordingly, the authors argue,

> [T]he specific rhetoric, genres, institutional contexts and uses of visual imagery can become lost in the more global identification of cultural trends and their epic narratives of transformations of consciousness in the rubric of postmodern culture.
>
> (Evans and Hall 1999: 2)

This book tries very hard not to lose the specificity of rhetoric, genres, institutional context and various uses of visual imagery in its analysis of whether contemporary popular culture artefacts support the dismissal of feminism. It is a core purpose of research here to pay attention to the ways in which meanings and use 'are regulated by the formats and institutions of production, distribution and consumption' (Evans and Hall 1999: 2–3). 'Representation is always an act of power. This power is at its peak if a form of representation is able to disguise its subjective origins and values' (Bleiker 2001: 515).

As Weldes argues (2006), the discipline of International Relations (IR) has, in the past, tended to ignore popular culture. Instead, 'mainstream' approaches to IR (that is, rationalist and/or positivist approaches) 'typically take a rather narrow view on the kinds of evidence appropriate' for analysing meaning, if, indeed, the question of 'meaning' arises at all (Weldes 2006: 177). The same is also true, I argue, of International Political Economy, where popular culture and 'the visual' are rarely considered trustworthy or legitimate objects and/or sources of social science enquiry. Thus, although 'popular visual language is increasingly the language that amateurs and experts rely upon in order to claim contemporary literacy' and despite much politics being 'conducted through popular visual language' (Weber 2008: 137), apart from media and cultural studies, IR and IPE academia have been hesitant to explore the power (political, economic, social, cultural) that visual and popular culture wield on and through world politics. In particular, these disciplines have been reluctant to see the intrinsic politicality of popular culture, failing to read the 'competing and contesting discourses and their various ideological effects and implicit power relations' that, as Weldes articulates, popular culture expresses, enacts and produces (2006: 180). Yet, the cultural basis of action, behaviour, theory, value, and so on, is so important because it is here that actions, behaviours, values, and so on, are made commonsensical (ibid.: 178).

The USA and its relationship with popular culture and militarization provide an interesting example here. Specifically, it is unclear how we might meaningfully engage with the extent of a society's (such as the USA's) level of militarization,

24 Analysing popular culture

and the effects of this, without considering the ways in which the acceptance of 'the military' has become so mundane, so commonsensical, that 'civilians' wear its camouflaged outerwear as fashion, or know what 'AWOL', 'jarhead' or 'ground zero' mean because they have grown up watching *MASH*, *Rambo* and *Black Hawk Down*. We might know that the USA is heavily militarized, and that its leaders make decisions based on 'natural' assumptions about military justifiability, but *how* we (and by 'we', I mean consumers and producers of popular culture) know this is 'in and through the mundane culture of people's everyday experiences' (Weldes 2006: 178). Elite rhetoric is, of course, important in understanding the form and function of, for example, US foreign policy and intervention, but the ways in which the options, strategy or policy initiatives of elites are represented in and through popular culture can make a world of difference. Popular culture provides a, if not *the*, 'background of meanings that hep to constitute public images of world politics and foreign policy' (ibid.). Boardshorts in camouflage, water pistols, even some of our words, would not exist if the military did not, and these would not have been made logical, commonsensical, if the cultural landscape of the USA had not absorbed, and did not depend on, the givenness of the military. Understanding that the US military is culturally constructed and located means, of course, that it is neither given nor inevitable but is an arbitrary institution, and the development of the military-industrial complex that pumps out war novels, video games and movies, is circumstantial. This means that representations of the military as natural become *even more* important, not least to those whose livelihoods depend on its existence. Popular culture, Weldes argues, to the extent that it 'reproduces the structure and content of dominant discourses', helps to 'generate approval for, or at least acquiescence to, familiar policies and prevailing world order' (Weldes 2006: 179). Popular culture 'is thus implicated in the "production of consent"' (ibid., quoting Hall 1982).

IR and IPE's dismissive, or perhaps simply defeatist (although I tend to think there is a pernicious laziness in refusing to engage with the visual world that is deliberately dismissive), attitude to visual representation is disappointing but also highly misleading, since, as Carver notes, international politics 'is rarely done in any direct sense by philosophers but rather by people whose intellectual horizons are largely formed by TV, movies, visual reports in the news and rather more remotely, textual journalism and verbal briefings' (2010: 426). 'Geopolitical realisms' (where the 'theoretical frameworks and methodologically correct protocols of IR' do have some purchase) are at work across the political world, but 'these discourses are arguably as much image-based as fact-based (in so far as the two could possibly be separated' (ibid.: 427). Popular culture is a particularly important site of discursive power (the power of meaning-making) precisely because it is so mundane and yet, as Weldes argues, so innately political. While it matters eminently whether, and how, feminism is being taken seriously in the halls of power (Chapter 4 considers this in more detail), I would argue that politics is more pervasively narrated, and thus reproduced, in everyday ways (across the news media, for example, in film, on television and social networking sites, and so on).

Stuart Hall, visual language and the importance of social practice

The more widely articulated and consumed a message or meaning, and the earlier it is learned, the more powerful that message is likely to be, and the least 'constructed' it will appear. The televisual sign, in particular, is noteworthy because it combines 'two types of discourse, visual and aural' and, moreover, constitutes 'an iconic sign' in that it '"possesses some of the properties of the thing represented"' (Hall, quoting Peirce 1931, 1999: 511). As Hall argues, visual culture of course needs to translate a three-dimensional world into two dimensions and thus, as such, reality exists, to a certain extent, outside language (1999: 511). This reality is, however, 'constantly mediated by and through language' and 'what we can know and say has to be produced in and through discourse' (ibid.). For Hall, 'naturalism' and 'realism' are nothing but products of discourse, since our 'knowledge' is 'the product not of the transparent representation of the 'real' in language but of the articulation of language on real relations and conditions' (ibid.). Since representation is the result of discursive practice, so too is the 'real', at least in Hall's influential analysis.

Hall, as this book does, centralizes the role of discourse in processes of communication and meaning-making, arguing that the 'discursive form of the message has a privileged position in the communicative exchange', at least if we consider the importance of circulation (1999: 508). For example, a 'raw' historical event relayed on television is being signified 'within the aural-visual forms of the televisual discourse': that is, an event cannot be transmitted as it is without some form of transformation and is, as such, 'subject to all the complex formal rules by which language signifies' (ibid.). To become a 'communicative event', then, the event must be told and the meaning of the event can only be understood through its telling.

Hall articulates the process of communication according to five distinct 'moments': of production, circulation, distribution, consumption and reproduction. These 'connected practices' create meaning and messages, which must be articulated into social practices if the 'circuit is to be both completed and effective' (Hall 1999: 508). The importance of social practices here is significant, since (while allowing for the possibility that it might be used or understood at least somewhat against the grain) a 'message' is, in Hall's analysis, most often receivable at a particular stage only where it is recognizable or appropriate (During 1999, summarizing Hall 1999: 507), which means that the message must make a certain amount of sense to us based on our existent social experiences. We cannot consume the message without taking its meaning, Hall argues, and thus if 'meaning is not articulated into practice, it has no effect' (ibid.). Already coded signs thus intersect with 'the deep semantic codes of a culture' taking on additional and different dimensions as they circulate (Hall 1999: 513). Several patterns of power and influence will be at play in any given form of communication, including the formal 'sub-rules' of discourse, the 'social relations in which the rules are set to work' and the 'social and political consequences of the event having been signified in this way' (ibid.). To an extent, production, Hall argues, 'constructs the message' and the institutional

26 Analysing popular culture

structures of broadcasting are therefore important (including the 'knowledge-in-use' of technical skills, routines of production, and so on) (1999: 509–10). At a certain point, though, broadcasting structures 'must yield encoded messages' to the wider structures of social practice, which are themselves framed by structures of understanding, 'as well as being produced by social and economic relations' (ibid.).

Hall uses advertising as an example to argue that every visual sign 'connotes a quality, situation, value or inference', which may be present 'as an implication or implied meaning, depending on the connotational positioning' (1999: 510). The sign, for example a sweater, might connote a 'warm garment', 'the coming of winter', or a 'cold day', and set against 'the right visual background and positioned by the romantic sub-code', it may connote a 'long autumn walk in the woods' (ibid.: 513). In the same way, according to the codes through which relations of power are made to signify in particular discourses, masculine and feminine imagery may connote certain culturally specific values or qualities, depending on time and place. The 'generic male stereotype', for example, may often be represented as active, 'in accordance with Berger's dictum that "men act and women appear"', but it may also be represented as androgynous in an effort to subvert the 'macho hero' and connote sensitivity rather than brute strength (Stern 2003: 221–2).

I have recently been struck (and irritated) by a particular campaign for the Kia (car) range in Australia (launched in January 2013 during the Australian Open tennis competition, which Kia currently sponsors). In 2010 Kia ran a campaign for their Sportage SUV (YouTube 2013a) in which a seemingly average Australian male is driving around the suburbs listening to Grandmaster Flash's 'The Message' (first released in 1983).[1] The hook here is that Grandmaster Melle Mel and Scorpio are actually in the car with the driver, so apparently evocative of long lost good times is this vehicle. The driver then pulls into his driveway, whereupon his wife/partner, who has been pruning the hedges, asks him if he 'remembered the nappies' (which he did not, because he was, presumably, so absorbed in driving his exciting Kia Sportage). This is a good example of a representation of the classic stereotype of men in action, with woman as a cameo and including a smattering of the much-loved 'nagging wife' cliché. In Australia, the 'macho male' stereotype of masculinity has been particularly pervasive and the idea that Australian men are intrinsically tough is so widely articulated and consumed as to pass for 'fact' in Australian society. A YouTube user's comment is particularly revealing in this regard.

> You own a KIA dont [sic] you champ? Your [sic] a trodden down house husband who has to drive one of these heaps of shit because your missus said so and are all bitter and twisted at those who drive SS Commodores with Chev badges because you wish you had one too.
>
> (Comment posted 2012, YouTube 2013b)

Then, in January 2013, Kia released a new campaign, targeting, in two separate commercials, the 'New Age Man' (YouTube 2013 c) and the 'Woman of My

Time' (YouTube 2013d). Kia borrows George Carlin's 'Modern Man' sketch to attempt to identify modern man and modern woman as independent, confident, technologically savvy and environmentally aware. The end result, online comments have noted, is a cringeworthy and rather arrogant pretentiousness with which very few seem able to relate.

> I'm not sure that being a 'man or woman of now' is at all a desirable attribute: they're shallow, stupid, pampered, pretentious and with the attention span of a...oh, that looks interesting. This is from the 'there's nothing to say about the product, so let's talk about the consumer' school of 5 minute strategic thinking.
>
> (Old CD Guy, January 2013)

> [T]he achingly appalling casting and performance has delivered a smarmy piece of self-indulgent heart ache for every unfortunate sombitch[2] who sits down to watch the tube, dinner on lap, tin in hand. If I met that dude (from the ad) in the street, I'd be happy to do time for caving his head in with a plastic spoon.
>
> (Jacob's Creek, January 2013)

The difference in popularity of the two campaigns is striking. The 2010 campaign speaks clearly to identifiable cultural codes, specifically gender stereotypes of Australian married men as browbeaten and constrained and thus appears to map social relations much more persuasively, and perhaps aspirationally, than its successor. The 'New Age Man' of 2012, on the other hand, represents so much of a mash-up of various 'new age' clichés that he is considered irrelevant and is widely criticized. This may be attributable to a simple misjudgement on the advertiser's part (the company Innocean). In many regards, this is just a poor advertisement that is badly written and badly performed. Yet it is also an advertisement that is misaligned somewhat with Australia's 'dominant cultural order', which remains resoundingly suspicious of 'new age' househusbandry and artyfartiness. The Woman/Man of Now adverts, as 'problematic events', breach our expectations and 'run counter to our "commonsense constructs"' (Hall 1999: 513). The message of Kia's 2012 campaign cannot be consumed and reproduced because the story it tells does not intersect with the semantic codes of Australian culture: it is not recognizable or appropriate to (many) Australians and it makes little sense to them based on their existent social experiences or the wider structures of social practice in Australia.

'Culture', popular culture and (erroneous) high/low binaries

Quoting Williams, Storey notes that culture is 'ordinary'; it is 'how we make sense of ourselves and the word around us' and it is where 'we share and contest

28 Analysing popular culture

meanings of ourselves, of each other, and of the world' (2003: x, quoting Williams 1958). Culture is not only, however, 'how we live nature (including our own biology)', it is, Storey argues, an 'active process': it does 'not lie dormant in things (that is, any commodity, object, or event that can be made to signify), waiting patiently to be woken by an appropriate consumer', rather, it is 'the practice of making and communicating meanings', often with a specifically social substance (Storey 2003: ix–x).

> Watching a soap opera and talking about what the characters are doing; arguing about who should have won a football match; remembering together the songs of a shared youth; debating the claims of politicians and big business; protesting at the injustices and economic inequalities of globalization. [...] To share a culture is to interpret the world – to make it meaningful – in recognizably similar ways.
>
> (Storey 2003: x)

Popular culture, Strinati notes, is often defined 'by how it is explained and evaluated' and is frequently used descriptively, 'as covering a specific set of artefacts' (2004: xviii). Strinati has very little hope that any agreement on a 'theoretically-informed definition' can be reached, since 'the attempt to achieve this involves competing conceptions of the nature of the social relationships (or the lack of them) within which these artefacts are located' (ibid.).

As has been well-noted, popular culture suffers still from an implied inferiority, as 'the culture that is left over after we have decided what is high culture' (Storey 2012: 5). This involves an erroneous, but somehow still pertinent, low/high distinction that posits popular culture as less venerable than 'high culture', which is viewed as the result of 'an individual act of creation' and deserving of a 'moral and aesthetic response', while popular culture 'requires only a fleeting sociological inspection to unlock what little it has to offer' (Storey 2006: 6). Popular culture, in this definition, thus becomes 'a residual category, accommodating texts and practices that fail to qualify as high culture' (ibid.: 5–6).

This is a powerful distinction that has led to descriptions of popular, 'mass', culture as the epitome of commercialization. This book refuses this distinction and does not argue that popular culture is interchangeable with 'mass culture' (see Strinati 2004: 2). This is not to deny the crucial commercial foundations that sustain and propel aspects of popular culture, but simply to sound a warning against a too-easy equation of popular with mass culture. The association with mass culture has arisen, Strinati suggests, due to the rise in new media and development in communication technologies that have made 'culture available to the masses' (2004, quoted in Milestone and Meyer 2012: 4). The introduction, for example, of 'mass production techniques' in the making of films means that, although films are not quite motor cars, there is an obvious commercial aspect to their production and distribution (Strinati 2004: 4). For some, this means that, as a cultural product, cinema cannot constitute 'authentic and genuine works of art' (ibid.)

Although popular culture is, of course, often commodified, whether it is enough to argue that popular culture is reducible to particular criteria of profitability and marketability remains unclear. Embodying 'high' culture with an intellectual/ aesthetic quality and 'low' culture with popularism rarely holds strong, in practice. Classical music, for example, is consumed by many; niche TV programming much less so. Important aspects of popular culture are also simply not equatable to mass or media culture. These include everyday practices that carry cultural meaning, such as celebrating a wedding or getting a tattoo done. The 'juxtaposition of high and popular culture' in ways that associate 'high' culture with 'a bygone golden age free of commercialization, where art thrived for art's sake' and popular culture with capitalism, profit and big business, is, Milestone and Meyer argue, highly problematic (2012: 4). First, such assumptions exhibit an obvious elitism that fails to recognize that there are no neutral or universal standards by which we might measure culture. Second, *all* forms of contemporary Western culture are shaped by, and produced in, the economic system of capitalism. As the authors note, 'there is no space totally free of commerce' (ibid.).

As Storey suggests, 'popular culture' is 'a category invented by intellectuals' and 'the idea of popular culture is often a way of categorizing and dismissing the cultural practices of "ordinary" people' (2003: xi–xii). This I find particularly true of some attitudes towards popular culture as a legitimate area of scholarly enquiry. Thus, although

> the term popular culture can be articulated to carry a range of different meanings, what all these have in common is the idea of *popularis* – belonging to the people. Therefore, each of the different ways in which popular culture is formulated always carries with it a definition of 'the people'.
>
> (Storey 2003: xii)

This is not to suggest that, in understanding popular culture as of/by/for 'the people', we should assume that popular artefacts are necessarily popular, in the sense of being widely favoured or well-liked, as noted above. A rather large amount of 'popular culture' fails the quantitative index, whereas 'high culture' products may often outsell their niche, or subculture, popular culture cousins. Sales of jazz and classical music, or 'high end' literature, for example, often outstrip sales of comic books and anime, and 'arthouse' cinema frequently outperforms heavily marketed and more widely distributed mainstream movies. In 2011 in the USA, for example, the black-and-white movie *The Artist*[3] outperformed two of the year's anticipated biggest films, *Red Riding Hood*[4] and *Scream 4*,[5] both of which were shown at almost double the number of theatres (Box Office Mojo 2013).

Similarly, in 2004, eighty-nine new editions or translations of the plays of William Shakespeare, the 'epitome of high culture' (Storey 2012: 6), were released in the USA and 657,000 Shakespeare titles were sold (this does not include the copies bought in bulk by libraries and schools). Industry experts suggest that ten million copies of Shakespeare's works are sold a year worldwide (Blakeley 2005). Shakespeare's plays are put on some 5,000 times each year in amateur and professional theatres worldwide and eight Shakespeare films were released in 2004, including an Indian version of *Macbeth* titled *Maqbool* and a new *Merchant of Venice* starring Al Pacino (Blakeley 2005).

In Australia, according to a 2005–6 survey by the Australian Bureau of Statistics, 38 per cent of people aged 15 years and over had attended a performing arts event in the previous 12 months ('performing arts' here includes theatre, dance performances, musicals, operas and other performing arts events). Approximately 2.6 million people (or 17 per cent) attended other performing arts events, such as variety shows, revues and circuses (ABS 2010). As Figure 2.1 shows, more Australians visited botanic and zoological gardens and libraries than attended popular music concerts. The final of Australia's most viewed TV show in 2012 (*The Voice*) captured an audience of 'only' 3,325,000, or 14.7 per cent of the population (the total population in Australia is 22,620,600).[6]

Despite the obvious popularity of cinema as a 'cultural event', and although sources suggest that this is in decline in the USA and elsewhere (see, e.g., Atkinson 2012; BBC 2012), in 2006 the Australian 'Adult Literacy and Life Skills Survey' found that reading was a favourite activity for 61 per cent of people aged 15 years and over' (ABS 2011a). Interestingly, from 2009 to 2010 Australians spent A$2,032 million on 'literature', which was the third highest 'cultural' expenditure behind televisions ($3,350m) and pay TV fees (A$2,295m) (ABS 2011b). The 'old certainties of the cultural landscape' (Storey 2012: 7) may not seem quite as stable when close attention is paid to people's everyday cultural practices.

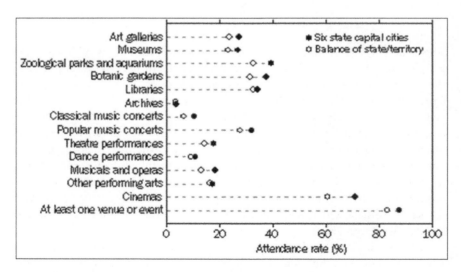

FIGURE 2.1 Attendance at cultural venues and events, by region.

Source: Australian Bureau of Statistics 2010.

Niche cultures (folk music, early rock'n'roll and '90s techno, for example) are various in origins, and many 'are the aftermath of mass cultures that have lost their currency with the general audience' (Westbury 2009). The same is also true of so-called 'high' culture. Theatre and opera were once popular, and well-populated, forms of entertainment, as were the works of Charles Dickens or, as Storey notes, 'film noir' (2012: 6). Perhaps the point most worth emphasizing here is that the high/low cultural binary does not allow for the dynamism of 'culture', fixing it as a static assemblage of artefacts rather than a variable and unstable process.

Popular culture and political economy

I am continually surprised that so little IPE scholarship considers the ways in which popular culture and economy are intertextual and mutually reproductive, since understanding popular culture has such relevance to economic questions of production, distribution and consumption. The following pages are concerned with some key points in understanding the relationship between popular culture, political economy and feminism. In this section, I turn to an older debate in the history of cultural studies concerning the troubled relationship between cultural studies and political economy. I then attempt to offer some clarity around how to approach consumer and popular culture, and why it is important to distinguish between the two.

Possibly one of the most famous, or at least the most commonly cited, 'political economy' engagements with the relationship between popular culture, consumerism, commercialism and capitalism is Adorno and Horkheimer's Marxist critique of the pernicious conservatism of popular culture (1999, originally published 1944). Adorno and Horkheimer describe a heavily managed, hierarchically ordered 'culture industry' that centrally produces to widely dispersed 'consumption points' (During summarizing Adorno and Horkheimer 1999: 33). They argue that popular culture is necessarily conservative, since it works in the interests of those in power, helping to maintain the status quo (existing relations of power) by pacifying the masses and justifying capitalism (cited in Milestone and Meyer 2012: 5). The modern culture industry thus produces safe, standardized products geared to the larger demands of the capitalist economy and it does so 'by representing "average" life for purposes of pure entertainment or distraction as seductively and realistically as possible' (During summarizing Adorno and Horkheimer 1999: 31). For Adorno and Horkheimer, popular culture and consumer culture were essentially indistinguishable and were compared to the much less dangerous 'high arts', since these were more technically and intellectually difficult. While popular culture and consumer culture are often intertwined, however, they should not be read as interchangeable. Popular culture was industrially produced mass culture designed to enrich the capitalist elite, and the 'culture industry', for Adorno and Horkheimer, was built to cultivate in individuals false needs that only capitalist production and consumerism could meet. '[T]he basis on which technology acquires power over society', Adorno and Horkheimer suggest, 'is the power of those whose economic hold over society is greatest' (1999: 33).

32 Analysing popular culture

It is worth noting that Adorno and Horkheimer wrote their 1944 essay when the cultural industry was much less variegated than it is today. The authors were not writing in an era of mass media, mass communications and 'new media' (on-demand, digital and/or internet-based media, including, email, digital radio, television, podcasts, blogs, wikis, websites, and so on). The rise of 'new media' has arguably opened the 'culture industry' to a level of creativity, reconfiguration and (possible) subversion that Adorno and Horkheimer were not privy to. New media have virtually eradicated the possibility of always controlling public use of technology. As Milestone and Meyer describe, new media and communication technologies 'blur the lines between producers and consumers and allow users much more flexibility', while also intensifying the 'connection between media and popular culture', such that, 'while popular culture and the media are not identical, they are increasingly intertwined' (2012: 5).

Approaches to 'culture' within International Political Economy (IPE), while they cannot be reduced to variations of Adorno and Horkheimer's critique, have, unsurprisingly perhaps, focused on the importance of the relationship between consumerism, commercialism and capitalism. As I will argue below, however, where other disciplines have produced lively and extensive debates on visual and popular culture, beyond Adorno and Horkheimer's analysis, IPE has fared relatively poorly in terms of speaking to popular culture. This is despite a large amount of critical IPE scholarship dedicated to analysing the concept of 'culture'.

Not all scholars of popular culture, of course, engage with political economy questions and this book does not suggest that cultural studies says all that needs to be said in terms of engaging economic life as cultural practice. A 1990s debate on 'culture' and the benefits and perils of political economy enquiry, summarized below, is perhaps instructive to understanding why IPE and cultural studies have followed rather separate tracks.

The (slightly troubled) relationship between cultural studies and political economy

> [C]ultural studies rests on the achievements of semiotics as a whole and stakes its distinctiveness upon the analysis of the symbolic, classificatory and, in short, meaning-making practices that are at the heart of all cultural production and consumption.
>
> (Evans and Hall 1999: 2–3)

A 1995 essay by Garnham, entitled 'Political Economy and Cultural Studies', argues that a 'founding antagonism' characterizes the relationship between Marxist political economy and cultural studies, based on cultural studies' 'profound misunderstanding of political economy'. The 'project of cultural studies', Garnham suggests, 'can be successfully pursued only if the bridge with political economy is rebuilt' (1995, in During 1999: 493). Cultural studies was

Analysing popular culture **33**

born 'of a set of assumptions about political economy' and needs desperately to reorientate itself to the capitalist mode of production rather than the cultural practices to which it 'assigns priority': the 'broken bridge', for Garnham, *must* be rebuilt for cultural studies to become a 'meaningful political enterprise' (ibid. 493–5).

Garnham's controversial piece argues that, by focusing overwhelmingly on 'cultural consumption rather than cultural production' and 'on the cultural practices of leisure rather than those of work' cultural studies has 'exaggerated the freedoms of consumption and daily life', playing politically 'into the hands of a right whose ideological assault has been structured in large part around an effort to persuade people to construct themselves as consumers in opposition to producers (1995, in During 1999: 495–6). Political economists, on the other hand, recognize, with Marx, 'that all commodities must have a use-value', they 'must satisfy some need or provide some pleasure' and that unequal power relations are 'embedded in the production, distribution and consumption of cultural forms as commodities' (ibid.: 496). We ignore at our peril the inherent relationship between the use-value of a commodity and its sources of production, distribution and consumption. Echoing Adorno and Horkheimer's critique, Garnham asserts that

> a delimited social group, pursuing economic or political ends, determines which meanings circulate and which do not, which stories are told and about what, which arguments are given prominence and what cultural resources are made available and to whom. The analysis of this process is vital to an understanding of the power relationships involved in culture and their relationship to wider structures of domination.
>
> (Garnham 1999: 496)

In a response to this piece, Grossberg argues that Garnham's analysis is a historical in its glorification of abstract capitalism (1995). Grossberg asks why it is 'that the USA is not the UK or Japan?', which is just a superstructural problem, and necessitates asking questions about the ways in which social relations develop 'beyond a simple binary distinction between the owners of the means of production and waged labour' (ibid.: 73). For Grossberg, Garnham is unable 'to consider such questions precisely because he refuses to engage the question of articulation' and it is articulation that is 'the principle way in which the relations between production, consumption, politics, and ideology are theorized in cultural studies' (Grossberg 1995: 73). Much work on consumption and reception in cultural studies, Grossberg notes, 'looks at the complex and even contradictory nature of consumption', and, while it does indeed conclude that consumption can produce pleasures and can be, in some ways, empowering, this 'need not and does not deny the exploitative, manipulative, and dominating aspects of the market' (ibid.).

Grossberg argues that, ultimately, production and consumption cannot be separated if we assume that 'the notion and practice of production are themselves

34 Analysing popular culture

culturally produced' (1995: 74). Marx himself noted the production involved in consumption/reproduction. A 'model of cultural analysis based on a separation of production and consumption is itself problematic, as is the reduction of production to waged labour', Grossberg notes, suggesting that the relations between production and consumption are more complex and less stable than Garnham suggests (ibid.). Responding to claims that cultural studies has reduced itself to uncritically 'celebrating' consumption, Grossberg argues:

> Cultural studies does not assume that opposition, resistance, struggle, and survival (coping) are the same; but it does assume that the possibilities for the first two depend in complex ways on the realities of the last two. The question of the relations and tensions among these forms of effectivity is important and needs to be explored.
>
> (Grossberg 1995: 75–6)

Grossberg stresses that scholars should pay attention to the small resistances and amendments that people make in their everyday lives, the ways in which they use 'the limited resources they are given to find better ways of living' and the methods by which they 'find ways of increasing the control they have over aspects of their lives' (1995: 75–6). Ignoring these moments of contestation and resistance only obscures a fuller understanding of 'the structures of power and inequality in the contemporary world and the possibilities for challenging them' (ibid.).

I should note here that I am not qualified to embroil myself in the debate about whether cultural studies has reduced itself to a form of 'cultural populism' and whether this has led to an exclusive focus on consumption and 'a corresponding uncritical celebration of popular reading practices' (Storey 2012: 219). I am also reluctant to suggest that cultural studies needs to do more political economy to remain 'politically credible' (Storey summarizes some of these debates, which he believes to be limited; see 2012: 232). This book is sympathetic to Grossberg's emphasis on the significance of (changing) social relations and articulation and is wary of offering a meta-capitalist framework for understanding the 'culture industry' or an exclusive focus on the domination and manipulation of the masses by powerful elites. Like Grossberg, my analysis assumes that 'people live their subordination actively'. This might also mean that 'they are often complicit in their own subordination' and 'that they accede to it', although power 'often works through strategies and apparatuses of which people are totally unaware' (Grossberg 1995: 75–6).

> [I]f one is to challenge the existing structures of power, then one has to understand how that complicity, that participation in power, is constructed and lived, and that means not only looking at what people gain from such practices, but also at the possibilities for rearticulating such practices to escape, resist, or even oppose particular structures of power.
>
> (Grossberg 1995: 75–6)

Analysing popular culture **35**

Storey notes that the media and communication industries are owned and controlled by an increasingly small number of powerful individuals and industries (2012: 232). I argue here, however, that popular culture is not reducible to 'industry' alone and is increasingly produced *by* the people as it is *for* the people (using technologies that are, of course, built and produced, by corporations, institutions and individuals, but which may, and often do, exceed their control). It is becoming increasingly difficult, in Australasia, the UK and the USA at least, to identify the 'delimited social group' that Garnham believes determines the meanings that circulate, particularly because social media has given such widespread prominence to non-elites. Yet, we should not ignore, of course, that Australian media ownership has often been noted for its high levels of concentrated ownership, with eleven of the twelve daily newspapers in Australia' capital cities owned either by News Corp Australia or Fairfax Media. Garnham's warning regarding the importance of paying attention to 'the power relationships involved in culture and their relationship to wider structures of domination' (1995 in During 1999: 496) remains important.

Grossberg's emphasis on the complexity of how people live their subordination is important, but I am equally convinced that there is work to be done *before* we can argue that people are, indeed, subordinated. Perhaps a more active grappling with power, access and resources than some in cultural studies might be willing to offer is needed. Consideration 'of what cultural resources are made available and to whom' (Garnham 1995 in During 1999: 496) remains a key component of analysis here. It might be problematic, for example, to assume that those that have access to social media are 'everypeople'. At A\$20 a ticket, at least here in Sydney, going to the cinema is not accessible to all, Foxtel, at a minimum of A\$90 a month, is too expensive for many and the A\$100 plus it requires to organize broadband powerful enough to download films, TV shows and music is out of reach to a considerable number of Australians, before we even begin considering the issues with availability and access that rural communities must face. As part of the power relationships necessitated by a wider consideration of cultural pro-duction, consumption and representation, the availability of wealth is important in understanding the 'significance and character of the values, norms and mean-ings' produced in the practices of consumption, which necessarily involves considering the 'complexity of the relationship between ownership and use of material goods, economic status, inequality and meaning' (Lury 2011: 11). Scholars should take seriously the (significant) proportion of the populations of so-called advanced consumer societies who are dispossessed and thus 'excluded from many forms of commodity consumption as they do not have access to the economic resources necessary for participation' (ibid.).

> The picture becomes even more stark if a global analysis is introduced: 20 per cent of the world's population − those residing in the rich nations − account for over 80 per cent of total consumer spending. Clearly, poverty places severe limits on the ability to participate in consumption insofar as it is linked to the purchase of commodities: economic status restricts the possible

36 Analysing popular culture

> extent of an individual's participation in consumption or practical freedom – as Bauman puts it [1990] – to exercise consumer 'choice'.
>
> (Lury 2011: 12)

This said, we should also be wary of assuming 'a direct or straightforward relationship between poverty and exclusion from consumer culture or wealth and inclusion' (Lury 2011: 12). While poverty, which should be appreciated in its relative and absolute forms, 'restricts the possibility of participation in the consumption of commodities', it does not necessarily or always prevent participation in consumer culture. Sometimes it may even incite this. As Lury notes, poorer US populations, for example, where they own a car, pay a higher proportion of their income on purchasing a luxury model (ibid.).

IPE and 'culture'

As Storey notes, our identities 'are not the expression of our "nature", they are a performance in culture' (2003: 91).

> [O]ur identities are made from a contradictory series of identifications, subject positions, and forms of representation which we have made, occupied, and been located in as we constitute and are constituted by performances that produce the narrative of our lives. Popular culture is a fundamental part of this process.
>
> (Storey 2003: 91)

IPE is highly attentive to understanding the power relationships involved in capitalist culture(s) and their relationship to wider structures of domination, as per Garnham's analysis. IPE also often deploys a critical analysis of culture as the environment where meanings are made and shared, as per Storey's analysis (2003, 2012). IPE scholarship on culture, rarely, however, goes as far as to articulate our identities as performances in culture and has generally failed to articulate popular culture as fundamental to any processes of identity-formation in IPE. While there is a lot of 'culture' in IPE, there is much less engagement than there might be with ideas about textuality, identity and difference, which are arguably more prominent in cultural studies. Cultural studies 'does not believe that all forms of power can be explained by capitalist relations or in economic terms' (Grossberg 1995: 78). IPE, as it stands, has proven rather uninterested in any meanings circulating in and through popular culture that might be relevant to understanding the realm of the 'economic'.

In IPE, critical scholars have often approached culture from a Gramscian tradition, as defined by relations of hegemony. This echoes, to a certain extent, Adorno and Horkheimer's critique and posits 'culture' and its reproduction as the preserve of a dominant capitalist elite. Germain's analysis, for example, of Harvey's work deploys culture as a mechanism of class power, with the 'dominant class's

Analysing popular culture **37**

cultural manipulations' forcing 'subordinate classes' to 'acquiesce to its rule' (Germain 2011: 67). For Germain, the dominance of neoliberalism in contemporary economic (and social) life is strengthened by its cultural value: this can be read as a form of Americanization where 'individual consumption and consumer choice have the effect, *pace* Robinson, of depoliticizing people, of inducing apathy so long as a certain lifestyle can be maintained' (ibid.: 67). Thus, 'culture is derivative of, rather than determinant to, the economy as understood in materialist terms' (ibid.: 69).

IPE has, historically, tended to separate production and consumption and has thus failed to highlight, as Grossberg suggests, the complex relations between production and consumption that render practices of production themselves culturally produced. Storey goes so far as to argue:

> Political economy's idea of cultural analysis seems to involve little more than detailing access to, and availability of, texts and practices. Nowhere do [political economists] advocate a consideration of what these texts and practices might mean (textually) or be made to mean in use (consumption).
> (Storey 2012: 233)

While I take issue with the monolithic picture of political economy that Storey has designed, I would agree overall with the general assessment that political economy has, generally, fared quite poorly in analysing the significance, and complexity, of popular culture. Storey suggests that post-Marxist hegemony theory has come closest to 'the promise of keeping in active relationship production, text and consumption', whereas 'political economy threatens, in spite of its admirable intentions, to collapse everything back into the economic' (2012: 233). For the 'new Marxists', for example, 'culture' has a role in the market economy as a means 'by which individuals can negotiate the hand dealt to them by existing class relations' (Germain 2011: 67). The 'consumption of, or engagement with, cultural products and artefacts provides an escape from the constraints of the market economy' (ibid.).

Neogramscians and other Marxists have also, as Best and Paterson suggest, invoked the notion of hegemony in global politics, 'opening up some space to talk about the cultural conditions of capitalism' (2010: 5). Scholars of 'cultural economy', the authors assert, share 'a belief in the crucial significance of economic life in determining differential life chances of people across the globe' and 'a rejection of the ability of orthodox models of economic life to fully capture the nature and dynamics of the economy' (ibid.: 3). In counterpoint to those that view culture as determined by the mode of production, Best and Paterson go on to note that scholars of cultural economy view culture, in its broadest sense as 'the meanings we give social life and material objects', as determining of 'concrete economic forms of life' (ibid.: 3). Such a focus highlights how 'cultural forms constitute what the economy is' and 'how cultural forms shape the operation of the economy in a number of concrete way' (ibid.: 4). Best and Paterson point to McDowell's

38 Analysing popular culture

(1997) analysis of the gendered character of financial markets or the evolving character of the 'work ethic' (as per Heelas' 2002 writing). A continued emphasis on class, however, 'has tended to reduce the question of culture to one of the means by which capitalist domination is reproduced and resisted' (ibid.: 5).

Lipschutz, for example, in his 2010 monograph, *Political Economy, Capitalism and Popular Culture*, suggests a fairly limited definition of popular culture, as essentially 'movies and novels', which are the products of a single 'capitalism' (2010: 2). While attentive to popular culture as reproductive of 'the tenets, principles, and practices that support existing social arrangements' (ibid.), Lipschutz's analysis is not specifically interested in the contested and complex nature of the meanings produced and consumed in and through popular culture (his analysis is deliberately organized around the insights popular culture might bring to both economics and political economy). For Lipschutz, a society's cultural products are not only reflective of the economic organization of that society, they are determined by it (that is, society's relations of production and reproduction). While economic practices and relations may, however, 'determine the distribution of practices and commodities', to argue that 'they determine which meanings circulate and which do not' (Grossberg 1995: 76) is a stretch. Articulating culture as a variable to the (pre-given) market economy, and class relations as fixed, is also problematic because it assumes, first, that social relations are fixed and predictable and, second, that there is some kind of neutrality to 'cultural products' wherein they are (re) produced separately to social relations and are simple vessels of pleasure. Material interests seemingly exist *a priori* to cultural products, which entertain rather than make and communicate meaning.

As Storey suggests, while almost 'everything we buy helps reproduce the capitalist system economically', everything we buy 'does not necessarily help us secure us as "subjects" of capitalist ideology' (2012). Lipschutz ultimately argues that popular culture is not 'a source of, or incitement to, revolutionary social action or transformation' (2010: 164). While, initially, I may have agreed with this proposition, I have found while writing this book that 'the capitalist system' is far too riddled with contradiction (as Marx so famously articulated) for the relationship between production, text and consumption to be so simple (and so bleak).

IPE needs to take 'more seriously than previously', argues Germain, culture as 'a cardinal aspect of political economy' (2011: 62). A 'cultural political economy' (CPE) approach takes 'the cultural turn seriously, highlighting the complex relations between meaning and practices', argue Jessop and Oosterlynck, while remaining attentive to the 'conjoint impact' of 'semiotic and extra-semiotic processes' on 'the constitution and dynamic of capitalist formations' (2008: 1156). As Best and Paterson argue, political economy, 'as conventionally understood, whether in neoclassical, public choice, institutionalist, statist or Marxist terms', is abstracted 'from its cultural constitution' (2010: 2). Orthodox political economy tends, Jessop and Oosterlynck suggest, to 'naturalize or reify its theoretical objects (such as land, machines, the division of labour, production, money, commodities, the information economy', while offering 'thin accounts, at most, of how subjects and subjectivities are formed and how different modes of calculation emerge, come to be institutionalised, and get modified' (2008: 1156–7). A move to incorporate culture, on the other hand, will likely 'transform our understanding of what political economy *is*' (Best and Paterson 2010: 2, emphasis in the original).

> Culture is too often [in IPE] a residual category of ideas that are simply apprehended and used in an instrumental manner, as ideological categories that rationalize particular decisions taken in the interests of more organic and somehow prior commitments. Culture, in this sense, confirms the modalities of world order, rather than shapes or undermines them.
>
> (Germain 2011: 62)

Not all political economists, of course, argue that capitalism is a monolithic system and not all want to run screaming at the suggestion that cultural emancipation may be possible through '"hitherto uncongenial economic mechanisms"' (Willis 1990, quoted in Storey 2012: 234). As Davies articulates, the 'cultural turn has provided some important innovations in recent studies of political economy', helping in particular 'to bring into question the conceptual and methodological dualism of culture versus economy' (2010: 49). While it is true that feminists have long 'recognized the importance of cultural struggle within the contested landscape of popular culture' (Storey 2012: 11), Gramscian and poststructural political economists also take seriously 'the contradictory mix of different cultural forces', the interactions 'between the discourses of the text and the discourses of the reader' and the 'political constructions of the people' that have animated cultural studies debates (see Storey 2012: 11).

> Post-Marxist hegemony theory at its best insists that there is always a dialogue between the processes of production and the activities of consumption. The consumer always confronts a text or practice in its material existence as a result of determinate conditions of production. But in the same way, the text or practice is confronted by a consumer who in effect *produces in use* the range of possible meaning(s) – these cannot just be read off from the materiality of the text or practice, or the means or relations of its production.
>
> (Storey 2012: 239)

Walker, however, argues that 'it is futile to expect the imminent arrival of a cultural political economy in any cohesive or integrated sense' (2010: 226). Since each of these terms, he suggests, already include each other, any strategy of inclusion is already thwarted and 'it is not so difficult to make any one of the terms do the work of the other two' (ibid.: 229). The term 'cultural political economy' also, Walker suggests, implies claims about value 'that are in profound contradiction with one another', with each part of the term, although already included in the others, working simultaneously to 'affirm autonomy from the others'

40 Analysing popular culture

(ibid.: 227). Thus culture, for Walker, as 'the value of identities and differences structured between potentially autonomous subject-nations and potentially collective communities' may be incompatible with politics as 'the value of a sovereign authority split between the sovereign state, the system of sovereign states and the sovereign subject-people', which may then compete with economy as 'the value established by property and the market' (ibid.: 230).

As someone who finds ideas about culture, politics and economy interesting and who thinks they are connected, I would prefer (and hope) to leave this book, semiotically and semantically, open in this regard. I rather like Vincent Mosco's definition of political economy (perhaps inserting a 'meaning' after 'consumption'), which leaves 'the discipline' relatively uncluttered by territorial claims. 'Political economy', suggests Mosco, 'is the study of the social relations, particularly the power relations, that mutually constitute the production, distribution, and consumption of resources' (2009: 2).

Storey adopts a Gramscian perspective to suggest that 'the cultural field is marked by a struggle to articulate, disarticulate, and rearticulate particular meanings, particular ideologies, particular politics' (2003: xi). He is wary both of 'economic reductionisim' (which sees meaning as determined by mode of production) and 'textual essentialism' (where meaning is an inherent property of things) and seeks to centre his approach more firmly on the activities and agencies that go into the making of meaning and, therefore, the 'politics of culture' (ibid.). Storey is concerned about 'the idea of popular culture' and how this is entangled 'with questions of social power' (2003: xii). Following Storey, this research starts from the assumption that 'meaning is not something fixed and guaranteed in nature' and 'is always the result of particular ways of representing nature in culture' (2003: x). My argument here is not, contra a certain amount of political economy scholarship, that class relations are the key causal force in world politics. I do not view 'culture' as *necessarily* something produced and/or consumed according to class relations (although I certainly concede that cultural artefacts may indeed be more readily available to/consumed according to resources, social relations and inequalities in these). Rather, as per Aitken's analysis, I am more interested in the ways that 'culture' is 'key to "economy" and to the ways in which "economy" could be (re)shaped' (2010: 68).

There may be aspects of cultural studies that are overly celebratory of popular culture (as per Garnham's critique), and it may be the case that a 'fear of economic reductionism' has led some in cultural studies, as per Hall's critique, to imply that the economic 'does not exist at all' (1996, cited in Storey 2012: 238). Attention to the 'conditions of existence' that generate cultural commodities and social relations still seems (at least to my untrained cultural studies eye) pervasive across cultural studies.

> [D]ominant ways of making the world meaningful, produced by those with the power to make their ways of articulating meaning circulate discursively in the world, generate the 'hegemonic truths' which seek to assume an

authority over the ways in which we think and act; that is, they invite us to take up 'subject positions' from which meanings can be made and actions carried out. It is this conflict – the relations between culture and power – which is the core interest of cultural studies.

(Storey 2003: x–xi)

This research is most interested in the popular cultural form of feminism, and how this might shape (or not) operations of the economy, noting the activities and agencies that go into making feminism (or antifeminism) meaningful. Several cultural studies ideas and innovations thus inform this book and I draw on these to provide a fuller picture of what I think are valid political economy questions, including how feminism (or antifeminism) are rendered meaningful across popular culture sites and how this might, as per Storey's argument, be entangled with questions of social power. Such ideas and innovations are various.

First, cultural studies places emphasis on *the media as symbolic institutions*, that is, as institutions whose products signify and in which language, practice and imagery convey messages, create narratives and construct meaning. Second, cultural studies underlines the significance of *questions of articulation*. Articulation is 'the principle way in which the relations between production, consumption, politics, and ideology are theorized in cultural studies' (Grossberg 1995: 73). Third, cultural studies focuses on *questions of identity*, engaging with important questions of *emergent identities*, which is significant for this book as people find new outlets for themselves through social media, and the relationship between identities, emergent and existent. Fourth, cultural studies highlights ideas around *textuality, interpretation and difference* to think both about the 'self-production' and social reproduction of culture, placing local practices in 'the wider context of the social structures of power' (Grossberg 1995: 73). Fifth, cultural studies underscores the *complex and contradictory* nature, not only of culture, but of the relationships between people, culture and power. Lastly, cultural studies is perhaps most significant to this research for emphasizing the extent to which culture (and its products) create and communicate *meaning* and is therefore, in and of itself, *meaningful*.

Consumer culture, consumerism and popular culture

Popular culture, including its processes, practices and products, is more than simply the commodities it produces and while we can argue to a certain extent the existence of mass media and communications, defining popular culture according to a notion of mass-produced commercial culture is, as I have argued previously, problematic. Certainly, popular culture, as per Storey's analysis the cultural practices of 'ordinary' people, will draw from the practices of consumer culture, and consumer culture borrows and deploys the representations of popular culture, but they are worth distinguishing. This is not only due to crucial historical and technological changes in the processes of production and availability but, relatedly, because, as outlined above, both popular and commercial

42 Analysing popular culture

culture are dynamic and their features subject to losing currency according to place, time and context.

Popular culture is rarely, today, wholly and systematically attributed to corporate and/or commercial interests. Popular culture can, and does, support and reproduce capitalist assumptions, but this is not a uniform process and must be analysed, not assumed. Both contemporary popular and consumer culture support and endorse 'material culture', which points, as Lury describes, 'to the significance of *stuff*, of *things* in everyday practices' but indicates also that 'this attention to the materials of everyday life is combined with a concern with the cultural, with norms, values and practices' (2011: 9, emphasis in the original). The rise of commercialism is more clearly, however, 'an artefact of the growth of corporate power' (Ruskin and Schor 2009, in Turow and McAllister 2009: 410).

It should also be highlighted that studies of consumption are not the same as, and ought not to be confused with, studies of 'consumer culture'. Australia, New Zealand, the UK and the USA can clearly be classified as 'consumer societies', for example, but their popular cultures are not equivocal, despite frequent intersections. As Miller articulates, it is true that 'the vast array of things that people buy in London are produced by some variant of the market or capitalism. So it is not surprising that we see the shopper as the end point of that system' (2012: 54). The shopper in London is not however, Miller suggests, merely the mannequin wearing the clothes that ensure the fashion industry (for example) remains profitable (Miller is summarizing Baudrillard here). In many instances 'the shopper has a quite extraordinarily precise idea of themselves in relation to the vast array of consumer goods' (ibid.).

Consumption is, of course, more than simply shopping, involving, as Lury notes, the consumption of things other than commodities, including gifts, self-produced objects, freely given services, and so on (2011: 12). As Miller articulates, consumption also entails the (social, not just individual) ways we transform the goods that we purchase, which is a 'much more active process' than shopping alone, 'shifting goods from alienable to inalienable' (2012: 64). The strong sense of identity that shopping imparts on the shopper is important, though, because it supports and reproduces the political identification of freedom with individual choice that is endemic to consumer culture (Lury 2011: 5–6). On 'owning' a thing, it no longer signifies the initial shop environment, and the chain of production that this entails, since the thing becomes the shopper's: it becomes 'a clear signal of [the] specific taste, personality and presence in the world [of the shopper in question]' (Miller 2012: 55). Clearly this process of self-identification in the face of a system (capitalism) that is otherwise alienating is partly a conceit of market ideology, but the various points up to which the shopper has achieved a precise sense of themselves are not explicable in reference to consumer culture alone.

Consumer culture, Lury notes, consists of a true diversity 'of things, processes, values, norms and practices' (2011: 5–6). It involves a variety of processes, sometimes 'pulling in different directions', based in some degree on forms of economic organization and divisions of labour (and driven by the pursuit of profit) but also dependent on relationships between different systems of exchange, regimes of

Analysing popular culture **43**

value, consumer politics and state action, 'expertise' and 'subcultures' and the 'political identification of freedom with individual choice' (ibid.). Consumer culture is as fundamental to our processes of identity formation as popular culture, and popular culture depends on consumption, but I would argue here that popular and consumer culture are worth separating, at least analytically. I borrow Lury's words to suggest that consumer culture is 'the use or appropriation of objects or things' in which 'the consumer emerges as an identity' in and of itself (2011: 9).

Popular culture, of course, uses and appropriates objects and things and popular culture can, and often does, support the reproduction of 'the consumer' as master identity category (although the consumer as 'master category of identity' does not always reside at its core). Importantly, popular culture is consumed in the sense of being bought and sold, and while everyday cultural meanings, including those circulating in popular culture, are important in understanding the ways in which consumer goods can, and often do, become an expressive instrument from which people create their lives, and their identities, popular culture also often eludes the profit motive of market capitalism. While popular culture is not, then, reducible to commercialism, we ignore at our peril the commercial imperatives that propel the production of cultural artefacts. As McRobbie articulates, these are particularly significant when we consider how feminists must, today, navigate the ways in which commercial imperatives might disarm feminist critique by reproducing a myth of choice, freedom and objection; a myth that is always pre-empted with irony in contemporary postmodern, consumer culture, since women (and men) are apparently free to choose how they are objectified (2009: 17).

Understanding the relationship, however, between popular culture as a site of meaning and the consumption of certain ideas about feminism demands consideration of the multiplication of identities that popular culture supports, only part of which can be accounted for by contemporary consumer culture. A limited commercial definition of popular culture may assume, for example, that profitability and marketability have taken 'precedence over quality, artistry, integrity and intellectual challenge' (Strinati 2004: 3). This assumption is flawed, however, because it does little more than describe consumers as the passive endpoints of economic activity, rather than being capable of actively transforming the world and being transformed by it. As Storey notes, we communicate 'through what we consume' and consumption is often 'the most visible way in which we stage and perform the drama of self-formation' (2003: 78). Consumption is also, then, a form of production. The kinds of books we read, the films we watch, the music we listen to: these are questions both of consumption and cultural identity and thus both are inextricably linked. Culture is not reducible to the products we consume, and I do not want to argue this here, but the relationship between consumption and cultural identity remains significant.

Using my investigation of the relationship between feminism and popular culture as a hypothetical, the relationship between popular and consumer culture is important. Commercial success can be measured in reference to the successful distribution, exchange and consumption of certain *stuff*, and this research is specifically

44 Analysing popular culture

interested in examining whether feminism (or antifeminism) can be argued to be commercially viable in the sense that they generate tangible profit for cultural producers. This research is also interested in asking whether feminism (or antifeminism) can be argued to be *successful* in the popular culture domain, which is not necessarily dependent on their commercial prowess but on their popularity, that is, the ways in which they generate support, debate and 'air time' and/or are more frequently represented in a positive light. This is difficult to measure (although easier to visualize) and is complicated by the ways in which people's sense of themselves (their processes of self-identification) in contemporary material culture have been inflected with the knowingness that comes with advanced information technologies. Popular culture, as a site of meaning-making, may enable the reproduction of certain conditions in which feminism is disparaged or dismissed. It may not do this uniformly and across artefacts, but a certain flourishing of antifeminism may take hold in particular (perhaps dominant) areas of popular culture, such as across network television programming, or in Hollywood film production. Depending on how extensive this reproduction of antifeminist meaning, consumer culture may also draw upon popular culture's representations and narratives of antifeminism to generate profit, supporting the production of antifeminist cultural products which are perceived as more commercially viable (that is, likely to generate profit), given prevailing popular culture trends. It is neither popular nor consumer culture alone that are individually responsible for sustaining and endorsing antifeminism, yet both may contribute to the perpetuation of a hostile environment for feminism. The more entrenched antifeminism becomes across dominant cultural sites, the more apparently normal and commonsensical antifeminism is and the more critical the feminist mass against such a hostile environment needs to be. The same might also be said of the militarization, sexualization, racialization, and so on, of popular and consumer culture. The social and cultural processes by which cultural artefacts are disseminated and reproduced are not a side issue to understanding politics, they are absolutely central to it.

Commercial viability and (cultural) popularity

As noted above, commercial success and popularity are not necessarily conflatable, nor should we assume either implies the other. Those movies and television programming considered 'cult classics' enjoy this status precisely because they are observed not to have experienced the commercial successes of big budget, Hollywood products. Very often, despite limited commercial success upon release, films, TV series, books, video games and so on become popular, perhaps explicitly because of their 'niche' status (*Napoleon Dynamite*, *Harold and Maude*, *Clerks*, *Little Britain*, *The Office (UK)*, *Community*). Some films and television series, especially within the science fiction and horror genres, have been produced specifically to achieve cult status (*Fear and Loathing in Las Vegas*, *Brazil*, *Pink Flamingos*, *Repo Man*, *The Evil Dead* films, *Twin Peaks*). In some instances, initial commercial failures yield to much bigger successes as artefacts gain popular momentum through video

Analysing popular culture **45**

and DVD distribution (*Fantasia, The Shawshank Redemption, This is Spinal Tap, The Rocky Horror Picture Show, Firefly, Futurama*, the video games *Eternal Darkness* and *Shadow Warrior*). Actor Bruce Campbell (of the much-loved and eminently 'cultish' *Evil Dead* films) once defined the difference between 'mainstream' and 'cult' by defining the former as 'a film that 1,000 people watch 100 times' and the latter as 'a film that 100 people watch 1,000 times'. Many 'cult' artefacts do, of course, also simultaneously attract both a particular subgroup of fans and a mass audience (Christopher Nolan's *Batman* Trilogy, in particular *The Dark Knight*, and the *Harry Potter* franchise are noteworthy here). While many film buffs would argue that a film cannot truly occupy 'cult' status when consumed by a mass audience, the relationship, and distinctions, between commercial success and cult following are difficult always to maintain.

Global/local contexts as platforms for success

As Waisbord argues, 'television is filled with national variations of programs designed by companies from numerous countries' and, for decades, 'formats of 'reality' and 'fiction' programming have been produced and sold in international markets' (Moran 1998, cited in Waisbord 2004: 359). 'Format television' has become one of, if not the, preeminent forms of commercial television, and its commercial successes are enormous. More than just another trend 'in an industry perennially hungry for hit shows and eager to follow them', the popularity of formats 'reveals two developments in contemporary television' (Waisbord 2004: 360). First, 'the globalization of the business model of television' is clearly evident here. Second, 'the efforts of international and domestic companies to deal with the resilience of national cultures' (ibid.). Analysis of both these developments, Waisbord argues, enables a reexamination of how 'economics and culture are related in the process of media globalization', with television becoming, in effect, 'an increasingly integrated' and singular business, 'governed by similar practices and goals' across locations (ibid.). While we might see this integration as a form of 'cultural homogenization', with a dozen media companies 'able to do business worldwide by selling the same idea' and audiences 'watching national variations of the same show', Waisbord prefers, however, to note how much formats 'attest to the fact that television still remains tied to local and national cultures' (ibid.). Television is 'both global and national', shaped both 'by the globalization of media economics and the pull of local and national cultures' (2004: 360).

This simultaneity applies to most forms of popular culture more broadly and the interplay of local and global contexts renders most arguments concerning cultural homogenization (normally read as Americanization) difficult to sustain. Privatization, liberalization, and deregulation of the airwaves have certainly 'opened television systems to flows of capital and programming', which has resulted in 'the increasing homogenization of systems on the principles of private ownership and profit goals' (Waisbord 2004: 360). While changes in the structure of television systems have, however, connected television systems that once functioned

46 Analysing popular culture

in relative isolation (ibid.), the cultural 'icons' produced by and in popular culture may not be universally known or recognized (Hollywood and Bollywood stars, for example, branded products renamed across location, national figures and symbols universally known but understood completely differently depending upon location). Cultural icons celebrated locally may have no popular reach beyond context and location but hold great popular sway *in* context. Countries may erect particular barriers to the availability of non-national products (France's Toubon Law mandating the French language and quota regulations enforcing 40 per cent French-language broadcast music spring to mind).

A cultural homogenization argument does not also, of course, account for the level of state control of the media experienced in countries such as Syria, China, Russia, Egypt and North Korea (which also themselves vary in terms of state intervention in and control of the media). It does not consider various media system models, as for example in Hallin and Mancini's famous analysis of the three media system models common to the Atlantic, northern Europe and southern Europe. Hallin and Mancini argue that the relative dominance of market mechanisms of commercial media is evident only in the 'Liberal Model' prevalent across Britain, Ireland and North America (2004: 11). The 'Democratic Corporatist' model evident in Northern Europe, they argue, is characterized by a historical coexistence of 'commercial media and media tied to organized social and political groups' and 'by a relatively active but legally limited role of the state', while the 'Polarized Pluralist' model of southern (Mediterranean) Europe is characterized by the 'integration of the media into party politics', the 'weaker historical development of commercial media' and 'a strong role of the state' (2004: 11). Even these relatively specific models, the authors suggest, can only be characterized as 'ideal types' that the media systems of individual countries fit 'only roughly' (2004: 11). In many instances, countries within models differ substantially (the UK to North America, for example, or Spain to Italy).

The diversity of media production outlets enabled by globalized capital and programming flows is also worth considering. The rise of multichannel, all-day, any-time programming has impacted media systems and their potential reach. Hollywood companies, Waisbord argues, enjoyed an early advantage, with 'extensive libraries, well-established distribution networks, and an unparalleled marketing machine', but as 'the principles of commercial television became standardized and industries matured, other domestic industries could also produce and export programming, particularly if they catered to niche audiences' (2004: 361). In Britain, the successes of Pearson (the originator of *Who Wants to Be a Millionaire*), in Holland of Endemol (*Big Brother*) and in Sweden of Strix television (*Survivor*) are evidence, Waisborg suggests, 'that the pool of producers is no longer limited to traditional Hollywood companies' (2004: 361).

Inequalities remain in the global trade of audiovisual products, as Waisbord notes, and, despite the successes of third world producers, 'Western domination of the global television market remains undisputed in terms of program sales' (2004: 362). Television programming has become diversified and more complex, but Hollywood studios continue to report huge profits. Despite no longer accounting for 71 per cent of the total world traffic in television material, as in the late 1980s, 'the six major Hollywood studios raked in $4.5 billion to $5 billion in 2001, more than the rest of the world combined' (Purcell 2001, cited in Waisbord 2004: 362).

> The popularity of television formats is at the crossroads of global and local dynamics of the cultural economy of television. Contemporary television is a Janus-faced industry that in the name of profitability needs to commodify real and imagined nations while being open to global flows of ideas and money. The global circulation of formats responds to programming strategies to bridge transnational economic interests and national sentiments of belonging. Such strategies neither follow patriotic concerns nor suggest that television dutifully respects the diversity of national cultures. Rather, they result from the intention to maximize profits while 'the national' continues to articulate cultural identities. In turn, television programming recreates and perpetuates national sentiments.
>
> (Waisbord 2004: 367–8)

The advantage of format shows is that they allow successful programs to be adapted to national cultures without running into the cultural incompatabilities that many foreign shows experience (Waisbord 2004: 368). Similarly, cable networks like MTV and ESPN have realized that programming in local languages can be more profitable than monolingual, English language broadcasts. General trends also suggest that the influence of internet access is increasingly influential in determining the consumption of media. In 2009, one-third of all internet traffic was video, a figure that rose to 40 per cent in 2010, and projections (Kerwin 2010) suggested that this figure would be at 91 per cent by 2014. Some of the highest consumers of video content, often through mobile communications technology, are found in the Global South, in countries such as Brazil, India and Mexico.

Commercial media (television, news media, magazines, print journalism) are designed to make a profit by delivering information and entertainment to individual (paying) consumers at the same time as they deliver the attention of these consumers to (paying) advertisers. The most successful Hollywood studios generate their profit (and pay for the countless flops) by finding ways to 'monetize the ancillary stream' (by, for example, selling pay-TV and overseas rights, creating tie-in video games, amusement-park rides, toys and other merchandise, and so on) (Davidson 2012). 'Worldwide spend on filmed entertainment is around $65 billion a year, of which the distributors' share is about $35 billion' and total 'revenues are split almost equally between the Domestic (North American) market and the Rest of the World' (Ritchie 2013). A film need not actually be terribly popular at the cinema in terms of bottoms on seats to be successful, if studios get their marketing stratgeies right, with theatrical (that is, cinema) revenues accounting for approximately 25 per cent only of the spend on filmed entertainment, while video (including DVD) takes around 40 per cent, television 28 per cent and ancillary

48 Analysing popular culture

revenues the final 7 per cent (ibid.). Studios regularly spend upwards of $50 million covering 'negative costs' (the costs incurred producing and shooting a film, but excluding distribution and promotion costs) and a further $30 million on marketing (up from approximately $8m and $3m respectively in 1980). While growth in the movie industry is projected to be fairly stable over the next few years, with predictions suggesting that growth will sit at around 0.6 per cent, growth in the *television* industry, with its ability to experiment with 'different models, distribution methods and ways of telling stories' is expected to be significant (Davidson 2012).

The importance of social media

Not-obviously-for-profit social media cannot necessarily be considered commercially successful in the same ways. While venture capitalism has very often providing the source funding for social media sites to overcome initially overbearing operational costs, this capital was forthcoming on the assumption that such social media sites would generate a method of 'monetarizing' their own success. Also, social media sites are often designed *not* to make a profit by delivering information and entertainment to individual consumers and by generating attention towards commercial advertisers. The more popular a website, the more money, generally speaking, it will be able to generate through advertising. In 2013, Twitter's annual expected global revenue from advertising was estimated at US$629 million, its projected 2014 revenue US$1.08 billion (*Sydney Morning Herald* 2013: 9). Social networking site Facebook has 1.15 billion active users and access to this enormous user base is highly valuable. Thus, 'advertisers might be willing to pay more for an ad on Facebook than for a comparable ad on a smaller social networking site' (Strickland 2009: 1). As Strickland notes, social media sites may also choose to charge a membership fee to users, which is a relatively less common but occasionally highly successful strategy (ibid.). Online dating sites are a good example of this, with many withholding key features from users until they choose to upgrade to a premium account. You might, for example, 'be allowed to browse for a potential match on a dating service, but you'd have to upgrade if you wanted to send your soul-mate-to-be a message' (ibid.).

'Developer fees' for social networking sites that incorporate applications and services into the community can also help generate revenue. Facebook, although it allows developers 'to create applications and incorporate them into Facebook for free', also has 'an optional verification program that requires developers to pay a fee to participate' (Strickland 2009: 1).

> For $375, Facebook will evaluate a developer's application. If the application meets Facebook's standards, Facebook will list it as a verified application. This means Facebook will feature the application prominently over apps that haven't been verified.
>
> (Strickland 2009: 1)

Analysing popular culture **49**

There are other potential options also, such as the establishment of special premium accounts for businesses, which would enable the businesses to leverage the social networking site as an advertising platform (Strickland 2009). The founders of Twitter have, for example, 'discussed a business model that would require companies to pay a verification fee to have an official company Twitter account' (ibid.: 1).

It is currently impossible to tell whether any link can be drawn between advertising spaces on social media site and the feminist (or otherwise) tone of user-driven content. Facebook has an 'advertising platform' that enables brands to build their digital assets on Facebook and drive traffic to their websites (Rodriguez 2013). The more the advertisers pay, the more frequently their advertisements appear on Facebook. Marketers generate 'leads' by posting Facebook advertisements that are directly linked to forms programmed on the Facebook domain. These forms collect a user's contact and personal information from users, including their personal data, interests, location, and the pages on which they click the 'like' button (known as 'psychographic content'). I, for example, only seem to attract sponsored advertising links to weight loss, fitness, jewellery, household and beauty products. This is presumably because marketers have made particular assumptions about my gender, lifestyle and habits, rather than my 'liking' certain weight loss, fitness, jewellery, household and beauty products, which I have never done. I have often wondered what, had I frequently posted psychographic content celebrating sexist, pornographic and/or sexualized content, my sponsored advertisements would look like. If I were male and heterosexual, might I expect to see more ads for *Playboy*? Despite, however, 'liking' and commenting on a number of feminist pages, I have seen little on my user page to reflect these tastes.

As Lyons notes, Facebook promised to 'reinvent media and advertising' and its 'grandiose promise' was that it 'could deliver targeted ads with pinpoint accuracy, delivering ads that were perfectly aligned with people's interests'. As Mark Zuckerberg famously intoned in 2007, 'Once every hundred years, media changes" (Lyons, 2013). If this is the case, Lyons asks,

> how come it's now 2013 and my Facebook homepage is littered with ads that remind me of the cheap one-column ads you used to see in the back pages of 'men's magazines,' back in the day? Why am I getting all these crappy, annoying ads featuring women with enormous breasts urging me to learn a second language or buy solar panels? [Figure 2.2] It's not just me. My buddy Lonn Johnston yesterday posted a copy of one of these obnoxious big-boob ads, because apparently they're popping up in his feed too.
>
> (Lyons 2013)

I (white, 35 years old, female, Australian resident), on the other hand, am more likely it seems to encounter the ads in Figure 2.3.

Most social media sites, including Facebook, will generally fail to police sexist content. When complaints are made, offending material is usually removed (either

FIGURE 2.2 Advertisement on Facebook.

Source: Lyons 2013.

FIGURE 2.3 Author's Facebook newsfeed, 8:14am, October 2013.

Source: Author screenshot.

Analysing popular culture 51

FIGURE 2.4 'Airbag by Porsche' (advertisement).
Source: People Against Sexist Advertising 2010.

by the user who posted the content or by Facebook itself), but this relies on Facebook users themselves to monitor content. Facebook can be a site to contest, and share opinions against, sexism (as in, for example, the pages 'People Against Sexist Advertising' (Figure 2.4), the various 'Slutwalk' pages, 'Feminist Frequency' and so on), or it can be a source of (perhaps inadvertent) sexist and derogatory speech, innuendo and discrimination.

Figure 2.5 shows the Facebook page of a motorbike group of over 4,500 members in Sydney, and is (meant to be) dedicated to the art of motorcycling. The group is a private group, requiring administrator permission to participate and administrator moderation. At this point in the day, I had already waded through at least five or six hilarious naked-women-draped-on-motorbike style pictures, which is not unusual for a group page this size and one dominated by male members. I was interested to know what reaction I would generate if I complained here. Although I generally ignore this kind of sexist content on social media, disregarding posts that I find stupid or offensive (there are simply so many), in person I would always make my views known. I thought that an experiment was in order. I reported the above picture and it was removed almost immediately, by the group member who originally posted it. Although I am probably now despised by at least five male motorcyclists in Sydney, I did receive the following from another male rider (all the comments shown in Figure 2.5 are from male members of the group).

Sydneys Riders   About   Events   Photos   Files

I would never....

43 minutes ago near Carlingford

He's on a ninja 250, no? That's the only way he's ever gonna see up there
37 minutes ago via mobile

I would.
35 minutes ago via mobile

Oh wait what? There is a bike in the picture??
34 minutes ago via mobile

Wait Wot?
34 minutes ago via mobile

i would
32 minutes ago

What ride a green bike ? Me either !
28 minutes ago via mobile

Once you've had black you never go back...
26 minutes ago via mobile

fuk that green shit bike
25 minutes ago

i wanna tap that ass
25 minutes ago

 Penny Griffin Really?? Laughing at harassment and sexist abuse? Please remove this misogynist rubbish. This is a group page, show some respect for the female riders here.
17 minutes ago

ooooooh its a joke relax and enjoy life its a pic
15 minutes ago

FIGURE 2.5 'Sydney Riders' Facebook Page, 17 July 2013.

Source: Author screenshot.

I saw your comment regarding that picture/post on Sydney Riders. Just want to say I wholeheartedly agree with you that women should be respected – not treated and viewed [as] sexist objects. I suppose comments like these are thrown about every day. What matters is that it doesn't go unnoticed! Safe riding!

(Sydney Riders' Facebook group page member, 2013)

Notes

1 Don't push me 'cause I'm close to the edge, I'm trying not to lose my head, It's like a jungle sometimes, It makes me wonder how I keep from goin' under.
2 According to Apple (2005), 'sombitch' is a variant of 'son of a bitch', 'used mostly by white male Southern Americans over the age of forty, in the process of getting killed during a War event on the popular Korean game Ragnarok Online. Sombitch is usually pronounced in an ear-splitting pitch that can be heard across the trailer park: 'YOU SOMBITCH! FUCK FUCK THESE FUCKING FUCKERS!' (real-life quote).
3 Distributor: Weinstein Company. Box office (US): $44,671,682. Theatres: 1756.
4 Distributor: Warner Bros. Box office (US): $37,662,162. Theatres: 3030.
5 Distributor: Weinstein Company. Box office: $38,180,928. Theatres: 3314
6 I should note that OzTAM, the ratings provider for Australian television, calculates ratings from 3,500 panel homes in Sydney, Melbourne, Brisbane, Adelaide and Perth and 1,413 homes nationally for subscription television.

3

POPULAR CULTURE, PRODUCED, REPRESENTED AND CONSUMED

In understanding the ways in which popular culture and feminist discourse support and contest each other, three discursive processes, in particular, are central. These are processes of production, representation and consumption. It is the interaction of these three processes that constructs, Milestone and Meyer argue, 'what we commonly identify as gender identities' (2012: 1). As Rowley asserts, however contested the relative importance of the themes of production, representation and consumption, 'we cannot account for the complex ways in which gender and popular culture matter in global politics without considering all three' (2009: 313). Understanding the power of popular culture texts by engaging with who produces popular culture, its representative, symbolic authority (and how visual and linguistic representations produce meaning) and the practices of consumption that drive and reproduce popular culture permits us a closer mapping of the relations of power, gendered forces, hierarchies and myths through which popular culture enables us to make sense of the world.

The production, representation and consumption of the visual consists of a sequence of processes and the simultaneous emersion of viewer-knowers in the world. As Carver notes, politicians and spokespeople across democracies and author-itarian regimes do not by happenstance deploy or make reference to allusions, quotations and 'lessons' from television and Hollywood: they do this because rulers must share the common language of the ruled (and vice versa), 'not just verbally, but in terms of symbolic references through which meaning is necessarily communi-cated' (Carver 2010: 427). Failing to communicate in popular terms would, in fact, render presidents, prime ministers and political figures less authoritative, at least in terms of their communication skills.

56 Popular culture, produced, represented and consumed

Production

The 'very notion and practice of production are', Grossberg argues, 'themselves culturally produced' (1995: 74). Grossberg notes that 'the relations between production and consumption' are complex and, often, unstable. Analysis that separates production and consumption is thus 'problematic', as is 'the reduction of production to waged labour' (which ignores what Marx himself had argued, which is 'the production involved in consumption/reproduction') (ibid.).

If the relations between production and consumption are complex and unstable, how then are we to understand the processes of who makes what, for whom, and where in the contemporary global political economy and how is analysis of the production of cultural products best approached? How might we position questions about gender identity and feminism in the production of popular culture, including television, cinema, music and social media? Asking apparently simple questions about who produces what, for whom and where requires more complex considerations of relations of cultural power than might at first seem obvious. We cannot assume that what is produced is what is consumed, but analysis that rigorously separates production and consumption is, for Grossberg and many cultural theorists, questionable.

Milestone and Meyer note how, although a good deal of attention has been paid by scholars to 'how culture is represented and consumed', production as a fundamental element of the processes of popular culture has 'often been overlooked' (2012: 6). More recently, they suggest, scholarly work has begun to engage more substantially with cultural production, particularly with the arrival of new cultural and media industries and technological and cultural shifts in working and production. The 'production of culture' remains however, Milestone and Meyer suggest, 'very different to other forms of production' (ibid.). 'Culture' is arguably not made on a production line and is generally held to be 'connected with the realms of the symbolic, identity and aesthetics' (ibid.). Issues of ownership and control remain, however, significant (and some would argue that there is evident across cultural production a 'production line' ethos in capitalist societies).

Asking what kinds of structures enable the production of Hollywood's cultural artefacts, for example, necessitates taking seriously the existing patterns, processes and systems through which Hollywood executives make sense of success and profitability. According to an Annenberg School for Communication and Journalism (part of the University of Southern California) study on the representation of women in film, 'Gender Inequality in 500 Popular Films', both onscreen and behind the camera over the course of five years, a discouraging picture of women's presence and representation emerges. The study notes that females are less likely to be represented on screen and are even less likely to appear behind the camera. When they appear on screen, they are more likely to appear in 'sexy attire' or partially naked. Worryingly, compared to females between 21 to 39 years of age, 'in 2012, females 13 to 20 years of age are more likely to be shown in sexualized attire and partially naked' (Smith *et al.* 2013: 1).

This, according to Hunter (2013), is not, however, necessarily about sexism; or at least it is not *only* about sexism. Although Hollywood *is* sexist, Hunter asserts, the sexism Hollywood reproduces is reflective of its profit motive, not the dismissal of women *per se*. Sexism in Hollywood is the result of structural factors, such as 'talent disinterest, industry laziness and the slow nature of societal change' (ibid.).

> Does sexism occur on a daily basis in Hollywood? Has Hollywood been one big boys' club since the very beginning? Are there still too few women making big (and small) movies? Yes, yes and yes. Is sexism the singular reason? Not even close. Profit is and always will be the main deciding factor.
>
> (Hunter 2013)

Producing a film is betting on its success, notes Hunter, 'and it makes sense that a business would try to ensure the best results by attaching known quantities to their biggest projects' (2013). Hollywood does best what it did before and, 'when studio decisions are working, as they did in 2012 to the tune of the highest domestic box-office tally in history, the industry is given no convincing reason to change their ways' (ibid.).

The Annenberg study examined the top one hundred grossing films from 2007, 2008, 2009, 2010 and 2012. No reason is provided for ignoring 2011, which, Hunter notes, included such 'female-friendly films' as *Harry Potter and the Deathly Hallows 2*, *The Twilight Saga: Breaking Dawn 1*, *Kung Fu Panda 2*, *The Help* and *Bridesmaids*.

> The past decade has seen only 41 women make films that landed in the year-end top 100 lists. Put simply: the male-to-female ratio among studio filmmakers is 15.24:1. The stats are about as bleak for female screenwriters, so there's your first problem – there aren't enough women given opportunities to create complex roles for women, and most male screenwriters and directors are either afraid to write good roles for women or bad at it.
>
> (Bailey 2013)

Hunter argues that it is movie studios' 'profit agenda' that leads them to hand 'very few big budget films' to inexperienced directors (2013). Studios instead choose names that evoke either a proven track record or at least a temporarily high profile (such as *Tron Legacy* director Joseph Kosinski, who had produced only a series of eye-catching, scifi-themed commercials). 'Only ten (non-animated features) of 2012's top 100 films were helmed by first-time feature directors' (ibid.). A director 'builds up' to directing a big action film, with 'an interest and aptitude in the film's more blockbustery elements' (that is, action and/or CGI) just as important and necessary as experience (ibid.). It is, Hunter suggests, 'not hard to imagine that a higher percentage of males show enthusiasm towards making movies loaded with cartoon violence and lackluster scripts' (ibid.).

58 Popular culture, produced, represented and consumed

What Hunter does not consider is that, if even a handful of studio executives also thought like this, it is not hard to imagine an environment in which no female is considered viable for a 'big action film'. It is also, then, not hard to see how women in film become more 'naturally' associated with independent cinema, as shown in a recent report sponsored by the Sundance Institute and put together by the USC Annenberg team that produced the 'Gender Inequality' report. This study, 'Exploring the Barriers and Opportunities for Independent Women Filmmakers' (Smith *et al.* 2013), found a much higher percentage of female film-makers (29.8 per cent) working in independent cinema (more specifically, films selected for the Sundance Film Festival between 2002 and 2012).

Hunter suggests that the report's 'presumed conclusion', that women make smaller films because they are unable to get 'the jobs in big Hollywood' may be false and that it could 'also be that many women are simply drawn to the more personal, intimate and smarter stories best served by smaller films' (2013). Hunter points to Oscar-winner Kathryn Bigelow's success as an example of how women in Hollywood count themselves out before they have even got close to the industry. He quotes Bigelow herself to suggest that 'many female filmmakers simply don't think they can be a movie director' (either through 'fear of big, sexist Hollywood' *or* 'a lack of self conviction or personal interest').

> If there's specific resistance to women making movies, I just choose to ignore that as an obstacle for two reasons: I can't change my gender, and I refuse to stop making movies. It's irrelevant who or what directed a movie, the important thing is that you either respond to it or you don't. There should be more women directing; I think there's just not the awareness that it's really possible. It is.
>
> (Bigelow 1990)

Given that women generally, in Hollywood and independent cinema, fare poorly in comparison to men, whether Hunter's feelings about women's preference for small and independent filmmaking are true or not seem somewhat beside the point. As the Center for the Study of Women in Film in Television notes, women's presence in domestic US cinema production (women as directors, executive producers, producers, writers, cinematographers and editors) decreased in 2013 by two percentage points from 2012 (Lauzen 2014). The Center also notes that practices of film criticism are themselves gendered, with 'popular film criticism' remaining a 'predominantly male activity' and 'films with male directors and writers' receiving 'greater exposure as male critics are more likely to review these films than films with female directors and writers' (Lauzen 2013: 2). Bigelow, who in 1990 had just released the film *Blue Steel*, starring Jamie-Lee Curtis, does not deny that there is 'specific resistance to women making movies' and notes only that she was able (or lucky enough) to ignore it.

The Sundance report points to five key areas in which women's career development in film is hampered. First, women face particular gendered financial barriers. Second, they face male-dominated industry networking. Third, they face stereotyping on set. Fourth, they struggle with work and family balance. Fifth, they face exclusionary hiring decisions (Sundance Institute 2013). The report argues that mentoring and encouragement for early career women, improving their access to finance and raising awareness of the problem would improve women's film prospects. Hunter suggests that we need to wait for the slow crawl of social change to disable the male-dominated production 'wheel' and that female-led cinema success is 'a game of dominoes or connect the dots' (2013). The 'sexist' line is both too reductive and too simple and it remains difficult 'to engender change of any kind when the status quo is so damned profitable' (ibid.). Such change might include the end of audiences 'turning big, dumb movies that objectify women into box office hits', instead going out of their way 'to find and support films that not only understand the Bechdel Test but pass it, too' (ibid.).

> Barring moviegoers making their collective voices heard, the change will need to come voluntarily from within. A quota system is out of the question so spontaneous effort is required from people in positions of power currently reaping the benefits and bonuses from unprecedented box office success. Good luck with that.
>
> (Hunter 2013)

Gendered disparities in television, radio and news media are slightly less shocking than those in film, although the numbers remain heavily skewed and (white) men predominate. According to statistics published by *Media Report to Women* (*MRW*), national public radio in the US shows a relatively high representation of female hosts. Reports from the fourth Global Media Monitoring Day (2009), in which observers in 130 countries monitored major media outlets, found that '24 per cent of the people interviewed, heard, seen or read about in mainstream broadcast and print news were female', which represented a 'significant change from 1995, when only 17 per cent of the people in the news were women' (*MRW* 2012). *MRW* notes that near parity now exists between women and men 'in the category of people providing popular opinion', although 'women are persistently underrepresented as experts and authorities' in the news (ibid.).

In US broadcast news reporting, while in 1987, 'men reported 73 per cent of stories', by 2007, 'men reported 48 per cent and women, 40 per cent' (the remaining 12 per cent were team efforts featuring reporters of each gender) (*MRW* 2012). In US newsrooms, however, 'women's participation has remained static, at roughly 36.5 per cent, since 1999' and white men remain responsible for 80 per cent of all major op-eds (ibid.). Women working full-time in daily newspapers total approximately 36.92 per cent in the USA, with minority women accounting 'for 19.3 per cent of female newsroom staffers'. Sports journalist jobs remain 'overwhelmingly white and male' (ibid.). In 2011, female TV news directors totalled 28.3 per cent and female radio news directors only 10.7 per cent. Female journalism and mass communication bachelor's degree graduates, however, fare better in

60 Popular culture, produced, represented and consumed

the job market than their male peers, since women 'disproportionately specialize in advertising and public relations, which have higher levels of full-time employment for their graduates than do other parts of the field' (ibid.).

The news media industry's structures of production of content and the industry itself remain heavily segregated between 'pink' and 'blue' collar areas. In the USA, according to Chemaly,[1] 'men outnumbered women in front-page byline coverage of the 2012 presidential elections at top newspapers by an almost 3 to 1 margin' (2014). On Sunday morning talk shows, 'one survey found that only 25 per cent of guests were female' and another concluded that 'only 14 percent of those interviewed and 29 percent of roundtable guests' were women (ibid.). Women remain 'concentrated in 'pink collar' areas in both new and old guard media', including 'food, family, furniture and fashion'.

> [A] review of the *New York Times* and *The Wall Street Journal* shows that just one-half of one per cent of op-eds were written by Latinos; for The Washington Post, that number was 0 per cent. Among those publications, Asian Americans wrote an average of 2 per cent; African Americans roughly 5 per cent.
>
> (Chemaly 2014)

The television industry remains similarly gender-segregated. In network television, 'male directors outnumbered females 4 to 1 in a review of 3,100 episodes of prime-time television' (broadcast and cable) (Chemaly 2014). In the 2010 to 2011 prime-time television season in the USA, 'women accounted for 25 per cent of all creators, executive producers, producers, directors, writers, editors, and directors of photography working on situation comedies, dramas, and reality programs airing on the broadcast networks' (*MRW* 2012). In the same season, while they made up 37 per cent of producers, women also constituted only 4 per cent of directors of photography (ibid.).

Representation

Put simply, engaging with (and understanding) the politics of representation means negotiating the symbolic references through which meaning is made and communicated. The above discussion of the production of sources of popular culture tells us that there are particular and obvious inequalities across the media industries in terms of who produces what, where and by what means. It might be the case that a lack of female directors, for example, of Hollywood action movies leads to a poverty of representations of women in action movies, but to make this argument, we would need to assume that the gender of a director relates directly to their ability to create meaningful representations. This is a somewhat tenuous and essentialist argument that assumes that men cannot write women, and vice versa (or, for example, that male directors cannot produce decent female characters and that female directors create better representations of women on celluloid).

While there is some anecdotal evidence to suggest that female writers and directors create more and better female characters,[2] this line of argument does not necessarily take us far in understanding how a set of desired attributes reproduced in representations of women and men across popular culture makes sense. To understand the social and cultural logics, and thus impacts, of gendered representations, we need to ask further, and different, questions, about the types of verbal and visual messages that content generated from such inequalities might yield. We need, for example, to understand the broader social settings by which it makes sense to people that certain, desirable, attributes of a male character in a movie or television show, for example, are likely, when expressed by a female/gay/non-white male, to incite condemnation.

Understanding the practices of representation through which our popular culture artefacts make sense to us requires interrogating the visual and verbal messages that are reproduced across popular culture. Practices of representation and structures of production are intimately entwined because the activities and agencies that go into making certain representations meaningful are, as per Storey's argument (2003, 2012), entangled with questions of social power. Producers, directors, script writers, editors, executives, and so on, are always situated culturally. They are located within networks of social mores and assumptions and their productions are readable in terms of the logics to which they speak. If women are understood, within a particular cultural and temporal location, to be more persuasively 'realistic' when represented by a 'damsel in distress' persona, this is a reflection of the embedded cultural biases of processes of production, representation and consumption, while the reproduction of these stereotypes also legitimates the further reproduction of these biases. Understanding, as per Grossberg's analysis, our notions and practices of production, representation and consumption as 'culturally produced' requires that we take seriously how popular culture is both conditioned by wider cultural practices and, in turn, conditions these. Popular culture's verbal and visual messages may tend, for example, to portray women as subservient and men as dominating; or, to stand out, to gain attention, they may do the opposite, which is radical and noticeable precisely where submissiveness is coded 'feminine'.

While writing this book I have often wondered whether scepticism towards visual analysis in IR and IPE derives of the various physicalities of visual and textual form. While both visual and linguistic culture are the subject of contestation, and both are as open to interpretation as each other, a written text may appear uniformly the same in its presentation across readerships, while imagery might more readily be assumed to be potentially deceptive, changing or too unstill. Perhaps it is this assumed potential for deception that makes many scholars uncomfortable, insecure even, in engaging visual language. Carver notes that visual communication has frequently been coded as 'insufficiently determinate' an academic source for serious study, which means that it requires 'too much interpretation' (and does not therefore constitute a reasonable source of knowledge) (2010: 424). Texts, on the other hand, give scholars a sense of confidence that

62 Popular culture, produced, represented and consumed

what they know, or what they 'are allowed to know', can be limited to what they can say 'that can be written down', repetitiously referring 'text to text, words to words' to create 'a certainty in sameness' (ibid.).

> By contrast, pictures do not tell us much that is instantly determinate, unless they have captions, simply because they do not put their meaning into words. And moving images – when analysed for meaning – are often conflated in works of interpretation with screenplays, where the on-screen words can appear in written form in a book or transcription.
>
> (Carver 2010: 424)

In counterpoint to those who might claim that analysis of popular and/or visual culture is not serious academic business, I would suggest that, to engage in any meaningful way with how we formulate knowledge about the world, and what therefore we know (or do not know) about the world, we need to consider the political processes of representation by which knowledge, reality and identity are selected, organized and transformed. Not only texts but images are central to our representations: in some contexts perhaps, images are today *more* central than texts in representing the world, in others, as Benjamin predicted, word and image are increasingly inter-dependent (1972, cited in Evans and Hall 1999: 7). By failing to consider the power visual language might wield, and the relations of power from which it emanates, we fail also to understand a crucial part of how people 'know' the world and how they then choose (or are able) to act within it.

Bleiker and Hutchison (2008) stress the 'influence that representations of emotion exert on political dynamics' in the realm of visual culture (quoting Bronfen 2005: 131), noting that:

> A growing body of literature examines how in the age of globalization various senses interact with the visual and how the latter has come to be seen as a particularly 'reliable,' even 'authentic' way of knowing the world. Some go as far as stressing that the real political battles today are being fought precisely within these visual and seeming imaginary fields of media representations, where 'affectively charged images' shape our understanding of political phenomena more so than the actual phenomena themselves.
>
> (Ibid.)

As Bleiker argues, referring to Guy Debord's influential work on 'spectacle', 'everything directly lived becomes distanced through representation' (2009: 7). Representation becomes part of 'spectacle', which is a social relationship between people 'mediated by images' (Debord 1992, in ibid.). Even the most thorough empirical analysis 'cannot depict its object of enquiry in an authentic way' and, as Bleiker notes, any representation of 'the real', visual or textual, remains a form of interpretation, reflecting angles and framing, colour choices or brush strokes (ibid: 7).

'Reading' the image

Importantly, all forms and practices of representation convey messages. Messages, because they depend inherently upon the interpretation of the observer, can be *read*, in the sense that they can be received and made sense of, although 'reading' itself has come to symbolize a fairly static and linear process based on the written form. A more expansive definition, and understanding, of 'reading' might instead focus on the ways in which it involves all sorts of human faculties, including perception, reception, study and utterance.

Perhaps the most well-known account of 'reading' the image is supplied by French literary theorist Roland Barthes. Images, in Barthes' analysis, deploy signs and values, each of which requires a general cultural knowledge to yield particular messages. Barthes was concerned for three types of message in particular: the *linguistic* message; the (coded) *iconic* message; and the 'non-coded iconic', or *literal*, message (1999 [1964]: 34–6). The 'overall structure of the image', Barthes suggested, is the 'final inter-relationship of the three messages' (ibid.: 36). Images 'given without words' are, Barthes argued, rare and the linking of text and image is a frequent occurrence (ibid.).

Among contemporary sites of popular culture, this is very clearly the case with print and broadcast media, wherein, although these sources deploy both images and language, language remains the more privileged system of representation. Images rarely appear, across the internet and in the blogosphere, unmoored from linguistic representations (through taglines, descriptions or other written devices) and visual news media, documentary film-making and factual media outlets will usually ground their reporting in some form of spoken monologue or dialogue.

> Today, at the level of mass communications, it appears that the linguistic message is indeed present in every image: as title, caption, accompanying press article, film dialogue, comic strip balloon. [...] What are the functions of the linguistic message with regard to the (twofold) iconic message? There appear to be two: *anchorage* and *relay*.
>
> (Barthes 1999 [1964]: 37, emphasis in the original)

All images, Barthes argues, are polysemous (that is, they are capable of carrying multiple meanings). The image's polysemy is potentially disorientating to the observer, and the presence of the text fixes, to a certain extent, the image's possible meaning(s). This helps the observer 'to choose *the correct level of perception*' (ibid., emphasis in the original). In terms of the symbolic message, the linguistic message guides not so much identification as interpretation, 'constituting a kind of vice which holds the connoted meanings from proliferating' (ibid.). Anchorage may also be ideological, directing the reader 'through the signifieds of the image', remote controlling the reading 'towards a meaning chosen in advance' (ibid.: 37–8).

64 Popular culture, produced, represented and consumed

> In all these cases of anchorage, language clearly has a function of elucidation, but this elucidation is selective, a metalanguage applied not to the totality of the iconic message but only to certain of its signs. The text is indeed the creator's (and hence society's) right of inspection over the image; anchorage is a control, bearing a responsibility – in the face of the projective power of pictures – for the use of the message. With respect to the liberty of the signifieds of the image, the text has thus a *repressive* value and we can see that it is at this level that the morality and ideology of a society are above all invested.
>
> (Barthes 1999: 38)

The function of 'relay' is less common, argues Barthes, but significant in understanding the juxtaposition of text and image where images are not fixed, as in, for example, film. Herein, dialogue functions 'not simply as elucidation but really does advance the action by setting out, in the sequence of messages, meanings that are not to be found in the image itself' (ibid.).

We never encounter a literal image in 'a pure state', whether images appear to us as coded or uncoded. Whereas, for Barthes, drawings are coded messages (since they are reproductions and lack an 'essential nature'), photographs would seem to constitute messages without codes (since they appear as recordings, not transformations). A photograph, 'although it can choose its subject, its point of view and its angle, cannot intervene *within* the object (except by trick effects)' (ibid.: 39). In a photograph 'the absence of a code clearly reinforces the myth of photographic "naturalness" and the mechanical that captures the scene is a guarantee of 'objectivity' (ibid.: 39–40). A photograph, as Sontag argues, is 'not only an image' but 'a trace'; it is something 'directly stencilled off the real, like a footprint or a death mask' (Sontag 1999 [1978]: 80–1). Whatever humans may do to photographs, there is a sense in which this is preceded by a 'brute' photograph, establishing in humans 'not a consciousness of the *being-there* of the thing', but 'an awareness of its *having-been-there*' and 'the denoted image naturalizes the symbolic message', making innocent the 'semantic artifice of connotation' (Barthes 1999 [1964]: 40). The more 'technology develops the diffusion of information (and notably of images), the more it provides the means of masking the constructed meaning under the appearance of the given meaning' (ibid.: 40).

'Reality has always been interpreted through the reports given by images', argues Sontag (1999 [1978]: 80). 'Philosophers since Plato have tried to loosen our dependence on images by evoking the standard of an image-free way of apprehending the real' (ibid.: 80). Sontag argues that our allegiance to the written word over the image goes back a significant way in history to Plato's suspicion of the image as something of a 'sham' (ibid.: 80–1). This 'naïve realism' equated the image with mere appearance; as 'no more than a resemblance' of the thing depicted and not the thing itself (ibid.: 81). Despite advances in humanistic and scientific thinking, which were anticipated to weaken the allegiance on images, images have become, however, and more than ever, substitutes for reality. Although, as Sontag notes, reality 'has always been interpreted through the reports given by images', images

Popular culture, produced, represented and consumed **65**

are, today, in effect, 'coveted substitutes for firsthand experience' that have become 'indispensable to the health of the economy, the stability of the polity, and the pursuit of private happiness' (ibid.: 80). For Sontag, the photograph revives the primitive equation of the image with the thing itself, wherein images and real things are simply two manifestations of the same energy or spirit.

Reading an image 'politically' involves abandoning the pretence that there is a thing itself, an authentic truth or reality, being represented. Rather, the point is to deconstruct the image as an interpretation, as per Bleiker's critique, of the real and a part of our social and cultural relationships. This necessitates, I suggest, adopting something of a poststructuralist understanding of the act of 'reading', in the style of Jacques Derrida, as an act of meaning-creation in itself. Scanning the eyes across a visual projection or a written page does not, as Derrida might have argued, allow us to decipher the 'given meaning' of a 'text' (text here is used in the loosest sense to refer to a physical representation of verbal or visual form),[3] rather, that act is itself 'part of creating' the meaning of the text (Zehfuss 2009: 138–9).

Abandoning Plato's suspicion of the image as 'mere appearance' and assuming that images and the visual world convey as much meaning as (if not more than) written sources allows us to open the visual world to the practices of deconstruction and to 'decode' the messages present across sources of visual culture. Deconstruction, for Derrida, was less a method than a 'critical sharpness' on the part of the researcher that could be applied to contextualizing, historicizing and seeking out the ambiguities and ambivalences in a given source. Derrida was highly sceptical of describing deconstruction as explicitly either method or tool of analysis, refusing any separation of text and exterior application of method, and advocating, rather, that deconstruction be considered always internal to the text. The point, for a deconstructive approach, is that the text always carries within itself its own undoing: the task of the analyst is simply to highlight the incoherencies, inconsistencies and problematic assumptions the text has otherwise rendered indiscernible (Griffin 2013a).

An audience is never left entirely to their own devices in decoding visual discourse and their relationship to hegemonic discourses, negotiated understandings and oppositional meanings is thus impacted heavily by cultural context, the choices of political elites and the methods of media professionals. The production of popular, visual, culture, the 'shooting and editing processes', as Carver terms them, through which visual language is constructed (these might be movies, news broadcasting, television, sports reporting, performances, photos, and so on), enable 'viewer-knowers' to engage in everyday practices of interpretation (2010: 426). Specifically visual elements, as Rowley notes, code characters in different ways' (2009: 316). Such elements, present across all forms of visual representation, are given 'layers of meaning' including, for example, certain props, costumes and other symbols (gestures, stylization, dressing, camera angles).

Stuart Hall discusses three hypothetical positions from which 'decodings' of televisual discourse can be constructed (Hall 1999: 515). The first position is that of the 'dominant-hegemonic' position, where the viewer is operating within the

66 Popular culture, produced, represented and consumed

dominant code, that is, taking meaning as it was intended from a television newscast (or other televisual product). 'This is the ideal-typical case of "perfectly transparent communication"', or 'as close as we are likely to come to it' (Hall 1999: 515). Within this, there may be a professional code at work, by which broadcasters encode messages that have already been signified in a hegemonic manner and assume that the audience is decoding a message within the dominant-hegemonic position. Broadcasting professionals are able both to operate relatively autonomously, but also to reproduce (sometimes in a contradictory way) 'the hegemonic signification of events' (ibid.: 516).

Hegemonic viewpoints are such because they define 'the mental horizon, the universe, of possible meanings of a whole sector of relations in a society or culture', carrying the 'tamp of legitimacy' to make their representations seem 'natural, 'inevitable' or common-sensical (Hall 1999: 516). Hall suggests that hegemonic interpretations are often generated by political and military elites (particularly as in the Northern Ireland 'troubles' as reported throughout the UK in the 1980s and 1990s, or the Chilean coup, the Industrial Relations Bill, and so on). It is possible to argue that, today, WikiLeaks has destabilized these elites' ability to dictate presentational formats, the selection of personnel, choice of images, staging of debates, and so on. I would argue, however, that news media reporting of asylum seekers in Australia falls largely into this dominant-hegemonic position. As Hall notes, conflicts and contradictions arise regularly between the dominant and the professional significations and their signifying agencies (ibid.).

The second position is the 'negotiated code'. Here, most audiences will understand adequately what has been dominantly defined and/or professionally signified (Hall 1999: 516). While they understand the (abstract) grand significations, however, they make their associations and applications based on situational context and local conditions. This may result in what 'defining elites' and professionals identify as a 'failure in communications', since local, context-driven associations may not always flatter broader-based and power-laden hegemonic discourses (of, for example, the 'national interest' or liberal economic policy-making).

The third position from which televisual discourse can be decoded is, Hall argues, the *oppositional code*, where viewers understand perfectly the literal and connotative inflections of a discourse but decode the message contrarily (1999: 517). This deliberate contrariness is a 'significant political moment', signalling perhaps a crisis point for a broadcasting organization and highlights the importance, as Hall terms it, of the 'politics of signification' (ibid.).

As Milestone and Meyer note, although Hall's model of multiple reading positions is more sophisticated than other grand theories of media audiences, 'it simplifies the complex process of audience responses and meaning production', condensing these processes 'into three reactions of agreement (preferred reading), disagreement (oppositional reading) and negotiation (negotiated reading)' (2012: 161). Hall's encoding/decoding model may work better for analysing factual media with strong ideological and political messages, but, Milestone and Meyer argue, performs poorly for fictional media, 'which may not contain any particular messages' (ibid.: 159). It is harder to find direct, connected, overall messages in sports programmes, reality television and talent contest shows, for example (ibid.: 160). Although they may contain strong narratives about, say, normative masculinity, how they are interpreted by certain audiences may vary enormously.

Gendered representations

> Militant feminists, I take my hat off to them. They don't like that.
> (Milton Jones, quoted in Mullinger 2012)

> The young feminists who are spearheading this new activism clearly have enormous energy, ambition and idealism, and in many cases are doing brilliant work. But the question of where the movement goes next, of what its prime focus should be, remains to be answered.
> (Cochrane 2010)

Popular culture and the successes, or otherwise, of feminism and antifeminism connect through various and powerful relations of representation. As Hollows and Moseley note, ideas about examining feminism *and* popular culture often presume 'that a "real" and "authentic" feminism exists outside popular culture', offering 'a position from which to judge and measure feminism's success or failure in making it into the mainstream' (2006: 1). A more useful approach, the authors argue, might be to consider how, by examining feminism *in* popular culture, our ideas about what feminism is or might be about have been formed 'through the popular' (ibid.).

Popular culture texts are central sites of meaning-making. More than simply the by-products of a society or culture, they constitute how we know ourselves and how we believe ourselves to be valid. Examining, for example, how contemporary Hollywood films create and depict women, or how TV shows reproduce ideas about the 'wife', the 'mother', tells us something about the struggles over the meaning(s) of gender identities that have actively shaped, and constrained, people lives. Popular culture texts may corroborate existing, and highly regulative, social narratives and assumptions, they may be tools of ideology and state, elite or group interest, but they might also offer important and subversive critiques of certain social narratives and assumptions. Popular culture, and its processes of production, representation and consumption, are saturated, at every level 'with ideas about how men and women should behave and what they have the right to do' (Milestone and Meyer 2012: 211). Rather than seeking to show how popular culture provides another source for scholars, say of IR or IPE, to add to the list in formulating their analyses, this book argues that popular culture resides at heart of understanding relations of power in global politics. It would be careless scholarship *not* to take seriously how our lives, behaviours, assumptions and possibilities are formed within the popular.

'Gender', as Milestone and Meyer articulate, is 'a deeply political, contentious and complex subject' (2012: 6). As a process of communication, the representational practices of popular culture depict and describe the meanings of

68 Popular culture, produced, represented and consumed

masculinity, femininity, maleness and femaleness that circulate through every society. Representation is so important 'because it is an active process of creating meanings' and how we represent a group of people or an event (through the words we choose or the images we use) shapes 'the meanings of these people and events' (ibid.: 7).

As a brief example, the United Nations Convention to Eliminate Discrimination Against Women (CEDAW) links 'stereotypes about women' directly to 'prejudice based on gender' (Liggett 2012). CEDAW sees a direct correlation between representations of women, femininity and femaleness in society and the prevalence of discrimination against women's bodies. Liggett proposes that 'sexist advertising harms women through objectification and diminishing of self-image', because 'through visual and verbal messages women are portrayed as subservient to men' (2012). The reproduction of this subservience, including women's portrayal as sex objects rather than, say, rounded human beings, only further legitimizes violence against women, harms 'women's self-image by portraying an ideal stylized body' and impacts negatively on men 'through stereotyped images of masculinity' (ibid.).

Representations of women and men across popular culture that may seem more innocuous are no less imbued with powerful gender prerogatives. A history of representing women, for example, as concerned with and in need of heterosexual relationships has created powerful forces for defining women in the West as predominantly heterosexual and fulfilled only by the presence of (heterosexual) romantic attachments. Similarly, defining men as romantic leaders, or as sexually non-committal and avaricious, is similarly constraining while being highly productive of powerful narratives about what men in the West are meant to be.

> [F]emales are depicted in domestic settings far more than males (especially in toy advertising), implying that they can do little outside the home; female characters in films and TV shows aimed at boys are rarely afforded the opportunity to be hero; female characters talk about and worry over their looks far more than male characters; a female's looks are, depending on the program, commented on by male characters and sometimes quite rudely [...]. Such images lay the groundwork for a boy's future attitudes about females, especially if these attitudes are reinforced by peers and ignored in the home environment.
> (The Achilles Effect 2010)

Sontag's discussion of the importance of acquisition in our relationship with images is a central point in understanding the power wielded by the visual. In many instances, we claim to know, and we claim knowledge, because we have *seen*. As Rowley articulates, although we live in a world that depends upon visual communication and communication through the visual, 'we are rarely *explicitly* taught how to read visual images' (2009, citing Howells 2003: 311, emphasis in the original). While reading a visual image may come naturally to most, decoding our 'coded' messages relies, as per Barthes argument, upon the cultural 'tool kits' we have at our disposal.

As feminists have shown, these tool kits may or may not draw upon feminism (Hall and Rodriguez 2003: 885). They do, however, draw upon and thus reproduce cultural and social assumptions about people's bodies, what people can, ought and will do and how they will behave. The relationship between gender codes and prevailing norms in and of visual culture is crucial to feminism, but feminism is perhaps not crucial to the reproduction of the codes that, for example, define the 'modern woman' as a digitally in-touch, corporate pioneering 'canteen-helping, fundraising, muffin-making, party-going, yoga lover' (Kia 'Woman of Now' advertisement, Australia, YouTube 2013d); the 'modern man' as 'free-range, free-spirited, free-willed, but on a leash' (Kia 'Man of Now' advertisement, Australia, YouTube 2013c); sexuality as who and how many we choose to sleep with and; material consumption as natural.

> Sarah Palin responded to her depiction on the cover of *Newsweek* (Figure 3.1) by saying that, when it comes to 'Sarah Palin', 'this "news" magazine has relished focusing on the irrelevant rather than the relevant. […] The out-of-context Newsweek approach is sexist and oh-so-expected by now' (Sarah Palin Facebook page, quoted in *Huffington Post* 2010).

FIGURE 3.1 *Newsweek* cover, 23 November 2009.

Source: *The Telegraph* 2009.

70 Popular culture, produced, represented and consumed

It is important not to misplace human agency in reading the visual. As Benjamin has so famously noted, people have a critical facility with visual and verbal communication that should not be forgotten (1972, cited in Evans and Hall 1999: 7). It is exactly the dangers of assuming a mimetic relationship between representation and represented that render our critical facilities so crucial and so potentially vulnerable. When we see women and men posed provocatively and sometimes abusively in advertisements, we may not actually believe that these images 'represent' what women and men are, should or could be. The quality of the representations of women and men that we are surrounded by in popular culture certainly do, nonetheless, have a direct impact on our sense of self, our sense of others and our expectations of both. The dangers of mimesis are often easily masked by powerful (and potentially damaging) representations of bodies, norms and ideas in popular culture. Photographic images, as Sontag describes, allow us to possess something we may have no experience of: they are so important, so powerful, because they furnish us with knowledge disassociated from and independent of experience (1999: 81). When an image is produced, photographed, circulated and acquired, in the sense that it enters our experiences, it becomes, as Sontag describes, 'part of a system of information, fitted into schemes of classification and storage' (1999: 82). Images give control: control to the observer to redefine their knowledge and experience and control over the thing being recorded, scrutinized and surveilled.

As Skrzydlewska notes, a noticeable tendency 'to present provocatively dressed women, in sexual poses' and for the lyrics of songs for young people to contain 'sexually suggestive content' marks many contemporary television programmes, computer games and musical video clips (2012: 4). This, I would argue, makes it much harder, when children are bombarded with images of their pop star idols as sexualized and sexually competent, to argue that the message equating preternaturally early sexual bravado with maturity and success has *not*, somewhere, been absorbed. This is not to disregard children's own critical facilities but to suggest that the casual observer would do well not to underestimate the processes of self-identification through which children associate their own lives and ambitions with those of their idols. Similarly, the prevalence of images of only women cleaning in advertisements for household cleaning products, while only men drive luxury car models, may prove effective because they corroborate, and then further reproduce, cultural assumptions that equate women with domesticity and men with superior motor skills and spatial awareness.

Consumption

While consumption is certainly related to acts of purchase and the reproduction of consumer capitalism, which will be considered below, it is also worth noting that a thorough understanding of 'consumption' necessitates broader engagement with not just the 'objects of consumption', but 'the organization of objects in environments, object worlds and spaces of consumer experiences' (Lury 2011: 10).

Popular culture, produced, represented and consumed   **71**

'Immaterial culture' needs also to be considered, which is not the world of ideas but the products and services 'whose important characteristics are the outcome of intellectual – or immaterial – labour' (ibid.). Consumer culture, Lury argues, depends on systems of trade, imperialism, the impact of various social groups, the state, other systems of exchange (such as the household and family), cultural inter-mediaries and subcultures (ibid.). Depending on the perspective, 'consumption' itself is largely understood as 'consumption as buying', 'consumption as having', 'consumption as being' and 'consumption as doing' (ibid.: 11).

Investigating consumption as crucial in and to popular culture thus involves thinking specifically about how people acquire, possess, process and respond to popular culture. In relationship to understanding feminism within (and thus repro-duced by) popular culture, this also necessitates thinking about consumption as gendered. Understanding consumption as (potentially) gendered means engaging with how the consumption of popular culture might depend on and (re)produce particular gender identities, entrench or reconfigure traditional gender categories or affect (even rewrite) how we perform our gender identities.

In understanding how feminism and antifeminism are consumed, it is worth, I suggest, considering four key points. First, it is important to reflect on the role of the 'commodity' in contemporary capitalist societies. The commercial viability of a commodity depends on its successful distribution, exchange and consumption. This research interrogates whether sufficient evidence can be marshalled to argue that antifeminism exists in commodity form and is commercially viable (at least, that is, more so than feminism). This depends on understanding how antifeminism is dis-tributed, exchanged and consumed. In the pages following, research here focuses on feminism and antifeminism in popular form, taking care to follow Hollows and Moseley's advice to examine feminism *in* popular culture and, therefore, as some-thing shaped and understood through the popular (rather than presuming a 'real' or 'authentic' feminism existing somewhere outside popular culture).

Second, analysis of consumption and gender might consider how women and men consume media and popular culture texts and how this varies (or not). Culture might be consumed privately and domestically, or it might be consumed more publically.

Third, as Rowley notes, considerations of cultural consumption have reflected particularly on audience reception and the interpretive processes through which audiences consume popular culture (2009: 318). As she also notes, the 'methodo-logical obstacles to accessing audiences' interpretations are not insignificant' (ibid.). This research is limited in how much it can, and should, say about how people 'make sense of and respond to media texts' (Milestone and Meyer 2012: 149). Analysis here of audience interpretations of feminism, and antifeminism, is very firmly restricted only to the direct experiences and interpretations cited by survey respondents to feminism, antifeminism, sexism and popular culture. Accessing and drawing conclusions from wider audience perceptions of popular culture was not a methodological goal of this research and it would be irresponsible of me to hazard what would be, at best, a sequence of guesses around interpretation and reception.

72 Popular culture, produced, represented and consumed

Fourth, as Milestone and Meyer discuss, analysis of popular culture and consumption might also reflect upon spaces of public consumption and how people are able, or not, to access public spaces, whether they are able to be 'active consumers' and cultural producers and what kinds of power struggles over consumption infuse public spaces (2012: 149).

The commodity in capitalist culture

Commodities exist as things that can be bought, sold or exchanged through a market. They are often, but need not be, physical objects, their core purpose being not the manifestation of themselves but of profit. 'Objects are everywhere in capitalism' (Jhally 2009: 416) and an immense collection of commodities must be sold for capitalism to sustain itself. Thus capitalism needs constantly to innovate and commodify (including ideational or physical objects) in order to increase its market base and, once produced, 'commodities must go through the circuit of distribution, exchange and consumption, so that profit can be returned to the owners of capital and value can be "realised" again in a money form' (ibid.).

> If the circuit is not completed the system would [slip] into stagnation and depression. Capitalism therefore has to ensure the sale of commodities on *pain of death*. In that sense the problem of capitalism is not mass production (which has been solved) but is instead the *problem of consumption*. [...] So central is consumption to its survival and growth that at the end of the 19th century industrial capitalism invented a unique new institution – the advertising industry – to ensure that the 'immense accumulation of commodities' are converted back into a money form.
>
> (Jhally, in Turow and McAllister 2009: 417, emphasis in the original)

Whether contemporary commodity capitalism renders gender, sexuality and the body (and its images) as objects of capitalist consumerism is open to debate, but I would argue that the body is today, in Western society, entirely open to commodification.

For Marx, although labour power ultimately resides in workers' bodies, the alienation of labour inherent in capitalist society meant that labour was always somehow external to the body of the worker, a commodity that the worker sold and that capitalists consumed. The worker themselves was thus estranged from the objects of their production. In post-Fordist capitalist societies, however, processes of industrialization and post-industrialization demand what Antonio Gramsci referred to (in *Americanismo e Fordismo*, written between 1929 and 1932 and published in 1949) as a new 'psycho-physical nexus', which requires different forms of participation, intelligence and attitude from the worker. Workers are specialists in flexibilized production systems, with their 'value' dependent on certain representations of their individuality and their minds and identities far more crucial to the commodities capitalism produces than ever before. In contemporary

Popular culture, produced, represented and consumed **73**

post-Fordist societies, it is arguably the case that every aspect of human life has been rendered, in essence, a commodity, with workers' own bodies (and thus their identities) shaped to yield tangible profit or success. While for Marx, capitalists purchased commodified labour power and, ultimately, consumed workers' bodies, in post-Fordist societies, the worker's very body, rather than simply their alienated labour, is for sale.

In a goods-driven society, the objects produced by capitalist modes of production carry meaning in and of themselves. Goods themselves have become, as Miller agues, 'highly expressive of relationships and culture' and 'extremely nuanced' (2012: 112). What consumer societies produce matters not because production and consumption are the result of need, but because demand reflects desire, which is quite far beyond the purview of economic rationalism to predict and justify. Successful advertising promotes the desirability of objects as much as, if not more than, the need for them. Value is not, therefore, objectively produced but is socially practised and subjectively sustained (or lost). The beauty, leisure and fashion industries do not, for example, succeed according to how much we need them but according to how much cultural value is placed on their products. Bodies are also readily manipulated to create their own appendage commodities, for example, through the diet and exercise industries and their representations of the need for constant bodily enhancement. The value placed on physical advancement cannot be understood objectively and 'rationally': it is, rather, a question of how and where the body is appropriated by capitalist prerogatives within particular cultural and social standards.

Strinati questions whether the emergence of culture in commodity forms allows 'the criteria of profitability and marketability' to take 'precedence over quality, artistry, integrity and intellectual challenge' (2004: 3). Profitability is certainly a central criterion by which the longevity of culture in commodity form is sustained. The music and network television industries are, in many ways, shaped by their ability to generate sales, as is Hollywood. Successful social networking and blog sites are also beholden, in crucial respects, to the advertising revenue they can generate. Feminism and antifeminism exist in commodity form in the sense that they, or at least symbols and narratives associated with feminism and antifeminism, can be said to generate or compromise the production of profit. This depends on how feminism and antifeminism are distributed and exchanged in commodity form.

It can be argued, for example, that the producers of the third season of *Veronica Mars* clearly supported the notion that associating the lead actor with an overtly feminist politics would be damaging to the character's credibility and the show's success and thus chose openly to disparage and ridicule feminist activism. The same could also be argued of the film *Legally Blonde* and the television show *Cagney and Lacey* (which are discussed further in Chapter 5). What cannot be known, however, is whether these examples would have been more or less profitable if different writing, production and representational decisions had been made. The highly popular US television show *Girls* frequently references feminism

74 Popular culture, produced, represented and consumed

positively and the show's lead character, Hannah, frequently self-articulates as feminist. Feminism is clearly a part of the writing and production team's *modus operandi* but it is not clear how successful the show would have been without a feminist narrative. Certainly, it would not have been the same kind of show without this and it may even have failed to speak to young, independent women as successfully as it has done, in which case it may be possible to argue that feminism is a crucial component of the show's commercial success.

As Hollows and Moseley note, the seemingly 'uneasy' relationship between feminism and popular culture has often been approached in terms of understanding 'the ways in which feminist ideas' are incorporated in popular culture sources 'in order to enable women to be addressed as consumers' (2006: 10). This is particularly true of discussions of *Sex and the City*, which have frequently focused on how the show constructs the feminine citizen as 'a shopping citizen' (ibid.). Here, feminist symbols and narratives are understood as manipulated in the service of consumer culture and feminism is, in every sense, a commodity to advance certain capitalist interests. Studies of the commodification of feminism within the popular 'have noted how modes of popular feminism are frequently centred around white, middle class femininities', cementing the idea that 'feminism is a movement for the privileged who can "have it all"' (ibid.: 7).

Understanding popular culture as it represents feminism, feminist ideas and feminist agendas in particular and selective ways is important in understanding feminism within the popular, but it is not all that we need to know. Studies that keep feminism somehow beyond the popular, as a separate authority figure from which producers of popular culture would do well to take heed, reproduce 'the idea that the feminist has good sense and therefore the moral authority to legislate on gendered relations', while perpetuating 'hierarchical power relations between "the feminist" situated outside the popular and "the ordinary woman" located within it' (Hollows and Moseley 2006: 11).

Women, men and the consumption of popular culture

The rise of digital consumption involves important considerations in analysing the power of media representations. The increase in the consumption of non-traditional media outlets allows consumers greater power and variety in the choices they make over which media channels and sources they consume. Consumers who are already adept at 'multi-tasking' between media outlets may be highly unlikely to devote attention to media that does not engage and stimulate them.

The amount of time, for example, that Australians spend online, in addition to the other sources of media they consume, is substantial and likely, according to recent research, only to increase (see Figure 3.2, which shows that in 2010 Australians spent just under 22 hours per week online). Brittain suggests that the 'Australian public want to be engaged and stimulated by the media they consume, and this is proven with a 58 per cent increase in online media consumption and a staggering 106 per cent increase in video consumption between 2007–2010' (2013).

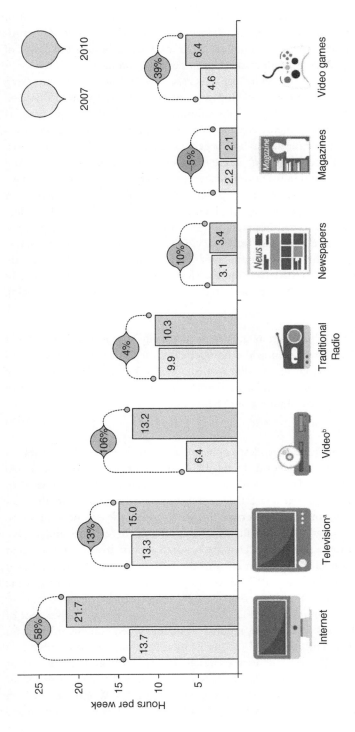

FIGURE 3.2 Average hours per week spent consuming media by online Australians aged 16 and over, 2007–10 ($N = 5,886$). Not all media types or activities are shown.

a Broadcast TV (not online); excludes time-shifted TV and Internet Protocol TV.
b Includes PC, video and DVD; excludes video using mobile devices.

Source: Nielsen 2011.

76 Popular culture, produced, represented and consumed

Traditional advertising and marketing tools are just not, he argues, 'as effective or cost effective as they used to be' (ibid.). Magazines, in particular, are not only struggling, their readership and consumption is in decline, although the costs of advertisements in magazines with readerships in decline continue to rise (ibid.).

Kerwin examines a 2010 white paper, *Global Media Habits 2010*, by Greg Lindsay, to look at how media are being consumed around the world, 'divorced from business considerations' (2010). She summarizes ten trends that are particularly interesting in shaping media consumption in traditional and emerging media market economies. No information here is gender disaggregated. As will be shown below, data on media consumption, where it is gender disaggregated, is patchy and over-estimates so-called significant differences (perhaps because 20 minutes' viewing time means more to an advertiser paying for time than a social scientist. A woman's daily 22 minutes on a seventh-generation console is 'significantly' different to a man's 48 minutes but in practical terms, this difference is less obvious).

The first key trend demonstrates that television has become a 'necessity' across the world, even in relatively poor populations. Kerwin notes that in 2010, 'nearly half of Indian households' had TV, 'up from less than one-third in 2001' (2010). In urban areas, however , 'that figure jumps to 96 per cent' (ibid., summarizing Lindsay 2010).

> In Kenya, the TV-penetration rate rose from roughly 60 per cent to 70 per cent from 2005 to 2009, even as the number of households measured increased by nearly half. Even in the slums of Sao Paulo, TVs are the top seller of Brazilian retail chain Casas Bahia, despite the fact that residents tend not to have electricity or running water.
>
> (Kerwin 2010)

The second trend indicates that, despite the internet, more television, not less, is being consumed across the world. In the USA, the 'average American watched 280 minutes of TV each day in 2009', notes the white paper, which is 'more than four-and-a-half-hours worth and a three-minute increase compared to the year before' (Lindsay, summarized in Kerwin 2010). A similar rise can be seen across the globe, with 'the average human being' consuming three hours and twelve minutes of television a day (ibid.). Deloitte research reports that, for 63 per cent of Australian respondents, television remains the preferred form of entertainment across all age groups (Deloitte 2012). According to Nielsen, in 2010 more online consumers reported watching video content on TV (90 per cent) than on a computer (86 per cent) in a month-long period (2012). In 2011 more than 80 per cent of internet respondents in 56 countries reported watching video content at home on a computer (84 per cent) or on TV (83 per cent) at least once a month (ibid.).

The third trend Kerwin discusses relates to the type of programming most commonly or frequently watched, which is sports, reality TV and soap operas. The most watched event in TV history was the 2010 FIFA World Cup, which was 'broadcast in every country (including North Korea) and garnering an average audience of 400 million viewers per match' (Kerwin 2010). More than a third of Afghanistan tunes into *Afghan Star*, the country's version of *American Idol*. Brazil's Globo network has broadcast locally produced soap operas since the 1970s, many of which regularly reach 80 million viewers (ibid.).

The fourth trend concerns the reduction in newspaper circulation in the USA and Western Europe, while the rest of the world apparently experiences a 'newspapers boom' (Kerwin 2010). 'In both number of titles and circulation, Asia, Africa and Latin America are climbing at an annual double-digit pace' (ibid.). China and India house almost half of the world's top 100 daily newspapers, where the average newspaper boasts a circulation of 109,000 or more (ibid.). In India, the number of paid dailies has increased since 2005 by 44 per cent, accounting for more than one-fifth of all newspaper titles on the planet (2,700 titles) (ibid.).

The fifth trend relates to Facebook's monopoly of the social media market (although more recent research has also suggested that Facebook's time might be numbered, see, e.g., Frizell 2014). Facebook, with a user base of 517 million people, 70 per cent of whom live outside the USA in 2010, occupied six hours of users time (per month) 'versus less than half that time for every other site in the top 10' (Kerwin 2010). According to a study of 1,642 international Facebook users, the average user is 31 years old and follows nine brands, with three-quarters (76 per cent) of these pressing 'like' to signal that they are a fan of a brand (ibid.). In 2010, Facebook's share of total minutes spent on the internet was a substantial 15.8 per cent (Smith 2014). According to Smith (2014), 30 per cent of Americans get their news from Facebook, which relates also to British studies that have found that, although time spent consuming media is increasing, few consumers seem willing to pay for their access (Wray 2010). A KPMG Media and Entertainment Barometer, for example, notes that 88 per cent of consumers polled in March said they got their online news free, which represented an increase from 84 per cent in September 2009 (ibid.).

The sixth trend concerns the importance of cyber cafes, which have helped spread internet use across emerging market populations. In South Korea, people can rent broadband access for roughly 80 cents an hour, eliminating the need for costly monthly subscriptions, and leading to Koreans' embrace of social networking and multiplayer online gaming, Kerwin notes (2010). Cyber cafes, or 'warnets', are also popular in Indonesia, where only 5 per cent of homes have a PC, and Brazil, where the cafes are known as 'LAN houses' and run at hourly rates as low as $1 (ibid.).

The seventh trend concerns online video consumption. According to the report, the BRIC countries (Brazil, Russia, India, China and also Indonesia) have the most avid consumers of online video. Internet users in China and Indonesia, for example, 'were 26 per cent more likely than the average user globally to watch online video, while Indian viewers were 21 per cent more likely and both Russians and Brazilians were 11 per cent more likely' (Kerwin 2010). In 2009, one-third of all internet traffic was video, rising in 2010 to 40 per cent. Projections by Cisco suggest this figure will be at 91 per cent by 2014. Although, as Lindsay's

78 Popular culture, produced, represented and consumed

white paper argues, PC ownership varies according to location, a 2012 Nielsen report found that 'watching video content on computers has become just as common as watching video content on television among online consumers' (Nielsen 2012. This report used survey data collated in 2011 from 56 countries in the Asia-Pacific, Europe, Latin America, the Middle East, Africa and North America). Although Nielsen suggests that in-home TVs and computers remain the most popular devices with which to watch video content, 'usage and growth in online and mobile technologies is making a sustained impact' (ibid.). The report also supports Lindsay's *Global Media Habits 2010* report in noting that, in certain locations, mobile phones replace the internet, with mobile video particularly prominent in Asia-Pacific and Middle East/African regions, 'where 74 and 72 per cent of online consumers, respectively, report watching video on mobile phones at least once a month' and 'almost 40 per cent (38 per cent and 37 per cent, respectively) say they do so at least once a day' (ibid.). While mobile video is less prominent in North America than in other parts of the world, North America 'is seeing the highest growth rates in mobile phone video consumption' (ibid.).

> The convenience of mobile connectivity has revolutionized how people are engaging with digital content and each other around the world,' said Dounia Turrill, SVP, Client Insights, Nielsen. 'With the growth of smartphones, mobile video consumption is on the rise for entertainment content, particularly in emerging markets where many consumers leapfrog home internet altogether in favor of the all-in-one smartphone.
>
> (Nielsen 2012)

The eighth trend relates to the differences in access costs between the internet and mobile phones in developing countries, with 81 million Indians (7 per cent of the population) using the internet, but six times as many (507 million) having mobile phones (Kerwin 2010). This pattern is repeated worldwide, with PC and mobile penetration rates for China at 20 per cent and 57 per cent, for India at 4 per cent and 41 per cent, Brazil at 32 per cent and 86 per cent and Indonesia at 5 per cent and 66 per cent respectively (Kerwin 2010).

The ninth trend includes the proliferation of new screens, netbooks, e-readers and tablets, which 'is expected to quadruple global IP traffic by 2014' (Kerwin 2010, noting predictions by Cisco). By 2014, it is suggested, the equivalent of 12 billion DVDs will be circulating online on a monthly basis. 'The biggest growth driver', Kerwin notes, 'is video', meaning 'data-rich 3D and HD streams' delivered directly to computers, TV sets and phones. The white paper estimates that this will lead 'global mobile traffic to double every year for the foreseeable future' (Kerwin 2010, summarizing Lindsay 2010). The proliferation of 'new screens' represents some interesting information in terms of how people consume with their various electronic devices. According to a 2012 Motorola Media Engagement Barometer, residents in Mexico, the UAE and Sweden are most likely to consume media in tablet or mobile form in the bedroom, while Sweden, the UK and Australia are the most likely to watch broadcast television (in the living room) (*Guardian* 2012). In Australia, a 2012 Deloitte 'State of the Media Democracy' survey of Australian media usage and preferences found that respondents (aged 14–75) tend 'to use all their screens and devices at once' (Deloitte 2012). According to Deloitte Media Partner Clare Harding, Australians are 'digital omnivores' and more than a quarter (28 per cent) of Australians own a laptop, a tablet *and* a smartphone and 71 per cent of Australians 'multi-task' while watching live TV (cited in ibid.).

Last, but not least, Kerwin summarizes the overall global media landscape as one defined by 'more' (2010). Time spent on and with computers has tripled, she notes, over the past decade among children aged between 8 and 18 (ibid.). Most of this group's time is spent on social media, followed by games, video sites and instant messaging, with the average child managing to fit a total of 10 hours and 45 minutes worth of media content into seven-and-a-half hours of media exposure per day (ibid.). A British survey conducted with over-sixteens in late 2009 through early 2010 noted similar results, with time spent consuming media (watching television, reading news, playing video games, updating social networking profiles and using video on demand services) 'ballooning' (Wray 2010),

A number of reports have suggested that women and girls use social media more than their male counterparts (see, e.g., Macale 2011). *Media Report to Women* (*MRW*) notes that, in the online environment, females slightly outnumbered males in 2010 (at 51.8 per cent to 48.3 per cent) (2012, citing Williamson 2008). The same research also found that men, however, visited more sites and stayed longer there per visit than women (ibid.). 'Men are more likely to use social networking for business', declares *MRW*, while women use social networking 'to build personal relationships', preferring video streams of TV programs 'while men prefer user-generated content sites such as YouTube' (*MRW* 2012, citing Kwik 2009). *The Guardian* argues that women 'now rule the web'. Women 'are 73 per cent more likely than men to have watched a full-length TV show online' and are '40 per cent more likely to play games on Facebook' (*Guardian* 2012). Eight out of the 10 Twitter users 'to have mustered 10 million or more followers are women' (ibid.).

Nielsen surveys have also indicated that women watch 'significantly' more television than men (by 40 minutes per day), although men spend slightly longer per day on connected (seventh-generation) gaming consoles, such as the Xbox (48 minutes, compared with women's 22 minutes each day) (Lunden 2012). There are also, of course, notable differences in terms of the gendered consumption of certain media products (*The Economist*, for example, and as will be discussed below, has a much higher male readership, as do, unsurprisingly, magazines such as *GQ*, *Esquire* and *Zoo*). Hollywood executives assume that their core market for action, science-fiction and horror films is teenage boys, but this is not necessarily born out in viewer statistics. In 2010, for example, the Motion Picture Association of America (MPAA) noted that women and men go to the movies in equal numbers

80 Popular culture, produced, represented and consumed

(Silverstein 2011). Similarly, video games designed specifically with a male player in mind are almost as often played by a female, although game producers and designers continue to assume a particular (white, male) audience.

In sum, gendered differences in terms of digital and online consumption, however, are difficult to establish, often conjectural and frequently concentrated on analysing small sectors of the US population. There is little sustained and reliable research that points to identifiable gender differences in the consumption of media, across age groups and locations. Gender differences may affect the ways in which people consume media, but no empirical evidence currently exists to prove this assertion. Men and women may use cultural texts to construct their masculine and feminine identities (Miletsone and Meyer 2012: 183), but assuming that they consume those texts differently based on whether they are male or female is dangerously essentialist, over-estimating unprovable differences and missing important other factors that affect consumption.

Audience reception and interpretation in and of popular culture

Understanding consumption as interpretation involves negotiating the interpretive processes through which audiences consume popular culture. This necessitates examining users' experiences of media and lends itself to audience participation and observation methods of research into what people do when they consume popular culture (for example by watching TV and films, playing video games, writing blogs, updating their social media accounts, and so on). Do, for example, video gamers think consciously and reflectively about cultural models of the world as they play, and do people make *gendered* meanings out of the games that they play? Rowley notes that little research 'has engaged in a sustained way' with these questions (2009: 321).

Establishing how consumers respond to the messages and images circulated across media has thus far been the task of media audience, or media reception, research (Milestone and Meyer 2012: 152). Such research 'has shown time and time again that consumers are neither uniform nor passive in their responses' to media and that women are, for example, often highly critical of the ways in which media products represent women (ibid.: 153).

Survey respondents in this research[4] tended to agree that we need 'more positive representations of feminism in contemporary popular culture' (Survey Question 33, see Appendix A) and that contemporary 'popular culture is heavily sexualised' (Survey Question 42). When asked if they could recall any examples of positive or adverse representations of femininity or masculinity in popular culture (Survey Question 37), respondents found much to fault. Their responses here were illuminating and wide-ranging, targeting: 'traditional representations of femininity' (Australian male, 65 plus); myths of beauty reproduced through the fashion and modelling industries (Australian female, 45–54); the equation of nudity with liberation across the music industry (Australian female, 25–34);

Hollywood films that construct women as powerless, dependent on men or permanently in need of rescue (Australian female, 25–34); troubling representations of femininity reproduced through the advertising industry (multiple female respondents, 25–54); endless news media 'stories' about cheating footballers, their 'hapless' wives and the manipulative women they cheat with (British female, 35–44); television shows such as *Ladette to Lady* and *The Farmer Wants a Wife*, which reproduce a core essence to femininity as constantly needful of marriage and babies (Australian female, 35–44); the prevalence of see-through blouses on Australian newsreaders (Australian female, 45–54); the reliance on sexualized violence in TV crime dramas and the reproduction of gay male stereotypes in TV comedies (Australian female, 35–44); in Australia, the media tirade against Julia Gillard (Australian female, 45–54), and; the rise of pink, ditsy, cute and fluffy 'girliness' across consumer and popular culture and the (growing) differentiation of boys' and girls' playthings (British female, 55–64).

On the other hand, survey respondents lauded and were quick to point out where popular culture produces representations of men and women, of diverse sexualities, displaying complexity, depth and courage. Respondents specified characters such as Omar and Griggs in *The Wire*, Spike in *Buffy*, Rick in *The Walking Dead*, Peggy in *Mad Men* and media coverage of Aung Sung Suu Kyi and Michelle Obama as notable in this regard. Not all respondents were able to offer concrete examples of what were, for them, positive or adverse representations of men, women, femininities and masculinities in popular culture (which is not surprising given that we each respond differently and in our own ways and time frames to media messages), but many displayed a high level of active engagement with the quality of popular culture representations. As Milestone and Meyer note, research on the influence of media has left behind a 'direct-effects' model that assumes that audiences directly, uncritically and passively absorb media messages, conceptualizing media effects 'in much more open, complex and sophisticated ways' (2012: 153). Audiences are more likely today to be described as active participants in processes of media consumption, 'actively involved in the process of meaning production', such that 'meaning' is always the outcome of both the media *and* the audience (ibid.: 154). The polysemy of cultural texts means that different interpretations are always possible, whether a cultural producer intends a particular meaning or not (ibid.: 154–5). It is then the semiotic elements of a text that become particularly interesting and that may seek to 'anchor', as Barthes (1999 [1964]) notes, a particular meaning to a text over another (by, for example, distancing a male character in a television show from something traditionally conceived of as a female task and a mundane chore). Ultimately, the audience may continue to make sense of the cultural text in ways other than producers intended, anchorage or no.

Conceptualizing the audience as active in the meaning-making process also, as Milestone and Meyer discuss, envisages audiences as active and critical in how they think about cultural texts and engage in 'interpretive resistance' (2012: 155). Interpretive resistance is evident at individual and collective levels, as audiences

82 Popular culture, produced, represented and consumed

deconstruct and subvert media messages (guerilla feminist campaigns are a good example of this subversion in terms of direct action, although subversion may produce no forms of material resistance). It is also important 'not to make a simple equation between media messages as bad, manipulative, wrong and regressive and resistance to media messages as good, right and progressive' (ibid.: 156).

Audiences respond to media texts variously and intimately, and the meanings they may promote at any given time depend on 'socio-individual factors', such as gender, class, age, knowledge, experience, politics, identity, and so on (Milestone and Meyer 2012: 160). As noted above, it is hard to prove that gender, for example, plays a role in affecting the ways in which people consume media, but since discourses of gender are so central to our forms of self-identification it seems self-evident to argue that they would have some role in shaping our interpretations of media. Yet social factors combine and analysis should be wary of privileging gender as 'more important than other social factors' in responses to media messages (ibid.: 161). Several survey respondents, for example, noted how wedding and marriage reality television programming depends on the reproduction and representation of certain ideas about 'traditional' femininity as home-bound and husband/baby-seeking. Whether, however, this is considered an 'adverse' representation of femininity in contemporary popular culture (Survey Question 37) depends entirely on the social and political context of the respondent. 'Adverse to whom?', as one respondent notes, would be a pertinent question here.

It is also worth thinking about how, as per Milestone and Meyer's discussion, consumers may be entirely inattentive to media messages according to the different modes of consumption that exist across audiences and media. A cinema environment, for example, may promote a more focused form of viewing, while a domestic living room 'may encourage intermittent, diffuse and inattentive viewing', the point being that a film studies' model of the cinema viewer cannot be considered a transferable model for all types of media consumption (Milestone and Meyer 2012: 162–3).

Power and spaces of consumption

Power and gendered use of space are important factors in understanding the constitution, interpretation and effects of popular culture. Analysis of popular culture and consumption would do well, then, to reflect upon spaces of public consumption and how people are able, or not, to access public spaces (Milestone and Meyer 2012: 149). Cultural and social norms may encourage or discourage access to certain spaces through forms of regulation and self-regulation that, for example, dictate that men should feel uncomfortable in a lingerie shop, or women in a bar on their own (ibid.: 184).

Milestone and Meyer discuss how the majority of spaces that we inhabit have been designed by men (urban planning and the modern city, for example) (2012: 184–92). The ramifications for women's access include the construction of the city as a natural space for men with restrictions to women's access and assumptions about their 'natural' domesticity. 'Victorian hang-ups about women "without a purpose" in public space' have lingered throughout the twentieth century and research on youth subcultures has often fetishized male experience and participation (ibid.: 192–6). In contemporary urban spaces, the success of the 'gay village', representing 'the colonization of a geographical space by a marginalized group', has been dominantly defined by male homosexuality and has represented the marginalization of lesbians in those spaces (ibid.: 202–4). 'While women are no longer absent from the city', as they once were, Milestone and Meyer argue, 'they are not yet free to exist in the city in the same ways as men' (ibid.: 209).

In terms of *virtual* spaces, which Milestone and Meyer do not discuss, I have found geek feminist discussions of sexualized environments striking on the point of the colonization of space and women's presence/absence in certain spaces of activity. Geek feminists have criticized sexualized environments across 'geek settings' (which are usually computer-based) for many reasons, but particularly as exclusionist spaces. Sexualized environments, as a method for heterosexual men to 'bond', are intrinsically 'othering', not only to women but to anyone who is not a heterosexual man (GeekFeminismWiki). This point is also returned to in Chapter 4.

The privatization of public space, and its effects, under the expansiveness of various Western neoliberal projects, would also be worth considering here in terms of how bodies are regulated in and able, or not, to access certain spaces. The contemporary urban space, for example, is frequently associated 'with opportunities for wealth generation', as noted by UN-Habitat in its report *State of Women in Cities, 2012–2013* (2013: 86). The creation of spaces designated as public but privately controlled and managed for private purposes has become one of the key symbols of modern neoliberalism, a 'stimulation of consumption' (Christopherson 1994: 418–19) that allows for the marketization of all areas of social life. This stimulation also, importantly, enables the regulation of bodies within the spaces designated private/public according, for example, to dominant ideas about the flexibilization of labour or, as Harvey terms them, the 'coercive laws of competition' forcing 'the continuous implementation of new technologies and organizational forms' that so characterize the contemporary urban space (2008: 24). Our urban areas, Harvey argues, are increasingly 'divided and conflict-prone', with the neoliberal turn having 'restored class power to rich elites', stagnating the incomes of the urban poor and etching the results of stagnation and degeneration 'on the spatial forms of our cities, which increasingly consist of fortified fragments, gated communities and privatized public spaces kept under constant surveillance' (ibid.: 32). For Harvey, the city is characterized more by a daily fight for survival than a sense of community or urban identity and privatized redistribution 'through criminal activity threatens individual security at every turn, prompting popular demands for police suppression' (ibid.: 32–33).

As Chant and McIlwaine note, gender and urban development are intimately interrelated and have long been recognized as such in feminist analyses of the urban environment (2013). For example, concomitant to the idea that the contemporary city is marked by 'opportunities for wealth generation' is the idea

84 Popular culture, produced, represented and consumed

that 'urban women supposedly enjoy greater social, economic, political opportunities and freedoms than their rural counterparts' (UN-Habitat 2013: 86). Chant and McIlwaine note that, demographically, the urban future is likely to be dominated demographically by women, yet 'social, economic and political gains lag behind' and, as the cityscape expands, especially across the Global South, 'barriers to female "empowerment" remain widespread, especially among the urban poor and/or those who reside in slums' (ibid.). Such barriers are evidenced, as UN-Habitat discusses, by 'notable gender gaps' in 'labour and employment, decent work, pay, tenure rights, access to and accumulation of assets, personal security and safety and representation in formal structures of urban governance', which demonstrate that 'women are often the last to benefit from the prosperity of cities with expanded economic, social and political opportunities' (2013: viii). Women living in peri-urban slums, which are often entirely devoid of services and infrastructure and constituted by low-quality shelter, are even more constrained, Chant and McIlwaine note, 'in their ability to connect with the rest of the city' and 'may be more challenged than their counterparts living in similarly marginalized but more centrally-situated neighbourhoods' (2013, citing Khosla 2009).

The importance of advertising in popular culture

> [A]s I remember being told by my first marketing director, '[marketing, sales and advertising] is a people business'. 'Like cannibalism', he added after a short pause.
>
> (O'Sullivan 2007)

> Advertisers use three main strategies to lure folks into buying their products: sexism, boobs and sexism.
>
> (Gamble 2009)

Advertising has sold smoking to women as a source of their empowerment (see Symon 2011). It has succeeded in asking us to use two Alka Seltzers when only one is required. It has made us take a 'coffee' break (rather than, say, just a break). It has normalized the idea of ordering bigger food, because selling small and cheap does not counter 'the social stigma in being seen ordering extra portions of anything' (Smallwood *et al.* 2012).

Advertising 'is pervasive in mediated messages' and 'has the power to influence social attitudes' (Liggett 2012). Importantly, advertising constitutes (and is constituted by) the simultaneous production, representation and consumption of culture. A marker and a creator of social mores, advertising mixes visual and verbal messages to shape and redefine the consumption of objects within cultural spaces (see Figure 3.3). These objects invariably include human bodies.

> Adverts occupy more public space than ever before in history. [...] In 2009 the UK became the first major economy where advertisers spend more on internet advertising than on television advertising. Through such dominance, ads

Popular culture, produced, represented and consumed **85**

FIGURE 3.3 'How to Synergize'.
Source: Meyer 2011.

contribute to attitudes and values. Due to their power to influence attitudes within a society, serious attention should be paid to the content of advertising.
(Liggett 2012, citing Sweeney 2009)

Whether advertisements possess 'any more influence than news or entertainment programming' remains open to some debate (see Liggett 2012). Technology enables viewers to eliminate advertisements from program content and, overloaded with 'messages of all kinds', we may effectively 'learn to screen out and limit their reception of information' (ibid.). Advertising, of course, includes 'a variety of body types, cultures, and ages' and can, if it chooses, 'define beauty outside traditional stereotypes' (ibid.). Advertising may also portray women in roles of power and success. Nevertheless, if I search for an advertisement for cleaning, beauty, anti-ageing, diet or cosmetic enhancement, the chances are, women will feature heavily (Figure 3.4).

FIGURE 3.4 Advertisement for Cif Cream cleaner. The tagline reads: 'Always a Beautiful Ending'.

Source: Cif 2014.

Arguments about advertising's influence notwithstanding, advertising is significant in terms of popular culture's processes of production, representation and consumption because it has so effectively blurred the lines between these processes. As well as being commodity-orientated, the production and dissemination of advertisements is also aesthetics-based and dependent upon certain ideas, and values, of artistic integrity (Box 3.1). Deploying linguistic and visual, coded and uncoded messages, advertisements are often extremely specific in cultural terms while adhering to universal demands for increasing profits. Successful advertisements have also become cultural icons in and of themselves, more representative of a social zeitgeist than of the products they are meant to be selling.

BOX 3.1 HOW DO ADVERTS GET MADE?

The creative process

Preparation

The creative team needs to absorb the brief given to them by their client. They will research and investigate the product, its marketplace, and their client's intended audience in order to become fully familiar with the issues involved. The team will then accumulate a multitude of rough ideas through brainstorming sessions and free association thinking.

Incubation

Once the preparation has been done and initial ideas generated, it is not unusual to reach a blocking point. At this stage it is often found best to switch off from the problem, and let the conscious mind give way to the subconscious.

Illumination

Often the flash of inspiration will come when creatives are away from the office environment. Suddenly the jigsaw comes together, the pieces fall into place and an innovative idea has emerged.

Verification

After the initial excitement of having an amazing idea, creatives need to be objective about their thoughts and check if the brainwave fits the brief. This verification process is one that will be ongoing, gradually whittling the wide variety of ideas down into a smaller and smaller group until a manageable number emerge as the strongest to take forward to the client.

Getting the message across

There are a wide variety of ways to advertise and while creative agencies will often try to invent (or re-invent) new ways all the time, the majority of advertising uses established techniques. The choice of which technique to use is an important one. Get it right, and the message will get through to the target audience, get it wrong and it could miss the audience altogether.

Content

- *Informational* – focusing on the facts.
- *Emotional* – plays on our emotions to develop an interest in the product.
- *Image* – tries to link the product to desirable qualities such as a certain lifestyle.

Approach

- *Hard sell* – tackles the sales issue head on and attempts to persuade the audience that this product is the one for them.
- *Soft sell* – a very much more subtle approach avoiding the sales issue and presenting an aspirational image.

Format

- *Factual* – puts forward the information in a simple and straightforward way, e.g. business-to-business advertising.
- *Demonstration* – an advert that focuses on showing how the product works.
- *Comparisons* – the advertised product is compared favourably against the competition.

(Continued)

88 Popular culture, produced, represented and consumed

(Continued)

- *Direct approach* – the actor speaks directly into camera.
- *Indirect approach* – the advertiser infers a view about the product but without directly speaking to the audience. Drama is often used.
- *Comedy* – an attempt to give an audience a positive emotional response to the product by linking it with laughter.
- *Problem solving* – the product answers a problem, for example, how to remove a stain on the carpet.
- *Endorsement* – a well-known figure directly endorses a product or does so indirectly by appearing within the advert.

(Source: Open University 2006)

Appendix B notes a number of other advertisements that proved quite instructive to the early stages of this research. These images uncritically celebrate sexual violence, women and gay men's promiscuity and sexual availability and asymmetrical relations of power and authority.

Notes

1 Chemaly cites here the Women's Media Center '2013 Status of Women in Media Report', the Fourth Estate Project, The Op-Ed Project, American University's Women and Politics Institute, Media Matters for America, the Columbia Journalism Review and Vida.
2 This is much debated, but there are some interesting examples of female directors choosing projects that include and focus more intently on well-developed female characters, including Penny Marshall's *A League of Their Own* (1992), Jane Campion's *The Piano* (1993), Kimberly Peirce's *Boys Don't Cry* (1999), Sofia Coppola's *The Virgin Suicides* (1999), Patty Jenkins' *Monster* (2003), Catherine Hardwicke's *Thirteen* (2003), Lynn Shelton's *Your Sister's Sister* (2011) and Ava DuVernay's *Middle of Nowhere* (2012). 2013 was a good year for female-helmed films, with the release of Nicole Holofcener's *Enough Said*, Lake Bell's *In a World …*, Sarah Polley's *Stories We Tell* and Haifaa al-Mansour's *Wadjda* (see Mirk 2014). *Frozen* (2013) was co-directed by Jennifer Lee, who was brought into the project initially for her writing skills, and seems generally considered the most feminist of Disney's blockbusters. According to a fellow co-director on *Fandango*, Chris Buck, Lee helped '[create] some of the best female characters we've ever done, the most fully realized, the most three-dimensional' (Amaya 2013).
3 For Derrida, the text was always much more than simply words on a page, such that it might be a theory, an image, a performance, a structure, an organization, event or artefact, and so on.
4 The only source of ethnographic participant observation data was that generated by the survey, which was limited to a small number of respondents. Most, but not all, survey respondents were located in Australia. This was a small sample of people (169 in total), answering questions designed to access respondent's immersion in and active engagement with representations of feminism, femininity and masculinity in and of popular culture.

4

FEMINISM(S), FEMINISTS AND THE (ENDURING) 'POPULARITY GAP'

> I'm not a feminist – I hail men, I love men. I celebrate American male culture, and beer, and bars and muscle cars . . .
>
> (Lady Gaga, quoted in Keller 2010)

> I think of myself as a humanist because I think it's less alienating of people who think of feminism as a load of strident bitches.
>
> (Susan Sarandon, quoted in *Marie Claire*, April 2014)

> A [feminist is a] person [...] who, while pushing for equality intellectually, [...] puts one group on a 'more equal' footing by hindering another's progress through law.
>
> (Survey respondent, Japanese male, age 18–24)

> Feminism implies many things to different people and I don't agree with them all. Some extreme forms of feminism can be characterised by the bra burning, hate men [stereo]type. However I think this is becoming less relevant [...]. I think real feminism is [about] accentuating the brilliant qualities that women possess and taking full advantage of them. I think that it's wrong to try to imitate men and women will only do themselves a disservice by doing so. Feminism is about bringing to the fore the best qualities of women.
>
> (Survey respondent, Australian female, age 18–24)

This chapter provides a background to beginning to understand where we might locate feminism within the popular today. Whereas Chapter 5 offers an examination specifically of examples of feminism and antifeminism within popular culture, this chapter contextualizes this discussion by considering feminist 'identity' in Western societies, such as Australia, the USA and the UK, in an era noted for the 'death of feminism' and the rise of so-called 'postfeminism'. During the 1990s and beyond, discussions around the nature of postfeminism point to an enduring ambivalence concerning feminism's place within the popular. Marked by reports

90 Feminism(s), feminists and the (enduring) 'popularity gap'

of its demise within the popular in tandem with its ascension in governance forms, feminism is at once debilitated and eminently powerful. Feminism's (contested) relationship with the neoliberal project suggests a need to look more closely at the resistances, popular or otherwise, that make complex our understandings of the relationship between feminism and popular culture.

Although frequently represented in singular form, varying social contexts for and of types of feminism are always worth considering and point to the impossibility of offering either a uniform or universal definition of 'feminism'. My hope over the following pages is to try to capture some of the diversities, and dissonances, within 'feminism' as it manifests in popular culture. Young women who have not, for example, grown up with the same 1970s/1980s, radical feminist/liberationist sources will not identify with feminism in the same way as someone who grew up responding to, say, *Spare Rib* magazine. Similarly, second-wave feminists may find little to recognize in the glorification of commercialism and sexual objectification characterizing the 'postfeminist' era.

Feminist 'successes': How feminists have changed things

> Feminism is not dead. This is not a postfeminist era. Feminism is still vibrant, despite declarations that it is over. Feminism is a success, although many gender inequalities remain. Feminism is taking powerful new forms, which make it unrecognizable to some.
>
> (Walby 2011: 1)

> Over the past four decades feminism has experienced unprecedented growth. In the words of Sonia Alvarez, 'The sites where women, who declare themselves feminists, act or may act have multiplied. It is no longer only in the streets, in autonomous or consciousness-raising groups, in workshops for popular education, and so on. Although feminists continue to be in those spaces today, they are also in a wide range of other cultural, social, and political arenas: the corridors of the United Nations, the academy, state institutions, media, and nongovernmental organizations (NGOs), among others.'
>
> (Alvarez 1998, cited in Hawkesworth 2004: 961)

Hawkesworth goes on to list the prevalence of feminist activities: in official institutions of state in Africa, Asia, Australia, Europe, Latin America and North America, through gender mainstreaming projects and the creation of 'national machinery' for women, gender equity efforts in major foreign policy initiatives, femocrats working within public agencies, four UN-sponsored world conferences on women, a Convention to Eliminate All Forms of Discrimination against Women (CEDAW), the proliferation of feminist non-governmental and civil society organizations (2004: 961–2).

Feminist ideas have been mainstreamed across the world in various governmental and non-governmental programmes, institutions, agencies, policy units, social formations, grassroot collectives, alliances, coalitions, crossing the broadest possible spectrum of engagements (environmental, military, welfare, health, development, pedagogy, juridical, employment, trafficking and justice based, among other things). Feminist campaigning has focused on securing equal pay, equal education and opportunities, access to (free) contraception and abortion, securing child-care provision (for women and men), women's legal and financial independence, ensuring women live free from intimidation and violence, an end to discrimination against same sex couples, equal representation, an end to the burden of poverty on women, access to resources, health-care provision, awareness of the practices and effects of armed conflict, protection of the human rights of women, fighting the stereotyping of women and challenging inequality in women's access to and participation in communication systems. The list goes on.

> The feminist movement has had an immense effect on American culture, laws, education and social relationships. [...] [F]eminism is the prevailing dogma on university campuses and in the book industry. The feminists are powerful enough in the media, in schools and colleges, and in politics and government to intimidate most of their opposition, especially men.
>
> (The Eagle Forum 2002)

Governance feminism (what I term 'The Feminist Project', which represents the liberal governance ambitions of certain, often US-based, feminist campaigners, and what Eisenstein refers to as 'hegemonic, mainstream feminism', 2009: ix), according to Halley, and as will be discussed in more depth below, has achieved great and widespread success. In national governments, international governance, and through inter- and non-governmental organizations, 'feminist justice projects have moved off the street and into the state' (Halley 2006: 20). This has been in large part, Halley suggests, because of the successes of family law, sexual harassment, domestic violence victories and highly effective feminist activism aimed at the ad hoc criminal courts in Rwanda and the former Yugoslavia. 'By positing themselves as *experts* on women, sexuality, motherhood, and so on', Halley argues, 'feminists walk the halls of power' (ibid.: 21).

> In some important senses, then, feminism rules. Governance feminism. Not only that, it *wants* to rule. It has a will to power. And not only *that*, it has a will to power – and it has actual power – that extends from the White House and the corporate boardroom through to the minute power dynamics that Foucault included in his theory of the governance of the self. Feminism may face powers greater than its own in its constant involvement with its opponents; but it deals with them in the very terms *of* power.
>
> (Halley 2006: 22, emphasis in the original)

Feminism and neoliberalism

The successes of feminism in institutions and mechanisms of governance has not, however, been without criticism, not only from such antifeminists as Phyllis Schlafly and *The Eagle Forum*, but from within the feminist canon itself. In particular,

92 Feminism(s), feminists and the (enduring) 'popularity gap'

the proximity between the neoliberal project and feminism has been examined at some length in various feminist analyses. Whereas the feminist absorption of neoliberalism has caused no small amount of concern, the neoliberal absorption of feminist ideas has been a quieter, and perhaps smoother, process, with neoliberal institutions and practices co-opting market-friendly feminist discourse and making good use of liberal feminism's sympathy for individualism.

Feminism has certainly been changed by virtue of its relationship with the influence of neoliberalism on political landscapes since the early 1990s. More particularly, feminism has been changed by virtue of the ways the development of neoliberal social relations have reconfigured people's (particularly young people's) assumptions of self-worth, social value and inequality. Neoliberal projects in the twentieth century have overseen (perhaps heralded, some would argue) broad shifts in social justice activism away, as Harris notes, from collective, hierarchical, state-oriented phenomena 'towards transitory engagements, heterogeneous movements and personal activities' (2010: 475). The rise of neoliberalism has given precedence to ideas about the market as the key, indeed the only, distributor of scarce resources, it has centred the power of private capital and has rendered increasingly fragile the links between economic security and prosperity.

Within this environment, the importance, and potential impacts, of 'the uneven and multiple significations of media imaging of feminism' (Hinds and Stacey 2001: 155) should not be underestimated. We should not then, perhaps, be surprised if young people place greater value on individual 'lifestyle choice' than, say, challenging sexual objectification. Harris argues that young women 'continue to pursue a feminist agenda through and around narratives of choice and individualisation, conditions of de-collectivisation and globalisation, a pervasive media culture and the emergence of new information and communication technologies' (2010: 477). Dismissing young people for their lack of 'activism' only obscures the private or less public activisms that are taking place, activisms that take better account of the 'encroachment of the culture industry' into every aspect of our lives (ibid.: 478).

The extent to which feminism has both legitimated and challenged neoliberalism is not clear, and feminists are not unified in their approach to understanding the dominance of social organization based on market mechanisms. Some feminists see feminism and neoliberalism as complementary and mutually reinforcing; some fear the incorporation of feminism into neoliberalism, or the *neoliberalization* of feminism, warning that neoliberalism, in its reproduction of economic inequality and de-democratization, is always intrinsically incompatible with, hostile even to, feminism (Walby 2011: 21). Eisenstein is critical, for example, of what she refers to as 'hegemonic, mainstream feminism' (2009: ix), which is the sort of feminism used by people with power in the name of the extension of 'capitalist democracy'. Halley's articulation of 'governance feminism', as will be discussed in more depth below, is intrinsically critical of the exclusions reproduced in the institutionalization of feminist justice projects, which lie at the heart of state-based organizations (including international organizations). Elias has found, in her analysis

Feminism(s), feminists and the (enduring) 'popularity gap' **93**

of governance discourse, as espoused by organizations such as the World Economic Forum (WEF), that gender analysis is often disconnected 'from more critical feminist perspectives such as those that elucidate how gender inequalities function within contemporary processes of capitalist expansion' (2013: 154). The neoliberalization of gender within and emanating from governance organizations is based, she argues, on 'deeply essentializing understandings of gender that stress women's shared and innate skills and characteristics', while it also ignores 'the divisions of race, class, and nationality that serve to grant certain groups of women (such as those participating in Davos meetings) privileged status in the current global order' (ibid.).

> It is certainly no bad thing that an organization such as the WEF has placed gender prominently on its issue agenda. Such practices do serve to legitimate a focus on gender issues within state and nonstate arenas and within international organizations. But there is an inevitability about the way in which gender issues are instrumentalized in order to link women's empowerment and gender equality straightforwardly to economic growth and competitiveness. [...] By disappearing feminism in favor of technical measurement and celebrity humanitarianism, the resulting Davos feminism reflects the dominance of postfeminist visions of gender whereby gender equality and women's empowerment are only understood in relation to [their] ability to serve the market economy.
>
> (Elias 2013: 166–7)

Arguing that 'the movement for women's liberation has become entangled in a dangerous liaison with neoliberal efforts to build a free-market society', Fraser has suggested that feminism has become capitalism's 'handmaiden' (2013). 'Neoliberal' capitalism, she argues, has made of feminism an individualist, and individualizing, discourse that has eschewed its former commitment to social solidarity, care and interdependence to instead yoke 'the dream of women's emancipation to the engine of capital accumulation' (ibid.).

Feminism, Walby suggests, 'has been opposed and misrepresented within neoliberalism' (2011: 23). Walby is particularly critical of what she describes as the 'hostile context' produced for feminism by neoliberalism. Feminism, Walby argues, 'thrives in conditions of democratization', but neoliberal tendencies are towards de-democratization, the use of private money to fund 'public' services and the post-9/11 securitization and reduction of civil liberties, all of which 'reduce the political opportunities for feminism' (ibid.: 158). Walby suggests, however, that there are 'alternative futures', of which social democracy is one possibility. She notes that 'neither the intensification of neoliberalism nor its replacement by xenophobic protectionism or by state capitalism is inevitable' (ibid.).

> While feminism in increasing in strength, the wider context is becoming increasingly hostile to the practical achievements of feminist goals. There are

94 Feminism(s), feminists and the (enduring) 'popularity gap'

> new as well as old threats to feminism from hostile forces. The neoliberal turn, with its concomitant features of increasing inequality, de-democratisation, financialisation, securitisation and environmental crisis, poses a challenge to feminism and to the achievement of gender equality.
>
> (Walby 2011: 157)

The environment produced by the global financial crisis has been particularly adverse for feminism, Walby argues, 'because the recession blocks economic expansion and rapid reductions in government budget deficits lead to cuts in jobs and public services disproportionately used by women', which directly exacerbates existent gender inequality(ies) (2011: 157–8). Though the crisis has, arguably, created space for a resurgent social democratic politics (across the West but also evidenced in the Middle East and North African social uprisings), it has also, however, enabled the creation and reproduction of a discourse of state failure, overseeing the policing of the modern state as a bureaucratic (rather than a democratic) entity. 'Corrupt', lethargic and ineffective states, such as Greece, Cyprus and Italy, are used in neoliberal discourse to re-entrench neoliberalism's advocacy of the market, not state, as deliverer of economic salvation, growth and individual choice.

As Prügl articulates (2011), something will *always* happen to feminist knowledge when it enters mainstream organizational contexts. There can be no such thing 'as pure feminist goals outside the mainstream', 'untouched by the workings of power' (2011: 73). 'Governance feminism' can be read simply as the 'governmentalization' of types of feminist knowledge, where feminist knowledges have been co-opted and adapted to serve the purposes of governance, which produces 'a particular kind of knowledge' (feminist legal expertise, expertise on how to mainstream gender or manage diversity, and so on) (ibid.: 72). Although it has become symbolic of The Feminist Project's claim to power, we choose whether we understand the sum total of feminism as it relates to its governance incarnations.

Janet Halley and feminists with blood on their hands

In her 2006 book *Split Decisions: How and Why to Take a Break from Feminism* Janet Halley goes one step further than most critical feminist analyses, arguing that we should relinquish our allegiance to 'feminism' precisely because feminism, or The Feminist Project, has become so ingrained a part of everyday, neoliberal, institutional life. Feminism, she argues, 'is running things' (in the USA, Canada, the EU, the human rights establishment, the World Bank) and feminists themselves 'walk the halls of power' (2006: 20–1). In becoming a central part of everyday institutional life, she argues, feminists and feminist scholarship have blood on their hands, having (consciously) overlooked both the power they wield and the damaging effects of the policy-making they have formalized.

Whether Halley's argument is entirely sustainable remains, in my mind, doubtful, but her analysis has been, however, at least for myself and this research, both provocative and inspiring. Halley captures something about The Feminist Project and governance feminism that has been, and is, troubling, that deserves attention and that is reflected perhaps in the uncertain ambiguity that many feel in response to questions about whether they would self-describe as feminist, or what they think feminism is. In a time of 'post' and 'hybrid' (socialist, antiracist, postcolonial) feminisms, taking a break from a Feminist Project that fails to see the wider social injuries that surround us (that is, as Halley articulates, those not related to feminism as cataloguing women's injuries) is not necessarily undesirable. Certainly, advertising and popular culture objectify men and their bodies too, which Halley would argue is a 'not feminist' point, and which my survey respondents found troubling and disempowering.

Halley reads feminism's power in the governance of sex harassment, child sexual abuse, pornography, sexual violence, antiprostitution and anti-trafficking, and prosecutable marriage rape laws. 'In family law alone', she argues, 'feminism has scored numerous victories that prefer the wife to the husband and the mother to the father', including 'the presumption that young children must spend substantial time with their mothers', 'the rise of alimony', 'the shift in common-law-property states to equitable division of property upon divorce', and so on (Halley 2006: 20–21).

> It would be a mistake to think that governance issues only from that combination of courts, legislatures, and police which constitutes the everyday image of 'the state'. Employers, schools, healthcare institutions, and a whole range of entities, often formally 'private,' govern too – and feminism has substantial parts of them under its control.
>
> (Halley 2006: 21)

Halley suggests that employers and schools in the USA put a 'tremendous' effort into regulating sexual conduct at work and sexual harassment and that feminist policy campaigns have had considerable effect within state and non-state entities beyond the sex/gender binary, elevating, for example, child sexual abuse as 'a serious enforcement priority' (2006: 21). She argues, however, that because feminist rape activism has focused so wilfully on child sexual abuse, it has forced 'other kinds of child neglect and abuse, other kinds of adult/adult interpersonal violence' into the background, because they 'lack the charisma of the sexual offences' (ibid.). This, Halley contends, is 'an effect of governance feminism' (ibid). Because, then, governance feminism represents itself as perpetual underdog, it fails to take responsibility for its pernicious effects, making it hard 'for feminists to see around the corners of their own construction' (2006: 33).

> Unless [feminism] Takes a Break from itself, it can't see injury to men. It can't see injury to men by women. It can't see other interests, other forms of power, other justice projects. It insists that all justice projects will track a subordination model.
>
> (Halley 2006: 3)

96 Feminism(s), feminists and the (enduring) 'popularity gap'

I initially found myself quite hostile to Halley's claims, and determined to debunk her view of feminism as a power-hungry, power-wielding, governance success story. I think much of this, though, has to do with not having grown up and lived in the USA. Australia, certainly, is not the bastion of feminist power that Halley articulates the USA to be. Although she attempts to talk more widely about feminism in relation to international governance projects, her discussion of feminism is bounded by US culture and politics. Whether the cultural specificity of her own (and US feminism's) circumstances renders her argument particular only to the US context is debateable. How much power feminists actually have wielded in the name of challenging patriarchal oppression beyond US politics is not certain. Certainly, the justice project successes that Halley notes for governance feminism in the USA are more widespread than the USA alone. Recent protests in Delhi are perhaps a good example of the strength with which women and men will fight for a justice project they believe in.[1] A quick glance at Australian politics, however, suggests that, despite a history of feminist activism and various feminist campaigning and project-building, feminists rarely walk the halls of power in Australian government. Having also researched, at some length, development organizations, particularly the World Bank, I do not, then, share Halley's confidence in feminism's seat at the table of power. Certainly, in interviews I conducted at the World Bank in 2005, gender unit staff noted their 'tokenism' and relative invisibility.

The (premature) burial of feminism

> A strange phenomenon has accompanied the unprecedented growth of feminist activism around the globe: the recurrent pronouncement of feminism's death. From the 1970s through the new millennium, journalists, academics, and even some feminist scholars have declared the demise of feminism and hailed the advent of the postfeminist age.
>
> (Hawkesworth 2004: 962)

> A late 1990s cover of *Time* magazine with the caption 'Is feminism dead?' featured photos of prominent feminist activists, including one of the flighty television lawyer character, Ally McBeal (Bellafante 1998). Such media pronouncements of the 'death' of feminism rest on widespread presumptions that young women do not appreciate gains made by the women's movement, are not concerned about discrimination, and do not support feminism. These suppositions have rarely been tested.
>
> (Aronson 2003: 903)

Perhaps Halley's most significant critique, especially in terms of how feminism is stereotyped and represented today (true or otherwise), lies, however, in the ways in which the Feminist Project has played on a certain marginalization lament. Halley argues that contemporary feminism self-represents (falsely) as the underdog. She suggests that feminism in the 1990s displayed a penchant for self-representation as abandoned and powerless. This resulted in a huge body of feminist literature from the 1990s 'laced with anger, pain, mourning, resentment, and fear' (Halley 2006: 31–2). The 'diagnoses of feminist paralysis, live burial, and so on were exactly wrong', however, and feminism '*experienced itself* as paralyzed (etc.), but it *wasn't*' (ibid.: 106, emphasis in the original). Instead, the 1990s was 'the decade par excellence of the emergence of governance feminism' (ibid.). 'If anything needs to be diagnosed here,' argues Halley, 'it is the profound rupture between the actual, real-world and theoretical power that feminism was exercising, and its experience of theoretic and institutional powerlessness' (ibid.: 32).

Feminism and feminists, thankfully, do not seem to have pursued lamenting their marginalization beyond the 1990s. During the 1990s, however, the English language media certainly wasted no time declaring the death of feminism (see, for example, Thornton 2013; *Time* 1998). In growth and activity, feminism was not, and as Halley and Hawkesworth both identify, paralysed, but the speed of the media's uptake of feminism's demise was unprecedented. As Hawkesworth writes, between 1989 and 2001, 'during a period in which the number of feminist organizations grew exponentially, a Lexis-Nexis search of English-language newspapers turned up eighty-six articles referring to the death of feminism and an additional seventy-four articles referring to the postfeminist era' (2004: 962–3).

Given 'the vibrancy and the variety of proliferating forms of feminist theory and practice', why, Hawkesworth asks, 'the premature burial of feminism' (2004: 963)? The obituaries for feminism first emerged in 1976, with the November publication of *Harper's* cover story 'Requiem for the Women's Movement' (Geng 1976), 'the first of many media pronouncements that "second-wave" feminism was dead' (Hawkesworth 2001: 963). Nothing had happened in 1976: the *Harper's* journalist, Geng, had simply decided that feminism was dead. As Hawkesworth notes, this account of feminism's demise, and the many others that have followed it, are noteworthy for their location of feminism's internal combustion. In 1976, the women's movement, had, apparently, 'lost its bearings, cut itself off from American women, and abandoned its original purpose' (ibid., citing Geng 1976: 964). Similarly, in 2012, we were witnessing the 'death of the feminist dream' (Kinchen 2012, writing in *The Times*) because women cannot keep up with 'the feminist concept of "having it all"' (ibid.).

The 'feminist' concept of 'having it all' is, of course, a myth, much as the death of feminism is a myth, created and sustained by the reproduction, often through the mainstream media, of (untested) presumptions that women *think* that feminism is concerned with 'having it all'. I have yet to find a feminist who has actually said that women can 'have it all', but this appears largely irrelevant to many 'popular' discussions of feminism. It is a useful device, and has been repeated so often, because it offers what Hawkesworth describes as 'a narrative of dissolution' that allows us 'not only to imagine feminism dead but to understand that its demise was caused by processes internal to feminism' (2004: 964–5).

> Feminism, of course, has been dead for decades. But like most progressive ideology, it continues a zombie-like existence, stumbling around the universities, popular

98 Feminism(s), feminists and the (enduring) 'popularity gap'

culture, and the media, devouring the brains of the stupid or badly educated. [...] The feminism that has burrowed into the women's studies caves in colleges and universities is something else: a species of progressive identity politics predicated on perpetual victimhood as a means for extorting more social and political clout. [...] [L]ike most cults, it is humorless, intolerant, conformist, illiberal, and lustful for the power needed to indulge the totalitarian impulse to silence the infidels and impose orthodoxy. In their gospel, the only 'choices' women have are to abort babies, hate men, despise conservative or religious women, and incessantly bite the liberal-capitalist hand that feeds them.

(Thornton 2013)

In such stories, there has been no foul play, no external intervention; feminism's time was simply 'up'. Hawkesworth detects in these narratives of the 'death' of feminism a moral code that is vital in understanding representations of feminism today in the popular media. As feminism has expanded and gained traction across multiple sites, in various ways and with numerous projects, it has decentred white, middle-class Western women. To cultivate an inclusive international feminism, Hawkesworth argues, feminism has had to learn to embrace 'the priorities of women of color and women of the global South', 'fighting racism, homophobia, heteronormativity, and cultural imperialism'. Such a dose of difference becomes, to many media commentators, a lethal dose and a 'familiar frame for the demise of feminism' emerges (2004: 965).

Feminism in a postfeminist era

[Y]oung women get the message loud and clear that the absolute last thing they should embrace is feminism. Indeed, as one reviews the media land-scape of the past 15 years, one is struck by how effectively feminism – a social movement that has done so much for women, and for men, for that matter – has been so vilified in the media that many young women regard it as the ideological equivalent of anthrax.

(Douglas 2011)

Whether located in putative popular revolts against feminism, academic criticism, women's consciousness in postindustrial society, or contemporary culture, postfeminism involves a mapping of social space that renders feminism homeless and groundless. The boundaries of the viable are redrawn to exclude any feminist presence. Within the narrative frame of evolutionary extinction, postfeminism is a marker of time as well as space, implying a temporal sequence in which feminism has been transcended, occluded, overcome. Invocations of postfeminism, then, could be read as banishments, command-ing us to imagine gender relations, higher education, individual psyches, and contemporary culture at large as spatial and temporal zones in which femi-nism has been eclipsed. Much like the obituaries in the popular media, assertions about postfeminism proclaim that feminism is gone, departed, dead.

(Hawkesworth 2004: 969)

Although, as Hawkesworth notes, the death knell for feminism had been sounded as early as 1976 (2004: 963–4), the media began to label women in their teens and twenties as 'postfeminist' in the early 1980s, with *The New York Times* publishing 'Voices from the Post-Feminist Generation' (Bolotin 1982). It was the 1990s that would be, however, the era of postfeminism par excellence, with Ebeling publishing 'The Failure of Feminism' (1990), Kaminer's suggestion that feminism is suffering an 'identity crisis' (1993) and Hogeland's proposal of a mass-scale 'fear of feminism' (1994). Today, postfeminism has become, Aronson suggests, the most frequently used depiction of the current cycle and stage of the women's movement (2003: 905).

The meaning of postfeminism, however, is unclear and subject to some contestation. It remains a term celebrated by some (e.g. Davidson 1988, Brooks 1997) and treated with suspicion (sometimes outright hostility) by others (e.g. Hawkesworth 2004; McRobbie 2009; Walby 2011). Positioned as a rejection of the victim-centred feminism of the second wave, the 'celebration of individual agency in general and raunch culture in particular' (sometimes invoking 'girl power' or 'grrrl style') has achieved widespread popularity, but has not been uncontested (Walby 2011: 19–20).

Often considered representative of a form of feminism 'entirely mainstreamed' and with 'its political content removed or marginalised' (Harris 2010: 475), post-feminism has been argued to be the '"simultaneous incorporation, revision and depoliticisation" of feminism' that indicates that women's worldviews may today 'include more feminist principles while being less explicitly feminist' (Aronson 2003, quoting Stacey 1987: 906). While 'third wave' has been a label attached to the contemporary feminism of young women (Walby 2011: 19), it is not clear whether 'third wave' and 'post' feminisms are interchangeable terms or are, indeed, even commensurate entities. Third-wave feminism is considered 'to explicitly embrace hybridity, contradiction, and multiple identities' (Aronson 2003: 905), offering perhaps a more reflective sense of intellectual purpose than the much-criticized term 'postfeminism', and all its associations with vacuity, commercialism and individualism. While the notion of a third wave, however, 'seemed to hold hopes for a new surge in imaginative and diverse but linked-up feminist practice purportedly less driven by the perceived ideological alliances of previous waves', the third wave's 'little sisters', Harris suggests, especially 'those young women now in their teens and 20s', have seemed 'less able to cash this out' (2010: 475).

What is perhaps most clear about postfeminism is that it has often been attributed with deciding, and then proclaiming, the 'death' of feminism (see, e.g. Davidson 1988). Hall and Rodriguez locate four key claims to the postfeminist argument (2003: 879). First, they highlight the (postfeminist) claim that support for the women's movement has decreased over the 1980 to 1990 period. Second, they note that postfeminism is associated with the claim that antifeminism has increased among 'pockets' of young women, women of colour and full-time homemakers. Third, they emphasize that postfeminism has claimed that feminism has lost support because it has become 'irrelevant', and, fourth, they highlight the development of a 'no, but ...' type of feminism, with women reluctant to

100 Feminism(s), feminists and the (enduring) 'popularity gap'

self-define as feminists but approving of equal pay, economic independence, sexual freedom, reproductive choice, and so on (ibid.).

As Hall and Rodriguez also stress, however, there exists little actual evidence to support the, postfeminist, claim 'that young women are less likely to support the women's movement than are older women' (2003: 888). While there was a short-lived decline in support for the women's movement/feminism in 1992, this was followed by an *increase* in support through the late 1990s (ibid.: 895). Aronson observes that since the mid-1980s, 30–40 per cent of women (in the USA) have called themselves feminist, which is the same percentage of people who label themselves Republican or Democrat (2003: 904). Women coming of age in the 1990s 'are more likely to support feminist goals and are more politically active in achieving these goals than women who came of age in the 1980s' (ibid.: 905). Feminism, it would seem, is not in decline, it is not unpopular and it is not unsupported. Studies have also linked feminist self-identification with self-esteem (Fischer and Good, 1994), self-efficacy (Foss and Slaney, 1986) and academic achievement (Valenzuela, 1993) (cited in Fischer *et al.* 2000: 15).[2]

Where there is more evidence to support a claim for feminism losing ground, however, rests in examining the media's relationship with feminism. Young women's development of a feminist perspective and identity 'is tied closely with institutions that support and nurture such a perspective' (Aronson 2003: 919). Aronson notes the availability of women's studies programs, in particular, but such institutions could feasibly consist of all the social and educative institutions young women submit themselves, and are submitted, to. 'Any survey of media's coverage of contemporary feminism over four decades', argue Hall and Rodriguez, 'reveals a persistent pattern of negative portrayals: women's lib, man hater, bra burner, unfeminine, lesbian and/or sexually deviant, feminazi (ugly, unable to catch a man, dyke), and whining victims' (2003: 880).

> If the ideology of postfeminism prevails, the women's movement will cease to exist because people perceive women to be equal. If feminism prevails, the women's movement will build on previous progress to address the remaining structural forms of gender inequity. Our research shows that *postfeminism is a myth*; women continue to support feminism and find it relevant in their lives. However, the emphasis on postfeminism in the popular media may create a future reality in which collective struggle is deemed unnecessary. This possibility is the ultimate danger of the postfeminist argument.
>
> (Hall and Rodriguez 2003: 899, emphasis added)

Postfeminism as the 'new feminist' backlash

> We don't need to be feminists in my generation.
> (Carla Bruni-Sarkozy, quoted in *Marie Claire*, April 2014)

> The feminist movement, like the civil rights movement, is one that almost everyone is afraid to criticize. If you attack feminism, you're obviously a sexist,

misogynistic male who wishes that women would just stay home and cook, clean and raise children. The issues I have with feminism have nothing to do with the idea of equality between men and women; I just feel that women can and will succeed without the now largely irrelevant feminist movement 'supporting' them.

(Enerson 2007)

If some have celebrated 'new', or post, feminism, despite or indeed because of its embrace of commercialism and materialism (see, e.g. Walter 1999; Moran 2012), perhaps more have shared Hall and Rodriguez's concern for the possible dangers represented by the postfeminist celebration of individualism and its apparent snub to collective struggle. While 'postfeminism', Walby contends, can be argued to form a 'more indirect' opposition to feminism than other attacks have assumed, in opposition it remains (2011: 19). Walby suggests that postfeminism, in declaring the world postpatriarchal and postfeminist, seeks to 'transform the feminist challenge to inegalitarian forms of sexual practice into an embrace of commercialized forms of sexuality' (ibid.). Herein, the 'substantive focus' of debates has centred on sexuality and popular culture, 'in particular raunch culture' (ibid.). The question, for Walby, is then 'whether these sexual and cultural practices are an extension of forms of feminism, or merely a variant of sexist culture' (ibid.).

For most feminists, it seems, the glorification of commercialism and sexual objectification is not feminist. A 'pervasive culture of post-feminism' has relegated previous women's movement politics to the past, constructing feminist work as 'complete' (Harris 2010: 476). Whelehan argues that 'new feminism' (such as that espoused in Natasha Walter's 1999 book of the same name) 'too casually claims that clear victories have been won' for young women, and 'that the way forward is in the form of lifestyle choices and self-definition' (2000: 11). As such, 'new' (or post) feminism, she suggests, 'misrepresents its scope, its political energy and its ability to learn from mistakes, as well as suggesting that the purview of 'new' feminism is much more inclusive than it actually is' (Whelehan 2000: 11). Commercialism, McRobbie argues, simply allows women (and men) the freedom to choose how they are objectified (2009: 17). McRobbie's particular concern is that 'postfeminism' has supervised conscious and overt attempts to 'enact sexism', partly as a way of telling feminism off, but also made complicated by moves to dismiss feminism as a thing of the past.

The rise of postfeminism in the 1990s is different to the backlash against feminist gains that took place in the 1970s and 1980s (perhaps most famously articulated in Susan Faludi's book of the same name). It is more complex, less obviously aggressive, to the point where, McRobbie argues, antifeminism is able to mimic the appearance of feminist solidarity, and enjoys the power afforded by the diversities of communication embodied in contemporary forms of popular culture (2009). As Mascia-Lees and Sharpe argue, 'postfeminism' can be used to describe a cultural context 'in which the feminism of the 1970s is problematized, splintered' and 'considered suspect' (2000: 3). In this new, and perhaps trickier to trace, backlash, feminism is appropriated by the current social and cultural landscape into a highly

102 Feminism(s), feminists and the (enduring) 'popularity gap'

individualistic discourse, rendered yet more hostile to ideologies of collective struggle by the prevalence of the 'self-help ideology' in popular culture that collapses the political into the therapeutic (ibid.: 93). 'Old feminism' is thus presented in media and popular culture as outdated, 'curdled' even, and, as Whelehan suggests, 'as having signally failed to speak to the majority of women' (2000: 11). 'Modern' ideas about women are instead aggressively disseminated, McRobbie argues, 'so as to ensure that a new women's movement will not re-emerge' (2009: 1). '[T]hrough an array of machinations, elements of contemporary popular culture are perniciously effective in regard to this undoing of feminism, while simultaneously appearing to be engaging in a well-informed and even well-intended response to feminism' (ibid.: 11).

While the media continue to run a background pastiche of feminism as humourless, unoriginal, unexciting and inaccurate, McRobbie suggests, young women are 'rewarded' for abandoning feminism with a highly individualized, and individualizing, discourse that promises freedom and independence through particular 'lifestyle choices'. The advocacy of a 'postfeminist' landscape across popular culture teaches young women, McRobbie argues, not to embrace feminism but commercialism as freedom within 'a hyper-culture of commercial sexuality, one aspect of which is the repudiation of a feminism which is invoked only to be summarily dismissed' (2009: 18). The rise of so-called 'raunch culture' is, as Levy articulates, a key component of this individualizing, commercialist discourse of postfeminist 'empowerment': 'a new raunch culture didn't mark the death of feminism [but] was evidence that the feminist project had already been achieved. We'd *earned* the right to look at *Playboy*; we were empowered enough to get Brazilian bikini waxes' (2006: 3–4, emphasis in the original).

Levy is particularly critical of the emergence of the 'tawdry, tarty, cartoonlike version of female sexuality' that has 'become so ubiquitous, it no longer seems particular' (2006: 5). 'What', she argues, 'we once regarded as a *kind* of sexual expression we now view *as* sexuality' (ibid., emphasis in the original). As Walby notes, feminism 'in all its waves has supported innovation and experimentation in forms of intimacy' (2011: 20). The rise of raunch culture, however, 'depoliticises exploitation and inequality', and 'the sexualisation of women limits options for women rather than providing them with sexually liberating choices' (ibid.).

While others have suggested that, in an age of hypercommercialism, we might celebrate the range of women's attitudes to feminism, McRobbie remains fiercely critical of attempts to pursue a defence of women's capacities to turn around or subvert the world of consumer culture in which they were invested. Locating her attack on feminist cultural studies in this regard, she argues that,

> [A] concern to understand dynamics of power and constraint [has given] way to celebratory connections with the ordinary woman, or indeed girls, who created their own, now seemingly autonomous, pleasures and rituals of enjoying femininity from the goods made available by consumer culture (e.g. television programmes like *Sex and the City*). If this could be done with

Feminism(s), feminists and the (enduring) 'popularity gap' **103**

what capitalism made available, then there seemed to be no real reason to challenge the principles upon which capitalism was based.

(McRobbie 2009: 2–3)

Stereotype threat ('I'm not a feminist, but ...')

Saddest of all is that the girls are just as likely as the boys to roll their eyes. I have thought long and hard about why this is, and the only answer I can muster is that the girls need to remain appealing to their male classmates, and a feminist is, well, just not date-able I guess. She is a threat. A threat to the status quo, a weirdo, an outsider. She won't let the boys be boys, or men, or whatever it is they are trying to be to impress these girls they chase.

(*Being Feminist* 2012)

[A] mind that is struggling with negative stereotypes and anxious thoughts is not in a psychologically optimal state for doing taxing intellectual tasks.

(Fine 2010: 34)

I wouldn't go so far as to say I am a feminist; that can come off as a negative connotation. But I am a strong female.

(Carrie Underwood, quoted in *Huffington Post* 2013)

Harris notes that there is considerable complexity in what young women say about feminism, and 'a focus on young women's attitudes has overshadowed a more productive investigation into contemporary young feminist practice, including its continuities with the past' (2010: 475). She suggests that a lack of a coherent feminist agenda or a singular movement has confused young women, and asks that the focus be less on what women say about being feminists than on what they actually *do* (ibid.: 480). We need, Harris states, to pay better attention to the complexity of women's attitudes towards feminism 'and the social conditions in which these are forged in order to identify the range of vibrant feminist practices in which they engage' (ibid.).

Harris argues that 'a considerable amount of feminist research' reveals 'young women's (lack of) identification with the label "feminist"' (2010: 476). In the research with young women about feminism that Harris cites, she notes three broad findings that are worrying: first, that young women today are not inclined to call themselves feminists; second, that young women believe that, to a large extent, the women's movement is a thing of the past; and last, that young women privilege the narrative of individual choice (ibid.). As she notes, this research *has not demonstrated* that young women today do not espouse notions of equality and choice, but that young women distance themselves from the label of 'big f' feminism (ibid.). Harris suggests that calling oneself a feminist and supporting 'feminist goals' might not go hand in hand: while young women might appreciate what feminism has thus far achieved, they tend not to identify themselves as 'feminist' (ibid.: 476).

Survey findings from this research support a certain ambivalence around engagement with 'big f' feminism: 67 per cent of women (of all ages) agreed with

104 Feminism(s), feminists and the (enduring) 'popularity gap'

the statement that 'feminism is accessible to young women in the 21st century' (Survey Question 16), while 69 per cent of 18- to 24-year-olds (male and female) agreed; 63 per cent of women agreed that 'feminism is accessible to women of all ages in the 21st century' (Survey Question 18), while 62 per cent of 18- to 24-year-olds (male and female) agreed.

> [W]hether or not young women call themselves feminists, they support feminist goals. In fact, the young women I interviewed were more support-ive of feminism than had been found in past research, and none expressed antifeminist sentiments.
>
> (Aronson 2003: 919)

Although there is little evidence to support the (postfeminist) claim that young women are less likely to support the women's movement than are older women, as the survey for this research also noted, what does seem apparent is that young women have been taught to fear and reject, unsurprisingly, negative representa-tions of the women's movement in the popular media, as Hall and Rodriguez argue (2003: 888–95). Feminism in the 1990s, and beyond, McRobbie suggests, became associated, especially among young Western women, with a 'seemingly tyrannical regime of feminist puritanism' (2009: 17; see also Figure 4.1). In their 2003 study, Hall and Rodriguez note how the battle for women's equality is repeatedly, according to media sources, declared 'already won' (ibid.: 884–5). 'By uncritically declaring that gender equality exists in the 1990s', the backlash against 'old feminism' that took place in the 1990s 'cast the women's movement as irrel-evant' (ibid.: 880). Hall and Rodriguez highlight a 1996 study by Bushman and Lenart, which classified one-third of the sample's women as postfeminist, because the women sampled believed that the women's movement had 'virtually elimi-nated discrimination' (ibid.: 884–5). According to Bushman and Lenart, young women in the 1990s were 'redefining feminism' to privilege self-definition and choice, such that 'postfeminist' women cited 'individual efforts' as 'the key to women's advancement' (ibid.).

> I am not a feminist, but I do believe in the strength of women.
>
> (Katy Perry, quoted in *Marie Claire*, April 2014)

'Stereotype threat' is the '"real-time threat of being judged and treated poorly in settings where a negative stereotype about one's group applies"' (Steele, Spencer and Aronson 2002, quoted in Fine 2010: 30). Stereotype threat induces, according to Fine, characteristically threatened psychological behaviour: jittery, anxious, stressed, angry or defensive responses that are characteristic of a 'mind under threat' (ibid.: 34). Whether there exists a threat in being associated with a fusty, out of date and puritanical ideology (such as feminism) has not been proven, but the prolific media stereotyping of feminists as man-hating, feminazi whiners would seem a good incentive for young women to disavow feminism.

FIGURE 4.1 'The Big Feminist But'.

Source: O'Leary and Reilly 2012.

106 Feminism(s), feminists and the (enduring) 'popularity gap'

> For me, feminism is bra-burning lesbianism. It's very unglamourous.
>> (Geri Halliwell, quoted in *Marie Claire*, April 2014)

As Aronson found, young women tend to be depoliticized and individualistic and many are heavily influenced by the media, which has supported the antifeminist backlash (Aronson 2003: 905). Among the postfeminist generation, concepts such as choice, power and independence have been heavily individualized, and these women show ambiguity in their responses to feminism (ibid.: 918). 'No, but…' feminism offers a new version of feminism that allows women to resist being labelled or labelling themselves as feminist, but still endorse feminist objectives of gender equity (Hall and Rodriguez 2003: 883–4). In this sense, it provides young women with an escape from the threat of the 'big f' stereotype, enabling them to redefine feminism in their own ways without fear of public ridicule. On the other hand, the 'I'm not a feminist, but …' phenomenon, while suggesting that 'a new version of feminism is finding credence among some women', encourages women to disidentify as feminist and disavow feminism itself and may, Hall and Rodriguez suggest, lead to a situation 'that could reduce support for the women's movement in the future' (ibid.: 898). Privileging self-definition and choice may also require closing down options for collective struggle and identification, further depoliticizing the women's movement. This is particularly worrying if these same women believe that the women's movement has already eliminated discrimination and needs no further support.

Australia and 'men in blue ties'

> If it's true … that men have more power generally speaking than women, is that a bad thing?
>> (Tony Abbott, then-Leader of the Opposition, 1998)

Australia, my home, and (possibly) the world's most sexist 'egalitarian' country, is an interesting example of the antagonisms that characterize the contemporary feminist landscape and the popular culture representations that define, in multiple ways, the limits of feminist ambitions in Western societies.

On 11 June 2013, former Australian Prime Minister Julia Gillard gave a speech at the launch of her 'Women for Gillard' campaign in Sydney. She warned that the 2013 election would be a decision that would determine whether 'we will banish women's voices from our political life' (Gillard, quoted in AustralianPolitics.com 2013):

> I invite you to imagine it. A prime minister – a man in a blue tie – who goes on holidays to be replaced by a man in a blue tie. A treasurer, who delivers a budget wearing a blue tie, to be supported by a finance minister – another man in a blue tie. Women once again banished from the centre of Australia's political life. […] [W]e know nothing worth fighting for ever came easy. Look at the suffragettes and what they faced. Look at the garment workers who went on strike, the feminists of the 1970s. Women's equality has always been hard-fought for, and we're entering a hard fight again.
>> (Gillard 2013)

Very few females in Australian politics have been able to use the 'f' word and maintain their credibility, or their careers. Before her famous 'misogyny' speech of 10 October 2012, Gillard's refusal to push an explicitly feminist agenda was well-commented upon. While feminist justice projects have, arguably, gained considerable traction in the USA, Gillard's references to feminism have been a risky strategy in an Australian political environment entirely dominated by White Men With Grudges. In July 2013 Gillard was unceremoniously deposed as Leader of the Australian Labor Party (ALP), and therefore as Prime Minister (many would suggest by the 'faceless men' who have long pulled the strings in the ALP).

> Before last week [and Julia Gillard's famous 'misogyny' speech] I bet there were millions of Australians who'd never even heard the word misogyny, let alone knew what it meant, but it was suddenly on the front page of newspapers and being mispronounced by TV hosts whose usual high-water mark is mastering the 'gangnam style' dance.
>
> (De Brito 2012a)

As De Brito notes, although in Australia attitudes 'about women, race, religion, violence, family, fatherhood and homosexuality' have shifted and continue to shift, traditional male roles have often been characterized by a 'spine of cruelty and dispassion' (De Brito 2012b). Within such an environment Julia Gillard's attack on sexism was risky but powerful, making international headlines as 'the first time an Australian leader', and 'possibly any world leader', had delivered 'such a forthright attack on misogyny in public life' (Rourke 2012):

> Gillard cited Abbott's past description of abortion as 'the easy way out'; his characterisation of Australian women as housewives who did the ironing; and his suggestion that men were better adapted than women to exercise authority and issue commands. [...] 'It's incredibly significant to have a prime minister powerfully state that she has experienced sexism. [...] That the sexism which is so deeply embedded in the Australian body politic was named may give some women licence to express and seek to counter the sexism they have experienced in their working lives'.
>
> (Rourke 2012, citing Professor Barbara Pini, Griffith University in Queensland)

In Australia, according to the Australian Human Rights Commission, one in five Australian women has experienced sexual harassment in the workplace. In this research, the statistics proved even more disconcerting, with an enormous 80 per cent of the survey respondents who answered the question, 'I am a woman who has experienced sexism' (Survey Question 25) agreeing that they had, indeed, experienced sexism.[3] My own personal sentiments and experiences on this topic echo the following respondent, who notes that '[Sexism has involved for me] too many instances to discuss actually. Overall, [it has left me with] a great sense of powerlessness and lack of self worth' (Australian female, age 45–54).

108 Feminism(s), feminists and the (enduring) 'popularity gap'

Women in Australia constitute less than one-third (30.1 per cent) of all parliamentarians in Australia's parliaments (Parliament of Australia 2012). Eight per cent of board members in Australia's top 200 listed companies are female, although more than half of those companies have no female directors at all (in Britain three-quarters of the FTSE 350 companies have at least one female board director; in the USA in 2010, women held 16 per cent of board seats at Fortune 500 companies and more than 50 per cent of companies had at least two women board directors) (Catalyst 2010). The gender gap in wages in Australia has changed little in two decades (remaining steady at between 16 and 17 per cent). A recent study by Monash University in Melbourne noted that 57 per cent of women who worked in the media had experienced sexual harassment. Women, it argued, were badly under-represented in the top levels of media management, holding 10 per cent of positions, compared with an international average of 27 per cent. 'The report's author', Rourke notes, suggests that her findings 'might go some way to explaining why much of Australia's mainstream media (much against the tone of social media commentary) concluded that Gillard's speech was a political disaster' (2012). As Lewis and Woods articulate (see Table 4.1), women of all age groups in Australia believe that sexism has worsened.

> For all the progress of the last 20 years – vastly improved educational outcomes for girls, increased numbers of female university graduates, more women in senior corporate and political positions, the freedom to delay getting married and having children – Gillard's speech tapped into a despair that women are still judged by their looks, weight, age, clothes, sexual behaviour, and relationships with men.
>
> (Lewis and Woods 2012)

Prior to his success at the 2013 election, Tony Abbott, Charlesworth argues, had established 'a very combative atmosphere' in which he 'explicitly used sexist and misogynist language' towards Julia Gillard (cited in Rourke 2012). Invoking 'a deep suspicion of successful women, which resides in Australian

TABLE 4.1 Do you think women face more or less pressure over their behaviour and appearance than they did 20 years ago?

Women	Total women	Aged 18–24	Aged 25–34	Aged 35–44	Aged 45–54	Aged 55–64	Aged 65+
Total more	58	68	58	50	59	62	58
Total less	25	15	28	29	23	24	22
About the same	14	8	10	16	16	13	20
Don't know	3	9	5	5	1	2	–

Source: Lewis and Woods (2012). Responses were gathered in October 2012 to questions in a weekly 'Essential Report', produced by Essential Media Communications.

culture generally', Abbott attempted to cast Gillard as 'untrustworthy', attacking her on policy but also repeatedly focusing on her gender (ibid.). Abbott's misogyny (and the media's reproduction of this misogyny) means that 'women in the workforce are constantly having to fight the sense that they are not legitimate' (Charlesworth, cited in ibid.).[4]

> To have our first female Prime Minister share her deep offense at being described as a man's bitch provided a powerful point of connection for women, many of whom may now have access to the trappings of equality yet still feel trapped by the straightjacket of society's judgement.
>
> (Lewis and Woods 2012)

As many scholars and activists have noted, Australian feminism has been responsible for one of the earliest achievements of women's suffrage.[5] It has significantly undermined legal and social barriers and has sought to eliminate discriminatory practices and discrimination against women. Women from non-English speaking backgrounds in Australia, however, 'remain one of the most marginalised groups' (Seibert and Roslaniec 1998), suffering higher levels of unemployment than any other group except for Aborigines and people with disabilities (the levels of discrimination these two groups experience puts every so-called 'advanced' liberal democracy to shame). They 'have poorer mental health relative to other women in Australia', 'they often suffer alienation and isolation' and they remain 'largely unrepresented in government bodies and in other sectors of the public sphere' (ibid.). Seibert and Rosianec attribute this state of affairs, in part, to certain feminist failures:

> [F]eminism, despite its claims, never fought for the rights of all women. The feminist movement has been largely a middle class pursuit, and while women all over the world have been fighting for rights, somehow western middle class Anglo-Saxon feminism gained supremacy over other women's movements.
>
> (Seibert and Roslaniec 1998)

The sexualization of popular culture and the recentralization of feminist concerns

In her 2011 study of why young British women sought involvement in feminist activism, Mackay notes that the 'sexual objectification of women in popular culture' triggered activism and feminist consciousness 'even above experiences of male violence, which the majority had been affected by' (Mackay 2011: 173). Many of these young women, Mackay suggests, understood male violence to include pornography and prostitution, in a connection with second wave, radical, feminisms that the media have long proclaimed dead and buried:

110 Feminism(s), feminists and the (enduring) 'popularity gap'

> [T]he women's liberation movement appeals to these young women today for many of the same reasons it appealed to their predecessors forty years ago. Experiences of sexism in mixed social movements, the impact of male violence and a resentment of the demeaning portrayal of their sex in the media and wider society, all gradually turned to an anger and political consciousness which led them to feminism as a form of resistance and protest.
>
> (Mackay 2011: 173)

The sexualization of popular culture remains a provocative and controversial topic: 97 per cent of survey respondents in this research agreed (with most agreeing strongly) that 'contemporary popular culture is heavily sexualised' (Survey Question 42). Popular culture, and its many and varied artefacts, are at the forefront both of women's experiences of sexism *and* their resistance of these. The impossibility of extrapolating subjugation and resistance in understanding the impact and reproduction of feminist ethics in contemporary societies is striking and makes for confusing times. At the same time, magazines, advertisers, studios, networks and media producers everywhere continue, apparently, to labour under the assumption that sexism is commercially viable. The imperative to reproduce impossible standards, unrealistic behaviours and derogatory stereotypes for and of female bodies alongside the apparent 'celebration' of female voices across magazines, music, television and cinema makes, I believe, popular culture the most important arena in which we can examine properly the complexities of modern feminisms, their impact and their significance. As vigorous and dynamic as feminist debate is, and, however 'smart' and informed our discussions, the power of corporate-sponsored sexism and misogyny remains pervasive and the constant sexualization of popular culture and advertising products continues.

Blurred lines

> I have a mom who's a feminist, she's an English professor, an intellectual. She really gave me the equipment to understand that you can celebrate yourself without putting yourself down or needing to apologize for the way you look.
>
> (Model and actress Emily Ratajkowski, who appears semi-naked for most of the video to the song 'Blurred Lines', responding to criticisms that the song promotes 'rape culture', quoted in Ayers 2013)

The release of Robin Thicke's pop song 'Blurred Lines' (which was nominated for a Grammy in 2014) in March 2013 sparked some high profile debates, even 'smart debates' (Ayers 2013), in the popular media and on social networking sites around suggestions that the video was sexist and promoted 'rape culture'. The music video, directed by Diane Martel and depicting Thicke and his collaborators, T.I. and Pharrell Williams, cavorting with models in various states of undress, was released in two versions, the first depicting the models topless, the second showing them covered. The topless version of the video was removed from YouTube on 30 March 2013 for violating the site's terms of service regarding nudity, but was later restored.

> I don't [think the 'Blurred Lines' video clip is sexist]. I really appreciate the people who watch out for that stuff, and I'm sensitive to those sorts of things. On the surface level, the naked women dancing, I understand that can be perceived that way. But we're directed to have a sort of confidence, a sarcastic attitude about the whole situation. That eye contact and that attitude really puts us in a power situation. The director, Diane Martel, is a woman, and so is the DP. We really worked on that and tried to convey that in the video. The way we are annoying them, being playful and having a good time with our body – it's something very important for young women today to have that confidence. I think it's actually celebrating women and their bodies.
> (Emily Ratajkowski, in Ayers 2013)

In her *Daily Beast* column, Romano criticizes the video's creators for engineering 'a fake controversy by making an unrated version' of the video 'featuring strutting, mostly naked supermodels' (2013). She notes that:

> The nudity might be fine if the song was called, 'Let's All Have Some Fun,' but it's called 'Blurred Lines', and the subject itself is enough to make some female music fans uncomfortable. The song is about how a girl really wants crazy wild sex but doesn't say it – positing that age-old problem where men think no means yes into a catchy, hummable song.
> (Romano 2013)

The video's director, Diane Martel, has defended the 'Blurred Lines' video project as 'more pro-woman than misogynist' (Ayers 2013). The suggestion, however, that the song, together with the music video, trivialize sexual consent (and thus can be argued to promote rape culture) is an important one. As Lisa Huyne describes, the phrase 'I know you want it' hardly encompasses 'the notion of consent in sexual activity' (quoted in Romano 2013).

In response to criticism, the song's principal performer, Robin Thicke, reportedly told music channel VH1 that 'for me, nudity is the least offensive thing in the whole world. Guns, violence, war? That's offensive' (quoted in Romano 2013). The video's lead female, Emily Ratajkowski, in an interview with *Esquire* magazine in July 2013, defended the video against criticisms of sexism. She was more equivocal on the subject of the representation of women's bodies across popular media sources, arguing that she 'loved' this kind of conversation about sexism, finding it 'so important now'. 'We see', she argues, 'so many images of nude women because of the internet. I think it's very important to make that distinction

112 Feminism(s), feminists and the (enduring) 'popularity gap'

[between 'super-gangster' sexism and celebrating women's bodies]. I think the video is a great way to do that' (quoted in Ayers 2013).

The survey conducted for this research produced mixed results in terms of responses to questions related to the objectification of women and the sexualization of popular culture. The strongest response received was to the statement that 'contemporary popular culture is heavily sexualised' (Survey Question 42), where an overwhelming 97 per cent agreed and *none* disagreed (3 per cent of respondents were 'neutral' in their response here). The statement that 'the objectification of women is unacceptable in the 21st century' (Survey Question 40) received a more mixed response, with 76 per cent of respondents agreeing, but 12 per cent actively disagreeing (only 14 per cent of those who agreed were male); 72 per cent of respondents agreed that they felt 'uncomfortable' seeing sex 'being used to sell products that are not related to sex' (Survey Question 43); and only 68 per cent of respondents agreed that the 'sexualisation of commercial products that are not related to sex is unacceptable' (Survey Question 44), with 14 per cent of respondents actively disagreeing with this statement.

A concern, then, that popular culture is sexualized is not accurately mirrored in this research in respondents' concerns for commercial culture. Expectations that commercial culture is more likely to be sexualized may be more prevalent here. How intimately Westerners have absorbed the idea that 'sex sells' is unclear, but they are certainly rarely surprised by the scope of advertisements that, in some way, play on a clichéd, provocative, heterosexist and male-directed picture of female sexuality. Understandings of and relationships to sexual objectification are, today, intricately entwined with commercial objectification: the term 'empowerment' itself maintains an association with economic independence that has made it easily malleable to the purposes of corporate exploitation. It clearly matters to survey respondents in this research how and where sex and sexuality are used in processes of production, representation and consumption. What is less clear is how we might articulate our own identities within circuits of popular culture that reproduce domination, subordination and resistance in unclear ways. It remains difficult for many, and understandably so, to articulate the desirability of women allowing themselves, choosing even, to be objectified, or submitting to objectification, as an expression of their empowerment, even power *over* men, even if their freedom also encompasses their sexual freedom.

Embracing the inner slut, and the effects of the sexualization of popular culture

The so-called 'Feminist Sex Wars' of the 1980s oversaw, in part, a battle by sex-positive feminists to overcome increasingly radical, no-men-allowed, all-sex-is-rape narratives to empower and enable women to embrace and represent their sexuality. This was a response to the kinds of structuralist, male-domination-based theorizing that offered women little to no meaningful agency, since male domination structured (in a power-over sense) not only sexuality, but, as Halley articulates, 'our very terms for apprehending social life, for having desires, for experiencing ourselves as embodied' (2006: 58). This feminism had described a system so heavily loaded, 'so permeated by male domination', that all its elements (from law, to education to the very fundamentals of social existence) could never be used against it (ibid.).

By the 1990s, so keenly had commercial machinery embraced women expressing their sexuality, that the pendulum had swung firmly in the favour of a knowing self-objectification. In this new, 'bimbo' feminism, accepting, and expressing, one's inner 'slut' (in a commodified context) became a goal, not a hindrance, and criticizing the sexualization of an environment merely reinforced the moral taboos that had maintained women, and their sexuality, in a position of oppression (see Figure 4.1).

> Now we have bimbo feminism, giving intellectual pretensions to a world where the highest ideal is to acknowledge your inner slut. I am woman, see me strip. Instead of peaceful havens of girl things and boy things, we have a society where women of all ages are striving to become self-actualized sex kittens.
>
> (Dowd 1997)

To critique the sexualization of popular culture within an environment of aspirational exploitation appeared puritanical and the suggestion that we should each hide our sexual expressiveness, our desires, our needs and urges clearly repressive. Sexual freedom became the ability to laugh (apparently ironically) at sexually provocative, objectifying and unedifying imagery and representational practices. The increasing sexualization of popular culture was defended as an opportunity for women's self-expression and freedom of speech, which also entitled magazines to adorn themselves with half-naked, white and superhumanly lean women. Popular media conspired, rather successfully, to reproduce circuits of commercial production, representation and consumption wherein those who complain about the needless sexualization of media products are easily cast as old-fashioned (and probably sex-starved) puritans intent on censoring imagination and crushing creativity. Such tropes will be explored in subsequent sections examining the gendered narratives of popular culture that reproduce feminism and antifeminism.

Serious concerns for the effects of the sexualization of popular culture and commercial artefacts have, however, emerged in recent years. Particularly in the guise of child protection, the fight against sexual objectification has become something of a force to be reckoned with, emboldened by successful and widespread social media campaigning and support.

A 2012 proposal from the European Parliament's Committee on Women's Rights and Gender Equality (CWRGE) for a 'Motion for a European Parliament Resolution on the Sexualisation of Girls' (2012/2047(INI) declares sexualization to consist of:

114 Feminism(s), feminists and the (enduring) 'popularity gap'

> [A]n instrumental approach to a person by perceiving that person as an object for sexual use disregarding the person's dignity and personality traits, with the person's worth being measured in terms of the level of sexual attractiveness; sexualisation also involves the imposition of the sexuality of adult persons on girls, who are emotionally, psychologically and physically unprepared for this at their particular stage of development; sexualisation not being the normal, healthy, biological development of the sexuality of a person, conditioned by the individual process of development and taking place at the appropriate time for each particular individual.
>
> (Skrzydlewska 2012: 4–5)

The report goes on to state that the manifold consequences of the sexualization of girls (focusing on girls from ages six to thirteen years) include their inhibited 'psychophysical development', reduced self-esteem, 'psychologically based eating disorders', 'self-objectification', the restriction of 'choice of professional aspirations' and the increased 'probability of aggressive behaviour towards [other] girls' (ibid.: 4).

> [B]esides the eroticised imagery of women used in advertising, an increase in the number of sexually charged images of children in that industry has been noted. [...] [T]he transformation of teenage stars into sex symbols in order to increase their chance of success in show business leads to establishing a conviction among girls that being sexually attractive causes others to perceive such a person as being more mature. [...] [D]egrading the value of women and presenting their image in a manner derogatory to their dignity, being a manifestation of sexualisation, contributes to an increase in violence against women, and to the intensification of sexist attitudes and outlooks, which in the long term lead to discrimination against women as employees, sexual harassment and to undervaluing their work and achievements.
>
> (Skrzydlewska 2012: 4)

The European Parliament report is focused exclusively on girls and does not state what the effects of sexualization on boys might be. Other research has, however, suggested that if it is true 'that our girls are being sexualized, then it is also true of our boys' and that we have 'created a society in which men and boys believe it is acceptable and normal to exert violence against women'.

> 'A five-year-old boy can buy a lad mag and learn that women are only sex objects and he has entitlement to their bodies. If he logs on to Zoo magazine's website, he can watch videos of girls stripping and lap-dancing, one set up as if the woman is being stalked and secretly filmed in her bedroom while she strips, another of a "ridiculously hot" girl being so frightened, she is screaming and crying uncontrollably in a ball. This is not just about

Feminism(s), feminists and the (enduring) 'popularity gap' **115**

sexualisation. Sexual harassment is being eroticised.' Boys are being violated and warped as they grow into men, and leaving the problem and the consequences of the problem in their hands is unfair, and unrealistic. We are not doing women any favours by ignoring this issue as it relates to boys. 'Boys who are not enthusiastic about (sexualised culture), or speak out against it, run the risk of being ignored or ridiculed, of being labeled "gay", "unmanly" or not liking sex. Boys and young men are under pressure to act out a model of masculinity in which power and control over women, and men, is normal. In which violence is normal.'

(Salvation Army n.d., citing Bell 2007)

As the Geek Feminism Wiki articulates, the sexualization of an environment (media or otherwise) is not just of concern for its impact on children. Women today 'are stigmatised as well as celebrated for being too sexual', which 'traps women into a double-bind when responding to sexualized environments, because even by getting the joke they may reveal themselves as too sexual' (2014). Across 'geek settings' (usually computer-based), geek feminists criticize sexualized environments for many reasons. As a way for heterosexual men 'to bond over their common attraction to women', sexualized environments are 'othering for anyone who is not a heterosexual man, including, obviously, women', which also contributes to women's 'invisibility' (ibid.). Within a geek environment, this 'sensation of exclusion is very visceral when in a small minority, as women can be in geek settings' (ibid.). A 'long tradition of sexual images, suggestions and approaches' have been used 'to shame, scare, harrass or brutalise women' (ibid.). These are common enough for 'most women' to have had personal experience of them and 'unknown men seeking to make a situation sexual' can make women 'feel mentally uncomfortable at best and physically intimidated often' (ibid.). Body image concerns are played on when 'sexy imagery' manipulates 'mainstream attraction stereotypes' and, for geek feminists, the 'feminist idea of sexual freedom', where 'all parties freely consent to sexual situations' means that an ethics of consent should be implicit when 'talking about sex or displaying images of it', regardless of whether legal consent is required (ibid.).

Geek feminists articulate other concerns that speak directly to, and might trouble, the supporters of sexualized environments across popular culture. Sites and arenas that seek to welcome members of cultures 'with different standards of expressing sexuality in public' may find a sexualized environment 'offputting' to people of various backgrounds (GeekFeminismWiki). Environments 'where participants are expected to bond over sexual ideas' are a concern for the presence of children and families (ibid.). Sexualized environments or sexualized behaviour in the workplace 'are commonly considered unprofessional' and sexualized environments 'may damage the reputation' and poison the environment of professional geek events, such as technical conferences (which are, geek feminists argue, 'inappropriately sexualised' through the presence of, for example, 'booth babes' or sexualized presentations) (ibid.). Of all geek environments, gaming is perhaps the most heavily sexualized, with 'advertisements, avatars, and communications between gamers' often highly sexualized (ibid.). The overlapping work and play spaces of geek technical and task-oriented communities can also reproduce and exacerbate sexual innuendo and intimidation and here the sexualization of an environment is a key impactor on women's ability to participate (ibid.) (see Figure 4.2).

FIGURE 4.2 Mouse pad with wrist support.
Source: guNjap 2010.

Notes

1 Mass-scale protests gripped India following the horrific gang rape and murder of a 23-year-old female medical student on a Delhi bus on 16 December 2012 (her male companion was also seriously injured). Viji Sundaram asks, in her piece on the protests, whether the widespread outrage throughout the country at the attack is a sign that India is 'on the verge of a Feminist Spring' (Sundaram 2012). India's parliament has since passed 'sweeping' new laws to protect women against sexual violence, making stalking, voyeurism and sexual harassment a crime, providing for the death penalty for repeat offenders or for rape attacks that lead to the victim's death and making it a crime for police officers to refuse to open cases when they receive complaints of sexual attacks. India's poor record of law enforcement remains a concern for feminist groups, including an insensitive police force and overburdened judiciary (Nessman 2013).
2 Disparity in assessment methods makes comparisons across studies of feminist tendencies difficult.

3 Of the men who answered 'I am a man who has experienced sexism', 50 per cent agreed that they have experienced sexism.
4 'As Gillard was neither married nor a mother (a conservative MP once described her as being "deliberately barren"), she challenged the norm of what was accepted as appropriate femininity in Australian society' (Charlesworth, in Rourke 2012).
5 New Zealand was the first country to grant women the vote at a national level, while Finland, as well as some American states, gave women voting rights at a state level before Australian women obtained that right across the nation. Aboriginal women were not able to vote in Australia until 1967 (Seibert and Roslaniec 1998).

5

IN POPULAR FORM
(FEMINISM AND ANTIFEMINISM
IN POPULAR CULTURE)

Asking what popular culture can tell us about feminism, rather than what feminism, or the feminist, can tell us about popular culture (Hollows and Moseley 2006: 1) allows for an understanding of the creation of feminism within popular culture, more than simply popular culture's reflection of existing feminist concerns. Engaging with how feminism is formed *within* the popular is important, not least because it tells us something about both the unevenness of feminist narratives and the complexities of popular representations. While it would be (relatively) easy to construct a narrative that charts a linear catalogue of feminism's incorporation into the mainstream, from 'monstrous outsiders' of the 1960s and 1970s to the incorporated Ms of the 1990s, 'such a linear account of the move towards reconciliation leaves little room for the uneven and multiple significations of media imaging of feminism during this time' (Hinds and Stacey 2001: 155).

This research examines feminism, in popular culture form, in order to understand how representative practices have come to constitute and shape feminism, our responses to feminism and feminism's popular success. The following pages thus cover what I consider to be some of the key gender tropes in popular culture. These tropes provide the parameters around how popular culture engages with feminism and feminism's concerns. Gendered popular culture tropes represent, I argue, our cultural tool kits for appropriating feminism (that is, the cultural mechanisms by which feminism is filtered through our everyday lives).

The following pages examine feminism as it is produced, represented and consumed in popular form, including how and where it is appropriated and/or practised across various popular culture sites. Popular culture deploys and disparages feminism in many and various ways. The embodiments of feminism that we encounter across popular culture sites are so important because of their relationship with how they make it possible, and acceptable, to self-articulate as feminist and articulate a feminist politics. The embodiments of antifeminism are equally important for the many

120 In popular form (feminism and antifeminism in popular culture)

channels they offer through which to encourage derogatory, violent and demeaning narratives of engagement and to dismiss feminism and feminist gains.

> For me, a definable thread runs through the language of culture, politics and the mass media that is quite simply anti-feminist and anti-equality. Anti-feminist arguments, contrary to popular belief, do not just affect self-defined feminists; they act as a powerful rejection of *all* women's autonomy.
>
> (Whelehan 2000: 3–4, emphasis in the original)

This chapter examines four key elements of popular culture and gender by looking at examples of *overt antifeminism, tacit antifeminism, overt feminism* and *tacit feminism*. These elements are filtered through multiple popular culture channels, and the following considers a selection of sources from film, television, news media, music, magazines, comics, video games, the internet and blogosphere and social media. Some elements (overt feminism) are widespread politically and across social media but remain marginal across popular culture sources, others (overt and tacit antifeminism) are widely visible across mainstream media, film and television programming but more likely to be criticized in social media and the blogosphere. Most elements, at various times and according to media type, vary in their visibility in mainstream popular culture.

Overt antifeminism (1): Why the development of decent female movie characters is not encouraged

> The real reason, I was informed, to put women in a script was to reveal things about the men. Any other purpose I assigned to the women was secondary at best, but I could do what I wanted there as long as the women's purposes never threatened to distract the audience from the purposes of the men.
>
> (Kesler 2008a)

> [Ben Stiller] needs all [his] versatility for *Walter Mitty*, a huge risk for studio and star, because it's a big-budget, special effects production that has to appeal to mainstream Hollywood audiences (teenage boys) with themes that are more suited to mature and female audiences.
>
> (Tulloch 2013)

> [W]hile I am personally drawn to the presence of a female action hero, it is currently a tough sell with the less than stellar way *Sucker Punch* was received. Ultimately, while I don't think [*Legend of the Red Reaper*] is for Legendary, I think the property has potential.
>
> (E-mail sent by a Legendary Pictures representative to Tara Cardinal,
> script writer of *Legend of the Red Reaper*, quoted in Pahle 2013)

Kesler, in her account of her time at film school, argues that film and TV production processes have long assumed, and continue to assume, that Hollywood's target

In popular form (feminism and antifeminism in popular culture) **121**

audience is composed solely of white, straight, insecure boys (2008a). This means, in the eyes of production houses and studio executives, that the lead character must be a white, straight male. Studios have decided that audiences pay more to see men in lead roles, but because studios believe that the male lead is more profitable, they create more films with male leads and films with female leads become anomalies. Actresses who find themselves in the unfortunate position of leading a big budget failure find themselves on Hollywood's discard pile much sooner than their male peers in similar positions. As Holmes surmises,

> In many, many parts of the [USA] right now, if you want to go to see a movie in the theater and see a current movie about a woman – *any* story about *any* woman that isn't a documentary or a cartoon – you can't. You cannot. There are not *any*. You cannot take yourself to one, take your friend to one, take your daughter to one. [...] Dudes in capes, dudes in cars, dudes in space, dudes drinking, dudes smoking, dudes doing magic tricks, dudes being funny, dudes being dramatic, dudes flying through the air, dudes blowing up, dudes getting killed, dudes saving and kissing women and children, and dudes glowering at each other. [...] They put up *Bridesmaids*, we went. They put up *Pitch Perfect*, we went. They put up *The Devil Wears Prada*, which was in two-thousand-meryl-streeping-oh-six, and we went (and by 'we', I do not just mean women; I mean *we, the humans*), and all of it has led right here, right to this place. Right to the land of zippedy-doo-dah. You can apparently make an endless collection of high-priced action flops and everybody says 'win some, lose some' and nobody decides that They Are Poison, but it feels like every 'surprise success' about women is an anomaly and every failure is an abject lesson about how we really ought to just leave it all to The Rock.
>
> (Holmes 2013)

Such rationalizations only further, of course, legitimize, the only-male-leads-are-generally-successful logic the studios themselves invented. The vicious cycle mentality is clear. The film industry, Kesler argues, 'has set women up to fail by giving them mostly crap shows and films to lead on those rare occasions they get lead roles, and then rationalizing successful examples of women leads into failures of epic proportions' (2008a).

Although Hollywood's 'Golden Age' demonstrated how profitable 'leading ladies' could be, the modern-day Hollywood studio has learned to rationalize male leads in supposedly economic terms but for reasons that are, it can be argued, purely sexist. Studios and networks have established a system 'based exclusively on promoting male leads', and despite, as Kesler notes, *Business Week* and the *Wall Street Journal* having reported consistently 'for a decade that women are a far more profitable audience' (2008a). One of the main reasons 'why 99 per cent of female characters', and female actresses, are sacrificed 'is to prop up the men' (ibid.).

Kesler was told that there were a high number of filmmakers who wanted to see the changes that she hoped for, she just needed to do 'what it took to get into

122 In popular form (feminism and antifeminism in popular culture)

the industry and accrue some power' and she then could start 'pushing the envelope' to see if 'maybe, just maybe, change would finally happen' (2008b). On writing scripts with multiple women, with names, talking to each other, about subjects other than men, Kesler found, however, the industry less encouraging. An industry professional finally imparted 'one blessedly telling explanation'.

> 'The audience doesn't want to listen to a bunch of women talking about whatever it is women talk about'. 'Not even if it advances the story?' I asked. That's rule number one in screenwriting, though you'd never know it from watching most movies: every moment in a script should reveal another chunk of the story and keep it moving. He just looked embarrassed and said, 'I mean, that's not how *I* see it, that's how *they* see it'.
>
> (Kesler 2008b emphasis in the original)

Blaming the audience is an obvious excuse, but the belief in Hollywood that 'if two women came on screen and started talking, the target male audience's brain would glaze over and assume the women were talking about nail polish or shoes or something that didn't pertain to the story' remains prolific (Kesler 2008b). There are, of course, still men in this world who would glaze over when women talk, but, shockingly, there are also men who love romance movies and women who prefer action/adventure, thriller and sci-fi genres to romantic comedies.

> Much to the frustration of those who campaign for greater visibility of women on screen, every successful venture from *Thelma and Louise* (1991) to *Bridesmaids* (2011) is hailed as marking a turning point. A turning point that never eventuates. 'Every time there's a movie starring women, the media is very excited to say, "Well, this changes everything"', Geena Davies told media organisation NPR earlier this year. 'That's what happened with *Thelma and Louise* … and nothing changed'.
>
> (Le Marquand, citing Geena Davies, 2013)

It is unclear exactly why Hollywood assumes that its target audience is teenage boys. Lyttelton argues that some evidence has backed the assumption that 13- to 24-year-old males are the biggest money-spinners, 'with superheroes and effects-driven tentpoles being consistently the biggest moneymakers' over the last 35 years (2012). Yet history's biggest grossing films, *Gone with the Wind* and *Titanic*, obviously fail to fit this mould, and 40 per cent of *The Avengers* opening weekend audience was female. In 2010, women bought 50 per cent of movie theatre tickets, which is slightly less than they did in 2009, when they bought 55 per cent of movie theatre tickets (Silverstein 2011).

Observers have suggested that Hollywood perhaps courts teenage boys for their association with 'fandom'. It has only recently '"surprised a lot of people" that girls are fans too' (Jeff Katz, former Fox movie executive, cited in Rogers 2009). Only

In popular form (feminism and antifeminism in popular culture) **123**

boys seem to be associated with 'geek' and fan culture in the minds of Hollywood executives and the success of 'geek-appealing' franchises such as *X-Men*, *The Lord of the Rings* and *Transformers* has sedimented Hollywood's view of its 'core' audience for blockbusters as nerdy 13- to 24-year-old males; 'not just teen boys, but teen boys at their pimpliest, stutteringest and downright geekiest' (Rogers, citing the *Washington Post*, 2009). 'Characters and a sweeping plot', more heavily associated with 'female-friendly' movie-making, are 'something that Hollywood has been turning away from, instead focusing on effects and production and big named stars' (Rogers 2009). As statistical reporting continues to suggest that boys are saving their movie-going pennies for games and DVDs, heading only to theatres for specific genre films and not generic action movies, Hollywood is seeing the profit generated by the *Twilight* franchise and acknowledging that women may be willing to spend more money than boys 'if the film is done with the right mix of romance and drama and suspense' (Lori Joffs, co-owner of 'The Twilight Lexicon' website, quoted in Rogers 2009).

Lyttelton argues that, by July 2012, only three of that year's top fifteen grossing (non-R rated) films thus far (*The Avengers*, *Men in Black 3* and *Wrath of the Titans*) were targeted directly to the teenage boy demographic (2012). MIB3 was an underperforming disappointment and *Titans* made half its predecessor's profit. 'The way-above-expectations' opening of *Magic Mike* 'is only the latest in a series of examples of female audiences', particularly older female audiences, arguably being 'more reliable than young men in terms of actually turning out at the box office' (ibid.). In 2011, two of the three original films in the US domestic box office top twenty (*The Help* and *Bridesmaids*, each of which grossed over $170 million) were aimed at women (2012). *Brave*, *Snow White and the Huntsman*, *Prometheus* and *The Hunger Games*, four of 2012 biggest action-adventure films, featured 'strong, impressive female leads' (ibid.). Each of these films also passes the Bechdel Test. As Lyttelton notes, it would be nice, of course, 'if a single one of the female-driven hits was actually directed by a woman' (*Brave* lost its co-helm Brenda Chapman half way through the shoot after she was fired) (ibid.).

The reverse side of Hollywood taking greater notice of female-driven profits is, however, a sense that Hollywood may seek to cut corners with film-making targeted at girls and women, turning a bigger profit by producing less high-quality films for female fans (something that the B-grade effects in the *Twilight* movies may attest to).

> The trend that I see coming is studios spending as little on 'female' movies as possible to take advantage of the huge profit. I guess it's within Hollywood's right to do so, but I think it reveals a condescending attitude towards female viewers. [...] Meanwhile Hollywood is tripping over itself at Comic-Con to make sure the tiniest details meet male-fan approval. 'Is this Iron-Man suit okay? You like?? Please don't trash us online!!' So Iron Man's suit is going to look amazing, but I don't think the studio behind *Twilight* is working as hard to make the werewolves look cool in *New Moon*. And I think it's because they

124 In popular form (feminism and antifeminism in popular culture)

> believe girls only care about how Taylor Lautner looks without his shirt on. Decent CGI is 'guy stuff.' Maybe I'm wrong though. I hope I am. We'll see.
>
> (Actor Mark McMillian, quoted in Rogers 2009)

In 2012, women accounted for a paltry 28 per cent of the characters in the year's top-earning films, although women also accounted for 51 per cent of the year's movie-going audience (Le Marquand 2013). A 2012 report by the British Film Institute showed that, while independent film fares better in employing female talent, women's numbers continue to remain low (with 11 per cent of independent films released in the UK between 2010 and 2012 directed by women, and 16 per cent written by women) (ibid.). As Prof. Stacy Smith notes, given that 'females go the movies as much as males', any 'lack of change' in the representation of women in film 'is likely due to entrenched ways of thinking and doing business' (cited in ibid.).

> [A]ccording to a study by the Annenberg School for Communication and Journalism, women made up only 29.9 per cent of the speaking roles in 2007's top movies. In the same year, Warner Bros CEO Jeff Robinov reportedly said that the studio would not develop any more movies with female leads after the latest Jodie Foster and Nicole Kidman vehicles underperformed.[1] [This] doesn't make sense – when *John Carter* and *Battleship* flopped, they didn't stop making movies with men; they stopped making movies with Taylor Kitsch.
>
> (Sargent 2012)

Films, TV shows, books, and so on, for, by or about women have, however, all produced substantial profit. So, the question remains, why discriminate if it does not actually generate profit? One answer lies in audience/market perception, or, more importantly, what this is believed to be (rightly or wrongly). Sigourney Weaver's famously accidental casting as Ripley, for example, in the *Alien* tetralogy betrays a wider perception that one might expect the pilots of spacecraft to be male. The 'shock value' of Ripley being female rather than male, and not only male but tough and resourceful, is perhaps more symbolic of sexist assumptions than any sign of Hollywood getting radical. The more recent, and much praised, *Gravity* (directed by Alfonso Cuarón and starring Sandra Bullock) has also been criticized for offering yet another tired representation of femininity that 'reduces the feminine to mere birth imagery and motherly yearning' (GenderBender 2013). As Sargent notes, even movies with strong female characters often do not pass the Bechdel Test[2] (*The Girl with the Dragon Tattoo*, *Star Wars*, *Lord of the Rings*, *Tomb Raider*, *Underworld*, even movies aimed mostly at women, such as *When Harry Met Sally*, *(500) Days of Summer* and *Kate and Leopold*) (2012). *Zero Dark Thirty* is one of very few 'action movie' exceptions in recent years to carry a female lead, pass the Bechdel Test *and* be directed by a woman (it was also widely snubbed at the 2013 Oscars for being too ambiguous a recounting of the CIA's use of torture,

In popular form (feminism and antifeminism in popular culture)   **125**

with the sugar-coated, much less demanding, and male-led, *Argo* taking the best picture prize).

Kesler argues that ego and laziness have created the conditions for Hollywood to ignore the fact that movies for, by or about women are profitable (2008b). Film professionals have been conditioned, and have too much ego invested, in believing that movies/TV shows by, for or about women that are successful are exceptions to the rule, because 'it was really the alien/Terminator/Hannibal Lechter people wanted to see, not the Ripley, Connor or Starling' (Kesler 2008b). If, however, these professionals were to acknowledge, *en masse*, that female-biased films really can be and are successful, 'suddenly everyone needs remedial classes' (Kesler 2008c). The work that would have to be put in, Kesler argues, to undoing the learned flaws in many studios' rationality looks enormous and threatens the status quo.

> Honestly, you write women [in films and TV shows] pretty much like you write men. But [film professionals] *think* it would mean learning something new, and to be fair, for many of them it would mean learning to write credible voices belonging to a group of people they associate with little more than high school rejection, being told to clean up their room, divorce and child support checks. It would also, for many of them, mean noticing someone who has never before existed to their eyes: women who don't fit the 'hot chick' profile.
>
> (Kesler 2008c, emphasis in the original)

Those producing shows and films discriminate, even though it does not profit them to do so, because they believe, and want to believe, that heterosexual, white masculinity will sell. Studios and networks have made a decision that male leads produce greater success, and they produce films and shows that support this decision, with male leads. Some of these films achieve great success, thereby prompting further support for films and shows with male leads. Ideas about what is profitable are not the same as what is actually profitable, but they matter more.

> I *had* to understand [on starting film classes at UCLA] that the audience only wanted white, straight, male leads. I was assured that as long as I made the white, straight men in my scripts prominent, I could still offer groundbreaking characters of other descriptions (fascinating, significant women, men of color, etc.) – as long as they didn't distract the audience from the white men they really paid their money to see.
>
> (Kesler 2008b emphasis in the original)

Overt antifeminism (2): Why women are in refrigerators

> In [superhero comics], men can fly and fight and do heroic things and meet girls and have a secret identity – you know, all the stuff men secretly want to do. Women ... not so much. In fact, outside of comic books specifically written

126 In popular form (feminism and antifeminism in popular culture)

> for women, female characters in superhero books have a pretty tough time of it. And by 'tough time', I mean horrible, horrible things happen to them.
>
> (Bricken 2008)

The popular culture trope 'Women in Refrigerators', giving rise to 'Women in Refrigerators Syndrome', has generated some heated discussion around sexism, the comic-book and film industries. The verb 'to fridge' refers to the concept of killing off a female character 'solely for the purpose of giving the story's main male hero a reason to angst', as *Gadzooks!* notes (2010). The name of this trope originates in a storyline in *Green Lantern* 'in which the villain Major Force leaves the corpse of Kyle Rayner's girlfriend, Alexandra DeWitt, literally stuffed into a refrigerator' for Rayner to find (*TV Tropes* 2013a). Popularized by comic book writer Gail Simone, her website, Women in Refrigerators, is dedicated to the 'superheroines who have been either depowered, raped, or cut up and stuck in the refrigerator' (2013). Simone realized that most of her favourite female comic book characters had 'met untimely and often icky ends' and set herself to compiling a list of instances of female comic book characters who were killed off as a plot device (ibid.). Simone's intention, she claims, was simply to point out to comic book creators that 'if you demolish most of the characters girls like, then girls won't read comics', but the site has become a trope in and of itself for feminist popular culture critique. The term has, however, come to be used more broadly, referring, over time, 'to any character who is killed off, abused, raped, incapacitated, de-powered, or brainwashed for the sole purpose of motivating another character' (*TV Tropes* 2013a).

That director Christopher Nolan has a 'woman problem' has been variously commented upon by a number of bloggers and reviewers (see, for example, Belinkie 2010; Quigley 2010; Black Cat Reviews 2012; Kessler 2012). As Kessler argues, 'Nolan is a great analyst of the human soul and the forces that drive men to go to the extremes of either horror or grandeur' (2012). His engagement with male characters' psychology has probably made him one of the most respected directors working in Hollywood today. Nolan's male characters 'are always complex, tortured, torn between good and evil, frantically mad or in a breathless search for justice. The subtleties and intricacies of their many layers can only be commended' (ibid.).

Nolan's female characters, on the other hand, are either dead or are 'one-sided, one-dimensional, archetypal roles, with often no other purpose than to push the male hero in one direction or the other' (Kessler 2012). These women fit the Women in Refrigerators trope to a 't'.

The Dark Knight trilogy, with a production budget of over US$585 million, was a hugely successful franchise, producing three of the biggest films of 2005, 2009 and 2012 and grossing over US$2 billion worldwide (Table 5.1). Unlike many of Hollywood's big budget, special-effects monsters, however, *The Dark Knight* was almost universally celebrated for its so-called viscerality, the grittiness of its context

In popular form (feminism and antifeminism in popular culture) **127**

TABLE 5.1 *The Dark Knight* trilogy

	Batman Begins	*The Dark Knight*	*The Dark Knight Rises*
Rated (US):	PG13	PG13	PG13
Distributor:	Warner Bros.[a]	Warner Bros.	Warner Bros.
Production budget:	$150 million	$185 million	$250 million
US domestic gross:	$206,852,432	$534,858,444	$448,139,099
Foreign box office:	$167,366,24	$469,700,000	$632,902,188
Worldwide total:	$374,218,673	$1,004,558,444	$1,081,041,287
	Domestic summary		
Opening weekend:	$48,745,440	$158,411,483	$160,887,295
	(No. 1 rank,	(No. 1 rank,	(No. 1 rank,
	3,858 theatres,	4,366 theatres,	4,404 theatres,
	$12,634 average)	$36,283 average)	$36,532 average)
Close date:	30 October 2005	5 March 2009	13 December 2012
In release:	142 days	231 days	147 days
	(20.3 weeks)	(33 weeks)	(21 weeks)

Note:
[a]As of 10 January 2013, Warner Bros. had 14.3 per cent of total market share (Box Office Mojo 2013).

and its apparently more complexly and realistically drawn characters. The films rose almost immediately to the top of IMDB's (user-derived) top films of all time. British Director Nolan, director of the much praised 'cult' film *Memento*, was chosen by Warner Bros. to refresh a franchise that had descended in to what was considered schlock campiness. Taking the 'realistic texture' of 1979's *Superman*, Nolan states that he 'wanted to make the Batman epic you expected to have been made in 1979' (quoted in Pulver 2005). The origin story 'was the bit that had never been told' and Nolan 'wanted to try to do it in a more realistic fashion' than had been tried in a superhero film before (Nolan, quoted in Pulver 2005). Thus *Batman Begins*, the first of the trilogy, 'deals with its central figure as a study in psychological damage' (Pulver 2005).

> Superheroes fill a gap in the pop culture psyche, similar to the role of Greek mythology. There isn't really anything else that does the job in modern terms. For me, Batman is the one that can most clearly be taken seriously. He's not from another planet, or filled with radioactive gunk. I mean, Superman is essentially a god, but Batman is more like Hercules: he's a human being, very flawed, and bridges the divide.
>
> (Christopher Nolan, quoted in Pulver 2005)

Yet it is not clear, reading *The Dark Knight* with any hint of gender sensitivity, exactly what divide Batman does bridge. The universe that *The Dark Knight* represents is entirely dominated by competing models of masculinity, much as was that of *Superman* in 1979, but without the humour (and humility) of Richard

128 In popular form (feminism and antifeminism in popular culture)

Donner's direction and Christopher Reeve's performance (especially the actor's surprisingly convincing portrayal of a Clark Kent so diffident and respectful it is impossible to imagine him even remotely considering cavorting with naked strippers *à la* Bruce Wayne).[3] As commentators have noted, the Nolan Batman franchise is an interesting, and troubling, example of Hollywood's penchant either for avoiding decent female characters altogether, or for actively writing them out of movies (see *Black Cat Reviews* 2012).

Given that *The Dark Knight's* director was looking in part to find 1979's *Superman* in his Batman trilogy, it is not clear why he created a series of vapid, ineffective female characters almost 30 years later. As *Black Cat Reviews* notes, canon female characters in the *Dark Knight* trilogy make up approximately 35 to 40 minutes screen time of their own accord, per film (2012). Of course filmmakers take liberties with their material, and not all canon male characters appeared in *The Dark Knight* trilogy. The slim pickings offered, however, by female characters Rachel Dawes, Martha Wayne, Holly Robinson, Catwoman/Selena Kyle and Talia/Miranda Tate compare tellingly to the 'fully realized canon male characters featured in the films' (from Heath Ledger's iconic Joker, to relatively unknown characters such as Bane and Ra's al Ghul) (ibid.). 'As far as canon female characters go', there is, *Black Cate Reviews* notes, 'a difference between not using *everyone*, and barely using *anyone*' (ibid., emphasis in the original). Moreover, 'not only were there plenty of opportunities to feature canon female characters' through-out the *Dark Knight* trilogy, 'there were moments in the films where to do otherwise required the filmmakers to diverge from established canon, and they did so anyway' (ibid.).

The Dark Knight's Rachel Dawes serves well as a hinging plot device, rather than, say, a realized characterization, throughout the first two films. As Pistelli points out at *Dissident Voice*, 'she spends her brief screen time torn between two men [Batman and Harvey Dent], before being brutally dispatched in a glaring instance of the "women in refrigerators syndrome"' (2008). A more arse-kicking *Dark Knight* female is Anne Hathaway's wily and manipulative Catwoman, who is 'always seductive' while remaining 'a little more relatable than other renditions of the character' (ibid.), despite wearing a black spandex bodysuit and four-inch spiked heels for most of the final *Batman* instalment, *The Dark Knight Rises*.

> Female action heroes are still accessed mainly as an object of sexuality, even if you can probably look past the Catwoman character [in *The Dark Knight Rises*] a little bit more (though mostly because she is supposed to act like a feline, which are famously sinuous and flexible creatures).
>
> (*Not Another Wave* 2012)

Not Another Wave points to a scene in *The Dark Knight Rises* that is particularly telling of the conventional gender tropes Nolan's *Dark Knight* relies so heavily upon. Here, Selena Kyle shifts from easy murderer to terrified screaming witness at a shoot-out, begging for help, then quickly reverting, again, to her killer

In popular form (feminism and antifeminism in popular culture) **129**

identity. This scene, 'embodies the two reactions you see for female characters in that situation' (*Not Another Wave* 2012). Female characters are either 'participating in and enjoying the killing, or they're so completely terrified that they just scream' (ibid.).

Women are not, of course, the only sex to fare badly in the superhero universe, and the 'Men are the Expendable Gender' trope is worth noting here. This trope is, *TV Tropes* suggests, a result of the 'double standard between male and female roles in the media', such that female characters apparently 'start with automatic audience sympathy' because women are (meant to be) seen as 'moral, innocent, beautiful or simply because they have sexual value' (2013b). Male characters, on the other hand, 'must earn audience sympathy by acting appropriately manly and heroic, which, more often than not, involves saving the Damsel in Distress' (ibid.). Women, therefore, do not lose (as much) audience sympathy as men 'for being helpless, incompetent or abandoning men to their fates in order to save themselves' (ibid.). The consequences of this are several. In the first instance, if stories require random anonymous characters to die, they will likely be male (ibid.). Female villains are more likely to be redeemed, and are also 'less likely to be taken seriously in their villainy' than male villains (ibid.). Male characters suffer more explicit and brutal deaths and male villains who target female characters 'are portrayed as more evil than those who target men' (ibid.).

Overt antifeminism (3): Why games with female characters don't sell

Anita Sarkeesian began her 'Tropes vs. Women in Video Games' project in 2012, seeking 'to examine the plot devices and patterns most often associated with female characters in gaming from a systemic, big picture perspective' (Feminist Frequency 2013). The project was funded solely through internet 'backers' donating through the 'Kickstarter' crowdfunding platform (6,968 people pledged upwards of $1 for Sarkeesian to fund production costs, equipment, games and downloadable content).

> The Tropes vs. Women in Video Games project aims to examine the plot devices and patterns most often associated with female characters in gaming from a systemic, big picture perspective. This series will include critical analysis of many beloved games and characters, but remember that it is both possible (and even necessary) to simultaneously enjoy media while also being critical of its more problematic or pernicious aspects.
>
> (Sarkeesian 2012)

In an effort to highlight the inherent sexism of gaming, which, perhaps even more so than Hollywood's big-budget cinematic efforts, is aimed at teenage and young men, Sarkeesian's project highlighted five particular tropes common across a variety of games. These tropes are: the *Damsel in Distress* (Video No. 1); the *Fighting F#@k Toy*

130 In popular form (feminism and antifeminism in popular culture)

(Video No. 2); the *Sexy Sidekick* (Video No. 3); the *Sexy Villainess* (Video No. 4); and *Background Decoration* (Video No. 5). The project also looked at other tropes in gaming, including *Voodoo Priestess/Tribal Sorceress* (Feministfrequency Video No.6); *Women as Reward* (Video No. 7); *Mrs. Male Character* (Video No. 8); *Unattractive Equals Evil* (Video No. 9); *Man with Boobs* (Video No. 10); and some *Positive Female Characters* (Video No. 11).

Some of the comments posted online in response to Sarkeesian's project (over a two-hour period in 2012), before her videos had even been made, are particularly telling:

> She needs a good dicking, good luck finding it though.

> Why do you put on makeup, if everything is sexism? Why don't you shave your head bald, stop wearing makeup and stop wearing huge slut earrings. You are a fucking hypocrite slut.

> 1940 – WE WANT TO BE EQUAL

> 2012 – WE ARE SUPERIOR!

> Yep … tits or gtfo.

> Yeah, I can't wait for the day we get to play 'ugly feminist ham planet: the game'. That would sell millions of units.
>
> (Quoted by *Feminist Frequency* 2012)

Sarkeesian responds to these comments with equanimity, referring to them as 'the types of silencing tactics often used against women on the internet who dare to speak up' (*Feminist Frequency* 2012), but the misogyny here remains astounding, not least given that Sarkeesian's modest aims to explore gendered representations in video games make no claim to seek to disable the traditional gaming industry.

Kuchera describes video games as a world in which 'male developers create games with male only heroes for an often overwhelmingly male audience' (2012). Not only this, but the games feature white male heroes, generally 'with a little bit of facial hair' (ibid.), in the assumption that they are for a white male audience. Citing EEDAR data (a research and data collection company working on video games), Kuchera finds 'almost no games with exclusively female heroes' (2012). The idea 'of a female-led game seems so toxic to publishers and marketing that there is barely enough examples from which to draw conclusions' (Kuchera 2012).

Having spent more of my adult life battling through *Zelda (Twilight Princess)* than I should probably admit to, I have long been sceptical of publishers' claims that the female audience for video games is insignificant. Estimates for 2008 suggested that between 38 and 40 per cent of the video gaming population was female; by 2012 this number had risen to 47 per cent (cf. the Entertainment Software Association). Sarkeesian's project also points to the number of women who do actually play

In popular form (feminism and antifeminism in popular culture) **131**

video games. As Reisinger notes, people often seem surprised 'that women really do play games and have a very real interest in the industry' (2008).

Kuchera looks at EEDAR data from 2012 to suggest that games 'that allow you to choose your gender are reviewed better than games that offer male-only heroes', *but*, 'games with male *only* heroes sold better' (2012, emphasis in the original). 'If you're finding a large-budget game and you see these numbers, you see that you lose sales by adding the capability to choose a female hero, and you lose *significant* sales by releasing a game with a female hero' (ibid., emphasis in the original). This is generally true except for the Nintendo DS console, where it is not often noted that female-optional games sell better than male-only games.

As Kuchera points out, however, this kind of conclusion is easily drawn by publishers, but fails to consider an important element of the gaming industry, which is marketing. Advertising (Sydney has been in 2013 awash with buses advertising *Grand Theft Auto 5* and its three male protagonists)[4] and shelf space in-store can dictate the ways in which a game will sell. Kuchera discovered that games 'with only female heroes are given *half the marketing budget as games with male heroes*' (2012, emphasis in the original). It would appear that publishers 'send female-lead games out to die without proper support' (ibid.) The *Tomb Raider* and *Portal* series remain possibly the only example of large-budget, well-marketed games with a female hero and, although perhaps their successes speak for themselves, there are so few examples of such well-supported, female-led games that conclusions are virtually impossible to draw (ibid.).

The sexism of the gaming industry itself is also worth considering here, since a perceived hostility to female gamers and industry professionals may be all it takes to maintain a discouraging stronghold for sexism over the gaming industry. As Liutongco argues, sexism in video games is hotly debated, but much of the controversy centres 'not on the question of whether sexism in video games exists, but rather if the industry should change to address it' (2013). Evidence that sexism in the gaming industry is actually ingrained and abounds is also, sadly, ample. Women represent only 12 per cent of the gaming industry in terms of personnel and both male and female professionals have named the gaming industry as 'an overall hostile environment for women', citing 'lower wages and a decreased occupational mobility for female employees', as well as 'a lack of respectful female representation in games' (ibid.). Given the outright, and abusive, hostility that Sarkeesian encountered throughout her 'Tropes' video project, the incentives *against* producing female-centred games for those, few, industry professionals who are female may be substantial.

> According to CNN, 'More than 60 percent of female students enrolled in game design programs at The Art Institutes said they believed male dominance in the industry is a deterrent to women pursuing a career in gaming, according to a survey commissioned by SOE'.
>
> (Reisinger 2008)

132 In popular form (feminism and antifeminism in popular culture)

Overt antifeminism (4): Why men are entitled to sex but (independent) female sexuality is unacceptable

> A spokesman for Michigan Speaker James Bolger said in a statement that [Michigan State Rep. Lisa] Brown would not be allowed to give her opinion on a school employee retirement bill Thursday because she had 'failed to maintain the decorum of the House of Representatives.'
>
> [...]
>
> 'What she [Brown] said was offensive,' [Republican Rep. Mike] Callton told The Detroit News. 'It was so offensive, I don't even want to say it in front of women. I would not say that in mixed company.'
>
> [...]
>
> 'If I can't say the word vagina, why are we legislating vaginas? What language should I use?'
>
> [...]
>
> Democratic Rep. Barb Byrum was also blocked from addressing the Republican-controlled legislature Thursday. The House forbid Byrum from introducing her amendment to the abortion bill, which would have banned men from getting a vasectomy unless they could provide proof that it was a medical emergency. 'If we truly want to make sure children are born, we would regulate vasectomies,' Byrum said Thursday.
>
> (Quoted in Roberts 2012)

The double standard that depicts the 'naturalness' of men's entitlement to sex against women's independent sexuality as unacceptable relates partly to the often-used trope of 'Damsel in Distress' across popular culture sources. Herein, since women are in constant need of rescuing, men must be characterized as assertive and able, with their sexuality depending on women needing them rather than, say, being able to rescue themselves. The double standard also, however, has strong links to nastier, 'rape culture', elements (even sensible, smart girls/women just really want a good-looking psycho to bend them over the table). Examples here are so plentiful it is hardly worth listing them, but a few, for me, stand out.

Outrageously promiscuous male characters in popular culture, such as Don Draper (*Mad Men*) or Christian Troy (*Nip/Tuck*), gain prestige from their woman-izing. Equally promiscuous female characters, however, usually end up humiliated, mutilated, diseased or dead, or they are 'daddyless', without appropriate father figures, and clearly in need of psychological intervention (Deborah Morgan in *Dexter*, Samantha Jones in *Sex and the City*, Catherine Tramell in *Basic Instinct*, Alexandra Forrest in *Fatal Attraction*, Mavis Gary in *Young Adult*, any slasher movie and most female characters in Bond movies, especially the 'evil seductress' types, and so on). *The Walking Dead*'s Andrea, perhaps one of the show's least popular characters,[5] is also one the show's two examples of a female character seeking sexual fulfilment without implied monogamy. The other character, Lori Grimes

In popular form (feminism and antifeminism in popular culture) **133**

(the protagonist Rick Grimes' wife) sleeps with another man (thinking, not unreasonably, that her husband is dead) and meets a particularly grisly death by caesarean section in Season Three. Andrea, promiscuous for this show having had non-monogamous sex at least twice, dies by her own hand having been set upon by a friend-turned-walker in Season Three. Taught that they are entitled to sex, men are 'trained from birth to see women as decoration', argues Wong (2012). Women are meaningful only in terms of their (hetero)sexuality and, even then, men are persistently told that they ought to be feeling frustrated, humiliated and powerless in the face of any assertion of this sexuality (ibid.).

As Sargent notes, US cinema censors seem much more likely 'to give a movie an NC-17 rating for sexual content (the most restrictively a film can be rated in the States) when the woman is shown enjoying herself a little *too much*' (2011, emphasis in the original). The former X-rating was threatened at *Boys Don't Cry* for a scene depicting a lengthy female orgasm, while *Scary Movie* received a no-quibbles R rating, 'despite a woman being plastered to the ceiling by a blast of semen' (ibid.). Long entrenched in slasher folklore, the trope that no woman who survives to the end of a movie will have been shown having had sex (the 'Final Girl' trope) remains, largely, unblemished. 'The MPAA [the Motion Picture Association of America] is under the impression that for moviegoers, the subject of female sexuality, even if it's just depicting women being *too* into sex, is scary and weird' (Sargent 2011, emphasis in the original).

Related to men's entitlement to sex versus women's sluttishness is the 'Sexist Jerk Who Scores' character. This is a common trope in popular culture representations, a result, Kesler suggests, of heterosexual male screenwriters' failures to 'pick up' women in bars and their ensuing rationalization that 'women really *should* be putting out for him and not the other guy' but are not, because 'he is a super nice guy, and the guy who can get women into bed is a jerk, and there's something wrong with those women that they prefer a jerk to a nice guy' (2008c, emphasis in the original).

> The thing about this writing trope is that it puts the men exclusively in the position of power. It depicts women as helpless things that need the constancy of relationships but sometimes get tricked into casual sex. It assumes women who have their own reasons for having casual sex are damaged goods. It assumes men are by nature sex seekers and women are by nature sex awarders, thereby stripping women of any power in the scenario, other than the power to award sex to the dull and/or obnoxious who are being framed as the 'right' choice.
>
> (Kesler 2008c)

The 'Sexist Jerk Who Scores' character also, importantly, serves as a warning note to 'promiscuous' women, since he is 'a punishment and warning to all those great-looking girls who turn down dull, boring and ugly guys in favor of attractive guys' (Kesler 2008c). While men 'are allowed to be incredibly shallow about women's looks', women who think like this will be punished (ibid.).

134 In popular form (feminism and antifeminism in popular culture)

> Even when male 'sexuality' is actually just a violent form of brutality that happens to resemble sex superficially, that important force must not be locked up. It must be allowed to roam free at any costs [...]. No, men mustn't pause to examine themselves, their motives or the likely consequences of their actions, ever, for if they do, it might distract them or even dissuade them from the quest society has handed them: the mindless screwing of everything in sight.
>
> (Kesler 2011)

That female characters exist only to promote male leads for network profits, in many studio executives and television professionals' eyes, makes it even less likely that women's sexuality will be explored fully and independently in films where male actors take the lead roles. Films produced to be dominated by female leads can, and do, allow for a greater exploration of independent female sexuality (*Boys Don't Cry, Martha, Marcy, May, Marlene, Thirteen, The Color Purple, Fried Green Tomatoes, The Help, The Hours*, and so on), but, as Holmes pointed out, anyone popping to a movie multiplex throughout the year will be lucky if they find a film in which women play more than a supporting role or are more than padding for an ensemble primarily focused on men (Holmes 2013).

Overt antifeminism (5): Why stupid girls are more profitable

> We're constantly being distracted from women's accomplishments with sexist fluff. Who cares about the accomplishments of the First Lady when black women are tearing out each others' weaves on *Basketball Wives*?
>
> (Sánchez 2012)

Since 1990, Joyner suggests, scripted shows, 'with continuous stories and character development that require teams of writers and set designers', have been increasingly pushed for space in television scheduling by the rise of so-called 'reality television' (2010). Wedding-hungry brides and toddlers in talent shows generate, Joyner argues, high-revenue returns and depend upon simple production values. Although they are not necessarily cheap shows to produce, with a 30-minute reality show, for example, costing between US$100,000 and $500,000 per episode (*E! Online*, cited in ibid.), they are certainly *cheaper* to produce than quality scripted shows. Each episode of *Mad Men*, for example, has a budget of between $2 and $2.5 million, while *Breaking Bad*, possibly the most critically celebrated scripted television show of the last ten years, reportedly cost $3 million per episode to produce.

In the reality TV universe, networks spend less on writers and less on 'stars' to populate their shows, which means also that smaller and emerging networks find reality shows particularly attractive. This is not to say that reality TV is 'unscripted', since it is heavily edited and particular scenarios clearly scripted for certain outcomes.

In popular form (feminism and antifeminism in popular culture) **135**

Joyner notes that product placement is much easier 'to digest' in reality television, generating advertising revenue for both the show and the network and the 'in-show placement' (for example, for Ford Motors in *American Idol*, or Snickers and Doritos in *Survivor*) that accompanies regular commercial breaks increases the value of paid advertising for reality show sponsors (2010). Even DVD sales of reality shows (including, for example, *The Simple Life*, *The Amazing Race* and *America's Next Top Model*) have unexpectedly outsold network dramas, despite studios' initial concerns (syndication revenue and retail DVD sales generate significant post-season profits for networks). Reality shows can be used to deliver new content to networks (and thus generate more advertising money) while networks' more expensive scripted shows are 'off-season'.

> By filling the majority of a calendar year with 'new' episodes of a show, networks and cable channels can capitalize on ad revenue for a longer time span – and there's little fear that a union strike will cease production in the meantime.
>
> (Joyner 2010)

'The more profitable so-called unscripted programming grows', argues Pozner, 'the more poisonous its representations of women become' (2004). Viewers continue to tune in to reality television shows 'because these shows frame their narratives in ways that both reflect and reinforce deeply ingrained societal biases about women, men, love, beauty, class and race' (ibid.). Realty TV exists, as *Who Wants to Marry a Multi-Millionaire* producer, *Married by America* and *Joe Millionaire* creator Mike Darnell has said, to provoke an audience reaction of 'Oh, my god! …What's wrong with you?' (quoted in Pozner 2004). The 'realities' that these shows represent are, however, manufactured, with reality TV show participants edited, coaxed, goaded and prompted in various ways and to reveal various 'truths'. Women are represented as gold-digging, money-grubbing sluts in an appeal to the basest, and most sexist, assumptions about women, but in buying into these representations, audiences only further reproduce the conditions wherein women are expected to value beauty, thinness and a rich spouse over intelligence, independence and professional accomplishment.

In recent years, a specific strain of reality TV has emerged that particularly troubles a number of feminists. Alexander notes that her search through Wikipedia for 'Wedding Television Shows' yielded an impressive 32 results, while US television currently hosts six 'different television shows about teen moms' (2013). Australian television currently airs at least nine wedding-based reality TV shows at any one time (*I Found the Gown*, *Something Borrowed*, *Something New*, *Don't Tell the Bride*, *Say Yes to the Dress*, *Mother of the Bride*, *Brides of Beverley Hills*, *Bridezillas*, *Whose Wedding is it Anyway?*, *Four Weddings*), plus *Deadly Women* (which deals largely in money-hungry, marriage-obsessed women whose superficial charms conceal murderous impulses towards their unsuspecting spouses) and the *Real Housewives* franchise. A number of these shows are US- and Canada-based, but not

136 In popular form (feminism and antifeminism in popular culture)

all, and in 2014 Australian audiences gained the dubious pleasure of *The Real Housewives of Melbourne* (produced by the network channel Arena). Both wedding and housewife reality shows have become ubiquitous; unique in the world of reality TV for their unwaveringly unflattering portrayals of the everyday woman.

Added to North America's *Who Wants to Marry a Multi-Millionaire*, *The Bachelor*, *Beauty and the Geek*, *Wife Swap*, *Say Yes to the Dress*, *America's Next Top Model* and any of the *Real Housewives* franchise (among others reality shows), these shows teach women, feminists have argued, that they can be fulfilled only through finding a husband, that they should aspire solely to a life of leisure, that they are valuable as decorative props for advertisers, that they are bad wives and mothers if they pursue professional or political interests outside the home and, as in VH1's *Flavor of Love*, that they ('especially women of color') are 'ignorant, violent, gold-digging' and promiscuous (Pozner 2010). As Sánchez notes, the *Real Housewives* franchise depicts middle-aged women as 'shallow, catty, greedy, and idle' (2012). These women's 'success' and identity 'are entirely dependent on the men they marry', and 'nearly every episode shows these women ripping each other to shreds over some frivolous transgression. It not only encourages pettiness, but also teaches girls that women can't be friends' (ibid.). While the Kardashian family themselves may not be unintelligent, 'what they are manufacturing and perpetuating is stupidity' (ibid.).

Pozner is interested in why it is that reality TV (or, more accurately, the networks, editors and writers behind reality TV) choose to present women as marriage-obsessed bimbos (2010). Beginning to monitor unscripted programming when *The Bachelor* debuted in 2002, Pozner sensed 'a new resurgence of a classic antifeminist media meme' (ibid.). 'Since then', she argues, 'reality television has emerged as America's most vivid example of pop cultural backlash against women's rights and social progress' (ibid.). 'Compare the accomplishments and experiences of American women over the past decade with their depictions through the unscripted looking glass, and a systemic pattern emerges' (ibid.). Pozner names this pattern a backlash against feminism, where, 'in the unscripted (but carefully crafted) world of dating, marriage and lifestyle shows' women should not be concerned 'with politics, law, athletics, activism or even careers in general' (unless, Pozner argues, they are 'competing for the supermodel/starlet/rock star gigs that populate ten-year-olds' daydreams, or have schoolteacher/flight attendant/professional cheerleader jobs that were acceptable in the pre-feminist 1950s'). Rather, 'reality TV producers, casting directors, editors and their product placement sponsors have collaborated to paint American women as romantically desperate, matrimonially obsessed and hypertraditionalist in their views about the "proper" role for wives and mothers, husbands and fathers' (ibid.).

Similarly, Sánchez bemoans the affected 'dumb girl voice' that characterizes US teenagers, but asks why she is actually surprised by the over-use of this voice, since 'women have always been encouraged to play dumb' (2012). The 'dumb girl trope is deeply ingrained in American culture and history', she argues, and women have been explicitly advised to 'play dumb' to catch a man (ibid.). SMS,

In popular form (feminism and antifeminism in popular culture) **137**

or Silly Me Syndrome, is 'a common female affliction', suggests Fernandes (2013). 'There is a dearth of quality men around and these women know that if they play smart, they will not have as many men as they would like. Hence, they are willing to compromise' (Varkha Chulani, clinical psychologist and counselor, quoted in Fernandes 2013). According to Chulani, women in the dating world thus not only cut themselves short personally, but in their careers also, ceding to men the 'upper hand' just in case the male ego is too fragile to handle the 'threat' of an intelligent woman (ibid.). Women may, in their earlier dating experiences, have been told 'that the man is intimidated' by a woman with knowledge and position, and family members will, according to Chulani, 'pressurise women into not showing their smart side just to impress a potential "good catch"' (ibid.).

Scripted television has, of course, not been entirely usurped by reality TV. In particular, children's and teenagers' television programming remains hugely popular, and widespread, with the increasing reach of television channels such as Disney and Nickelodeon. These channels, Sánchez argues, 'have the power to dictate and even create teen and tween culture in the United States' (2012). US teenagers number 33 million, the largest generation of teens in American history, and in 2011 spent $100 billion ('while influencing their parents' spending by $50 billion') (ibid., in reference to Nielsen data). 'The 'huge cultural and economic influence' of the teenage programming market 'allows media to manufacture anti-feminist ideologies that are targeted to young girls' (ibid.). Sánchez points to shows such as *JESSIE* and *Shake it Up* as reproductive of tropes of young women as ditsy, shallow and vain, but always 'cute' (ibid.).

> Glorifying stupidity in girls is highly profitable because it means that these young consumers will focus their attention on their appearance. They will never be the most popular girl in school if they don't have the latest doodad or lip gloss. Insecurity is lucrative.
>
> (Sánchez 2012)

Kang notes the example of a Cartoon Network show, *Tower Prep*, which was cancelled because network executives (its writer, Paul Dini, believes) were openly hostile to young females watching the show. The executives claimed that girls do not buy merchandise produced for cartoon TV shows. In a discussion with director Kevin Smith, Dini describes how cable network executives 'urged him to focus his storylines on his male characters' and to situate his female characters 'always "one step behind the boys"', to make them 'not as smart as the boys' and certainly 'not as interesting as the boys' (quoted in Kang 2013). Dini proceeded to create fully realized female characters regardless, even giving them developed back stories, and the Cartoon Network axed the show (ibid.). 'We don't want the girls because the girls won't buy toys', the executives told Dini. While boys 'buy the little spinny tops, they buy the action figures', girls 'buy princesses' and the network is 'not selling princesses' (ibid.).

138 In popular form (feminism and antifeminism in popular culture)

Why would young women 'want to be smart when they only see sexiness being rewarded' (Sánchez 2012)? Why would they strive for professional, political or personal achievement, when they lack interesting, intelligent female characters to engage with and look up to, or when these characters are persistently denied fulfilment or happiness because they need to be punished for their complexity? Teenage girls are not only watching shows aimed at teens, they are also watching, and absorbing, the lessons of reality television, and its persistent glorification of women's value according to their physical appearance. As Pozner articulates, the concern with reality television relates less to its impact on its participants, than 'the millions of viewers, scores of whom are young girls', who absorb 'these misogynistic spectacles uncritically, learning that only the most stereotypically beautiful, least independent women with the lowest-carb diets will be rewarded with love, financial security and the ultimate prize of male validation' (2004). Reality television's obsession with money- and marriage-obsessed 'bimbos' only interacts, from a wider cultural vantage, with the absence of representations of nuanced, intelligent and independent women in other arenas. This only discourages girls 'from having the audacity to be unapologetically intelligent' (Sánchez 2012), while robbing them of the confidence to interrogate patriarchal assumptions and discriminations as adults.

Beyond reality television, when networks do manage to create a scripted female character that is intelligent, strong and capable, this woman is often, as Dockterman describes, inexplicably incapable of making good choices 'when the man of her affection enters the picture' (2013). An old-style sexism pervades choices to disarm women before the men they admire, to render them powerless before male characters they are consumed by or to crumble them in the face of their male-centred obsessions. Recent shows such as *Scandal, Revenge, Homeland, The Newsroom*, even *Game of Thrones*, establish complex and important female characters, only to have them stumble before the objects of their affection. The trend to present female characters as derailed by men is so prevalent, Dockterman argues, that there exist few examples of a strong female protagonist on a popular TV show who does not make a poor decision because of a man at one point or another.

> Joan and Peggy on *Mad Men* are two of the only women not completely flustered by the opposite sex. And these women live in the 1960s, where a doctor tries to shame Joan out of using birth control and Peggy gets locked out of copywriter meetings simply because she's a woman. [This is] not to say that Joan and Peggy are not flawed; both characters have major pitfalls. It's just that their flaws are not men-centric.
>
> (Dockterman 2013)

Unlike male characters, who knowingly walk into disastrous situations to 'save' their girlfriends, wives, sisters or mothers, and whose 'seemingly idiotic actions are meant to be heartwarming and heroic', women blinded by love on television are reminded consistently that their decisions are destructive and selfish, yet they continue with them regardless (Dockterman 2013). They are not set up to be seen as sacrifices for the greater good and these women's decisions invariably entail significant costs, robbing them of audience sympathy and rendering the characters trivial.

Perhaps there is so little complaint at the media-circulated assumption that stupid women are more successful at finding love, marriage and eternal happiness because the movies and television shows written today to target younger generations are written for people who have, in a sense, grown up beyond feminism. Young people today have often grown up around women doing everything and there is, therefore, nothing surprising in women doing what, once upon a time, would have been the preserve only of men. Many of this generation 'would need it explained to them why *Cagney and Lacey* was revolutionary, because many of their moms had worked in fields once dominated by men' (Kesler 2008b). Too young to remember the second wave, even why we might have needed it, a generation that has grown up with Ellen Ripley and Sarah Connor as action heroes finds themselves in 'a media climate hostile to female characters and audiences' (Kang 2013). In this regard, young women are likely less aware of the dangers of self-representing as 'perpetually dumb' because they are not fighting the same gender battles as previous generations, while being surrounded by representations of women and girls as secondary, dependent and/ or appearance-obsessed.

Overt antifeminism (6): Why feminists can only be characterized negatively in popular culture

> 'Feminism' means so many different things that it appears to mean very little. Its theoretical advocates constantly contradict each other and themselves. In casting off feminine reserve and modesty they seem to have learned intellectual shamelessness as well. […] Antifeminism is thus nothing more than the rejection of one of the narrow and destructive fantasies of an age in which such things have been responsible for destruction and murder on an unprecedented scale. It is opening oneself to the reality of things.
>
> (Kalb 2004)

> I consider the term 'Feminazis' to be a fairly accurate description of members of what is now undoubtedly a hate movement.
>
> (MasculistFeminist 2013)

Stereotypes about and of feminists are everywhere in popular culture. Very few, if any, are flattering (Figure 5.1). According to such media representations, feminists are 'Feminazis', childless, gay, hysterical, aggressive, anti-men, angry, unattractive, whiny, anti-sex, sex-starved, bra-burners, averse to shaving, disrespectful of stay-at-home mothers, lacking a sense of humour, defensive, mentally (or emotionally) unstable and female.

Sarkeesian refers to the media and Hollywood's construction of certain tropes about feminists, or common and/or recognizable patterns and attributes to feminist

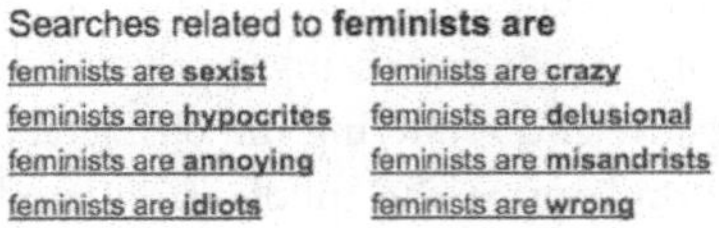

140 In popular form (feminism and antifeminism in popular culture)

> Searches related to **feminists are**
>
> feminists are **sexist** feminists are **crazy**
> feminists are **hypocrites** feminists are **delusional**
> feminists are **annoying** feminists are **misandrists**
> feminists are **idiots** feminists are **wrong**

FIGURE 5.1 Searches related to 'feminists are' at www.google.com.au.

Source: Author screenshot.

characters, as the creation of 'Straw Feminists'. Feminist characters, she argues, do not often make it through the production process and when they do, Hollywood offers only a 'distorted and warped version of feminism which [bears] little resemblance to actual feminist movements' (*Feminist Frequency* 2011).

The Straw Feminist works 'by deliberately creating an exaggerated caricature of a feminist', which writers then fill with various 'oversimplifications, misrepresentations and stereotypes to try to make it easy to discredit or delegitimize feminism' (*Feminist Frequency* 2011). Sarkeesian points to the third season of *Veronica Mars*, a show that had previously seemed to take some care to establish an independent, feisty and sympathetic leading female character. A group of Straw Feminists here become the 'villains' of the piece, spouting anti-male rhetoric and staging a 'fake rape' to incriminate a fraternity. 'Characters like these', Sarkeesian argues, 'serve to undermine and discredit feminist movements', but they also serve 'to separate female leads which are smart, strong and witty, in this case, Veronica, from any association with feminism' (ibid.).

> The Straw Feminist character is part of a fictional post-feminist world that only exists in Hollywood: the trope is a tool that's used to promote the fallacy that everyone is already equal. What's exceptionally frustrating is that these characters often bring up legitimate feminist concerns about women's rights and women's equality but those concerns are quickly undermined by the writers making the characters seem over the top, crazy, and extremist.
>
> (*Feminist Frequency* 2011)

Rush Limbaugh's frequent tirades against 'Feminazis' aside, we need only scratch the surface of popular culture to reveal the 'current of white-hot rage' that flows beneath. Wong argues that popular culture supports an environment in which modern men are 'made to feel that their manhood has, at some point, been stolen from them' (2012) (Figure 5.2). Wong points to the front pages of male discussion sites, such as Reddit.com, and the speed with which one can find 'several thousand men bemoaning how all women are gold diggers (7,500 upvotes) and how crazy and irrational women are (9,659 upvotes) and how horrible and gross and fat women are (4,000 upvotes)' (ibid.). 'A once-great world of heroes and strength and warriors and cigars and crude jokes has been replaced by this world of grumpy

In popular form (feminism and antifeminism in popular culture) 141

FIGURE 5.2 'Rush Vs Feminism'.
Source: Piascik 2012.

female supervisors looming over our cubicle to hand us a memo about sending off-color jokes via email' (ibid.).

> I don't know about anyone else, but when I hear the word ['feminist'], I think of an episode of *Family Guy* where there is a female lawyer named Gloria Ironbox who wears pantsuits and teaches sexual harassment classes, representing to men all that is 'wrong' about feminism to the show's male adolescent target audience. At the end of the episode, she tells Lois Griffin that she is fighting so that women like her can be 'more than just a housewife,' ending with Lois defending her housewife status in a catfight striptease. I think that people need to see through the stereotype [of] self-righteous tomboys who hate men and any woman who isn't CEO of Ms. Magazine or an OBGYN. Every feminist is different just like every woman is different and [has] a diverse range of opinions and beliefs that fall within the feminist spectrum. I wouldn't call Lois Griffin a great feminist, but I wouldn't say that Gloria Ironbox represents all feminists either.
>
> (SavvyRed 2010)

Tacit antifeminism (1): Why 'strong female characters' have become boring

For a long time, my favourite fictional character in popular culture was Brenda Chenowith, from *Six Feet Under* (whose creator, Alan Ball, has since gone on to

142 In popular form (feminism and antifeminism in popular culture)

create my next favourite television character, *True Blood*'s Lafayette). Brenda is highly intelligent but volatile, difficult and clearly flawed. Reactive and often emotionally disjointed, she is wry, sarcastic and often rather cold. She is perhaps not, on paper, an obvious role model for young women. Thinking about Brenda and reflecting on the power of popular culture representations of women in my own life, I have recently been pondering my discomfort at the lead female character in a new Fox show, *Sleepy Hollow*, which, despite its innate daftness, has become something of a so-called 'breakout' success for Fox.

Sleepy Hollow, very loosely based on the Washington Irving short story 'The Legend of Sleepy Hollow', began airing in September 2013, with a second season commissioned for 2014. On paper, the show's lead, Lieutenant Abbie Mills, is an excellent example of a strong female character. She is smart, competent and focused. Not motivated in the slightest (at least so far) by romance, Abbie acts as an anchor for all the otherwise bizarre supernatural goings on, maintaining her credibility by seeking only to get her job done. She is 'a relatable and capable narrator' and, Gennis argues, 'a fully realized hero', displaying vulnerability, strength and rationality, which is 'a pleasantly shocking change of pace compared to the often reductive women of network TV' (2013). Actor Tom Mison, who plays Abbie's partner Ichabod Crane, has said he was particularly attracted to the show because the two female leads are not 'defined by a man' (referring also to his character's wife, Katrina Crane) (quoted in Gennis 2013).

> [Y]ou don't see [independent female characters] enough. All too often ... the women are the girlfriend or the daughter and they have very little to do other than support the male characters' stories. [But with *Sleepy Hollow*], from the start and throughout, the female characters have been rounded and clear and individual.
>
> (Mison, quoted in Gennis 2013)

The 'Strong Female Character' (SFC) has, according to some commentators, however, become an over-used and tiresome trope in popular culture, a 'cheap, insincere nod toward equality' that replaces the important struggles women face with a glib evocation of perpetual toughness (Silverstein and Kang 2013). SFCs may, they argue, have been useful 'a few years ago when there was a dearth of women on film and most were so rubber-limbed, glass-ankled, or prone to fainting spells they literally needed to be carried out of danger by a man' (ibid.). Great female protagonists were, for a long while, always 'the exceptions' and films 'with strong female characters were anomalies, not the pattern' (ibid.). Today,

> Hollywood has taken our love of strong female characters and converted it into something dully literal. Strong female characters have become Strong Female Characters, a mutant sub-genus that has less to do with actual women than T-Rexes: physically intimidating, but mentally nonthreatening.
>
> (Silverstein and Kang 2013)

Strength, the authors argue, has become a substitute for personality where female characters are concerned. For McDougall, the SFC is one who displays a penchant for violence over dialogue because she always starts with an 'underlying deficit of respect', which she is then 'required to overcome by whatever desperate, over-the-top, cartoonish means' spring to hand (2013).

> That a female character is allowed to get away with behaviour that, in a male character, would rightly be seen as abusive (or outright murderous) may seem [...] an unfair imbalance in her favour. [But the Strong Female Character is] in a hole, and acts that would be hair-raising in a male character just barely bring her up to their level. [...] The Strong Female Character has something to prove. She's on the defensive before she even starts.
>
> (McDougall 2013)

What would vastly improve women's representation in popular culture is not more SFCs, Silverstein and Kang argue, but rather *the creation of women and girls with agency* (Silverstein and Kang 2013). Popular culture needs less women on celluloid to whom things happen, even if they kick ass when events overtake them, than female characters that actively drive plots forward (ibid.). Studios, networks, writers directors and producers need, McDougall argues, to 'get away from the idea that sexism in fiction can be tackled' by relying on depicting 'a single personality type', in the belief that 'you just need to write one female character per story right and you've done enough' (2013). Stories with a single SFC per script, surrounded only by and speaking only to men (as per *The Avengers*, *Salt*, *Shrek*, *Iron Man*, *Inception*, *Captain America*, *Thor*, and so on), do not a mountain of sexism in Hollywood overcome. Rather, a 'wealth of complex female protagonists' is required, each with the freedom to be 'strong or weak or both or neither', tough but also 'interesting', women who can be 'shy and quiet and do, sometimes, put up with others' shit because in real life there's often no practical alternative' (ibid.). Heroines are still needed, but so too are female characters 'in as many and varied secondary and character roles as men', including 'female sidekicks, mentors, comic relief, rivals, villains' (ibid.).

> If a director or screenwriter is interested in meeting the bare minimum of feminist standards, a female character should have the wits and a big enough part in the story to propel and shape the plot significantly on her own accord. We all enjoy seeing women kicking ass, but we'd enjoy even more watching a woman whose decisions are important and taken seriously by the characters around her.
>
> (Silverstein and Kang 2013)

Sleepy Hollow's Abbie Mills has been well received critically and popularly, as has the show, and seems to be perceived generally as 'a strong, resilient and courageous' person (see Martinez 2013). Yet I have not quite bought into her character and something to me seems a little off-kilter about her. At the moment, Abbie exhibits

144 In popular form (feminism and antifeminism in popular culture)

symptoms of being something of a caricature of what an SFC consists of. While her male partner, Ichabod Crane, is given extensive background (and also opportunity for emotional vulnerability) in each episode, with ample opportunity to ponder his life, and grieve his past life, the space allowed Abbie for self-reflection is relatively tiny. She remains continually, and reliably, unflappable, powering through any obstacles in ways that give little sign of any emotional response, rendering her, at the moment, a little dull. Where *Six Feet Under*'s Brenda Chenowith is given a good deal of room to explore herself, and is allowed to be persistently flawed and disagreeable (simultaneously strong, weak and neither), Abbie enjoys no such freedom.

Abbie's (thus far) rather one-dimensional toughness may exist partly because, as an African American woman, the character is also bound by reference to stereotypes that white characters never need face. Martinez suggests that Abbie's traits of resilience and strength may 'possibly trap her character into the "strong black woman" stereotype' and asks whether Abbie, and her sister Jenny, are 'too strong', 'too independent' and not 'vulnerable enough' (2013).

This is also a good example, however, of the 'damned if you do and damned if you don't' in writing female characters. Male characters currently outnumber female characters on screen by five to one (Silverstein and Kang 2013). If Abbie were visibly emotional in every episode, her ability to carry the mantle of saviour of the world would likely be questionable. If she needed to be protected, rescued and saved, her character would be another pretty girl 'under too much stress' who needs to be shielded from the world, a 'damsel in distress' and 'a white man's "sidepiece"' (Martinez 2013). As Martinez notes, the series' writers have avoided pushing Abbie's character into 'sassy black woman' territory and she certainly embodies the kind of agency that other television shows disallow their female leads. Perhaps I am simply uncomfortable with Abbie because I am uncomfortable with all the ways that female characters cannot appear vulnerable without appearing weak, while 'toughness' in women still appears to require the routing out of any hint of emotion. Representations of women on television simply do not enjoy the freedom of multiplicity that male representations revel in. As McDougall notes, 'Sherlock Holmes gets to be brilliant, solitary, abrasive, Bohemian, whimsical, brave, sad, manipulative, neurotic, vain, untidy, fastidious, artistic, courteous, rude, a polymath genius' (McDougall 2013). Female characters get to be supportive, sexy, dispensible, mad or dead. Or now, 'Strong'.

Tacit antifeminism (2): Why Hollywood is not good at 'girl power'

> Gravity is nominated for best film. It's the story of how George Clooney would rather float away into space and die than spend one more minute with a woman his own age.
>
> (Tina Fey and Amy Poehler, Opening Monologue,
> Golden Globes 2014, 13 January)

In a deceptively light-hearted article in *Cracked*, author Liang examines a number of examples, in recent cinema history, of Hollywood's attempts to represent women favourably. Not only, she argues, are these 'positive' representations, upon further investigation, not terribly favourable but they also highlight a deeply rooted 'woman problem' in Hollywood, a problem that movie studios are keen to disguise with attempts at so-called 'girl power' (2008).

Lord of the Rings: The Two Towers and *The Return of the King* were 2002 and 2003's biggest movie releases. Both films are also rather short on decent female characters. As McDougall notes, the movies are so short, in fact, on SFCs that the screenwriters of *The Lord of the Rings* sought fit to, rather clumsily, expand Arwen's role from the books by having her 'wander on screen, put a sword to her boyfriend's throat and boast about how she'd sneaked up on him' (2013). Actress Liv Tyler is later reported to have commented that 'you don't have to put a sword in [Arwen's] hand to make her strong' (quoted in ibid.).

The trilogy's Eowyn is probably the movies' closest approximation of an SFC. On the face of things, she is fairly tough, with a thirst for battle and an unwavering confidence in her fighting abilities. Introduced in the second film as a noblewoman of Rohan, 'an able ruler, and a trained warrior', Eowyn is, however, 'told to stay behind and help protect the women and children of Rohan while all the men go off to ride horses and stab things' (Liang 2008). Eowyn rebels and, disguising herself as a man, abandons her responsibilities to fight with Aragorn (who she is also in love with. He, however, is betrothed, which he fails to mention to the mooning, lovestruck Eowyn).

In *Return of the King*, Eowyn disguises herself as a man and travels with the Riders of Rohan to the Battle of the Pelennor Fields. It is during this battle that she, as per Tolkien's original book, confronts the Witch-King of Angmar, who, believing that she is a man, attacks her, since 'no living man' can hinder him. Eowyn, of course, is a woman, as she informs the Witch-King shortly before he meets his demise and, her thirst for battle apparently sated, she hangs up her shield, marries Faramir and lives, we assume, happily ever after. 'The lesson here, impressionable young girls, is that playing soldier is all well and good in emergencies, but you're not really complete until you land a husband. *Any* husband' (Liang 2008). As Liang notes, 'take that, patriarchy!' (ibid.).

Padme, of the *Star Wars* prequels (two of which sit in the highest-grossing films of all time, not adjusting for inflation), is also a potentially strong, inspiring vision of intelligence and steely fighting spirit. That is, as Liang notes, until she gets pregnant: 'As everyone in Hollywood knows, a uterus makes women do crazy things' (2008). In movies, pregnancy (generally) turns 'a heroine into a useless, whining, fragile creature' (ibid.) and the pregnant Padme spends the rest of her time on screen 'crying and wondering when Anakin will come home' (ibid.).

> After confronting her baby daddy about his experimentation with the Dark Side, she's injured and goes into labor. While giving birth to future ass kickers Leia and Luke, Padme decides to die. [...] [T]he movie makes it pretty clear:

146 In popular form (feminism and antifeminism in popular culture)

> she just gives up. No serious injury, no difficult birth, no blood spurting onto the table. What about the two children she has to live for? Nope. She'll have none of that. The uterus will not allow it.
>
> (Liang 2008)

Joss Whedon has been infinitely and tirelessly held up as possibly the only writer/ director/producer in Hollywood able to consistently produce decent female characters. Unashamed to admit, publicly and in private, that he finds women inspiring, Whedon has said (on creating perhaps his most enduringly loved female character, Buffy) that he 'wanted to create a female icon' but that he also 'wanted to be very careful to surround her with men who not only had no problem with the idea of a female leader, but were in fact, engaged and even attracted to the idea' (part of Whedon's 2006 'Equality Now' speech, transcribed in film ick (2006)). While Whedon's television shows and movies are littered with strong, smart and interesting female characters, and it is clear that Whedon sits somewhat against the grain of Hollywood's woman problem, were Buffy not also surrounded by interesting and developed *female* characters, she would very easily fit into the token SFC. Under close examination, very few of Whedon's productions actually offer a true wealth of complex female protagonists and one of his most commercially successful ventures, *The Avengers*, is a classic example of the SFC that so troubles a number of feminist commentators. With Joss Whedon's work, it has often been assumed, argues Liang, 'that all the female characters will be ground breaking paragons of feminist virtue' (2008). This may be because 'Whedon genuinely respects strong female characters', or it may be because he is 'intimidated by a cult fanbase that demands every show of his have another Buffy in it' (ibid.).

Whedon's *Firefly*, the television series, was cancelled by Fox before its first season had finished airing, but gained a cult following and impressive DVD sales. *Serenity*, *Firefly*'s spin-off theatrical release, opened in the US domestic box office at number two, but failed to make back its budget until its home media release. Both the television series and the movie constitute Whedon's homage to the genre of the Hollywood western (with a sci-fi twist). Herein, men are captains and leaders, women are (generally, if not always) whores, subordinates or mothers. In the form of 'River', the genius sister of *Serenity*'s (also the name of the ship) doctor, Simon, the women are, Liang notes, 'barking mad' (2008). In River's case, the reason for this is that she has been tortured and reprogrammed to be an assassin, with psychic abilities.

River's fighting prowess is certainly stunning and she saves the day (and the men) on a few notable occasions, rendering her a seemingly perfect fit for a (nutty) Buffy Part II. Herein, however, lies the problem with *Firefly/Serenity*, Liang argues (2008). River is so clearly superior in all forms of warfare that the fact she uses her gifts to the benefit of the crew so rarely is troubling. Instead, the character, 'driven insane by her experiences', ends up spending 'most of her time saying crazy things and throwing up in her brother's bed' (ibid.). Thus,

In popular form (feminism and antifeminism in popular culture)   **147**

'protecting River' constitutes 'the backbone of no less than five out of thirteen episodes' of *Firefly*, 'plus the theatrical movie' (ibid.). This is, Liang notes, 'an awful lot' of needing to be rescued for a feminist hero (ibid.). Fans have reacted fiercely to *Firefly/Serenity* and Whedon's apparent diminution of women, with some even suggesting that Whedon has stripped his female characters of their integrity and takes pleasure in displaying potentially powerful women as cowed, 'gleefully' demonizing female power and selfhood (fan *Livejournal* comments, cited in Liang 2008).

A brief note, here, on Hollywood award ceremonies is worth making. 2014 marked the second year that Tina Fey and Amy Poehler hosted the Golden Globes, taking over from the acerbic Ricky Gervais, who had hosted for the previous three years. Award shows in Hollywood are almost never hosted by women (Whoopi Goldberg and Ellen Degeneres are the only women to have hosted, solo, Oscar award ceremonies) and Fey and Poehler's MC-ing was 'widely acclaimed as a breath of fresh air in the stuffy, awkward world of awards-show hosting' when they took to the stage in 2013 (Pulver 2013). Not long followed by Seth MacFarlane's crude, crass and blatantly sexist opener to the 2013 Oscars (held on 17 February), including the 'song' 'We Saw Your Boobs', it has not taken the Hollywood machine too long to start the backlash, with the *New York Post*'s Kyle Smith claiming that we might as well have referred to 2014's Golden Globes as 'Girls' (see Smith 2014). The night was, Smith suggests, 'a deep dive into a pool of estrogen' (2014). Fey and Poehler, 'in accordance with the tiresome defense mechanism of female nightclub comics', made it all about 'gender', before their hecklers could get going (ibid.). Berating the duo's *Gravity* inspired joke, Smith complains that 'Bullock had ten times as much screen time as her co-star', with 'Clooney being reduced to playing her coach' (ibid.).

If, in terms of its representations of women, Hollywood is not good at 'girl power', in its actual use of female talents, it is considerably worse. An 'excess of estrogen' is not, as Chemaly notes, a problem that Hollywood suffers from. Citing data generated by Women and Hollywood, The Geena Davis Institute on Gender in Media, the Writers Guild of America, the Representation Project and USC's Annenberg School for Communication and Journalism's Gender Equality in 500 Popular Films' study, Chemaly notes that in 2012, men were 95.6 per cent of directors, 91.8 per cent of writers and 80 per cent of producers in Hollywood (a behind the screen ratio of five men to every one woman behind the camera) (2014). Of the 4,475 speaking characters on screen in 2012, only 28.4 per cent were female and only 6 per cent of the top-grossing films in 2012 featured a balanced cast (ibid.). Two of the ten Golden Globe 'best picture nominees had stories primarily about women and almost all failed the Bechdel Test' (ibid.). In television, 'women made up only 18.6 per cent of executive producers for television shows' between 2011 and 2012, while 'men of all ethnic/racial backgrounds combined' constituted 81.4 per cent (ibid.). Only 24 per cent of TV pipeline pilots for 2012 had at least one female writer (ibid.).

148 In popular form (feminism and antifeminism in popular culture)

Tacit antifeminism (3): Why women shouldn't read *The Economist*

> Leader writers [in news media] are generally white, middle-aged men and they have no perception of gender bias. They don't want to acknowledge that it happens within their newsrooms, and they certainly wouldn't be open to challenging some of those positions and changing the public discourse either.
>
> (North, cited in Rourke 2012)

The Economist is an English-language weekly news and international affairs publication. Describing itself as a newspaper rather than a magazine,[6] the publication is half-owned by the British *Financial Times* and is edited and produced in London. In 2013, *The Economist* enjoyed a circulation of 1,546,511 (representing a year-to-year growth of 5.63 per cent) and an online readership of 7,712,831, with 31,778,106 page views during August 2013 (The Economist Group 2013). It describes itself as the 'web's most trusted source of global news analysis' (*The Economist* 2014a).

As Hooper notes, *The Economist* has historically targeted itself at 'an international readership largely composed of elite men' and is a publication 'saturated with images of masculinity' (2001: 117). Currently, only 13 per cent of its readers are female (Hess 2011). The remaining 87 per cent, as Hooper also notes, are not just normal men, they are the financial and business elite (ibid.). 'Worldwide, the average reader's personal income is $175,000. His average net worth is $1,688,000' (Hess 2011). Forty-six per cent of readers are employed as senior managers in their companies and a quarter of these hold Chief-level ('C-level') positions (ibid.). These are the 'accomplished, influential people' the *Economist* is marketed at.

The Economist's readers receive the same editorial matter, regardless of location, except perhaps for varied section running order and, occasionally, different covers (*The Economist* 2014b). The advertisements featured in the magazine differ consistently, however, according to geographical location, which is particularly important in understanding how significant media sources, such as *The Economist*, are in reproducing the iconography and symbolism of the wider cultures in which they are produced, as Hooper shows (2001). Images within the magazine are carefully chosen to convey a sense of elitism, luxury and masculinity, fixing 'the overall meaning in favour of masculine corporate power' (ibid.: 127). The 9 January 2014 cover, for example, which is the same across the print versions produced for Latin America, North America, Europe, the Middle East, Asia, Africa and the UK, pushes the benefits of government-backed privatization, and clearly locates the task of unburdening governments with potential lucrative assets on the shoulders of a male subject (whose legs are seen struggling beneath various boxes of state-owned goodies).

In November 2011, *The Economist*, having commissioned two studies that found that women, although increasingly obvious in the business world, represented only a small percentage of the magazine's market share, ran an advertisement for a select demographic of potential (North American) subscribers. 'Why should women read *The Economist*?' a circular attached to the magazine asked (Figure 5.3).

FIGURE 5.3 *The Economist*, slip-cover.
Source: Odell 2011.

'They shouldn't'. Folded inside the pamphlet was the tagline: 'Accomplished, influential *people* should read us. People like you'.

The Economist, Hess notes, responded cynically 'to the new imperative to sell itself to women' by asserting that 'appealing to women is unnecessary': if an overwhelming majority of the accomplished, influential people it wants reading its pages happen to be men, the newspaper seems to be suggesting, 'perhaps it is because they have simply accomplished more' (2011). The newspaper offers no bylines, is presented in a monolithic editorial voice and argues 'that what is written is more important than who writes it' (*The Economist* 2014c). Anonymity keeps the editor 'not the master but the servant of something far greater than himself' (former editor Geoffrey Crowther, quoted in ibid.).

This hint at the dominance of the (anonymous) masculine voice is not random. We know, for example, that none of *The Economist*'s editors has been female and less than a quarter of its editors, writers, and bureau chiefs are women (Hess 2011). The mask of anonymity is, however, a trope common to the discipline of Western economics more broadly, a 'scientific' framing of current events that allows what might otherwise be viewed as subjective journalist commentary to be represented as factual knowledge (rather than, say, conjecture). By refusing to put names to ideas, *The Economist* can more easily obscure the context and partiality of those ideas, while also concealing where and from whom they came. Opinions can thus be stated as though they are 'bald facts or commanding imperatives' (Hooper 2001: 133).

150 In popular form (feminism and antifeminism in popular culture)

The magazine's style, or 'tone of voice' has remained distinctive throughout its time in publication. Developed by Crowther, it, as Hooper describes, is a 'terse, urgent style with short, punchy sentences' intended to convey object truth to articles' content (2001: 133). 'In Economese, as it is called, "the aim is to squeeze out un-necessary metaphors, adjectives and other argument obscuring figures of speech so that the ... point is got across clearly and economically"' (*The Economist* 22 December 1990, cited in Hooper 2001: 133).

The ways in which the magazine flattens its perspective by anonymizing its writing and obscuring any diversity of perspective is significant, Hess argues, because it allows the magazine to 'elude the gendered criticisms that often haunt any feminine byline' (2011). *The Economist* claims that 'what is written is more important than who writes it', but it is 'unclear how veiling the identity of the magazine's writers mitigates the masthead's surplus of male perspective' (ibid.).

> [With the 'women shouldn't read *The Economist*' advertising campaign], the magazine has attempted to claim [its] masculine perspective as a human one. The difference is that women are now administered explicit invitations to the club, so long as they think like the 'accomplished, influential' men who have produced and consumed this 'universal' worldview since 1843. Why should women read *The Economist*, again?
>
> (Hess 2011)

While it may be the case, however, that the magazine has not upped its female audience (the offending advertisement was dropped soon after it ran), *The Economist* remains a strong market performer (and one of the biggest-selling upmarket 'digitals' in the UK and USA). 'Thoroughly saturated with the signifiers of masculinity, in its self-promotions, its content, layout, house style, use of language, and advertising' (Hooper 2001: 146), *The Economist* has sought to encourage women into its ranks, while being unable to offer women a clear vision for their stable positioning within the business world. Clearly not sure what 'to do' with women and their otherness, *The Economist*'s efforts at inclusion are not extensive. While the magazine does not shy away from discussing such 'women's issues' as corporate boards, female breadwinners, gender gaps and female labour power, its pages remain saturated with the visual symbols of elite masculine power (images of men in power, men holding the power, men with expensive gadgets, men in major corporations, and so on). Examining the 'upmarket' *The Economist* also hints at the sexisms (and phobias) inherent in the genre of 'men's lifestyle', as will be discussed further below.

> I'm no woman, and I am not one of those 'C-level' professionals who feasts on *Economist* fare. But I [tend to] think that a lot of accomplished women will respond simply to the 'shouldn't' part of this pitch and continue to steer clear of *The Economist*.
>
> (Wemple 2011)

Tacit antifeminism (4): Why men's lifestyle magazines reflect sexual paranoia

> The price of female self-determination and steady strides towards formal equality, rather than being pictured as a pair of scales, is more like a see-saw: if women go up, men must hit rock bottom.
>
> (Whelehan 2000: 113)

The relationship between femininity, masculinity and consumption is a particularly good example of the unevenness and multiplicity of the media's 'imaging' of feminism, which is important to consider in any account of feminism and popular culture. Historically, a long-established association between masculinity and production has given rise to femininity's supposedly strong connections with consumption. This resulted, Gill argues, in a certain 'lavender whiff' to early twentieth century commodity culture (2007). Although consumption-based masculinities had actually been rather powerful in the West during the late nineteenth century (ibid. 205–6), by the post-war period (and a significant commercial boom), efforts were required to remasculinize consumption and the advertising and media and new service industries went into overdrive with efforts to present 'an easy natural masculine character' to modern consumption (Osgerby 2003, quoted in ibid.: 206). As the advertising industry, media and new service sector rapidly expanded in the post-war consumer boom, the relationship between masculinity and consumption deepened, which also increased the 'proliferation and fragmentation of representations of masculinity' (ibid.). By the 1980s, 'the templates of masculinity on offer were increasingly diverse' (ibid.: 207). 'Perhaps what we are currently witnessing at the start of the 21st century is nothing less than the emergence of a more fluid, bricolage masculinity, the result of "channel hopping" across versions of "the masculine"' (Beynon 2002, quoted in ibid.: 207).

The magazine industry has 'discovered men', declared *The New York Times* in the spring of 1990 (Draper 2012: 45). So-called 'liberated men' (who now apparently embraced their feelings and domestic responsibilities) were suddenly faced with 'an onslaught of new titles that went beyond the special-interest topics traditionally used to appeal to these readers' (that is, sports, sex, cars, or the outdoors) (ibid.). Fashion, grooming, relationships, politics, careers, cooking, entertainment, and health became serious men's topics and, despite a major economic recession, a flurry of men's lifestyle magazines were launched (and then often folded).

Although the magazine industry first announced that it was taking serious, public, notice of men in 1990, the industry had actually been targeting men as a particular demographic since the 1930s, with the launch of *Esquire* in 1933 'the magazine industry's first attempt to organize an audience around men specifically as a gendered demographic' (Draper 2012: 46). What is particularly important here, Draper argues, in charting the rise of men's lifestyle as a targeted genre of the magazine (and thus advertising) industry is 'the disavowal of homosexuality' that 'has been the most integral rhetorical strategy in the development of the industry' (ibid.: 47). Editors and publishers needing to gain support from advertisers have historically been

152 In popular form (feminism and antifeminism in popular culture)

exceptionally wary 'of having their products associated with potentially gay audiences', seeking instead to 'convince heterosexual male audiences that their masculinity would not be undermined if they read magazines targeting them through fashion and other lifestyle-based consumption' (ibid.). *Esquire* in the 1930s thus attempted 'to manage the potentially feminizing threat of fashion-based consumption' by emphasizing the utility of its clothing, rather than its style and aesthetics, 'boasting that the magazine features "men's clothes that are men's clothes – not fashions"' (*New York Times* 1933, cited in ibid.: 50). *Esquire*'s first editor, Arnold Gingrich, carefully crafted style-oriented consumption as a 'masculine' practice 'by including not only fashion content but also pin-up girls, lewd cartoons, literary stories by the likes of Ernest Hemingway that excluded or sexualized women, articles and imagery that emphasized rugged activities such as sports and hunting' (ibid.: 51). In the same ways as *The Economist* today impersonates the abstract, masculine tones of global finance in its efforts to exert an authoritative voice, the editorial voice chosen by *Esquire* in the 1930s and 1940s imitated 'barroom banter between tough guys' throughout the magazine's efforts to self-portray as the choice of rugged, red-blooded manliness (Pendergast, cited in ibid.).

Significantly, misogyny was central to the magazine's character, with aspects of domesticity otherwise fatally associated with housewifery reappropriated as manly pursuits. Women were thus depicted 'as lacking taste and skills in home décor', or men as better drink-mixers and cooks (Draper 2012: 52). 'This editorial strategy established *Esquire* as a space of "appropriate" heterosexual masculinity rooted in misogyny as well as homophobia, giving permission to straight readers to freely conceive of themselves as tasteful consumers' (ibid.).

The arrival of *Playboy* in the 1950s further sedimented the heteronormativity of the genre of men's lifestyle. Using 'sexualized images of the female form and other heterosexual signifiers to protect its readers against accusations of homosexuality' (Draper 2012: 54), *Playboy* also promoted a more hedonistic model of masculinity that frequently sought to challenge the staticness of the breadwinning ethos that had 'found new footing in the postwar emergence of a new middle class' (ibid.: 55). Hugh Hefner's editorial skills sought to cast the playboy 'as an embodiment of masculinity marked by individualism, youthful consumption, and the appreciation of women', escaping the shackles of domestic slavery through escapades represented as virulently heterosexual (should the observer mistakenly think the *Playboy* man was escaping marriage because he was a little bit 'queer') (ibid.).

During the 1980s, feminist advances and industrial changes that enabled the growing influence of the consumer sphere engaged, Draper suggests, a 'gendered media script' in the UK and USA that postulated men as 'more attentive to women, fatherly, narcissistic, stylish, and consumption-driven' (2012: 60). As increasing numbers of women entered the workforce, men were told they needed to keep up to look as good. The 'New Man' was created as 'a particular coding of masculinity' to draw men into consumer culture, while also counteracting the 'female threat' that was disadvantaging men in the style and beauty stakes (ibid.: 61). Men needed help to navigate the changes caused by second-wave feminism and a 'man's interest in fashion was no longer an indication that he was gay', rather that 'it had become a necessity for him in order to remain competitive in the corporate world' (ibid.: 62).

Since the industry assumed that gay men would read men's magazines no matter who they were marketed at, very little attention was paid to gay audiences in the 1980s. The threat of the lavender whiff has not, of course, been vanquished, and anxieties about how to address heterosexual men without losing the appeal of gay audiences have exercised the advertising industry. A concern that the 1980s 'New Man', with his emotional availability and domestic capacity, was a wimpy, feminized incarnation that emasculated 'real' men emerged in the 1990s.

'Anxieties about how to address heterosexual men' at this point were resolved, Gill argues, 'in two ways' (Gill 2007: 207). First, through the adoption of a 'laddish' tone, male editors and journalists were able to address readers as 'mates', while, second, 'an almost hysterical emphasis on women's bodies and heterosexual sex', when 'juxtaposed alongside avowedly homoerotic photographs', supposedly 'allowed magazines to appeal directly to a gay audience, while still defensively asserting the heterosexuality of their text' (ibid.).

The 'New Lad' phenomenon, embodied perhaps most clearly in magazines such as *Loaded* (1994–), *FHM* (1995–), *Maxim* (1995–2009) and *Stuff* (1996–), responded specifically, and dismissively, to the supposedly fashionable, vain and sensitive-to-women 'New Man' of the 1980s with the gendered script of 'a more boorish, misogynistic man less invested in attending to his appearance than in "authentically" male interests such as cars, sports, beer, and electronic gadgets' (Draper 2012: 79). Thus, although the style press has, in the twentieth century, pioneered 'radically new ways of representing masculinity', according both to Gill (2007) and Draper (2012), homophobic anxieties remain pronounced.

Feminism's role herein is clearly rarely conceived of as positive as far as the media's script for masculinity has developed in the late twentieth century and beyond, particularly in relation to the rise of 'lad culture'. Rather, feminism has become an important player in the media's reflection (and, in many instances, creation) of anxiety around heterosexual masculinity and, in the late twentieth century and beyond, the media finds itself frequently reflecting on feminism's impact(s) on men. As Whelehan argues, a classic 'explanation' offered for increasing reports of male depression and dispossession has been 'that changes in women's lives and aspirations over the past thirty years have offered new identities for women, but precious little for men' (2000: 113). What such claims conceal, thinly, is that women's economic productivity is threatening: to men's breadwinner status and economic supremacy, but also to the media industry's male-dominated canons of power. In conjunction with constant characterizations of feminists as whiney, bra-burning, man-haters (as noted above), 'politically correct' feminist concerns have been easily derided, and dismissed, with the explosion of lad culture. Reliant on postmodern 'irony', the use of naked or nearly naked women as adornments, crass humour and a juvenile tone, lad culture has contributed ample ammunition to the antifeminist canon.

154 In popular form (feminism and antifeminism in popular culture)

Interestingly, lad's magazines became, to a certain extent, victims of their own success: although upscale men's magazines (such as *GQ* and *Esquire*) could not compete in terms of sales, 'low brow' lad's magazines (such as *Maxim*, which labels itself 'the ultimate guy's guide') found themselves unable to attract the same type of fashion advertising and certainly could not command the same advertising rates (Draper 2012: 83). Luxury advertisers 'considered the lad readerships to be lowbrow', or 'nobrow', and 'thus undesirable', seeking instead a classier, more intellectual and demanding 'psychographic' (ibid.). In 2003, Wal-Mart banned sales of *Maxim*, *Stuff* and *FHM*, under pressure from Christian and some consumer groups to stop carrying the magazines. The effect, Draper argues, 'was more symbolic of the slowing enthusiasm for lad magazines' than an economic breaking point, since 'lad' titles were already experiencing a downward trend (ibid.).

While magazines, generally, have struggled to gain the sales in the twenty-first century they experienced in their 1980s/early 1990s heyday, we should be wary of dismissing the magazine as a thing of the past. *Guardian* writer Reynolds notes that *The Economist* and men's upmarket lifestyle magazines as *GQ* and *Esquire* 'are among those titles leading the digital charge', according to figures released by the Professional Publishers Association (PPA) (Reynolds 2013). *Men's Health* comes in third with digital sales of 12,081 in the UK, down 1 per cent in 2013, while *GQ*, 'which sold a monthly average of 12,231 copies digitally', is up 27 per cent on the year. In the UK, *The Economist* (which we know prefers to call itself a newspaper) performs strongly digitally; its sales rose a substantial 43 per cent in 2013 (ibid.).

Concerns that men are in a constant state of potential emasculation remain, however, clearly evident across contemporary popular culture sites, so much so, it seems, that in Australia a Liberal Member of Parliament deemed it acceptable to publically proclaim that the mining industry is being 'pussy whipped' by former Prime Minister Julia Gillard. The post-2003 re-emergence of an upscale, fashion-focused character to men's lifestyle magazines, the rise of 'metrosexuality' and the high visibility of gay culture from the 1990s onwards has resulted in 'a general shift away from overt homophobia particularly since the middle of the 1990s' (Draper 2012: 86). This is less the case, however, for sexism, where the eroticized display of the nearly (or actually naked) female form remains routine throughout men's magazines. In *GQ*, for example, semi-naked women jostle for space among the high-end designer ads, a 'Beach Bag Grooming Essentials' section and a brief survey of the pros and cons of *Victoria's Secret* versus *Agent Provocateur* models (see *GQ* 2014). *Agent Provocateur* models win because they are 'naughtier'. 'There's something seductively confident about a woman reliving her favourite Sharon Stone moments from *Basic Instinct*', suggests *GQ*.

Tacit antifeminism (5): Why the media promotes 'enlightened sexism'

Feminism has had many attempts made on her life, but the latest is to shove the hoary old dame into retirement by telling her she's been so successful, her services are no longer required. Apparently, women have achieved such completely equal status, it's safe to go back to celebrating our 'femininity' and our sexiness, source of the new empowerment.

(Souter 2010: 23)

Thank God girls and women can now turn their backs on stick-in-the-mud, curdled feminism and act dumb in string bikinis to attract guys. In fact, now that women allegedly have the same sexual freedom as men, they actually prefer to be sex objects because it's liberating. According to enlightened sexism, women today have a choice between feminism and antifeminism, and they just naturally and happily choose the latter because, well, antifeminism has become cool, even hip. Rejecting feminism and buying into enlightened sexism allows young women in particular to be 'one of the guys.' Indeed, enlightened sexism is meant to be making patriarchy pleasurable for women.

(Douglas 2010: 12)

Douglas's 2010 book, *The Rise of Enlightened Sexism*, documents how, since the early 1990s, the 'postfeminist' media has been selling women the lie that their (and feminism's) battles have been won. Douglas argues that the media has created 'fantasies of power' for women to which their actual lives barely correspond but that are powerful enough to reproduce the false assumption that there remains no urgency to feminist politics (2010: 1–9).

Douglas probably would not argue that enlightened sexism is *tacit* antifeminism, since, for her, enlightened sexism is an outright repudiation of feminism, the kind of 'good, old-fashioned, grade-A sexism that reinforces good, old-fashioned, A-grade patriarchy', but with a slightly better disguise (Manolo Blahniks and an Ipex bra) (2010: 10), but I position her argument here, as a form of tacit antifeminism, for the ways in which it is possible for popular culture and media artefacts to be superficially empowering while promoting an antifeminist agenda.

On the one hand, Douglas argues, 'embedded feminism' has become a cultural force to be reckoned with. 'Feminism is no longer "outside" of the media as it was in 1970' and 'feminist gains, attitudes, and achievements are woven into our cultural fabric' (2010: 9). On the other, enlightened sexism responds to 'the perceived threat of a new gender regime' (in which women stand up for themselves and may even occupy positions of greater power than men) by insisting 'that women have made plenty of progress because of feminism' so that it is now okay, 'even amusing, to resurrect sexist stereotypes of girls and women' (ibid.). Moreover,

[E]nlightened sexism sells the line that it is precisely through women's calculated deployment of their faces, bodies, attire, and sexuality that they gain and enjoy true power – power that is fun, that men will not resent, and indeed will embrace. True power here has nothing to do with economic independence or professional achievement: it has to do with getting men to lust after you and women to envy you.

(Douglas 2010: 9–10)

156 In popular form (feminism and antifeminism in popular culture)

Hence, Douglas argues, the popularity of the Pussycat Dolls, or TV shows such as *The Bachelor*, or Kate Moss on all fours of the January/February 2014, 60th anniversary edition of *Playboy*. 'Because women are now "equal" and the battle is over and won', Douglas argues, 'we are now free to embrace things we used to see as sexist, including hypergirliness. In fact, this is supposed to be a relief' (2010: 12).

The components of enlightened sexism, Douglas argues, are produced week in and week out by the media, and include 'anxiety about female achievement', a 'renewed and amplified objectification of young women's bodies and faces', the 'dual exploitation and punishment of female sexuality', the 'dividing of women against each other by age, race, and class' and 'rampant branding and consumerism' (2010: 10). Importantly, enlightened sexism is 'feminist in its outward appearance', telling women that they have the power to be anything they want, acting dumb in string bikinis to attract men because this is their *choice* (ibid.: 10). It is, however, 'sexist in its intent', 'making patriarchy pleasurable for women' and supporting women's equality, but making sure no feminist goals are pushed (ibid.). Since equality might lead to 'sameness', girls and women need to be constantly reminded that they 'are still fundamentally female, and so must be emphatically feminine' and so 'enlightened sexism takes the gains of the women's movement as a given' and uses them 'as permission to resurrect retrograde images of girls and women as sex objects, bimbos, and hootchie mamas still defined by their appearance and their biological destiny' (ibid.: 10).

> Today, we once again have what Betty Friedan famously called 'a problem with no name.' Millions of young women – the girl power generation – have been told that they can do or be anything, yet they also believe their most important task is to be slim, 'hot,' and non-threatening to men. Once they get out in the work force, though, they learn that there still is pay discrimination, inflexible work places, women slotted into low paying, dead end jobs more often than men and a glass ceiling in so many lines of work.
>
> (Douglas 2011)

Overt feminism (1): Young women *are* interested in and *actually practice* feminism

> If inequality between men and women is structural, a web of discrimination in which the dearth of women in politics intersects with the portrayal of women in pornography, which intersects with the tendency for women to be paid less than men, the depiction of women as obsessed with shoes, the likelihood that female plaintiffs will be disbelieved in rape cases, the attempts to undermine women's abortion rights; if the situation of women in Britain has an impact on women in France, the US, Iraq, Afghanistan and the Democratic Republic of Congo, then which threads do we pull to make the most impact in bringing the whole web down?
>
> (Cochrane 2010)

In popular form (feminism and antifeminism in popular culture)   **157**

Cochrane notes how, when scholar Catherine Redfern started the feminist website *The F Word* (in 2001), she felt that 'there was a general perception that young women weren't interested, and that the movement was therefore gasping its last' (quoted in 2010). In terms of my own academic environment and practices, I found when I began my career teaching in Australian universities a lack of overtly feminist students. Between 2007 and 2012, there seemed among my student cohort a pronounced disinterest in, even active hostility towards, feminism. This was one of the reasons that I began this book. I could not understand why young Australians were not more engaged. Even the more obviously feminist responses to the survey conducted for this research maintain a certain critical distance between the respondent and 'feminism'.

> [What comes to mind when I think of a feminist?] In a stereotypical way, initial images are of the feminists who engaged in protests of the 60s and 70s, but deeper thought brings to mind women who truly excel at what they do and portray the best of the female gender.
> > (Survey respondent, Australian female, age 18–24)
>
> [When I think of a feminist], I think of a whole bunch of different women – stay at home mums, businesswomen, female students. Just ordinary people.
> > (Survey respondent, British male, age 45–54)
>
> [I think of a feminist as someone who is] strong-willed [and] ambitious.
> > (Survey respondent, Australian female, age 18–24)

Despite, however, teaching the same courses in the same Australian university, the last couple of years of teaching have, strangely, offered different sorts of students engagements with feminism. I have not been able to put my finger exactly on it, but I have noticed a sea change in qualitative student engagement with feminism in the areas in which I teach, International Political Economy and International Relations. Students have been more vociferous in voicing their horror at, for example, women dying in Bangladeshi sweat shops in ways they were not a couple of years ago.

My students' more open embrace of feminism might have been a result of Julia Gillard's tenure as Prime Minister of Australia, and the active, heavily mediated and often heated discussions around sexism in Australian politics (and culture) that followed her famous 'misogyny speech' (made to Parliament on 9 October 2012). These discussions have revealed an anger, among a wide cohort (of female *and* male students), at the ways in which Australian politics remains invariably dependent on unimaginative gender and sexual stereotypes, inequalities and patterns of discrimination and exploitation. Gillard's speech made global headlines and the spotlight it shone on the obstacles Australian women continue to face, in public, professional and personal life, was acute. My female and male students were, reasonably enough, upset that this should be the image of their country that the world beheld and doubtless felt frustrated that a reality not of

158 In popular form (feminism and antifeminism in popular culture)

their own making had commandeered so much public attention. Beyond the unease that students may have felt personally, the debates that flourished in the wake of Gillard's speech were also surprisingly intelligent in a media landscape more often dominated by polarized reporting. Informed journalism was mixed with intellectual commentary in a way that allowed the public in Australia to engage meaningfully with questions that had not really been on the agenda for some time, relatively unencumbered by the usual tabloid nonsense (although there was, of course, plenty of this).

Young Australian women have been active in the women's movement for as long as feminism has been alive and kicking in Australia and young Australian women's activism remains dynamic (for example, in indigenous politics, health and social protection, human rights, refugee, LGBTI, peace and democracy regimes, among others). As Maddison describes, however, this activism has been 'less visible to the general public than the feminist activism of previous generations' (2004: 236). During the 1990s, media attention on the 'I'm not a feminist, but …' of young women's self-articulations overshadowed the 'presence and visibility' of the Australian women's movement (ibid.: 243). While young women continue to work to maintain a political space for feminist activism in Australia (ibid.: 249), the Australian media has chosen (largely) to ignore them and their efforts.

My survey asked all respondents (female and male)[7] to state whether they agreed or disagreed that feminism is accessible to young women in the twenty-first century (Survey Question 16. For the full content of the survey, see Appendix A); 67 per cent of female respondents agreed, while 54 per cent of male respondents agreed. Allowances for age, however, reveal interesting differences in response here.

The only age group of respondents *more* convinced of feminism's accessibility than the survey's youngest respondent group was the '65 or older' group (Table 5.2). The most cynical group of the survey's respondents were from my own age group (at the time), the 25–34-year-old group (which covers those born between 1976 and 1985). Residency appeared to have little impact on respondents' views here, with between 64 and 67 per cent of Australian, British and US residents agreeing that feminism is accessible to young women in the twenty-first century and 71 per cent of those who classified as 'other' in terms of residency agreeing.

TABLE 5.2 Survey Question 16, 'Feminism is Accessible to Young Women in the 21st Century' (age)

Age	*Percentage agree*
18–24	69
25–34	58
35–44	67
45–54	63
55–64	69
65 or older	88

In popular form (feminism and antifeminism in popular culture) **159**

Perhaps the most interesting diversity of opinion in Question 16 appeared when adjusting for level of education, with every level of education agreeing in the majority that feminism is accessible to young women in the twenty-first century, *except* those with doctoral degrees (Table 5.3).

In a response to a 2011 article by Jayson in *USA Today*, which argued that, for 'a movement so vocal when it began', feminism remains 'largely under the radar of most younger Americans today, except maybe from gender studies classes or history books' (Jayson 2011), young feminist activists Herold and Knox write:

> Contrary to the article's claims, we know our movement's history, and we are carrying it into the future. We don't just identify with feminism; we live it day to day. We fight for reproductive, economic, racial and social justice online, in the streets, and side by side with our friends and family members. We're questioning, bending and breaking down social norms, including sexuality, gender, age, class and race. We are abortion clinic escorts, online organizers, rape crisis center volunteers, radical journalists and sometimes even presidents of NOW [National Organization for Women] chapters.
>
> (Herold and Knox 2011, quoted in *USA Today* 2011)

Authors such as Walby, Hawkesworth, Valenti, Power, Walter, Aune and Redfern are convinced of feminism's vibrancy among young women. They are also able to offer evidence for their arguments, including young women's involvement in political and legal battles over reproductive rights, sexuality, sexual violence, gender gaps, and so on. Feminism is, Aune and Redfern argue, as relevant as ever and 'growing exponentially' (2010: ix). Mackay argues that 'a so-called "resurgence" of feminist activism in the UK is currently being reported by journalists, commentators and academics, with young women seemingly at the fore' (2011: 152). New organizations, festivals, websites and networking groups are constantly emerging, but people are not hearing about them, the authors argue; in part because of constant comparisons to a 'golden age' of feminism in the 1970s but also because 'established feminists' are not recognizing or are dismissing younger feminists' work (Aune and Redfern 2010: 10–11). It does not help, Aune and Redfern argue, that the 'mainstream media' is so prone to pronouncements of feminism's 'death' or that 'pro-feminist commentators' seem to accept the 'idea of feminism's decline unquestioningly' (ibid.: 1–2).

TABLE 5.3 Survey Question 16, 'Feminism is Accessible to Young Women in the 21st Century' (education)

Education	Percentage agree
High school	74
Diploma/certificate	86
Bachelor's	59
Postgraduate degree	82
Doctoral degree	49
Other	50

160 In popular form (feminism and antifeminism in popular culture)

Despite, as noted in Chapter 4, the prevalence of 'stereotype threat' and the ambivalence that people show in their engagements with 'big f' feminism, in the survey for this research, 41 per cent answered the question 'I would describe myself as a feminist' in the affirmative (Survey Question 7). 'Considering all the negative publicity feminism gets', it is 'incredibly encouraging' that a quarter of British women are happy to describe themselves as feminists, Aune and Redfern contend (2010: 5). Surveys show 'consistently' that 'most people have feminist attitudes' in the UK, whether they would describe themselves as 'feminists' or not (ibid.: 4). I would certainly argue that, although it is worth noting the extent to which people feel comfortable in adopting the 'big f' moniker, the type of politics that people espouse is *at least as interesting* as their use of the self-description 'feminist'.

> What's heartening is that feminism [seems] to be reaching beyond the ivory towers of academe to a broad range of women. Redfern points out that there have recently been feminist articles in *Elle* and *Company* magazines, while Walter says she was surprised to see pieces debating the importance of feminism in *The Sunday Times* and *The Daily Telegraph* this year [2010]. Power says that, even just a year and a half ago, when she wrote *One Dimensional Woman* 'the situation didn't seem remotely as optimistic, but so much has been happening, and there just seems to be a mainstream acceptance that feminism's still around, that it's not finished, it's not uncool, and it's not depressing. It suddenly has a contemporary sheen that makes it exciting, which wasn't really true in the 80s or 90s at all.'
>
> (Cochrane 2010)

This 'suddenly' exciting sheen to feminism has been paralleled in media reports that have declared that '2013 was when feminism hit the mainstream' (Turner 2014). Overt discussions of feminism have been quite prevalent, I would argue, across media outlets since the 1970s, particularly throughout the 'death of feminism' heyday of the 1990s. Over the last couple of years, however, these discussions have assumed a more reflective and sympathetic tone, perhaps propelled by a blogosphere unafraid to root out sexism and misogynist injustice. In 2013, Turner argues, challenges to 'media images', 'retrograde attitudes', and 'the thoughtless words of men' were not limited to only 'a few voices' and a 'handful of columnists'; these challenges numbered in their 'thousands' (ibid.).

> The shrugged indifference into which lads' mags were launched two decades ago – hey, they're harmless fun – was over. Women [in 2013] were emboldened and angry. And not just harridans like me, who recall the women's groups and feminist campaigns of the early '80s. [...] In 2010, I talked to a group of educated, thoughtful, hip young women; not one called herself a feminist. Puh-lease! That was something your mum used to be. Not any more.
>
> (Turner 2014)

In popular form (feminism and antifeminism in popular culture) **161**

Turner suggests that the tide changed with the publication of Caitlin Moran's book, *How to be a Woman*, a 'feminist work that wasn't academic or self-consciously clever but warm, inclusive' and 'welcoming, even to men' (Turner 2014). For Turner, Moran 'helped redefine feminism for a generation who didn't want it to preclude fun or fashion or having a boyfriend' (ibid.). This perhaps credits Moran with too much effect. 2013, in Australia at least, was a year of woeful political commentary and backsliding, a post-'Misogyny Speech' landscape in which it was no longer acceptable for a future Prime Minister to bluster his way through an election describing female candidates as having 'sex appeal'. As Turner also points out, Ariel Castor's imprisonment and torture of three women in Cleveland, Ohio, the gang rape and murder on a New Delhi bus in December 2012 of Jyoti Singh[8] and the sexual abuse scandals that have tarnished once golden British and Australian household names have fuelled young (as well as older) women's anger and emboldened these women to speak up (ibid.). US comedian and talk show host Jon Stewart's obvious awe in the presence of Malala Yousafzai was well-publicized and the media keen to relay her message to educate girls despite the repressions of political regimes. Lena Dunham's *Girls*, despite openly and non-ironically making various references to the terms 'feminism' and 'feminist', has been enormously successful and Dunham's overtly feminist profile has been high across popular culture sources. Miley Cyrus has stated that 'most music is sexist' and Beyoncé has sampled Chimamanda Ngozi Adichie's speech on feminism. In 2013 the BBC released *The Fall*, featuring a female lead both careerist *and* likable in Stella Gibson, a woman who is impressive, complex and capable of actively advancing the careers of her female colleagues. Importantly, Stella never appears overcome, pathetic or unstable in the face of her romantic entanglements.

> Women saying 'I'm not a feminist' is my greatest pet peeve. Do you believe that women should be paid the same for doing the same jobs? Do you believe that women should be allowed to leave the house? Do you think that women and men both deserve equal rights? Great, then you're a feminist. People think there is something taboo about speaking up for feminism. I know for a long time that I was embarrassed to call out misogyny because I was then going to be that complaining girl who can't let it go. But the fact is, we can't let it go – not until we feel like we have been heard.
>
> (Lena Dunham, quoted in Mulkerrins 2013)

When Joseph Gordon-Levitt, without any apparent hint of self-consciousness, asked 'who wouldn't be a feminist?' on *Ellen* in January 2014 the blogosphere, twitter and Facebook erupted in universal applause.

The shame and stigma young women, and men, have felt self-articulating as openly feminist seems, at this moment in time, less tangible (see also Figure 5.4). This is not to say that the scales will not once again tip towards the backlash that, every now and then, insists on rearing its ugly head, or that feminist campaigning has won in, to borrow Turner's words, 'a narcissistic age of selfies and hyper-grooming'. Women who

162 In popular form (feminism and antifeminism in popular culture)

FIGURE 5.4 'What is Feminism?'
Source: RainbowWish 2008.

put their voices, and faces, to public campaigns continue to risk a gamut of misogynist abuse and threats of violence.[9] *The Feminine Mystique* (first published in 1963) and *The Female Eunuch* (1970) remain, I would argue, as relevant today in their chastisement of sexist repression and hierarchy as ever. It has become somewhat 'fashionable' again to campaign (and to be seen campaigning), perhaps because of the financial crisis, the visibility of popular protest and the public vilification of government-led 'austerity'. Social media is, these days, so 'swift and limber' that it has the capacity to immediately and publically challenge any perceived outrage. 'Stalled in the trenches for a decade', feminism has, Turner argues, 'moved forward, reclaiming long-lost public space and political ground' (2014). 'The idea of feminism is completely natural', suggests singer Lorde: it 'shouldn't even be something that people find mildly surprising. It's just part of being a girl' (2014, speaking to *Rookie Magazine*).

Given that there is, then, a relatively strong argument for the existent, perhaps increasing, vibrancy of feminism, it is worth asking what feminism's strongest variants might currently be.

Overt feminism (2): The enduring strength(s) of liberal feminism(s)

Halley's mind is, for one, settled on the question of what feminism's strongest variants might, at the moment, be. For Halley, 'every currently articulable feminist

In popular form (feminism and antifeminism in popular culture) **163**

position is liberal in some way', although 'some aspire more than others to a critical relationship to their own inevitable importation of liberal tenets' (2006: 79). Fudge, in a piece for *Bitch Magazine*, argues this point also, describing liberal feminism as what everyone else would call 'just plain feminism' (2005).

I would argue that Halley and Fudge are probably right in terms of the *praxes* of feminism, and that movements for equality and social rights across the globe (varying according to locality and regional content) form the mainstay of most, if not all, contemporary feminist activism. Theoretically, however, the case is less clear. Radical, socialist, 'third wave', antiracist and postcolonial feminisms are far less attached to liberal precepts and, across the academy at least, feminist commitments are more varied and variable than Halley articulates (Box 5.1).

BOX 5.1 'MY FEMINISM'

My feminism doesn't judge women based on how many men, or women, they've slept with.

My feminism doesn't judge women based on how many men, or women, they've dated.

My feminism doesn't judge women based on whether they choose to have sex, abstain from sex, or dislike sex entirely.

My feminism doesn't attack a woman who has chosen stereotypical 'feminine' career.

My feminism doesn't tell women they're wrong if they like to be treated like a princess.

My feminism doesn't tell anyone that their sexual practices are 'humiliating' or 'misogynistic'. If you like the kind of sex you're having, and it's consensual, my feminism supports it.

My feminism doesn't berate women for acting feminine. It doesn't tell women they have to act masculine or independent in order to be a feminist.

My feminism laughs in the face of misandry, and tells men to accept what's coming to them for once.

My feminism doesn't tell anyone that it's wrong or right to shave your legs, arms, pits, face, or anything else.

My feminism is the belief that women should be treated as equals, and should be able to do what they want.

My feminism doesn't care if you choose to be feminine or masculine, as long as it is *your* choice, and no one else.

(This post applies to all women. Cis, trans*, and everything else. If you identify as female, even partially, even temporarily, this post is for you, and I love you. ♥)

MY feminism.

(Navi Dean 2010)

164 In popular form (feminism and antifeminism in popular culture)

Liberal feminism remains feminism's most obviously powerful embodiment because it has arguably had the most *impact* (on hearts, minds and bodies), due largely to its relationship with the mechanisms and practices of national and international governance. Liberal feminist tenets are pivotal in understanding the power of 'governance feminism' and feminism has been implemented widely in national governments, international governance and through inter and non-governmental organizations (as noted in Chapter 4).

In terms of ideas about women, society and human relationships, liberal feminism has perhaps been most significant for its focus on several key tropes. These form the foundation of a number of feminist networks, organizations, campaigns and activities, including campaigns and organizations (across the globe) for social justice, bodily integrity, political rights and representation, reproductive rights, rights to equal education, to working opportunities and to contraception. These tropes are: equality; freedom of choice and expression; self-ownership; independence; empowerment; feminine subordination; justice; and social transformation (specifically through policy reform projects designed to remedy women's disadvantage). The centrality of (private) ownership within liberalism, and thus its philosophical derivatives, lends liberal feminism its focus on rights and property, both of which are particularly important in understanding liberal feminism's conceptualization of the female body and the sanctity of a woman's capacity to exert control over that body. The focus on equality, wherein debates of course exist around whether the state is indeed an appropriate vehicle for promoting the best life for women, has produced a faith in the centrality of public policy, specifically policy reforms that negate women's disadvantage.

> The idea of being a feminist—so many women have come to this idea of it being anti-male and not able to connect with the opposite sex—but what feminism is about is equality and human rights. For me that is just an essential part of my identity. I hope [*Girls*] contributes to a continuance of feminist dialogue.
>
> (Lena Dunham, quoted in Ruiz 2013)

For a number of feminists the proximity between feminism and liberal mechanisms of governance has become increasingly problematic, for feminist projects themselves and also for the different types of women, and men, who are excluded from participating in contemporary hierarchies of power and governance. Feminism is not only evident, Halley argues, in the formal mechanisms of state and legislature, but in everyday processes and practices, including from employers, 'schools, healthcare institutions, and a whole range of entities, often formally "private"' (2006: 21). Feminism's reach, she argues, is substantial, and feminism, Halley goes so far to say, has 'substantial parts' of everyday processes and practices 'under its control' (ibid.). Halley notes that particularly across (domestic) US policy regimes, liberal feminism dictates the governance of areas such as child sexual abuse, pornography, sexual harassment, sexual violence and family law

(Halley 2006: 21). Fraser worries that the 'dream of women's emancipation' has been yoked 'to the engine of capital accumulation' (2013). Elias offers an analysis of what may get erased from the agenda when feminism is 'neoliberalized' and gender equality rendered compatible with market-led forms of economic growth (2013) (see Chapter 4).

For some feminists, this is to be expected. The Feminist Project that has become powerful in contemporary domestic and world politics cannot but be touched by the hierarchies of power and authority it works with and for in the name of legislating rights and equalities. As Prügl argues, successful governance feminism strategies have had to make gender available for governmental ends in ways that advance feminist agendas ambiguously (2011: 84).

In terms of the media as message and messenger, then, liberal feminism remains the predominant form of feminism in popular culture today. 'Celebrity feminism', however, constitutes possibly the most prevalent of feminism's popular embodiments, making it, in some sense, liberal feminism's vessel of choice. Feminists use social media to offer a variety of campaigns based, at some level, on the protection and promulgation of rights-based discourse. The visual power of celebrity endorsements of feminism, on top of the hive of activity that is feminism within social media, is considerable. The reproduction of celebrity imagery and the credibility that celebrity endorsements bring to feminism have come, I argue, to constitute and shape many of our responses to feminism. Celebrity feminism is, in many ways, feminism today, with the principles of liberal feminism at its core.

Overt feminism (3): The (increasing) popularity of celebrity feminism

> I do call myself a feminist, absolutely. It's worth paying attention to the roles that are dictated to us and [realizing] that we don't have to fit into those roles, we can be anybody we want to be.
>
> (Joseph Gordon-Levitt, *Ellen*, 9 January 2014)

> I like being a mouthpiece for the issues I think young females face today. It's always shocking when people question whether [*Girls* is] a feminist show. How could a show about women exploring women not be? Feminism isn't a dirty word. It's not like we're a deranged group who think women should take over the planet, raise our young on our own and eliminate men from the picture. Feminism is about women having all the rights that men have.
>
> (Lena Dunham, speaking to *Playboy* magazine, quoted in Beck 2013)

> I'm a feminist because I believe in women […]. It's a heavy word, feminism, but it's not one I think we should run from. I'm proud to be a feminist.
>
> (Sheryl Sandberg, quoted in Ruiz 2013)

The term 'celebrity feminsm' refers to a 'welter of contradictory discourses related to corporate populism, promotional culture, the cult of the celebrity, commodity feminism, postfordism, corporeal discipline, and individualism', each of which

166 In popular form (feminism and antifeminism in popular culture)

address women, Cole and Hribar argue, as consumers (1995, summarized in MacKay 2005: 83). Celebrity feminism has been much criticized by feminist social commentators and maligned for its identification with *accumulation* (particularly the conspicuous consumption of material goods). Sharing features with liberal feminism's prioritization of ownership and property rights, celebrity feminism often specifically invokes the romanticization of consumption and material accumulation. As such, celebrity feminism (as in, for example, *Sex in the City* and its obsession with the mantra of shopping-maketh-the-self) is seen to constitute a commercialized form of feminism, which offers a seductive, but problematic, feminist (or what some may term 'postfeminist') narrative.

Celebrity feminism's commercial, celebrity-endorsed narratives have, Levy argues, offered not 'the egalitarianism and satisfaction that was feminism's initial promise' but have summoned 'many of the corruptions of feminism', including a 'sexual marketplace' that prioritizes endless self-questioning, acquisition and commodity fetishization (2006: 174–5). Based on representing the modern woman's self-worth through the commercial and consumption choices that she makes, this kind of feminism tells women to seek empowerment through the freedom to shop, which is for Levy and for McRobbie (2009), among others, clearly and simply commercialism (and all its machinations, mechanisms and glossy advertising strategies) reproducing itself.

Celebrity feminism (such as that espoused by Oprah Winfrey, Ellen Degeneres, Geena Davis, Patrick Stewart, Joss Whedon *et al.*) is often viewed by its critics as frivolous and 'the ideologically suspect "other" of academic feminism' (Hollows 2000, citing Wicke 1994: 199). Celebrity feminism's critics, Hollows argues, have, however, failed to recognize that 'the energies of the celebrity imaginary are fuelling feminist discourse and political activity as never before' (ibid.). *Oprah*, for example, although not promoted as a 'feminist' show, was inherently woman-centred and often addressed the injustices at the heart of much feminist campaigning (job discrimination, male violence, sexual abuse, and so on), creating not only 'a televisual space for a form of popular feminism, but one defined by black feminism' (Squire 1997 in ibid.).

The power of the celebrity voice and the importance of the interplay between popular culture and celebrity figures should not be underestimated. The not inconsiderable furore over BIC's attempt to launch a pen 'for her' in 2012 shows, for example, how quickly and widely feminist ideas and concerns can be articulated and heard across mainstream media (BIC n.d.). The offending pens 'escaped notice for a while', that is 'until Margaret Hartmann from *Jezebel* heard about them from a reader' (Vinjamuri 2012). This lead to a number of women and men contributing (some rather witty) reviews on Amazon.

FINALLY!

Someone has answered my gentle prayers and FINALLY designed a pen that I can use all month long! I use it when I'm swimming, riding a horse,

In popular form (feminism and antifeminism in popular culture) **167**

walking on the beach and doing yoga. It's comfortable, leak-proof, non-slip and it makes me feel so feminine and pretty! Since I've begun using these pens, men have found me more attractive and approachable. It has given me soft skin and manageable hair and it has really given me the self-esteem I needed to start a book club and flirt with the bag-boy at my local market. My drawings of kittens and ponies have improved, and now that I'm writing my last name hyphenated with Robert Pattinson's last name, I really believe he may someday marry me! I'm positively giddy. Those smart men in marketing have come up with a pen that my lady parts can really identify with. Where has this pen been all my life?

(Amazon Reviewer, cited in Lang 2013)

The popularity of the viral campaign was then captured by Ellen Degeneres on her daily show, *Ellen*, in October 2012:

Women, we've made a lot of progress towards equality. We're allowed to vote, I think since 1982 now. We can wear pants, we can drive at night, all those things have happened. And then I saw something that makes me think we still have a ways to go. Well, it's a new product from BIC, the pen company, and they have a new line of pens called 'BIC for Her', and, this is totally real, they're pens just for ladies (I know you're thinking 'it's about damn time, where have our pens been?'). Can you believe this, we've been using man pens all these years? Eughhh. And they come in both lady colours, pink and purple, and they're just like regular pens except they're pink, so they cost twice as much (that is absolutely true as well). The worst part is, they don't come with any instructions, so how do they expect us to learn to write with them, you know? I was reading the back of the pack (well, I had a man read the back of the package to me) and it said it's designed to fit a woman's hand (this is all true, I'm not making any of this up). 'Designed to fit a woman's hand'. What does that mean? So, when we're taking down dictation for our bosses we'll feel comfortable and we'll forget we're not getting paid as much? I mean, just think over the last 20 years, companies have spent millions of dollars making pills that grow men's hair and fix men's sex lives, and now ladies have a pen. We have, we've come a long way baby.

(*Ellen*, The Ellen Degeneres Show, October 2012, Warner Bros. Television)

Against the grain of mainstream media programming, famous, and popular, female voices have achieved success promoting a feminist agenda, generally (but not only) by being funny. The appeal of figures such as Ellen Degeneres, Amy Poehler, Margaret Cho and Tina Fey has inveigled feminism into the mainstream quietly but effectively in recent years. Lena Dunham's *Girls*, although criticized for its lack of ethnic diversity or class consciousness, has been much praised for its angsty, honest view of young (white) women in Brooklyn, New York. *Girls* is a 'superior work of fictionalized anthropology', according to Stuever in *The Washington Post*

168 In popular form (feminism and antifeminism in popular culture)

(2012), that is 'raw, audacious, nuanced and richly, often excruciatingly funny', according to Poniewozik in *Time* (2012).

One of my favourite plays on (and with) 'celebrity feminism' is the 'Hey Girl', Feminist Ryan Gosling meme, which began as a blog by Danielle Henderson. Henderson was, then, a 'newly minted, academically frustrated graduate student looking for an outlet' (Henderson 2012). As she points out, there is 'no way to tell if Ryan Gosling is actually a feminist': he has simply said a few nice things about his mum and ex-girlfriends. Henderson was, however, overwhelmed with the response to the website, which was 'overwhelmingly positive', especially from those 'new to feminism or feminist theory' (ibid.). That Gosling has never publically disavowed his supposed feminism, or the meme, is encouraging.

While researching types of feminism prevalent across popular culture, I have been particularly struck by arguments around whether Buffy and *The Hunger Games'* Katniss are better role models to teenage girls than the, enormously popular, Bella of the *Twilight* series. At the time, only the first *Hunger Games* movie had been released and, although the first instalment set opening records in the USA, the *Twilight* series had scaled such significant financial heights during its existence (2008–12) that it was hard to measure the relative success of *The Hunger Games*. Katniss, although popular, was perhaps not quite as widely adored as Bella. *The Hunger Games'* second instalment, *Catching Fire*, has since then opened to enormous financial success (a domestic opening weekend of over US$158 million, compared with *Breaking Dawn: Part I*'s $138 million).

In an article in *The Atlantic*, Berlatsky asks 'if Bella fought Katniss, who would win?' and argues that commentators have overwhelmingly decided on the 'stereotypically girly' Bella getting stomped (2011a). This, Berlatsky argues, is because 'even women and feminists (especially women and feminists?)' are nervous about being associated with anything 'girly' (ibid.). According to this logic, negative reactions to Bella reveal a 'relative discomfort with Bella' that reflects 'a larger discomfort with femininity' (ibid.). On the other hand, Katniss is 'an extremely competent, tomboyish young woman who is athletic, focused, responsible, and able to take care of herself': (ibid.). She is 'politically engaged', 'not especially interested in boys' and 'doesn't have sex, or even really think about sex for almost the entire series': Katniss is, in other words, 'the ideal second-wave feminist daughter; smart, fierce, independent, and sexually restrained' (ibid.). While 'Bella is in many ways stereotypically feminine (passive, focused on romance and motherhood)', Katniss 'is in many ways stereotypically masculine (competent, deadly, not focused on romance)' (ibid.).

In comments directed at Berlatsky's article and 'popular feminist' dislike of Bella, Small notes that 'a lot of popular feminism' is not 'very attentive to the history of cultural gendering', wherein certain traits have been gendered 'female' and others 'male', with 'male traits' generally portrayed as 'better and more worthwhile' (cited in Berlatsky 2011b). Preferencing 'tomboys' in popular culture shows simply that the valuing of masculine traits remains prevalent, she argues, although it is a difficult issue (ibid.). It is hard for most feminists (myself included) to

In popular form (feminism and antifeminism in popular culture) **169**

preference the clumsy, mopey and indecisive Bella over the much more obviously self-composed Katniss. Buffy has the perpetual advantage of being well-written. Small contends that 'a lot of people seem to think that the point of feminism is making "masculine" behavior acceptable for women', or 'separating the behavior from the bodies of the people who perform the behavior and not judging women who prefer those historically masculine traits' (ibid.).

> A lot of the distaste for Bella is genuine distaste for the historically 'feminine' categories and behaviors and values and aesthetics, but it's generally expressed without even the slightest recognition of how problematic and limiting – and historically patriarchal – that attitude is. Part of the appeal of characters like Katniss is that they challenge conventional gender without completely eradicating it. Part of the appeal of characters like Bella is that they subvert conventional gender without really challenging it at all. [...] Girl power is great – except when it moves beyond allowing people with female bodies to behave any way they like and becomes a new set of restrictive, normative, angry, prejudiced norms that bully people with female bodies into behaving a certain way.
>
> (Small 2011, cited in Berlatsky 2011b)

To be tempted, Small argues, by the seductiveness of 'masculine' characteristics and to thus pretend that a woman's 'relationship to authority and strength and power and violence is transformed' just because she engages in them is not feminist at all (cited in Berlatsky 2011b). Nor is 'perpetuating biases and prejudices against historically gendered-feminine traits' desirable (ibid.). 'A feminism that can't make room for Bella is a feminism that's going to have a lot of trouble getting purchase with women who like Bella, and that seems like a tremendous mistake to me' (ibid.).

Overt feminism (4): 'Riot grrrl', sextremism and guerilla feminisms

> One of the main goals of riot grrrl within the third wave movement was to make feminism cool again in the hopes that it would spur young girls to get involved. By the late 80s feminism had faded from popular culture and been laid to rest in the mausoleum of academic discourse. The only people still talking about it were intellectual types [whose] expressions had become far too complicated and high-minded for the general public to understand or care about. Riot grrrl brought real, everyday, down-to-earth, issues back into the feminist spotlight and began to re-involve the people they affected. The punk/DIY scene was the perfect way to attract young, angry women to an arena where they could put the angst of teenage-girlhood to positive use in changing the landscape of gendered culture in their communities and the larger world.
>
> (Freeman 2014)

The riot grrrl movement is possibly most associated with an underground subculture of punk rock magazines and bands such as Bikini Kill, Bratmobile,

170 In popular form (feminism and antifeminism in popular culture)

Huggy Bear and Team Dresch, who sought to create punk music focused on representing women. Applied, inaccurately, to less political female alternative rock acts as Babes in Toyland, Hole and PJ Harvey, riot grrrl had splintered by the mid to late 1990s, with more radical voices concerned that their movement had been co-opted by Spice Girls' 'girl power' and/or any band with a woman in it. Riot grrrl's influences can be seen on performers such as Beth Ditto and numerous internet fan sites and, infiltrating pop culture, Bagnato argues, 'with the creation of strong female characters in TV shows such as *Buffy the Vampire Slayer* and *Xena: Warrior Princess*' (2013).

Riot grrrl's 'DIY' ethic and focus on female empowerment is clearly visible in the Russian band Pussy Riot (although they have yet to produce an album and have no set number of members) and the Ukrainian 'sextremist' topless protest group Femen, as is the punk yell-for-the-cause approach to activism. These two groups have particularly captured global headlines in recent years, although, as Vitchers notes (2013), many mainstream media commentaries have missed the point and the context of their activisms, turning Femen, for example, 'into a spectacle' without properly educating audiences 'on the form of protest the movement uses' (ibid.).

Femen's style of feminist activism is 'a direct outgrowth of post-Soviet youth movements', which focuses on empowering young women 'to become active participants in Ukrainian civic society in order to change the status of women's rights in Ukraine' (Vitchers 2013). The group, currently operating from exile in Paris, has most directly targeted sex tourism, poverty, unequal access to job opportunities and higher education, and the lack of female participation and leadership in Ukrainian government, using protest with bare breasts ('the symbol of their femaleness') to 'highlight their focus on issues affecting Ukrainian women and culture' (ibid.). Femen was also the subject of a not-terribly-flattering 2013 documentary, *Ukraine is Not a Brothel*, which reports that the Femen group was masterminded in its early years by Victor Svyatski, 'who supposedly hand-picked the prettiest girls to front the organisation' (MacNab 2014). The group's leader, 23-year-old Inna Shevchenko, declares this an 'out-of-date' snapshot of the group, which has since removed Svyatski (MacNab 2014).

Pussy Riot's Maria Alekhina and Nadezhda Tolokonnikova were, in December 2013, granted amnesty in what many believe is 'the Kremlin's attempt to soothe criticism of Russia's human rights record ahead of the Winter Olympics in Sochi in February' (*Daily News* 2013). Another member of the band, Yekaterina Samutsevich, was released on a suspended sentence a few months after all three had been found guilty of 'hooliganism motivated by religious hatred' and were sentenced to two years in prison for their performance at Moscow's main cathedral in March 2012 (ibid.).

Guerrilla feminism emerged as an anti-sexism stickering and graffiti campaign (Figure 5.5) that developed into a Facebook group (https://www.facebook.com/guerrillafeminism) and which also exhibits something of a punk, 'hooligan'

FIGURE 5.5 Examples of guerrilla feminism.

Sources: http://3.bp.blogspot.com/__0F6ZjAg9LU/TD5FToZMfqI/AAAAAAAAAIM/p_q7qojBZis/s1600/feminist_revolution.JPG; http://www.wordsoverpixels.com/warning-reflections-in-this-mirror-may-be-distorte/17226193f6cedc90e1bb046a369a0004.html

172 In popular form (feminism and antifeminism in popular culture)

approach to social activism. The group debates sexism, advertising, pornography and women's bodies openly and, often, stridently. Guerrilla feminist work is often witty, inspired and subversive, perhaps with a lighter touch than its feminist cultural antecedents, such as riot grrrl (which has been frequently described as 'angry' and, according to Courtney Love in *Spin* magazine, October 2005, doctrinaire and censorious). Guerrilla feminists are no less serious, however, in their campaigning against sexism. Their Facebook page describes the movement as 'a band of irregular soldiers that uses guerrilla warfare, harassing the enemy by surprise raids, sabotaging communication and supply lines'. Guerrilla feminism, the group argues, 'is not about violence', it is about 'utilizing the element of surprise' (https://www.facebook.com/guerrillafeminism).

> We paper/graffiti our cities with feminism, unbeknownst to the mainstream community. This is not a one day activist endeavor – it's everyday activism, so that we may seep into the mainstream psyche; little by little. Even if this never happens, we're still showing our existence. We're creating visibility.
> (https://www.facebook.com/guerrillafeminism. See also http://guerrillafeminism.tumblr.com/about)

Tacit feminism: Supportive but not self-professed

Only one type of feminism is discussed here under the 'tacit' category, a category that I found the hardest to populate since being secretly supportive of feminism necessarily lends itself to secrecy. Anyone, or any project, that does not self-describe as feminist but that supports 'feminist' goals might be included here, as also those who admire 'strong' female characters and role models but who may be ambivalent about 'big f' feminism or feel that describing themselves as feminist may be perceived negatively. There are, of course, other reasons for ambivalence around feminism and important challenges to the whiteness and elitism behind (some) dominant feminist projects have not, for many, yet been adequately addressed. In Australia, as feminists questioned women's roles and began to campaign for women's rights, voice and liberation, children of Australian Aboriginal and Torres Strait Islander families were being forcibly removed from their families by Australian Federal and State government agencies and church missions. It would not be much of stretch to imagine how, for some, feminism is associated with the complicity of the white settler government's brutalization of the indigenous population.

The survey conducted for this research counted 8 per cent of responses to the statement 'I would describe myself as a feminist' (Survey Question 7) as 'not sure'. This suggests a certain unease with self-identifying as feminist for a number of survey respondents. One respondent ticked the 'other' box to this question, stating that while they 'believe in equity for everyone, regardless of gender', as an Aboriginal woman, they did not feel 'that feminism has a place' for them

(Australian female, 45–54 years old). Another stated that, while they do not 'identify as a feminist', they 'do agree with some of the more contemporary feminist theories/politics' (Australian male, 35–44 years old). Such sentiments might, I would suggest, create the space for future feminist successes without labouring under the false impression that 'woman' or 'feminism' is necessarily a meaningful or uniform category. As Walter writes, many women 'who might not identify with any particular organization are still being moved to take action when they see something that has an impact on their lives' (2010: 236). 'Unplanned' anger can often produce real social change.

> I wouldn't say [I'm a] feminist, that's too strong. I think when people hear 'feminist', it's just like, 'Get out of my way, I don't need anyone.' And I think that's bad, because actually I don't believe that's what the word 'feminism' stands for. But that's how people relate to that word. I love that I'm being taken care of, and I have a man that's an actual leader. I'm not a feminist in that sense ... but, when it comes to music, I am a little bit more ballsy, but I think that's different.
>
> (Kelly Clarkson, speaking to *Time*'s Belinda Luscombe, October 2013)

Cagney and Lacey, a US television show that aired from 1982 to 1988 and starred Sharon Gless and Tyne Daly as the two female detective leads, Christine Cagney and Mary Beth Lacey, was one of the first 'adult' television programmes I remember watching as a child. I loved this show but I particularly loved the two female leads, who to me, at the tender age of six, were endlessly funny, smart and confident. At a period in life where I was desperate to know how women acted, watching any and all women avidly, Cagney and Lacey left a mark. I still recall quite clearly Cagney's wise-cracking and Lacey's seemingly constant efforts to balance her family and work.

As D'Acci notes, although Cagney and Lacey stood in many ways for an openly feminist politics, the show's feminism was only ambiguous and 'tacit', particularly as it progressed and the producers sought more and more to distance themselves from the 'feminist label' (1994: 161). Coproducer Shelley List and story editor Kathryn Ford noted that their policy with regard to feminism was to 'avoid hard-line statements that would alienate the audience' (summarized in ibid.). After a couple of years, the show's earlier radical politics and focus on women's solidarity was eschewed in favour of implicit depictions that might be read by some viewers as feminist. Indeed, Sharon Gless was the third incarnation of Christine Cagney, with her predecessor, played by Meg Foster, deemed by CBS 'too aggressive', 'too harshly women's lib' and too likely to be perceived as a lesbian by the audience (unnamed CBS programmer, quoted in ibid.: 30). Cagney even assumes, at certain points later in the series, positions that 'could be called antifeminist', while remaining 'associated with actions and behaviours that many would consider independent, empowered, or liberated' (ibid.: 162).

174 In popular form (feminism and antifeminism in popular culture)

'Tacit feminism' is thus, in D'Acci's terms, an invitation to read independent, spirited and intelligent characters that just happen to be women as feminist, but without making explicit feminist links on screen. It remains a fairly common theme across popular culture and is possibly the reason why independent, spirited and apparently intelligent celebrity figures such as Madonna, Taylor Swift, Susan Sarandon and Katy Perry shy away from labelling themselves, and being labelled, as 'feminist'. The many various cases of young women declaring 'I'm not a feminist, but ...' before listing a sequence of feminist objectives, an approach that has so irked feminist commentators (including myself) would also fit here.

In presenting this research and making arguments about antifeminism, I have often been asked 'well, what about [*insert strong female character*]? Isn't she evidence that feminism is alive across popular culture?'. Examples of spirited, 'gutsy' female characters (such as Sydney Bristow in *Alias* or Samantha Jones in *Sex and the City*) abound and are readily accessible across popular culture sources. Much like latter-day Cagney and Laceys, however, such characters may at certain times be read to correspond to certain feminist ideals but are rarely able, or allowed, to self-identify as feminist.

As Hogan describes, the sound of a journalist asking a female celebrity if she identifies as a feminist is liable to make the best among us cringe. Not because of the question, which many of us would happily answer, but 'because of the inevitable lose-lose reverberation it creates around the Internet' (2013). Those women that demure, and admit to not knowing what feminism might mean, are portrayed as 'ignorant disappointments to womankind' (ibid.). If 'a female celebrity answers that she is *not* a feminist and then follows up with an inaccurate definition of feminism' (as in Taylor Swift's much criticized discussion of feminism as 'guys versus girls') she is 'a traitor and a moron' (ibid.). Whereas 'if a female celebrity answers that question by saying she is 'one of the biggest feminists in the world', as per Miley Cyrus, or 'that she is a "modern day feminist"', as per Beyoncé, 'of course we then ask ourselves how often those female celebrities appear in their underwear in public and allow men to spring boners to their antics' (ibid.). It becomes *our* decision, not theirs, 'whether or not those male-gaze-mongers can *truly* call themselves feminists' (ibid.), which is, of course, rather hypocritical. The question 'Are you a feminist?' tells us 'much more about the feminist movement's own branding failures than it does the beliefs of the women prompted to respond', argues Hogan (ibid.).

> The main thing I learned from writing *Girldrive* is that the question, 'Are you a feminist?' is boring. We asked that question and got some generic-sounding, bullshit answer. Once we moved on and asked about women's actual lives, we learned the real stuff.
>
> (Nona Willis Aronowitz, author of *Girldrive: Criss-Crossing America, Redefining Feminism*, cited in Hogan 2013)

Notes

1 According to CBS News, Warner boss Jeff Robinov was reported, on the website Deadline Hollywood Daily, to have issued a decree stating that, 'We [Warner Bros.] are no longer doing movies with women in the lead' (CBS News 2009). Subsequent failures of films like *Catwoman* and *Aeon Flux* have led to some studio executive types declaring that 'any film that was not a rom-com led by a woman was pretty much doomed to failure' (Lyttleton 2012).

2 A number of Swedish cinemas have begun implementing their own Bechdel rating (the 'Test' itself has been around since 1985 and has become common film parlance). To receive an 'A' rating (for 'Approved'), a film must: contain at least two female characters; these two characters must converse, and; they must talk about something other than men (Greenfield 2013).

3 Having recently had the misfortune to sit through the 2013 'reboot' of *Superman, Superman: Man of Steel*, I was particularly struck by how undercooked a heroine 2013's Lois Lane appears on celluloid, particularly when compared to 1979's far sassier and, for me, interesting Lois (I should note at this point that Margot Kidder's talkative Lois Lane was as hated by many as she was loved by others).

4 The only women featured in *Grand Theft Auto 5* are peripheral, at best: strippers, hookers, a particularly whiney daughter, a bored housewife, a female taxi driver, etc.

5 From the Facebook page 'We Hate Andrea From The Walking Dead' to endless threads online hating Andrea, it is not exactly clear why she was so loathed. That her death was not written into the third season of *The Walking Dead* until shooting the finale began suggests that producers were not initially planning to write her out of the show, perhaps until fan disgust became so pronounced. The reasons for hating her seem to be that Andrea failed to shoot a gun properly (shooting a friend instead) and then failed to kill Season Three's evil nemesis, 'The Governor'. As Rothwell (2013) writes:

> There is a scary amount of Andrea hatred out there. People want that woman dead, now. I won't go into the misogyny of the hatred, nope. [...] Please, don't even get me started on the One African American at a Time rule on that show.

6 I refer here to *The Economist* as a magazine but note that this is not how the publication describes itself.

7 No one identified as ether 'intersex' or 'other' when asked to select their gender (Survey Question 2).

8 Indian law prohibits the identification of sex crime victims for their protection, but Singh's name was released to British newspaper *The Sunday People* by her father, who stated that he wanted 'the world to know her real name.' 'My daughter didn't do anything wrong, she died while protecting herself. I am proud of her. Revealing her name will give courage to other women who have survived these attacks. They will find strength from my daughter' (quoted in Ralph 2013).

9 Turner recounts how British journalist Caroline Criado-Perez, on beginning a small campaign to replace Elizabeth Fry, removed by the British government from the £5 note, with another female figure was sent a rape threat via Twitter, and a female MP and other female journalists received a bomb threat when Jane Austen was put on the £10 note.

6

CONCLUSIONS

The trouble with IPE

International Political Economy (IPE) embodies, to my mind at least, a commitment to political enquiry into economic life in a variety of shapes and forms. IPE scholars, in the critical tradition, have focused on understanding the historical formation of social interactions, the dynamics of actors and processes within the international system and the structures of 'world order'. While the generation and production of cultural products, read often in terms of transnational structures of production, is of interest to many in IPE, critical scholarship tends still to focus on class as the core unit of analysis, deploying 'class' both as context and meaning (to the detriment of, for example, gender, sexuality, race and disability as key identity categories).

IPE's use of class as the key (indeed, the only) causal force in society, with culture relegated to reflections of class interest, is, I argue, limited and limiting. In counterpoint to those who might claim that analysis of popular and/or visual culture is not serious academic business, I would suggest that, to engage in any meaningful way with how we formulate knowledge about the world, and what therefore we know (or do not know) about the world, we need to consider the political processes of representation by which knowledge, reality and identity are selected, organized and transformed. Not only texts but images are central to our representations. In some contexts, images are *more* central in representing the world. By failing to consider the power visual language wields, and the relations of power from which it emanates, we fail to understand a crucial part of how people 'know' the world and how they then choose (or are able) to act within it.

Popular culture offers sites and sources of meaning-making. More than simply the by-products of a society or culture, popular culture's artefacts constitute how we know ourselves, what we think we are capable of and how we believe ourselves to be valid. Examining, for example, how contemporary Hollywood films create

178 Conclusions

and depict women, or how TV shows reproduce ideas about the 'wife' and the 'mother', tells us something about the struggles over the meaning(s) of gender identities that actively shape, and constrain, people's lives. Popular culture, and its processes of production, representation and consumption, are saturated, at every level 'with ideas about how men and women should behave and what they have the right to do' (Milestone and Meyer 2012: 211). Popular culture artefacts may corroborate existing, and highly regulative, social narratives and assumptions and they may be tools of ideology and state, elite or group interest, but they might also offer important and subversive critiques of social narratives and assumptions. Rather than seeking to show how popular culture provides another source for scholars, of, say, International Relations (IR) or IPE, to add to the list in formulating their analyses, this book has argued that popular culture resides at the heart of understanding relations of power in global politics. It would be careless scholarship *not* to take seriously how our lives, behaviours, assumptions and possibilities are formed within the popular.

I have hoped with this book to help generate IPE enquiry that is more attentive to popular culture. As a political economist, I also think that it behoves the analyst to remember the aspects of 'the popular' that are 'of the people' and to think carefully about popular culture in terms of its accessibility. Popular culture artefacts are not universal and those who have access to, for example, social media, who go to the movies, can afford Foxtel, or have broadband powerful enough to download films, TV shows and music are not 'everypeople'. The proportion of populations that are dispossessed and thus are, as Lury argues, 'excluded from many forms of commodity consumption', since they lack 'access to the economic resources necessary for participation' (2011: 11), are an intrinsic component of the global political economy, and popular culture scholarship, in this vein, would do well not to forget them. This is not to argue that poverty, in both its relative and absolute forms, is a determinant of participation in the consumption of commodities, since it may, in some cases, even incite participation in consumer culture, as Lury notes (ibid.: 12). IPE scholarship is more attuned than most forms of political enquiry, I would argue, to the unevenness and inequalities that mark access to resources and opportunity in the global political economy. We should, however, assume nothing about those who consume popular culture without first enquiring into the everyday workings of their lives, routines and social circumstances.

Feminism, gender tropes and popular culture

This book has sought to explore the intimate and varied connections between the politics of feminism and the cultural practices of modern, Western, consumer society. It has explored feminism 'made sensible' through visual imagery and popular culture representations, examining feminism's popular and commercial value. It has investigated the extent to which popular culture is produced, represented and consumed to reproduce the conditions in which feminism is valued, or dismissed. It has asked where and how the sexualization of cultural products is

Conclusions **179**

maintained. It has asked whether sufficient evidence can be marshalled to argue that antifeminism exists in commodity form and is commercially viable.

This research has focused on feminism and antifeminism in popular form, examining some of the forms of feminism and antifeminism that I have found to be particularly prevalent and well-represented within popular culture. It has examined feminism and antifeminism, in popular culture form, in order to understand how representative practices have come to constitute and shape feminism, our responses to feminism and feminism's popular success. I have tried to heed Hollows and Moseley's advice and have not presumed any 'real' or 'authentic' feminism existing somewhere outside popular culture. Instead, this book has examined feminism within popular culture and, therefore, as something shaped and understood through the popular. Understanding how feminism, and antifeminism, are distributed, exchanged and consumed is central to understanding what feminism and antifeminism mean within the popular and understanding what feminism and antifeminism mean within the popular is central to understanding, I argue, how popular culture is such a powerful purveyor of our ideas about the world.

Popular culture deploys and disparages feminism in many and various ways. Gender tropes in popular culture, including, for example, why feminists are cast negatively across popular culture, why stupidity in girls is perceived as more profitable, or why 'strong female characters' have become more dull than inspiring, are powerful. They represent our cultural tool kits for appropriating feminism and are the cultural mechanisms by which feminism is filtered through our everyday lives. These tropes also provide the parameters around how popular culture artefacts engage with feminism and feminist concerns, which are so important because of their relationship with how they make it possible, and acceptable, to articulate a feminist politics or to encourage derogatory, violent and demeaning representations to dismiss feminism and feminist gains.

The relationship between gender codes and prevailing norms in and of popular culture is crucial to feminism but this research has, I think, shown that feminism is perhaps not crucial to the reproduction of these codes. An awful lot of the representational politics of popular culture remains galling, alarming and problematic. When we see female television characters cleaning, berating their hen-pecked husbands, bemoaning their wrinkles, or, worse, humiliated, objectified or dead, and when we encounter women and men posed provocatively (sometimes abusively, but nearly always suggestively) in advertisements, we may not actually believe that these representations 'are' what women and men are, should or could be. Yet the quality of the representations of women and men reproduced through and within popular culture certainly do have a direct impact: on our sense of self, our sense of others and our expectations of both. Popular culture's representations form the basis for our identifications with the world. Photographic images allow us, as Sontag has described, to possess something we may have no experience of (1999: 81). Images give control: control to the observer to redefine their knowledge and experience and control over the thing being recorded, scrutinized and surveilled. Images are

180 Conclusions

vital, and so powerful, because they furnish us with knowledge disassociated from and independent of experience. They allow us to 'know', in our own ways and according to the paths of knowledge, and sources of meaning-making, we have already available to us.

The extent to which we can, then, expect people to stand apart from prevailing representations and narratives created and sustained in and through popular culture is highly debatable. As I hope this book has shown, representations matter. How we are represented, and how then our cultural products are consumed and recirculated, sustains our knowledge of the world and conditions how that knowledge organizes us. The representative practices of contemporary popular culture are more than simply an aside to feminism's waning or ascending influence, they have come to constitute and shape feminism and our responses to feminism.

Is antifeminism more commercially viable than feminism?

If the research for this book has taught me anything, it is that ideas about what is profitable are not the same as what is actually profitable, but matter more.

Twenty years ago it seemed that what was often called 'feminism' had become code for a particular stereotype of man-hating radicalism that, although not representative of the feminist movement, saturated media and popular culture sites. The backlash against feminist gains that characterized the 1980s (in the USA especially, but elsewhere also) was further complicated in the 1990s, with, as McRobbie has argued, an array of 'machinations' and 'elements' of contemporary popular culture that were 'perniciously effective' in regard to 'undoing' feminism, although they appeared, and were made to appear, 'to be engaging in a well-informed and even well-intended response to feminism' (2009: 11). The 1990s, and the so-called rise of 'postfeminism', fed the myth that women had achieved equality and that feminism was, now, surplus to requirements. Popular culture artefacts, across television, film, news media, magazines, social media and music sources, have at various times contributed to representing feminism as outmoded, irrelevant or 'uncool'. Popular culture has seemed very much to be reproducing the conditions, as McRobbie, Whelehan and Levy have argued, in which feminism could be dismissed, with the rise of 'raunch culture' championing the nonsensical idea that commercialism and mass-scale consumption allow women (and men) the freedom to choose how they are objectified.

In many ways, contemporary Western societies are more discriminatory, perhaps even more misogynistic, than they have ever been. 2013 might well have been 'The Year of Feminism' (Turner 2014), but for all 'big f' feminism's successes, the persistence of (in many cases, increasing) wage gaps between men and women in all Western (and most non-Western) countries, the prevalence of sexual and domestic violence (or 'family violence', as it is termed here in Australia) and the under-representation of women in all aspects of political and public life, may suggest a lack of infiltration of feminist policy-making. Julia Gillard's 'Misogyny Speech' opened media, including social media, reporting and debate to

Conclusions **181**

a different level of intellectual engagement with prejudice, sexism and opportunity in Australia. It did not, however, rout this social blight, much as the Tazreen garment factory fire (November 2012) has not rendered female sweatshop workers any less expendable in the global political economy. I certainly, in this research, found it easier to uncover examples of antifeminism, tacit and overt, filtered through multiple popular culture channels, than I did examples of feminism. Yet there remains a true vibrancy to underground feminism(s) that is not well served by mainstream, and often alternative, media and popular culture representations and engagements.

I have been most struck I think, in this research, by the contradictions involved in engaging with the representational practices of popular culture. Only a couple of years ago, I would have argued that young women are not as concerned with feminism as past generations and that the, now rather clichéd, 'I'm not a feminist, but . . .' refrain was undoing feminism among my student cohort. I do not now think that this is true, and examining in greater depth popular engagements with feminism has taught me that people are rarely as naïve in their appreciations of relations of power as I might once have worried. Positive representations continue to jostle for space with disappointing caricatures and unflattering stereotypes but, for every example of a derogatory portrayal of girls, women, feminism or feminists, a genuine and affirming engagement exists to lift the spirits.

I have been surprised, for example, with the diversity and prevalence of feminist messages across various social media sites. Yet social media is not, of course, without its drawbacks and while feminist voices find multiple outlets, and varying levels of visibility, through the channels afforded by the explosion of social media, they fight simultaneously for space with some of the worst and most offensive that the internet has to offer (see Figure 6.1). I have found, as did McRobbie, the existence of a certain 'undoing' of feminism' (2009), but I have also appreciated the complexity of how women view their own opportunities and obstacles, how they perceive and experience gender discrimination and how they identify themselves with respect to feminism. In this regard, the survey conducted for this research was particularly enlightening and the gap between dominant representations of feminism (such as those found, for example, in the mainstream Australian news media) and more personal, intimate, engagements with feminist politics has often been substantial. Representations of feminism as old-hat, irrelevant, fusty and outdated did not correspond either to popular debates on a variety of feminist topics or to the importance that respondents ascribed their experiences of sexism and the sexualization of popular culture and commercial artefacts.

Research for this book has told me that the so-called 'death of feminism' is entirely irrelevant to understanding either the complexity of social relations in capitalist, liberal societies such as Australia, or the significance of feminist imaginings within popular culture and popular culture imaginings of feminism. The important question today is not 'where has feminism gone?' but 'where is feminism embodied?'; the answer to this is, I suggest, that feminism is vibrant but fragmented and it is this that makes it, perhaps, an easy target for its detractors. Yet even this very

"This week, Zoo magazine posted the following image on its Facebook page, asking the question "Left or right, but you've got to tell us how you got to that decision."
The comments came rolling in, here are some (warning – highly offensive comments):

FIGURE 6.1 The Facebook page of *Zoo Weekly*[1] magazine (Australia), 2012.
Source: Collective Shout 2012.

Conclusions **183**

fragmentation is ambivalent, rendering feminism incomplete to some and vital to others. Arguing, however, that feminism has many, various, definitions, to different people, does not make feminism redundant. Proposing that feminism means many things does not, as per Kalb's analysis, mean that feminism means nothing at all. There seem to be cycles of feminism's stigmatization and, at the moment, we are in an upswing. This will likely give way to further apathy, criticism and dismissal at some point in the future, perhaps even by the time this book is published. Throughout, and despite however many times popular media have heralded, and will continue to herald, the death of feminism, feminism continues to relate, in multiple ways, to the different challenges people pose to sexist, hierarchical and restrictive practices, structures and institutions. People arrive at feminism, or they do not, for all sorts of reasons. Refusing to police the boundaries of the political and defining feminism according to its multiplicity constitutes part of the strength, not the weakness, of our engagements with the term.

Note

1 *Zoo Weekly*, the magazine that brought us a 'hottest asylum seeker' competition, is one of Australia's biggest-selling 'men's lifestyle' magazines. Each week the magazine sells 28,000 copies to Australian boys aged between 14 and 17 years. Its circulation is unrestricted despite pornographic and frequently offensive content and it is 'conveniently positioned and priced for young readers to purchase in convenience stores, service stations and Coles and Woolworths' (Collective Shout 2012).

APPENDIX A: SURVEY QUESTIONS

Part 1: Demographic details

Question no.	Question	Response type
1	Please select your age group from the list below	Select one (8 choices)
2	Please select your gender	Select one (4 choices)
3	Please specify your ethnic or cultural background	Select one (9 choices)
4	Where do you currently reside?	Select one (5 choices)
5	Please select the highest level of education you have completed	Select one (6 choices)
6	Your present occupation	Select one (11 choices)

Part 2: The relevance of feminism today

Question no.	Question	Response type
7	I would describe myself as a feminist	Yes/No/Not sure
8	Being a feminist is one of a number of things that make up my identity	7-point scale
9	Feminism is personally relevant to me	7-point scale
10	Feminism is professionally relevant to me	7-point scale
11	Feminism is relevant to Australian society in the 21st century	7-point scale
12	Feminism is as relevant to men today as it is to women	7-point scale
13	Feminists largely see men as the enemy	7-point scale

186 Appendix A: Survey questions

Part 3: The popularity and/or accessibility of feminism today

Question no.	Question	Response type
14	How would you describe feminism?	Short answer
15	What comes to mind when you think of a feminist?	Short answer
16	Feminism is accessible to young women in the 21st century	7-point scale
17	Feminism is accessible to young men in the 21st century	7-point scale
18	Feminism is accessible to women of all ages in the 21st century	7-point scale
19	Feminism is accessible to men of all ages in the 21st century	7-point scale
20	I feel that men are sensitive to feminist issues	7-point scale
21	Men often feel uncomfortable engaging with feminist issues	7-point scale

Part 4: Practices of feminism today

Question no.	Question	Response type
22	I care very deeply about men and women having equal opportunities in all respects	7-point scale
23	I don't think there is one "right" way to be a feminist	7-point scale
24	Some of the men I know seem more feminist than some of the women	7-point scale
25	I am a woman who has experienced sexism	Yes/No/Not sure
26	I am a man who has experienced sexism	Yes/No/Not sure
27	If yes, what was the impact, do you think, of this experience?	Short answer
28	When I think about sexism, my first reaction is always anger	7-point scale

Part 5: Popular culture and feminism

Question no.	Question	Response type
29	Feminism is generally represented in a positive light on television	7-point scale
30	Feminism is generally represented in a positive light on the Internet	7-point scale
31	Feminism is generally represented in a positive light in film	7-point scale
32	Feminism is generally represented in a positive light in newsmedia	7-point scale
33	We need more positive representations of feminism in contemporary popular culture	7-point scale
34	Can you recall any particular examples of representations of feminism in the media in your lifetime?	Short answer

35	How would you describe the ways in which femininity is represented in contemporary popular culture?	Short answer
36	How would you describe the ways in which masculinity is represented in contemporary popular culture?	Short answer
37	Can you recall any examples of positive and/or adverse representations of femininity and/or masculinity in contemporary popular culture?	Short answer
38	What does this image say to you, if anything, about feminism today?	Short answer
39	'The feminist movement, like the civil rights movement, is one that almost everyone is afraid to criticise. If you attack feminism, you're obviously a sexist, misogynistic male who wishes that women would just stay home and cook, clean and raise children. The issues I have with feminism have nothing to do with the idea of equality between men and women; I just feel that women can and will succeed without the now largely irrelevant feminist movement "supporting" them' (Enerson 2007). Do you agree?	7-point scale
40	The objectification of women is unacceptable in the 21st century	7-point scale
41	The objectification of men is unacceptable in the 21st century	7-point scale
42	Contemporary popular culture is heavily sexualised	7-point scale
43	I feel uncomfortable when I see sex being used to sell products that are not related to sex	7-point scale
44	The sexualisation of commercial products that are not related to sex is unacceptable	7-point scale
45	Feminism is important in challenging problematic representations of men and women and/or masculinity and femininity in contemporary popular culture	7-point scale

Check this question list against

APPENDIX B: DOLCE AND GABBANA

At the time that research for this book was first taking shape, I had been reflecting on the relationship between advertising, art and feminism and the many, and varied, ways in which the sexual objectification of the human body is transmitted through popular culture artefacts. To give the reader a better idea of the specific imagery I was reflecting upon, included below are a number of images from Italian fashion house Dolce and Gabbana, purveyor of high-end fashion and luxury goods. Dolce and Gabbana (D&G), established in 1985 by Domenico Dolce and Stefano Gabbana, has been no stranger to controversy and is well known for its use of stylized eroticism and manipulation of 'typical' Western gender roles. Its advertisements are usually highly sexualized and 'often depict women as submissive to male supremacy' (Barbaric Poetries 2012). At the time of their release, several of these images (particularly Dolce and Gabbana's 'gang rape' and 'knives' campaigns) incited extensive social commentary and, in some cases, government intervention. While Dolce and Gabbana is certainly not a fashion house that seeks to avoid attracting public scrutiny or controversy, its advertising imagery remains interesting to this research for its uncritical celebration of sexual violence, women (and men's) promiscuity and sexual availability and its consistent reproduction of asymmetrical relations of power and authority. While Dolce and Gabbana clearly seek to commission campaigns that are deliberately provocative (and, therefore, eye-catching), this imagery was made more significant, here, for the designers' resounding (but perhaps unsurprisingly) public failure to engage with the politicality of their representational practices, denying both that the advertisements themselves were anything other than 'art' and that 'art' could be political.

190 Appendix B: Dolce and Gabbana

The March 2006 *Esquire* campaign

Founded in 1933 in the USA and published (digitally and in hard copy) by the Hearst Corporation, *Esquire* magazine numbers a readership of 725,000 and claims to be the 'only general-interest lifestyle magazine for sophisticated men', defining, reflecting and celebrating 'what it means to be a man in contemporary American culture' (Hearst 2014). The magazine publishes twenty-seven international editions, including publications specific to, for example, China, the United Kingdom, Japan, Greece, Colombia, Russia, South Korea, Ukraine and Thailand.

In 2006, Dolce and Gabbana ran a campaign featuring an image of a woman being pinned down by one male as four other males looked on (Figure B.1(a)). Not very long after, the fashion house withdrew the image from both Spanish and Italian publications to 'protect their creative liberty' (*Daily Mail* 2007), after authorities in Spain declared the campaign humiliating to women and potentially 'illegal', the Italian union CGIL's textile workers' division called for a boycott of Dolce and Gabbana products and human rights group Amnesty International stated that the advertisement risked 'excusing violence against women' (Reuters 2007). The fashion house instead ran a replacement image (Figure B.1(b)), with four men in suits watching as the same half-dressed female apparently writhes beneath them. 'We were looking to recreate a game of seduction in the campaign and highlight the beauty of our collections', Dolce and Gabanna have said, adding that it was never their intention 'to offend anyone or promote violence against women' (quoted in ibid.).

> Spain's Labour and Social Affairs Ministry branded the campaign [...] humiliating to women, saying the woman's body position had no relation to the products Dolce and Gabbana were trying to sell. 'One could infer from the advertisement that it is acceptable to use force as a way of imposing oneself on a woman, reinforced by the passive and complicit manner of the men looking on,' the Ministry said in a [2007] statement.
>
> (Reuters 2007)

What surprised me most about Dolce and Gabbana choosing this image of gang rape was less its shock value (clearly the pictures were designed for maximum provocation, despite the designers' disingenuous claims to the contrary) but that the designers would bother choosing to defend the campaign as art and then claim that art has nothing to do with 'real life'. In comments originally reported by *La Vanguardia*, the designers ask '"What has an artistic photo got to do with a real act?" You would have to burn museums like the Louvre or the paintings of Caravaggio' (Reuters 2007). Sadly, no one seemed to have asked Stefano Gabbana and Domenico Dolce whether the designers intended their 'artistic photos' to dirty themselves with the 'real act' of selling things.

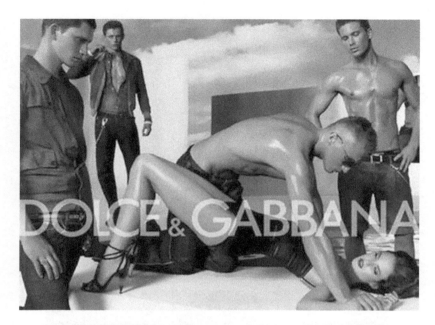

FIGURE B.1 D&G *Esquire* campaign images.

Sources: (a) Wagner (2008); (b) If It's Hip, It's Here (2007).

The October 2006 'knives' campaign

This particular campaign, featuring models in various states of undress brandishing knives (Figure B.2), was noteworthy in the British media for the criticisms levelled against it. The British Advertising Standards Authority (ASA) upheld more than

FIGURE B.2 D&G 'knives' campaign images.

Sources: (a) Taylor 2007; (b) Greaves and Mercado 2011.

Appendix B: Dolce and Gabbana **193**

150 complaints against Dolce and Gabbana 'from people concerned that the pictures glorified and condoned violent crime' (BBC 2007). The fashion house, avoiding the substance of the complaints, responded with the claim that the ads were heavily stylized and mimicked early nineteenth century art: 'In defence of the adverts, Dolce and Gabbana claimed they were "highly stylised and intended to be an iconic representation of the Napoleonic period of art, emphasising the theatrical effects of that genre"' (ibid.).

The advertisements themselves were run in the well-read and widely distributed newspaper *The Times* and *The Daily Telegraph* magazine supplement. The ASA's adjudication, which was hardly a stinging chastisement, was to remind Dolce and Gabbana 'of its duty to prepare ads with a sense of responsibility to consumers and to society', telling D&G and *The Times* 'to take greater care in the placement of similar ads in future' (ASA 2007).

The 2007/08 'objectifying men' campaign

Perhaps attentive to the complaints previously levelled at them, Dolce and Gabbana launched an autumn/winter campaign in 2007/08 that offered a sequence of images designed to present the woman as dominatrix (Figure B.3). Deploying a 'raunchy aggressive look complete with metal detailing, slicked back hair and whips' (Moss 2007), the images, shot by photographer Stephen Klein, display women accompanied by naked male models in various states of submission, set against a futuristic backdrop (the futuristic setting perhaps a nod to the designers' efforts to turn the tables on past criticism and point to a future of male, rather than female, objectification). Speaking about the campaign, Stefano Gabbana said,

> Since these images have offended someone, we want to stress that we wanted to represent a strong and dominatrix woman, as is today's woman. It's the vision of a dream more than reality, where the whip symbolizes women's power and where the naked models refer to a classic beauty inspired by Michelangelo. We wanted to place this artistic reference above everyday reality, but there was no intent to be vulgar or offend anyone's human dignity.
>
> (Stefano Gabbana, quoted in WWD 2007)

Women tend, statistically speaking, to be objectified more than men across modern sources of popular culture, including advertising, magazines, music videos, television, cinema, and so on. For women, their sexual objectification has meant that they are, as Heldman notes, considered 'less competent and less worthy of empathy by both men and women', with repeated exposure to images of sexually objectified women causing male viewers 'to be more tolerant of sexual harassment and rape myths' (2012).

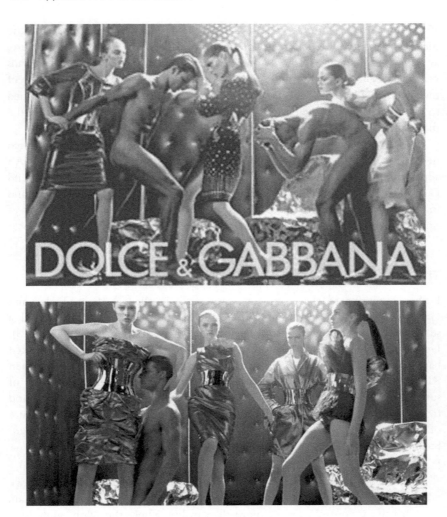

FIGURE B.3 D&G 'objectifying men' campaign images.
Sources: (a) WWD 2007; (b) newemotion 2007.

Pop culture sells women and girls a hurtful fiction that their value lies in how sexy they appear to others; they learn at a very young age that their sexuality is *for* others. At the same time, sexuality is stigmatized in women but encouraged in men. We learn that men want and women want-to-be-wanted. The yardstick for women's value (sexiness) automatically puts them in a subordinate societal position, regardless of how well they otherwise measure up. Perfectly sexy women are perfectly subordinate.

(Heldman 2012, emphasis in the original)

While sexual objectification is nothing new, simply reversing the trick by depicting men in sexually humiliating poses does little to subvert the harm in reducing human bodies to simple objects of desire for the pleasures of others. The sexual objectification of a body is, in essence, the dehumanization of that body, female or male, and there is no evidence to suggest that flipping the coin, and objectifying men rather than women, challenges this dehumanization or allows women greater agency over their sexual expression. A society that places value only on the sexualized body, within a culture of widespread sexual objectification, harms men *and* women. Here, Dolce and Gabbana's 'dominatrix' campaign is shocking, because advertisers so rarely portray women as anything other than passive, submissive or domesticated, but also conservative, preserving a space within popular culture for the primary significance of the body as sexually objectified (and objectifiable).

GLOSSARY

Abbott, Tony

Abbott is the current Prime Minister of Australia and key target of Julia Gillard's famous 'Misogyny Speech' of 9 October 2012. Infamous in feminist circles, Tony Abbott has been quoted as saying: 'I think it would be folly to expect that women will ever dominate or even approach equal representation in a large number of areas simply because their aptitudes, abilities and interests are different for physiological reasons'; 'I think there does need to be give and take on both sides, and this idea that sex is kind of a woman's right to absolutely withhold, just as the idea that sex is a man's right to demand, I think they both need to be moderated, so to speak'; 'What the housewives of Australia need to understand as they do the ironing is that if they get it done commercially it's going to go up in price and their own power bills when they switch the iron on are going to go up, every year', and, on Julia Gillard: 'Gillard won't lie down and die' (What's the Run Dude? 2012).

Activism

Activism in this book refers to any effort to advance, instigate or impede social and political change. Activism may be direct or indirect, visible or otherwise and targeted at instigating change in dramatic or subtle ways. It is not a synonym for banner waving, although it might involve this, and includes multimedia methods of organization, communication or protest.

AWOL; jarhead; ground zero

These are military terms that have entered common (civilian usage) due to the intersections between military and popular culture. This is particularly evident in

198 Glossary

the USA, but also elsewhere, in part, perhaps because of the dominance of US popular culture artefacts.

'AWOL' stands for absent without official leave and is a term that, officially, indicates the desertion of a military post and dereliction of duty (which is punishable by law), although in popular usage it has come to symbolize a more general sense of being missing or absent.

A 'jarhead' is a US slang term, sometimes considered derogatory, for a member of the US Marine Corps. Used in a 2005 film of the same name (directed by Sam Mendes and based on Anthony Swofford's 2003 autobiography), the term originated from, and references, the 'high and tight' hair cut that many US Marines display.

Technically with several meanings, the term 'ground zero' was popularized following the Second World War bombings of Japan. In military usage, 'ground zero' refers to the point directly above or below a massive (usually nuclear) explosion. It also means a centre point of rapid, intense or violent activity and can be used to refer to the origins, or very beginning, of something. The term came into widespread usage across North American media reporting of the World Trade Center bombings, in September 2001. Today, 'Ground Zero' (capitalized) is generally understood to refer to the site in Manhattan of the former World Trade Center.

The Bechdel Test

A movie is said to pass the Bechdel Test when:

1 It has at least two (named) women in it.
2 These women talk to each other.
3 These women talk to each other about something besides a man.

The fifty greatest films to pass the Test, according to Seddon (2014), include *Boogie Nights*, *Halloween*, *Donnie Darko*, *Life of Brian*, *Goodfellas* and *The Godfather Part II*. Films that fail, perhaps surprisingly, have included *Avatar*, *Harry Potter and the Deathly Hallows: Part II*, *The Lord of the Rings* and original *Star Wars* films and *Run Lola Run*.

A full list of movies that both pass and fail the Bechdel Test can be found at http://bechdeltest.com.

The blogosphere

Literally, the 'world of blogs', the blogosphere consists of all blogs and their interconnections. A single blog (web-log) is usually a discussion, informational or autobiographical site published on the internet. It might be single or multi-author and is textual, art, photo, video, music or audio based. Corporations frequently use blogs to appeal (sell their brand or products) to the social media masses and approximately 40 per cent of blog sites are income generating, although quantities vary widely. The traffic passing through blogs is counted by statistical tools such as Google Analytics and StatCounter. Estimates suggest that a new blog is created somewhere in the world every half-second and that there exist more than 180 million blogs, although with around a million new blog posts produced every day, this is difficult to track. According to Nielsen (2011), 6.7 million people publish blogs on blogging websites, another 12 million write blogs using their social networks (such as Tumblr and Pinterest) and most bloggers are female (Nielsen estimates that one in three bloggers are mothers). North America (including the USA) produces by far the largest number of blog sites, followed by the EU countries. Before San Francisco-based Pyra Labs created the 'Blogger' service for creating and maintaining personal web spaces in 1999, it is thought that there were less than one hundred blogs in existence.

Britpop

According to Hann a 'cultural abomination that set [British] music back', Britpop embodied 'quirky representations of Britishness' during the early 1990s that quickly degenerated into 'a generation of bands and fans who resembled nothing so much as a parody of the football hooligans of a generation before' (2014). Symbolized perhaps most famously by the bands, and their rivalry, Blur and Oasis, the slogan 'Cool Britannia', Noel Gallagher's Union Jack guitar and support of the newly elected Labour government (led by a then relatively youthful Tony Blair) and ending with Oasis's indulgent and over-hyped 'Be Here Now' album, Britpop was heavily associated with 'lad' culture and football (after the release of New Order's 'World in Motion' for the 1990 World Cup). Unusually it saw women take a leading role, with female singers such as Sleeper's Louise Wener, Echobelly's Sonya Madan, Catatonia's Cerys Matthews and Elastica's Justine Frischmann featuring prominently. Championed as 'indie', by 1997 Britpop had become 'such a part of the establishment that the Labour party even had its own unofficial Britpop liaison officer, a man named Darren Kalynuk' (Hann 2014).

The Eagle Forum (Phyllis Schlafly)

One of the leading antifeminist conservative interest groups in the USA, the Eagle Forum describes itself as a 'pro-family movement' and reports over 80,000 members. Its president, Phyllis Schlafly, who also publishes a weekly column on the Forum's website ('The Phyllis Schlafly Report'), has been tireless in her quest to undo advances in women's status and rights. As a lawyer and activist, Phyllis Schlafly was probably best known for her successful 1973 campaign to stop the passage of the Equal Rights Amendment in the USA. The Forum supports conservative issue areas and has worked with the Republican Party on numerous occasions. It is resoundingly pro-marriage, opposes the legalization of abortion, opposes international oversight by the UN or ICC, supports English-only education in schools, opposes same-sex marriage and resists sex education in schools.

200 Glossary

Schlafly argues, of feminists, that they are robbing women of the choice to be homemakers rather than paid workers (2012) and have killed the 'American nuclear family' (2014).

Galifianakis, Zach

A US actor and comedian, possibly most famous for his *The Hangover* movie roles but probably most celebrated for his cultish 'Between Two Ferns' mock-interview comedy series, hosted by online video channel 'Funny or Die'. Galifianakis claims that the shows are improvised and guests are not told what will happen in advance. Rather, the show is designed to reify 'inappropriateness', while making fun of the 'sycophantic' way the 'Hollywood machine runs' (Galifianakis, speaking to ABC News 2010).

Gaming culture

Gaming culture, or video game culture, is possibly one of the largest of contemporary popular culture's sub-cultures. Gamers have been said to comprise over 70 per cent of those aged from 6 to 49 in the USA, with most players being in their twenties and thirties. Online and LAN (local area network) gaming increase the social aspects, while significantly expanding the scope and scale of gaming culture. Gaming culture has produced a number of neologisms that have ventured into everyday usage, such as 'lol' (laugh out loud), 'noob' (beginner, in a slightly pejorative sense) and 'gg' (good game).

Notoriously masculinized and plagued by the sort of sexist, racist and homophobic bigotry that makes a hateful, but noisy, minority seem so abundant across the internet and social media more broadly, gaming culture has been heavily criticized over the years for its reification of sexist, violent and exclusionary content (fighting game culture has been particularly criticized). Female gamers are ambivalent about the levels of sexism and hostility that exist across the gaming environment, with some suggesting that 'the idiots are always vastly outnumbered by intelligent and respectful people' (MacDonald 2012), while others note that they are 'disappointed in the amount of sexism inherent in the titles that are coming out' and the 'bad attitude towards female gamers' that remains prevalent (Ballou 2014). Female gamers are no longer, however, the minority of gamers that they were once (a 2014 UK report suggests that women make up 52 per cent of the gaming audience in Britain), with women as likely to play games designed with male players in mind as men, a phenomenon that has been linked to the rise of the smartphone. This said, most games continue to be designed and produced with a male gamer in mind and most continue to feature male characters as leads (as per, for example, huge sellers such as the *Grand Theft Auto*, *XCOM*, *Assassin's Creed*, *Batman*, *Call of Duty* and *Battlefield* games. A few games do stand out for their use of female protagonists, including *Tomb Raider*, *Beyond: Two Souls*, *Resident Evil*, *Alien: Isolation* and *The Last of Us*, which still does not allow the player to play as a female for most of the game, but, as yet, female-led games remain in the minority).

Geek culture

Once used pejoratively for people considered eccentric and freakish, the term 'geek' is now more often used self-referentially and without malice to describe non-mainstream, often technologically obsessed (although the obsession may also relate to a hobby or intellectual pursuit) experts or enthusiasts.

Different categories of 'geekdom' include science geeks, math(s) geeks, computer geeks, history geeks, gaming geeks, popular culture geeks and so on. While geeks are assumed to 'do' things (that is, use new technologies to achieve certain ends), 'nerds' are assumed to know things and 'dweebs' are generally confused about everything (although on occasion 'geek' and 'nerd' are still used interchangeably). The US TV show *The Big Bang Theory*, and its enormous popularity, has been argued to have made 'geek' mainstream, although the show remains controversial across geek culture, with main characters that many geeks perceive as crude 'stereotypes' and a marginalization of female characters that has been labelled sexist (uzerfriendly 2014).

Geek culture, which is debated in terms of both content and meaning, is arguably becoming pop culture and is everywhere, with an explosion of people engaging in their hobbies and media with unbridled enthusiasm across the internet (in Japan, the term *otaku* is used to described someone obsessed with *anime* and *manga*). Generally considered non-conformist, sometimes hyper-rational, geek culture tends to embrace all things comic book, especially superhero stories, and collectable, geek culture also embodies a focus on 'cultishness', particularly of cinema, but of also music, gaming, video, art, photography and so on. 'Geek chic' embraces stereotypically geeky clothing and accessories (especially prevalent with 'hipsters' wearing geek glasses, messenger bags, cardigans, and so on, although many would argue that if a geek thinks they are 'cool', they are not a true geek). 'Geek Pride Day' is celebrated on 25 May.

Gender pay gap

The difference between male and female earnings expressed as a percentage of male earnings, the gender pay gap (or GPG) is sometimes also known as the gender wage, earnings or income gap. In Australia in 2014, the gender pay gap exceeded 18 per cent, to sit at a record high of 18.2 per cent (news.com.au 2014). In the USA, the Bureau of Labor Statistics tracks wage differences, in Europe the EU aggregates the calculations of its member states and in Australia the Workplace Gender Equality Agency calculates the national gender pay gap using Australian Bureau of Statistics' Average Weekly Full-Time Earnings data. Globally, the OECD collates and compares national data (this covers OECD member countries, plus Russia, Brazil, China, India, Indonesia and South Africa).

202 Glossary

Gillard, Julia

Australia's 27th Prime Minister and the Australian Labor Party (ALP) and country's first female leader. The first female Deputy Prime Minister of Australia following the ALP's victory in the 2007 federal election, Gillard became Prime Minister after former PM Kevin Rudd lost the support of his party and resigned. On 26 June 2013, Gillard lost the leadership of the Labor Party to Kevin Rudd, with her resignation as Prime Minister taking effect the following day. Strongly associated, across the Australian media landscape, with 'backstabbing' Kevin Rudd, Gillard, although a gifted politician and well known for her strong negotiating and debating skills, was frequently vilified while in power for her apparent connivances in a highly sexist and derogatory manner.

The Misogyny Speech.

The following is a full transcript of Gillard's speech, delivered on 9 October 2012 to the House of Representatives (Australia's lower House) in response to the Opposition's motion to have Peter Slipper removed as Speaker over sexist comments he was alleged to have made.

> Thank you very much Deputy Speaker and I rise to oppose the motion moved by the Leader of the Opposition. And in so doing I say to the Leader of the Opposition I will not be lectured about sexism and misogyny by this man. I will not. And the Government will not be lectured about sexism and misogyny by this man. Not now, not ever.
>
> The Leader of the Opposition says that people who hold sexist views and who are misogynists are not appropriate for high office. Well I hope the Leader of the Opposition has got a piece of paper and he is writing out his resignation. Because if he wants to know what misogyny looks like in modern Australia, he doesn't need a motion in the House of Representatives, he needs a mirror. That's what he needs.
>
> Let's go through the Opposition Leader's repulsive double standards, repulsive double standards when it comes to misogyny and sexism. We are now supposed to take seriously that the Leader of the Opposition is offended by Mr Slipper's text messages, when this is the Leader of the Opposition who has said, and this was when he was a minister under the last government – not when he was a student, not when he was in high school – when he was a minister under the last government.
>
> He has said, and I quote, in a discussion about women being under-represented in institutions of power in Australia, the interviewer was a man called Stavros. The Leader of the Opposition says 'If it's true, Stavros, that men have more power generally speaking than women, is that a bad thing?'
>
> And then a discussion ensues, and another person says 'I want my daughter to have as much opportunity as my son.' To which the Leader of the Opposition says 'Yeah, I completely agree, but what if men are by physiology or temperament, more adapted to exercise authority or to issue command?'

Then ensues another discussion about women's role in modern society, and the other person participating in the discussion says 'I think it's very hard to deny that there is an underrepresentation of women,' to which the Leader of the Opposition says, 'But now, there's an assumption that this is a bad thing.'

This is the man from whom we're supposed to take lectures about sexism. And then of course it goes on. I was very offended personally when the Leader of the Opposition, as Minister of Health, said, and I quote, 'Abortion is the easy way out.' I was very personally offended by those comments. You said that in March 2004, I suggest you check the records.

I was also very offended on behalf of the women of Australia when in the course of this carbon pricing campaign, the Leader of the Opposition said 'What the housewives of Australia need to understand as they do the ironing …' Thank you for that painting of women's roles in modern Australia.

And then of course, I was offended too by the sexism, by the misogyny of the Leader of the Opposition catcalling across this table at me as I sit here as Prime Minister, 'If the Prime Minister wants to, politically speaking, make an honest woman of herself …', something that would never have been said to any man sitting in this chair. I was offended when the Leader of the Opposition went outside in the front of Parliament and stood next to a sign that said 'Ditch the witch.'

I was offended when the Leader of the Opposition stood next to a sign that described me as a man's bitch. I was offended by those things. Misogyny, sexism, every day from this Leader of the Opposition. Every day in every way, across the time the Leader of the Opposition has sat in that chair and I've sat in this chair, that is all we have heard from him.

And now, the Leader of the Opposition wants to be taken seriously, apparently he's woken up after this track record and all of these statements, and he's woken up and he's gone 'Oh dear, there's this thing called sexism, oh my lords, there's this thing called misogyny. Now who's one of them? Oh, the Speaker must be because that suits my political purpose.'

Doesn't turn a hair about any of his past statements, doesn't walk into this Parliament and apologise to the women of Australia. Doesn't walk into this Parliament and apologise to me for the things that have come out of his mouth. But now seeks to use this as a battering ram against someone else.

Well this kind of hypocrisy must not be tolerated, which is why this motion from the Leader of the Opposition should not be taken seriously.

And then second, the Leader of the Opposition is always wonderful about walking into this Parliament and giving me and others a lecture about what they should take responsibility for.

Always wonderful about that – everything that I should take responsibility for, now apparently including the text messages of the Member for Fisher. Always keen to say how others should assume responsibility, particularly me.

204 Glossary

Well can anybody remind me if the Leader of the Opposition has taken any responsibility for the conduct of the Sydney Young Liberals and the attendance at this event of members of his frontbench?

Has he taken any responsibility for the conduct of members of his political party and members of his frontbench who apparently when the most vile things were being said about my family, raised no voice of objection? Nobody walked out of the room; no-one walked up to Mr Jones and said that this was not acceptable.

Instead of course, it was all viewed as good fun until it was run in a Sunday newspaper and then the Leader of the Opposition and others started ducking for cover.

Big on lectures of responsibility, very light on accepting responsibility himself for the vile conduct of members of his political party.

Third, Deputy Speaker, why the Leader of the Opposition should not be taken seriously on this motion.

The Leader of the Opposition and the Deputy Leader of the Opposition have come into this place and have talked about the Member for Fisher. Well, let me remind the Opposition and the Leader of the opposition party about their track record and association with the Member for Fisher.

I remind them that the National Party preselected the Member for Fisher for the 1984 election, that the National Party preselected the Member for Fisher for the 1987 election, that the Liberals preselected Mr Slipper for the 1993 election, then the 1996 election, then the 1998 election, then for the 2001 election, then for the 2004 election, then for the 2007 election and then for the 2010 election.

And across these elections, Mr Slipper enjoyed the personal support of the Leader of the Opposition. I remind the Leader of the Opposition that on 28 September 2010, following the last election campaign, when Mr Slipper was elected as Deputy Speaker, the Leader of the Opposition at that stage said this, and I quote.

He referred to the Member for Maranoa, who was also elected to a position at the same time, and then went on as follows: 'And the Member for Fisher will serve as a fine complement to the Member for Scullin in the chair. I believe that the Parliament will be well-served by the team which will occupy the chair in this chamber. I congratulate the Member for Fisher, who has been a friend of mine for a very long time, who has served this Parliament in many capacities with distinction.'

The words of the Leader of the Opposition on record, about his personal friendship with Mr [Slipper], and on record about his view about Mr Slipper's qualities and attributes to be the Speaker.

No walking away from those words, they were the statement of the Leader of the Opposition then. I remind the Leader of the Opposition, who now comes in here and speaks about apparently his inability to work with or talk to Mr Slipper. I remind the Leader of the Opposition he attended Mr Slipper's wedding.

Did he walk up to Mr Slipper in the middle of the service and say he was disgusted to be there? Was that the attitude he took? No, he attended that wedding as a friend.

The Leader of the Opposition, keen to lecture others about what they ought to know or did know about Mr Slipper. Well with respect, I'd say to the Leader of the Opposition after a long personal association including attending Mr Slipper's wedding, it would be interesting to know whether the Leader of the Opposition was surprised by these text messages.

He's certainly in a position to speak more intimately about Mr Slipper than I am, and many other people in this Parliament, given this long personal association.

Then of course the Leader of the Opposition comes into this place and says, and I quote, 'Every day the Prime Minister stands in this Parliament to defend this Speaker will be another day of shame for this Parliament, another day of shame for a government which should already have died of shame.'

Well can I indicate to the Leader of the Opposition the Government is not dying of shame, my father did not die of shame, what the Leader of the Opposition should be ashamed of is his performance in this Parliament and the sexism he brings with it. Now about the text messages that are on the public record or reported in the [media]– that's a direct quote from the Leader of the Opposition so I suggest those groaning have a word with him.

On the conduct of Mr Slipper, and on the text messages that are in the public domain, I have seen the press reports of those text messages. I am offended by their content. I am offended by their content because I am always offended by sexism. I am offended by their content because I am always offended by statements that are anti-women.

I am offended by those things in the same way that I have been offended by things that the Leader of the Opposition has said, and no doubt will continue to say in the future. Because if this today was an exhibition of his new feminine side, well I don't think we've got much to look forward to in terms of changed conduct.

I am offended by those text messages. But I also believe, in terms of this Parliament making a decision about the speakership, that this Parliament should recognise that there is a court case in progress. That the judge has reserved his decision, that having waited for a number of months for the legal matters surrounding Mr Slipper to come to a conclusion, that this Parliament should see that conclusion.

I believe that is the appropriate path forward, and that people will then have an opportunity to make up their minds with the fullest information available to them.

206 Glossary

But whenever people make up their minds about those questions, what I won't stand for, what I will never stand for is the Leader of the Opposition coming into this place and peddling a double standard. Peddling a standard for Mr Slipper he would not set for himself. Peddling a standard for Mr Slipper he has not set for other members of his frontbench.

Peddling a standard for Mr Slipper that has not been acquitted by the people who have been sent out to say the vilest and most revolting things like his former Shadow Parliamentary Secretary Senator Bernardi.

I will not ever see the Leader of the Opposition seek to impose his double standard on this Parliament. Sexism should always be unacceptable. We should conduct ourselves as it should always be unacceptable. The Leader of the Opposition says do something; well he could do something himself if he wants to deal with sexism in this Parliament.

He could change his behaviour, he could apologise for all his past statements, he could apologise for standing next to signs describing me as a witch and a bitch, terminology that is now objected to by the frontbench of the Opposition.

He could change a standard himself if he sought to do so. But we will see none of that from the Leader of the Opposition because on these questions he is incapable of change. Capable of double standards, but incapable of change. His double standards should not rule this Parliament.

Good sense, common sense, proper process is what should rule this Parliament. That's what I believe is the path forward for this Parliament, not the kind of double standards and political game-playing imposed by the Leader of the Opposition now looking at his watch because apparently a woman's spoken too long.

I've had him yell at me to shut up in the past, but I will take the remaining seconds of my speaking time to say to the Leader of the Opposition I think the best course for him is to reflect on the standards he's exhibited in public life, on the responsibility he should take for his public statements; on his close personal connection with Peter Slipper, on the hypocrisy he has displayed in this House today.

And on that basis, because of the Leader of the Opposition's motivations, this Parliament today should reject this motion and the Leader of the Opposition should think seriously about the role of women in public life and in Australian society because we are entitled to a better standard than this.

(*Sydney Morning Herald* 2012)

Global gender gap

A series of reports by the World Economic Forum (WEF) chronicle the national gender gaps of 136 countries in terms of economic, political, education and health-based criteria. The WEF provides a 'Global Gender Gap Index' (begun in

2006). In 2013, Iceland led the rankings, Finland came in at second position, Norway at third and Sweden in fourth. The Philippines and Nicaragua sat in fifth and tenth positions respectively, while the UK ranked 18th, the USA 23rd and Australia 24th.

GTFO

An internet acronym for 'get the fuck out', GTFO is usually used to express exasperation or displeasure at perceived stupidity or incompetence. It is also used in response to something that is unwelcome.

KPMG

A global accountancy (professional services) firm.

Multitasking (with media)

Especially attributed to younger people, Millennials (Generation Y) and Generation Z, and students (although probably as common among Gen X), there has been some debate as to whether multitasking with media devices (for example, 'watching' television while checking the internet on a mobile device) is bad for us, with recent studies suggesting that 'excessive' media multitasking is linked to 'cognitive, social and emotional problems' and a recent British study linking media multitasking with brain structure differences (specifically, lower grey matter density in the anterior cingulated cortex of those who often use several media devices at the same time). Previous research has linked high levels of media-multitasking with depression, anxiety and poor attention when faced with distractions, although the authors of this research note that they have established a link, not cause and effect (*Medical News Today* 2014).

Neoliberalism

Neoliberal discourse is pervasive across institutions and practices of governance and advocates for the capitalist 'free market' as the only reliable distributor of scarce resources across economic policy-making. Neoliberalism is based on the assumed centrality of marketization, privatization, deregulation and flexibilization and expounds the 'opening up' (through marketization, liberalization and industrialization) of national economies to world monetary flows. In times of crisis, neoliberal policy-makers have promoted strategies of so-called economic austerity, such as cuts in welfare benefits and freezes in public sector wages, which are associated with the enforced contraction of the public sector.

New age man

Although the New Age movement emerged in the 1970s as a Western spiritual movement, 'new age men', 'new age guys' or the 'sensitive new age guy (SNAG)' emerged most clearly in the 1990s, particularly as a *Sex and The City* favourite, and liked to talk about his motivations, feelings and concerns (hence the 'new age' aspect). Some have argued that the first appearance of the (hyper-masculine, sexist, homophobic and consumption-obsessed) 'lad' was a reaction to the SNAG, fuelled by men's magazines such as *Maxim*, *FHM* and *Loaded*. The 1990s new age man is a little metrosexual (in the sense of being in touch with his feminine side), but more sensitive, than the 'average' man. Dense clusters of SNAGs, can be found, according to the *Urban Dictionary*, at women's rallies. Since SNAGs exhibit such 'feminine' characteristics as timidity and sensitivity they have 'lost the core qualities of Masculine Man' because they were 'raised by emancipated females and a society that told [them] how important it is to be nice to women' (Pua Wiki 2014). They are, the Pua Wiki suggests, essentially 'nice guys' or 'wussies' (ibid.). Once considered a refreshing change for those critical of 'traditional' manhood and its emotional repressiveness, the new age man has been subjected to some ridicule and criticism, especially from those sceptical of men parroting gender equality rhetoric as a tool of seduction.

New media

Chiefly, any media that is internet based or reliant, such as websites, computer multimedia, video games, DVDs and blogs, is considered 'new media'. Most of the technologies described as 'new media' are digital and 'new media' provide on-demand, accessible content, often accessed through digital devices such as smartphones or tablets. User feedback is often immediate and interactive and users participate in content generation, which means that content is 'democratic' and also often uncensored at the time of generation.

Old media

This refers to the media that existed before the advent of the internet, and includes broadcast television and radio, newspapers, books, magazines and cinema (although many of these media now regularly use the internet). Where 'new media' have an intrinsically dynamic quality, 'old media' are generally considered more static and driven 'from above'.

Pink collar

'Pink collar', as opposed to 'blue' (skilled or unskilled manual labour) or 'white' (office-related) collar, refers to types of employment traditionally associated with female workers, particularly low-paid jobs and jobs in the service industry, nursing, primary school education and secretarial work.

Social media

User generated and internet based, social media involves the creation, exchange and interaction of information and ideas across various virtual spaces. These include social networking sites such as Facebook, professional networking sites such as Linked In, blogs and microblogs such as Twitter and Tumblr, content communities such as YouTube, collaborations such as Wikipedia, virtual inspiration 'boards' such as Pinterest, virtual worlds such as Second Life and game worlds such as Borderlands and Half-Life. Social media depend on mobile and web-based technologies and differ from traditional media in a number of ways, particularly in terms of the extent of their reach (and therefore, perhaps, their influence), dynamism, permanence and regulation.

Women in Refrigerators

This pervasive popular culture trope refers to a popular culture source or artefact's penchant for using the abuse, mutilation or murder of a female character as a motivating device for the (male) protagonist. The trope's name originated in a *Green Lantern* comic book storyline, which saw the hero's girlfriend stuffed, quite literally, into a refrigerator. It has since been popularized by comic book writer Gail Simone and her website, Women in Refrigerators, which is dedicated to the 'superheroines who have been either depowered, raped, or cut up and stuck in the refrigerator' (Women in Refrigerators 2013).

BIBLIOGRAPHY

A Woman Against Feminism (2009) 'A Woman Against Feminism', accessed March 2009, http://awomanagainstfeminism.blogspot.com/.

The Achilles Effect (2010) 'How Does Female Sexualization Affect Young Boys?', *The Achilles Effect*, 28 September, accessed March 2014, http://www.achilleseffect.com/2010/09/how-does-female-sexualisation-affect-young-boys/.

Acton Foundation for Entrepreneurial Excellence (2009) 'Logic, Emotion, Intuition and the Marketplace', *Action Foundation for Entrepreneurial Excellence*, accessed February 2014, http://alumni.actonmba.org/PDFs/Fall_Semester/Entrepreneurial_Journey/Logic%20Emotion%20Intuition%20and%20the%20Marketplace-%2007.pdf.

Adorno, T. and Horkheimer, M. (1999) 'The Culture Industry: Enlightenment as Mass Deception', in S. During (ed.) *The Cultural Studies Reader*, 2nd edn, London: Routledge, pp. 67–90.

Aitken, R. (2010) '"To the End of the Earth": Culture, Visuality, and the Embedded Economy', in J. Best and M. Paterson (eds) *Cultural Political Economy*, London: Routledge, pp. 29–43.

Alexander, V. (2013) 'Let's Ban Weddings and, While We're at It, Baby Showers Too', *The Huffington Post*, 12 December, accessed February 2014, http://www.huffingtonpost.com/valerie-alexander/lets-ban-weddings-and-baby-showers_b_4428778.html.

Alvarez, S. (1998) 'Feminismos Latinamericanos: Reflexiones Teóricas y Perspectives Comparatives', in M. Hawkesworth, 'The Semiotics of Premature Burial: Feminism in a Postfeminist Age', *Signs*, 29(4): 961–85.

Amaya, M. (2013) 'Jennifer Lee: Disney's First Female Feature Animation Director', *Rotoscopers*, 16 November, http://www.rotoscopers.com/2013/11/16/jennifer-lee-first-disney-female-director.

Andersen, N.A. (2003) *Discursive Analytical Strategies: Understanding Foucault, Koselleck, Laclau, Luhmann*, Bristol: Policy Press.

Angry Harry (n.d.) *Angry Harry* Blog Page, accessed March 2009, http://www.angryharry.com/.

Anti-Feminism Page (n.d.) *Anti-Feminism* Blog Page, accessed March 2009, http://www.jtest28.com/Anti-feminismpage.html.

Anti-Feminist UK (n.d.) *Anti-Feminist UK* Blog Page, accessed March 2009, http://anti-feminist-uk.blogspot.com/.

212 Bibliography

Apple (2005) 'Sombitch', *Urban Dictionary*, 25 April, http://www.urbandictionary.com/define.php?term=Sombitch.

Aronson, P. (2003) 'Feminists or "Postfeminists"? Young Women's Attitudes Toward Feminism and Gender Relations', *Gender and Society*, 17(6): 903–22.

ASA (2007) 'What You Looking At? Drawing the Line on Violence in Advertising', *Event Report of the Advertising Standards Authority*, 21 November, accessed July 2009, http://www.asa.org.uk/~/media/Files/ASA/Reports/ASAViolenceinAdsEventReport21Nov07.ashx.

Ashtari, S. (2013) 'Rush Limbaugh Slams Democrats for Turning Women "Into Abortion Machines"', *Huffington Post*, 6 November, http://www.huffingtonpost.com/2013/11/06/rush-limbaugh-abortion-machines_n_4228659.html

Atkinson, C. (2012) 'Chiller Theatre: Movie Attendance Sinks to 1995 Level', *New York Times*, 24 July, accessed January 2013, http://www.nypost.com/p/news/business/chiller_theater_ueJY1P6EzJQ9tjkStXgh0O.

Aune, K. and Redfern, C. (2010) *Reclaiming the F Word: The New Feminist Movement*, London: Zed Books.

Australian Bureau of Statistics (ABS) (2010) 'Attendance at Selected Cultural Venues and Events, Australia, 2009–10 Report No. 4114.0', 21 December, accessed January 2013, http://www.abs.gov.au/ausstats/abs@.nsf/Products/4114.0~2009-10~Main+Features~Characteristics+of+persons+attending?OpenDocument.

Australian Bureau of Statistics (ABS) (2011a) 'Arts and Culture in Australia: A Statistical Overview, 2011', 19 December, accessed January 2013, http://www.abs.gov.au/ausstats/abs@.nsf/Products/4F45E5DB10D157FECA257968000CB4F5?opendocument.

Australian Bureau of Statistics (ABS) (2011b) 'Arts and Culture in Australia: A Statistical Overview, 2011 Report No. 4172.0', 19 December, accessed January 2013, http://www.abs.gov.au/ausstats/abs@.nsf/Products/C1C150105240CC44CA257968000CB657?opendocument.

AustralianPolitics.com (2013) 'The Blue Tie Speech: Prime Minister's Address to Women For Gillard', 11 June, accessed March 2014, http://australianpolitics.com/2013/06/11/women-for-gillard-speech.html#sthash.Yw8VINkm.dpuf.

Ayers, M. (2013) 'Q&A: Emily Ratajkowski on "Blurred Lines" and Her Song of the Summer', *Esquire* Magazine, 22 July, accessed March 2014, http://www.esquire.com/blogs/culture/emily-ratajkowski-interview-blurred-lines.

Bagnato, D. (2013) 'Feminism 101: What in the World is a "Riot Grrrl"?', *Lip Magazine*, 15 August, accessed March 2014, http://lipmag.com/culture/feminism-101-what-in-the-world-is-a-riot-grrrl/.

Bailey, J. (2013) 'Guess What: Hollywood's "Bridesmaids" Revolution Never Happened', *Flavorwire*, 14 May, accessed February 2014, http://flavorwire.com/391410/guess-what-hollywoods-bridesmaids-revolution-never-happened.

Bakhtin, M.M. (2004) 'The Problem of Speech Genres', in A. Jaworski and N. Coupland (eds) *The Discourse Reader*, London and New York: Routledge, pp. 121–32.

Ballou, E. (2014) 'Sexism in Gaming Culture: Women Can Be Gamers Too, and Don't You Forget It', *Bustle*, 23 July, accessed August 2014 http://www.bustle.com/articles/32730-sexism-in-gaming-culture-women-can-be-gamers-too-and-dont-you-forget-it.

Barbaric Poetries (2012) 'Dolce and Gabbana: Do These Advertisements Go Too Far?', *Barbaric Poetries: Blog of Aestheticized Violence*, 9 May, accessed November 2014, http://barbaricpoetries.blogspot.com.au/2012/05/dolce-gabbana-do-these-advertisements.html.

Bargad, A. and Hyde, J. (1991) 'A Study of Feminist Identity Development in Women', *Psychology of Women Quarterly*, 15: 181–201.

Bibliography   **213**

Barthes, R. (1999) 'The Rhetoric of the Image' (originally published 1964), in J. Evans and S. Hall (eds) *Visual Culture: The Reader*, London: Sage, pp. 33–40.

Bartle, P. (2009) 'The Meaning of Culture', *Community Empowerment Collective*, 28 June, accessed September 2009, http://www.scn.org/cmp/modules/per-culm.htm.

BBC (2007) 'D&G Criticised Over Knife Adverts', *BBC News*, 10 January, accessed July 2009, http://news.bbc.co.uk/2/hi/uk_news/6247347.stm.

BBC (2012) 'Movie-Going Declines in Some Eurozone Countries', *BBC News*, 18 June, accessed January 2013, http://www.bbc.co.uk/news/entertainment-arts-18483804.

Beauty Redefined (2011) 'Bright Young Thing', *Beauty Redefined*, 25 March, accessed June 2013, http://www.beautyredefined.net/victorias-little-secret/.

Beck, L. (2013) 'Lena Dunham Loves Feminism, Paper Date Planners and Cadbury Cream Eggs (Join the Club)', *Jezebel*, 15 March, accessed November 2013, http://jezebel.com/5990694/lena-dunham-loves-feminism-paper-date-planners-and-cadbury-cream-eggs-join-the-club.

Being Feminist (2012) 'The Uncool Civil Rights Movement', *Being Feminist* Official Blog, 24 September, accessed June 2013, http://beingfeministblog.wordpress.com/2012/09/24/the-uncool-civil-rights-movement/

Belinkie, M. (2010) 'Christopher Nolan has a "Woman Problem"', *Overthinking It*, 29 July, accessed 26 October 2014, http://www.overthinkingit.com/2010/07/29/christopher-nolan-feminism/.

Bell, R. (2007) 'Our Sexual Obsession Damages Boys as well as Girls', *The Independent*, 22 February, accessed June 2013, http://www.independent.co.uk/voices/commentators/rachel-bell-our-sexual-obsession-damages-boys-as-well-as-girls-437307.html.

Bellasugar (n.d.) 'Tom Ford For Men Advertising Campaign', image, accessed July 2009, http://www.bellasugar.com/626923.

Benjamin, W. (1972) 'A Short History of Photography', *Screen*, 13(1): 5–26.

Bergeron, S. (2001) 'Political Economy Discourses of Globalization and Feminist Politics', *Signs: Journal of Women in Culture and Society*, 26(4): 983–1006.

Berlatsky, N. (2011a) '"Twilight" vs. "Hunger Games": Why Do So Many Grown-Ups Hate Bella?', *The Atlantic*, 15 November, accessed October 2012, http://www.theatlantic.com/entertainment/archive/2011/11/twilight-vs-hunger-games-why-do-so-many-grown-ups-hate-bella/248439/.

Berlatsky, N. (2011b) 'Tween Horror', *Hooded Utilitarian*, 18 November, accessed October 2012, http://hoodedutilitarian.com/2011/11/tween-horror/.

Best, J. and Paterson, M. (eds) (2010) *Cultural Political Economy*, London and New York: Routledge.

Beynon, J. (2002) *Masculinities and Culture*, Buckingham, UK: Open University Press.

BIC (n.d.) 'BIC® for Her', image, accessed January 2014, http://www.bicworld.com/en/products/details/421/bic-for-her.

Bigelow, K. (1990) 'Kathryn Bigelow Discusses Role of "Seductive Violence" in Her Films', *The Tech: Online Edition*, 16 March, accessed September 2014, http://tech.mit.edu/V110/N13/int.13a.html.

Black Cat Reviews (2012) '*The Dark Knight* (2008)', *Black Cat Reviews*, 20 July, accessed June 2013, http://blackcatreviews.tumblr.com/tagged/Aaron-Eckhart.

Blakeley, K. (2005) 'William Shakespeare, Millionaire', *Forbes*, 27 October, accessed March 2014, http://www.forbes.com/2005/10/26/shakespeare-william-earnings_deadceleb05_cz_kb_1027shakespeare.html.

Bleiker, R. (2001) 'The Aesthetic Turn in International Political Theory', *Millennium: Journal of International Studies*, 30(2): 509–33.

Bleiker, R. (2009) *Aesthetics and World Politics*, Basingstoke: Palgrave Macmillan.

214 Bibliography

Bleiker, R. and Hutchison, E. (2008) 'Fear No More: Emotions and World Politics ', *Review of International Studies*, 34: 115–35.

Bolotin, S. (1982) 'Voices from the Post-Feminist Generation', *The New York Times Magazine*, 17 October, accessed February 2015, http://www.nytimes.com/1982/10/17/magazine/voices-from-the-post-feminist-generation.html

Box Office Mojo (2013) accessed February 2014, http://boxofficemojo.com.

Bricken, R. (2008) 'The 10 Worst Women in Refrigerators (i.e. Cases of Violence Against Women in Comics)', *Topless Robot*, 30 June, accessed June 2013, http://www.toplessrobot.com/2008/06/the_10_worst_women_in_refridgerators_ie_cases_of_v.php.

Brittain, M. (2013) 'How Australia is Changing the Way that We Consume Media', *DBC2*, 15 June, accessed September 2013, http://www.dbc2.com.au/blog/how-australia-is-changing-the-way-that-we-consume-media/.

Bronfen, E. (2005) 'Reality Check: Image Affects and Cultural Memory', *Differences: A Journal of Feminist Cultural Studies*, 17(1): 20–46.

Brooks, A. (1997) *Postfeminisms: Feminism, Cultural Theory, and Cultural Forms*, London and New York: Routledge.

Butler, J. (1990) *Gender Trouble: Feminism and the Subversion of Identity*, London: Routledge.

Byrne, Z.S., Felker, S., Vacha-Haase, T. and Rickard, K.M. (2011) 'A Comparison of Responses on the Attitudes Toward Women Scale and Attitudes Toward Feminism Scale: Is There a Difference Between College-Age and Later-Life Adults with the Original Norms?', *Measurement and Evaluation in Counseling and Development*, 44: 248–64.

Callot, A. (2009) 'The Expired Feminism of Joss Whedon', *Overthinking It*, 23 December 2009, accessed February 2014, http://www.overthinkingit.com/2009/12/23/joss-whedon-feminism/.

Carver, T. (2002) 'Discourse Analysis and the Linguistic Turn', *European Political Science*, 2(1): 50–53.

Carver, T. (2010) 'Cinematic Ontologies and Viewer Epistemologies: Knowing International Politics as Moving Images', *Global Society*, 24(3): 421–31.

Carver, T. and Hyvärinen, M. (eds) (1997) *Interpreting the Political: New Methodologies*, London and New York: Routledge.

Cast Iron Balcony (2009) 'The Spike-Heeled Feminist Jackboot of Doom!', *Cast Iron Balcony*, image, accessed February 2014, http://www.castironbalcony.com/2009/05/27/clive-james-is-a-massive-tool/.

Catalyst (2010) *The 2010 Catalyst Census: Fortune 500 Women Board Directors*, Catalyst, December, accessed July 2013, http://www.catalyst.org/knowledge/2010-catalyst-census-fortune-500-women-board-directors.

CBS News (2004) 'Women's March CBS', photograph, accessed June 2013, http://www.cbsnews.com/news/slim-fast-trims-whoopi-from-ads/.

CBS News (2009) 'No More Female Leads in Movies?', 9 October, http://www.cbsnews.com/news/no-more-female-leads-in-movies.

Channel Nine Television (Australia) (2009) 'Aussie Ladette to Lady', accessed July 2009, http://channelnine.ninemsn.com.au/aussieladettetolady/.

Chant, S. and McIlwaine, C. (2013) 'Gender, Urban Development and the Politics of Space', *E-International Relations*, 4 June, accessed February 2014, http://www.e-ir.info/2013/06/04/gender-urban-development-and-the-politics-of-space/.

Chemaly, S. (2014) '"Too Much Estrogen": The Golden Globes, Chris Christie and Men Who Don't Want to Share Culture', *Huffington Post*, 13 January, accessed April 2014, huffingtonpost.com/soraya-chemaly/too-much-estrogen-the-gol_b_4589941.html.

Bibliography **215**

Christopherson, S. (1994) 'The Fortress City: Privatized Spaces, Consumer Citizenship', in A. Amin (ed.) *Post-Fordism: A Reader*, Oxford: Blackwell, pp. 409–27.

Cif (2014) 'Always a Beautiful Ending', image, accessed March 2014, http://www.cifclean.co.uk.

Cochrane, K. (2010) 'Feminism is not finished', *The Guardian*, 24 July, accessed April 2013, http://www.theguardian.com/lifeandstyle/2010/jul/24/feminism-not-finished-not-uncool.

Cole, C.L. and Hribar, A. (1995) 'Celebrity Feminism: Nike Style Post-Fordism, Transcendence, and Consumer Power', *Sociology of Sport Journal*, 12: 347-69.

Coleman, L. (2007) 'The Gendered Violence of Development: Imaginative Geographies of Exclusion in the Imposition of Neo-liberal Capitalism', *British Journal of Politics and International Relations*, 9(2): 204–19.

Collective Shout (2012) 'Zoo Weekly: Because Chopping Women in Half is "Men's Lifestyle"', *Collective Shout*, accessed October 2013, http://www.collectiveshout.org/zoo_weekly_because_chopping_women_in_half_is_men_s_lifestyle.

Connell, R. (2009) *Gender*, 2nd edn, Cambridge: Polity.

Coontz, S. (2010) 'Why *Mad Men* is TV's Most Feminist Show', *Washington Post*, October 10, accessed July 2013, http://www.washingtonpost.com/wp-dyn/content/article/2010/10/08/AR2010100802662.html.

Crave Online (2012) 'Still from *Legally Blonde*', image, in W. Bibbiani, 'B-Movies Extended: The Top Ten Movie Bunnies', *Crave Online*, 17 December, accessed 30 October 2014, http://www.craveonline.com.au/film/articles/201777-b-movies-extended-the-top-ten-movie-bunnies.

D'Acci, J. (1994) *Defining Women: Television and the Case of Cagney and Lacey*, Chapel Hill: University of North Carolina Press.

Daily Mail (2007) 'Dolce and Gabbana Pulls Spanish Advertising After Uproar Over "Humiliating" Campaign', 13 March, accessed November 2014, http://www.dailymail.co.uk/news/article-442074/Dolce−Gabbana-pulls-Spanish-advertising-uproar-humiliating-campaign.html.

Daily News (2013) '2 Pussy Riot Members, Maria Alekhina and Nadezhda Tolokonnikova, Released from Prison in Russia', *Daily News*, 23 December, accessed Bebruary 2014, http://www.nydailynews.com/news/world/pussy-riot-member-released-prison-article-1.1556170.

Dalby, S. (2009) 'The Geopolitics of the International System and Globalization', paper presented at the *International Studies Association Annual Meeting* 'Multidisciplinarity in International Studies' panel, 15, February.

Davidson, A. (2012) 'How Does the Film Industry Actually Make Money?', *New York Times*, 26 June, accessed 15 September 2013, http://www.nytimes.com/2012/07/01/magazine/how-does-the-film-industry-actually-make-money.html?_r=0.

Davidson, N. (1988) *The Failure of Feminism*, Buffalo, NY: Prometheus Books.

Davies, M. (2010) 'Works, Products, and the Division of labour: Notes for a Cultural and Political Economic Critique', in J. Best and M. Paterson (eds) *Cultural Political Economy*, London: Routledge, pp. 48–64.

De Brito, S. (2012a) 'The "Yeah, But" Speech', *The Sydney Morning Herald*, 17 October, accessed July 2013, http://www.smh.com.au/executive-style/culture/blogs/all-men-are-liars/the-yeah-but-speech-20121013-27jls.html#ixzz2AG9U9AFs.

De Brito, S. (2012b) 'Strange men', *Sydney Morning Herald*, 22 October, accessed July 2013, http://www.smh.com.au/executive-style/culture/blogs/all-men-are-liars/strange-men-20121022-28070.html-ixzz2AAOVnyOW.

Debord, G. (1992) *Society of the Spectacle*, Oakland: AK Press.

216 Bibliography

Deloitte (2012) *Vox Populi: State of the Media Democracy Survey: Australia's media usage and preferences 2012*, accessed September 2013, http://www.deloitte.com/assets/Dcom-Australia/Local Assets/Documents/Industries/TMT/Vox Populi_State of the Media Democracy Survey.pdf.

Divine, M. (2009) 'Yearning to Liberate the Inner Lady', *Sydney Morning Herald*, 28 February, accessed July 2009, http://www.smh.com.au/federal-politics/yearning-to-liberate-the-inner-lady-20090227-8k7k.html.

Dockterman, E. (2013) 'TV's Strongest Female Characters Share One Stupid Flaw', *Time*, 10 October, accessed February 2014, http://entertainment.time.com/2013/10/10/tvs-strongest-female-characters-share-one-stupid-flaw/.

Douglas, S.J. (2010) *Enlightened Sexism: The Seductive Message that Feminism's Work is Done*, New York: Times Books.

Douglas, S.J. (2011) 'The Rise of Enlightened Sexism', *On The Issues* Magazine, Winter, accessed July 2012, http://www.ontheissuesmagazine.com/2011winter/2011_winter_Douglas.php.

Dowd, M. (1997) 'How to Snag 2000 Men', *The New York Times*, 2 July, accessed July 2009, http://www.nytimes.com/1997/07/02/opinion/how-to-snag-2000-men.html.

Downing, N.E. and Roush, K.L. (1985) 'From Passive Acceptance to Active Commitment: A Model of Feminist Identity Development for Women', *The Counseling Psychologist*, 13: 695–709.

Draper, J. (Jr) (2012) 'Negotiating the "Lavender Whiff": Gay and Straight Masculinities in Men's Lifestyle Magazines, 1990–2010', PhD dissertation submitted to the University of Michigan 2012, accessed October 2013, http://deepblue.lib.umich.edu/bitstream/handle/2027.42/95996/draper_1.pdf?sequence=1&isAllowed=y.

During, S. (ed.) (1999) *The Cultural Studies Reader*, 2nd edn, London and New York: Routledge.

Eagle Forum (n.d.) 'Eagle Forum', accessed March 2009, http://www.eagleforum.org/era/.

Eagle Forum (2002) 'Understanding Feminists and Their Fantasies', *Eagle Forum*, accessed July 2009, http://www.eagleforum.org/psr/2002/dec02/psrdec02.shtml.

Ebeling, K. (1990) 'The Failure of Feminism', *Newsweek*, 18 November, accessed February 2015, http://www.newsweek.com/failure-feminism-205870.

The Economist (2014a) Tumblr web-page, accessed February 2014, http://theeconomist.tumblr.com.

The Economist (2014b) Front Cover, 9 January, image, accessed April 2014, http://www.economist.com/printedition/covers/2014-01-09/ap-e-eu-la-me-na-uk.

The Economist (2014c) 'About Us', accessed February 2014, http://www.economist.com/help/about-us#About_Economistcom.

The Economist Group (2013) 'Media Information', accessed February 2014, http://www.economistgroupmedia.com/planning-tools/circulation/.

Eisenstein, H. (2009) *Feminism Seduced: How Global Elites Use Women's Labor and Ideas to Exploit the World*, Boulder, CO: Paradigm.

Elias, J. (2013) 'Davos Woman to the Rescue of Global Capitalism: Postfeminist Politics and Competitiveness Promotion at the World Economic Forum', *International Political Sociology*, 7(2): 152–69.

Elias, J. and Beasley, C. (2009) 'Hegemonic Masculinity and Globalization: "Transnational Business Masculinities" and Beyond', *Globalizations*, 6(2): 281–96.

Enerson, C. (2007) 'From the Right: Why Feminists are Irrelevant', *The Eagle*, 19 February, accessed January 2009, http://media.www.theeagleonline.com/media/storage/paper666/news/2007/02/19/Opinions/From-The.Right.why.Feminists.Are.Irrelevant-2727458.shtml.

Enloe, C. (2007) 'Forward', *British Journal of Politics and International Relations*, 9(2): 183–4.

The Entertainment Software Association (n.d.) accessed April 2014, http://www.theesa.com/.

Esquire (UK) (2009) accessed June 2009, http://www.esquire-magazine.co.uk/homepage/?T=1246871825&JTID=105569511&OGID=98&network=MSN.

Evans, J. and Hall, S. (1999) *Visual Culture: The Reader*, London: Sage.

Faludi, S. (1992) *Backlash: The Undeclared War Against Women*, London: Vintage.

Feminist Frequency (2011) 'Tropes vs. Women: #6 The Straw Feminist', *Feminist Frequency*, 23 September, accessed July 2013, http://www.feministfrequency.com/2011/09/tropes-vs-women-6-the-straw-feminist/.

Feminist Frequency (2012) 'Harassment, Misogyny and Silencing on YouTube', *Feminist Frequency*, 7 June, accessed July 2013, http://www.feministfrequency.com/2012/06/harassment-misogyny-and-silencing-on-youtube/.

Feminist Frequency (2013) 'Damsel in Distress (Part 1) Tropes vs Women', *Feminist Frequency*, 7 March, accessed July 2013, http://www.feministfrequency.com/2013/03/damsel-in-distress-part-1/.

Fernandes, R. (2013) 'Why Smart Girls Play Dumb!', *The Times of India*, 30 March, accessed November 2013, http://articles.timesofindia.indiatimes.com/2013-03-30/man-woman/29867973_1_insecure-women-boyfriend-or-husband-sms.

film ick (2006) 'Transcript of Joss Whedon's Equality Now Speech', *film ick*, 12 July, accessed November 2013, http://filmick.blogspot.com.au/2006/07/transcript-of-joss-whedons-equality.html.

Fine, C. (2010) *Delusions of Gender: The Real Science Behind Sex Differences*, New York: W.W. Norton & Co.

Fischer, A.R. and Good, G.E. (1994) 'Gender, Self, and Others: Perceptions of the Campus Environment', *Journal of Counseling Psychology*, 41: 343–55.

Fischer, A.R, Tokar, D.M., Mergl, M.M., Good, G.E., Hill, M.S. and Blum, S.A. (2000) 'Assessing Women's Feminist Identity Development: Studies of Convergent, Discriminant, and Structural Validity', *Psychology of Women Quarterly*, 24: 15–29.

Foss, C.J. and Slaney, R.B. (1986) 'Increasing Nontraditional Career Choices in Women: Relation of Attitudes Toward Women and Response to a Career Intervention', *Journal of Vocational Behavior*, 28(3): 191–202.

Fraser, N. (2013) 'How Feminism Became Capitalism's Handmaiden, and How to Reclaim It', *The Guardian*, 14 October, accessed December 2013, http://www.theguardian.com/commentisfree/2013/oct/14/feminism-capitalist-handmaiden-neoliberal.

Freeman, N. (2014) 'Riot Grrrl: The Feminism of a New Generation', accessed April 2014, https://www.mtholyoke.edu/~freem20n/classweb/Message.html.

Frizell, S. (2014) 'Facebook is About to Lose 80% of Its Users, Study Says', *Time*, 21 January, accessed March 2014, http://time.com/1405/facebook-is-about-to-lose-80-of-its-users-study-says/.

Fudge, R. (2005) 'Everything You Always Wanted to Know About Feminism But Were Afraid to Ask', *Bitch Magazine*, accessed July 2013, http://bitchmagazine.org/article/everything-about-feminism-you-wanted-to-know-but-were-afraid-to-ask.

Gadzooks! (2010) 'The Deep Freeze: Christopher Nolan's Woman Problem', *Gadzooks!*, 31 July, accessed November 2013, http://rachelmariemohr.blogspot.com.au/2010/07/deep-freeze-christopher-nolans-woman_31.html.

Galifianakis, Z. (2010) 'Zach Galifianakis: Comedy's Sensitive, Sarcastic Sensation', 6 October, accessed September 2014, http://abcnews.go.com/Entertainment/zach-galifianakis-ferns-hangover-kind-funny-story/story?id=11807074&singlePage=true#.T4rmFbNabAw.

218 Bibliography

Gamble, C (2009) '8 TV Ads That Hate Women', *Cracked*, 11 February, accessed July 2013, http://www.cracked.com/article_17036_8-tv-ads-that-hate-women.html.

Garnham, N. (1999) 'Political Economy and Cultural Studies', in S. During (ed.) *The Cultural Studies Reader*, London: Routledge, pp. 492–503.

Geek Feminism Wiki (2014) accessed April 2014, http://geekfeminism.wikia.com/wiki/Geek_Feminism_Wiki.

GenderBender (2013) 'Gravity is the Mother of All Sci-Fi Duds: A Feminist Perspective', 17 October, accessed November 2013, http://talkbacker.com/movies/gravity-is-the-mother-of-all-sci-fi-duds-a-feminists-perspective/id=11576.

Geng, V. (1976) 'Requiem for the Women's Movement', *Harper's Magazine*, November, accessed April 2014, http://harpers.org/archive/1976/11/requiem-for-the-womens-movement/.

Gennis, S. (2013) 'The Secret to *Sleepy Hollow*'s Success is Abbie Mills', *TV Guide*, 4 November, accessed January 2014, http://www.tvguide.com/news/sleepy-hollow-abbie-1072972.aspx.

Germain, R.D. (2011) 'New Marxism and the Problem of Subjectivity: Towards a Critical and Historical International Political Economy', in S. Shields, I. Bruff and H. Macartney (eds) *Critical International Political Economy: Dialogue, Debate and Dissensus*, Basingstoke: Palgrave Macmillan, pp. 61–79.

Gifford, A. (2007) '15 Ads That Prove Sex Sells Best', *Inventor Spot*, accessed January 2009, http://inventorspot.com/articles/ads_prove_sex_sells_5576.

Gill, R. (2007) *Gender and the Media*, Cambridge: Polity.

GQ (2011) 'Mario Testino Retrospective', *GQ Australia*, 21 October, accessed November 2013, http://www.gq.com.au/gq+girls/girl+of+the+week/mario+testino+retrospective, 14887.

GQ (2014) 'Girl of the Week: Agent Provocateur vs. Victoria's Secret', *GQ Australia*, accessed January 2014, http://www.gq.com.au/girls/girl+of+the+week/agent+provocateur+vs+victoria+secret,19067.

Greaves, S. and Mercado, J. (2011) 'Print Ad Analysis: Passivity and Violence', 15 April, accessed February 2015, http://academic.reed.edu/anthro/adprojects/2011/greaves_mercado/Passivity%20and%20Violence%20Analysis.html.

Greenfield, B. (2013) 'Is This Film Feminist Enough? Swedish Theaters Add New Rating System', *Shine*, 6 November, accessed November 2013, http://shine.yahoo.com/healthy-living/is-this-film-feminist-enough–swedish-theaters-add-new-rating-system-202236913.html.

Griffen, V. (1989) 'Women, Development and Empowerment: A Pacific Feminist Perspective', report from the *Workshop on Women, Development and Empowerment*, Fiji, March 1987.

Griffin, P. (2007) 'Refashioning IPE: What and How Gender Analysis Teaches International Political Economy', *Review of International Political Economy*, 14(4): 719–36.

Griffin, P. (2009) *Gendering the World Bank: Neoliberalism and the Gendered Foundations of Global Governance*, Basingstoke: Palgrave Macmillan.

Griffin, P. (2013a) 'Deconstruction as Anti-Method', in L. Shepherd (ed.) *Critical Approaches to Security: An Introduction to Theories and Methods*, London and New York: Routledge, pp. 208–22.

Griffin, P. (2013b) Screen shot of author's Facebook newsfeed, image, author's file.

Griffin, P. (2014) Screen shot of searches related to 'feminists are' on www.google.com.au, image, author's file.

Grossberg, L. (1995) 'Cultural Studies vs. Political Economy: Is Anybody Else Bored with This Debate?', *Critical Studies in Mass Communication*, 12(1): 72–81.

Bibliography **219**

Guardian (2012) 'Motorola Media Engagement Barometer', image, accessed on 2 November 2014, http://www.theguardian.com/media-network/motorola-partner-zone/interactive/infographic-media-devices-home.

guNjap (2010) 'Mouse Pad With Wrist Support', photograph, accessed 30 October 2014, http://reggiocomics.wordpress.com/2010/08/02/wonder-festival-2010-summer-new-breast-mouse-pad-others/.

Hall, E.J. and Rodriguez, M.S. (2003) 'The Myth of Postfeminism', *Gender and Society*, 17(6): 878–902.

Hall, S. (1982) 'The Rediscovery of "Ideology": Return of the Repressed in Media Studies', in M. Gurevitch, T. Bennett, J. Curran and J. Woollacott (eds) *Culture, Society and the Media*, New York: Methuen, pp. 52–86.

Hall, S. (1986) 'Gramsci's Relevance for the Study of Race and Ethnicity', *Journal of Communications Inquiry*, 10(2): 5–27.

Hall, S. (1996) 'When Was the "Post-Colonial"? Thinking at the Limit', in L. Chambers and L. Curti (eds) *The Postcolonial Question*, London and New York: Routledge, pp. 242–60.

Hall, S. (1999) 'Encoding, Decoding', in S. During (ed.) *The Cultural Studies Reader*, 2nd edn, London: Routledge, pp. 507–17.

Halley, J. (2006) *Split Decisions: How and Why to Take a Break From Feminism*, Princeton, NJ: Princeton University Press.

Hallin, D.C. and Mancini, P. (2004) *Comparing Media Systems: Three Models of Media and Politics*, Cambridge: Cambridge University Press.

Hann, M. (2014) 'Britpop: A Cultural Abomination That Set Music Back', *The Guardian*, 25 April, accessed April 2014, http://www.theguardian.com/music/2014/apr/24/britpop-cultural-abomination-music-blur-oasis.

Harris, A. (2010) 'Mind the Gap: Attitudes and Emergent Feminist Politics Since the Third Wave', *Australian Feminist Studies*, 25(66): 475–84.

Harvey, D. (2008) 'The Right to the City', *New Left Review*, 53(Sept-Oct): 23–40.

Hawkesworth, M. (2004) 'The Semiotics of Premature Burial: Feminism in a Postfeminist Age', *Signs*, 29(4): 961–85.

Hearst (2014) '*Esquire*', accessed April 2014, http://www.hearst.com/magazines/esquire.

Heelas, P. (2002) 'Work Ethics, Soft Capitalism and the Turn to Life.', in P. du Gay and M. Pryke (eds) *Cultural Economy: Cultural Analysis and Commercial Life*, London: Sage, pp. 78–96.

Heldman, C. (2012) 'Sexual Objectification, Part 2: The Harm', *Ms.* Magazine Blog, 6 July, accessed November 2014, http://msmagazine.com/blog/2012/07/06/sexual-objectification-part-2-the-harm/.

Henderson, D. (2012) *Feminist Ryan Gosling: Feminist Theory as Imagined by Your Favorite Sensitive Movie Guy*, Philadelphia: Running Press.

Herold, S. and Knox, S. (2011) 'Letter to *USA Today*', *USA Today*, 31 October, http://usatoday30.usatoday.com/news/opinion/letters/story/2011-10-31/feminism-young-feminists/51019404/1.

Hess, A. (2011) 'Why Should Women Read *The Economist*?', *Good*, 12 November, accessed January 2014, http://magazine.good.is/articles/why-should-women-read-the-economist.

Higate, P. (2009) 'Putting "Mercenary Masculinities" on the Research Agenda', Department of Politics, University of Bristol Working Paper No. 03–09, accessed July 2010, http://www.bristol.ac.uk/politics/workingpapers/03-09phpaper.pdf.

Hinds, H. and Stacey, J. (2001) 'Imaging Feminism, Imaging Femininity: The Bra-Burner, Diana and the Woman Who Kills', *Feminist Media Studies*, 1: 153–77.

220 Bibliography

Hogan, H. (2013) 'How to Tell if You're a Feminist: An Easy Graphic Guide', *After Ellen*, 19 November, accessed November 2013, http://www.afterellen.com/how-to-tell-if-youre-a-feminist-an-easy-guide/11/2013/.

Hogeland, L.M. (1994) 'Fear of Feminism', *Ms. Magazine*, November/December, accessed February 2015, http://www.rapereliefshelter.bc.ca/learn/resources/fear-feminism-why-young-women-get-willies.

Hollows, J. (2000) *Feminism, Femininity and Popular Culture*, Manchester: Manchester University Press.

Hollows, J. and Moseley, R. (2006) *Feminism in Popular Culture*, Oxford: Berg.

Holmes, L. (2013) 'At the Movies, The Women Are Gone', *Monkey See*, 14 June, accessed November 2013, http://www.npr.org/blogs/monkeysee/2013/06/14/191568762/at-the-movies-the-women-are-gone.

Hooper, C. (2001) *Manly States: Masculinities, International Relations, and Gender Politics*, New York: Columbia University Press.

The Hoopla (2013) 'I Cannot Believe I Still Have to Protest This Shit', image, accessed November 2013, https://www.facebook.com/photo.php?fbid=544234525635453&set=a.181103431948566.45526.179775462081363&type=1.

Howells, R. (2003) *Visual Culture*, Cambridge: Polity Press.

Huffington Post (2010) 'Sarah Palin: Newsweek Cover Showing My Legs "Sexist"', 18 March, accessed February 2014, http://www.huffingtonpost.com/2009/11/17/sarah-palin-newsweek-cove_n_360334.html.

Huffington Post (2013) '10 Celebrities Who Say They Aren't Feminists', 17 December, http://www.huffingtonpost.com/2013/12/17/feminist-celebrities_n_4460416.html.

Hunter, R. (2013) 'Audiences are Ruining the Quiet Horror Movie Experience', *Film School Rejects*, 11 September, accessed November 2013, http://filmschoolrejects.com/tag/chaps-my-hide.

If It's Hip, It's Here (2007) 'Menacing or Marketing? D&G's Controversial Ad', 24 March, accessed November 2014, http://ifitshipitshere.blogspot.com.au/2007/03/menacing-or-marketing-d-controversial.html.

The Internet Movie Script Database (n.d.) *Legally Blonde* Shooting Draft, 31 July 2000, accessed January 2014, http://www.imsdb.com/scripts/Legally-Blonde.html.

Jayson, S. (2011) 'As NOW Marks 45 Years, is Feminism Over the Hill?', *USA Today*, 26 October, accessed July 2013, http://yourlife.usatoday.com/mind-soul/story/2011-10-26/As-NOW-marks-45-years-is-feminism-over-the-hill/50939774/1.

Jessop, B. and Oosterlynck, S. (2008) 'Cultural Political Economy: On Making the Cultural Turn Without Falling into Soft Economic Sociology', *Geoforum*, 39(3): 1155–69.

Jhally, S. (2009) 'Advertising at the Edge of the Apocolypse', in J. Turow and M. Mcallister (eds) *The Advertising and Consumer Culture Reader*, London and New York: Routledge, pp. 416–28.

Jones, A. (2010) *The Feminism and Visual Culture Reader*, 2nd edn, London and New York: Routledge.

Joyner, S. (2010) 'Why Networks Love Reality TV', *Investopedia*, 30 April, accessed July 2013, http://www.investopedia.com/financial-edge/0410/why-networks-love-reality-tv.aspx.

Kalb, J. (2004) 'Anti-Feminist Page', *Turnabout*, 12 February, accessed July 2009, http://antitechnocrat.net:8000/node/2.

Kaminer, W. (1993) 'Feminism's Identity Crisis', *The Atlantic*, 1 October, accessed February 2015, http://www.theatlantic.com/magazine/archive/1993/10/feminisms-identity-crisis/304921/

Kang, I. (2013) 'Blood-Boiler of the Day: TV Show Canceled for Having Too Many Smart, Interesting Girl Characters', *Indiewire*, 19 December, accessed February 2014, http://blogs.indiewire.com/womenandhollywood/blood-boiler-of-the-day-tv-show-canceled-for-having-too-many-smart-interesting-girl-characters.

Keller, J. (2010) '"I'm Not a Feminist... I Love Men": Rethinking Lady Gaga's Postfeminist Rhetoric and Its Potential for Social Change', *In Media Res*, 2 August, accessed February 2014, http://mediacommons.futureofthebook.org/imr/2010/08/01/im-not-feminist-i-love-men-rethinking-lady-gaga-s-postfeminist-rhetoric-and-its-potential.

Kerwin, A.M. (2010) '10 Trends That are Shaping Global Media Consumption', *Ad Age Global*, 6 December, accessed 15 October 2014, http://adage.com/article/global-news/10-trends-shaping-global-media-consumption/147470/.

Kesler, J. (2008a) 'Female Characters Exist to Promote Male Leads for Network Profits', *The Hathor Legacy*, 27 June, accessed July 2013, http://thehathorlegacy.com/female-characters-exist-to-promote-male-leads-for-network-profits/.

Kesler, J. (2008b) 'Why Film Schools Teach Screenwriters Not to Pass the Bechdel Test', *The Hathor Legacy*, 30 June, accessed July 2013, http://thehathorlegacy.com/why-film-schools-teach-screenwriters-not-to-pass-the-bechdel-test/.

Kesler, J. (2008c) 'Why Discriminate if It Doesn't Profit?', *The Hathor Legacy*, 9 July, accessed July 2013, http://thehathorlegacy.com/why-discriminate-if-it-doesnt-profit/.

Kesler, J. (2008d) 'The Misogynist Who Gets the Girls is a Male Fantasy', *The Hathor Legacy*, 22 April, accessed July 2013, http://thehathorlegacy.com/the-misogynist-who-gets-the-girls-is-a-male-fantasy/.

Kesler, J. (2011) 'Rape Culture and Male Entitlement to Sex', *The Hathor Legacy*, 1 March, accessed 26 October, http://thehathorlegacy.com/rape-culture-and-male-entitlement-to-sex/.

Kessler, A. (2012) 'It's a Man's Man's Man's World... The Cinema of Christopher Nolan', *The f Word*, 24 October, accessed July 2013, http://www.thefword.org.uk/reviews/2012/10/Films_of_Christopher_Nolan.

Khosla, R. (2009) 'Addressing Gender Concerns in India's Urban Renewal Mission', *UN Development Program* (UNDP India), accessed July 2013, http://www.undp.org/content/dam/india/docs/addressinggenderconcerns.pdf.

Kinchen, R. (2012) 'Death of the Feminist Dream', *The Australian*, 2 July, accessed July 2013, http://www.theaustralian.com.au/news/world/death-of-the-feminist-dream/story-fnb64oi6-1226413850603.

Kuchera, B. (2012) 'Games With Exclusively Female Heroes Don't Sell (Because Publishers Don't Support Them)', *Hammer Fist Gaming*, 21 November, accessed June 2013, http://www.hammerfistclan.com/forum/f14/games-exclusively-female-heroes-don-t-sell-because-publishers-don-t-support-552905/.

Kwik, P. (2009) 'Men and Women Use the Internet Differently', *The Tech Desk*, 15 April, http://www.tpltechnology.blogspot.com.au/2009/04/men-and-women-use-internet-differently.html.

Ladies Against Feminism (n.d.) 'Ladies Against Feminism', accessed July 2009, http://www.ladiesagainstfeminism.com/artman/publish/index.shtml.

Lang, N. (2013) 'The 10 Best Amazon Reviews of "BIC Pens For Her" So Far', *Thought Catalog*, 1 February, accessed January 2014, http://thoughtcatalog.com/nico-lang/2013/02/the-10-best-amazon-reviews-of-bic-pens-for-her-so-far/.

Lauzen, M.A. (2013) 'Gender @ the Movies: On-Line Film Critics and Criticism', *Centre for the Study of Women in Television and Film*, accessed April 2014, http://womenintvfilm.sdsu.edu/files/2013_Gender_at_the_Movies_Exec_Summ.pdf.

Lauzen, M.A. (2014) 'It's a Man's (Celluloid) World: On-Screen Representations of Female Characters in the Top 100 Films of 2013', *Centre for the Study of Women in Television and Film*, accessed April 2014, http://womenintvfilm.sdsu.edu/files/2013_It's_a_Man's_World_Report.pdf.

Le Marquand, S. (2013) 'In the Loop: Women Making News', *The Sunday Telegraph, Sunday Style Magazine*, 15 December.

222 Bibliography

Levy, A. (2006) *Female Chauvinist Pigs: Women and the Rise of Raunch Culture*, London: Pocket Books.

Lewis, P. and Woods, J. (2012) 'The Real Context: Sexism is Getting Worse', *The Drum*, 23 October, accessed July 2013, http://www.abc.net.au/news/2012-10-23/lewis-and-woods-sexism/4327520.

Liang, J. (2008) 'Hollywood's 5 Saddest Attempts at Feminism', *Cracked*, 1 September, accessed July 2013, http://www.cracked.com/article_16587_hollywoods-5-saddest-attempts-at-feminism.html.

Liggett, R. (2012) 'This House Would Ban Sexist Advertising', *International Debate Education Association*, accessed July 2013, http://idebate.org/es/node/17609.

Lindsay, G. (2010) 'Ad Age Insights: Global Media Habits 2010', November, accessed July 2013, http://www.greglindsay.org/articles/ad_age_insights_global_media_habits_2010/.

Lipschutz, R.D. (2010) *Political Economy, Capitalism and Popular Culture*, Plymouth: Rowman & Littlefield.

Liutongco, H. (2013) 'Sexism in the Video Game Industry', *Examiner*, 28 November, accessed March 2014, http://www.examiner.com/article/sexism-the-video-game-industry.

Lorde (2014) Interview with Tavi Gevinson, *Rookie Magazine*, 2 January, http://www.rookiemag.com/2014/01/lorde-interview.

Lunden, I. (2012) 'Nielsen: Women Watch More TV than Men, but Connected Games Consoles are Changing That', *Promaxbda*, 5 October, accessed February 2014, http://promaxbda.org/home/redirect?ID=23878dff-69cc-486d-a01f-057b0b690b7f.

Lury, C. (2011) *Consumer Culture*, 2nd edn, Cambridge: Polity.

Lyons, D. (2013) 'Seriously, Facebook, What is Up with These Obnoxious, Sexist Ads?', *readwrite*, 9 March, accessed March 2014, http://readwrite.com/2013/03/08/sexist-ads-on-facebook.

Lyttelton, O. (2012) 'Discuss: Does "Magic Mike" Prove That Female Audiences are Now More Reliable Than Hollywood's Staple Teen Boy Targets?', *Indiewire*, 2 July, accessed November 2013, http://blogs.indiewire.com/theplaylist/discuss-does-magic-mike-prove-that-female-audiences-are-now-more-reliable-that-hollywoods-staple-teen-boy-targets-20120702.

Macale, S. (2011) 'Social Media – Women Do It Longer, but Men Do the Talking', *The Next Web*, 22 September, accessed July 2013, http://thenextweb.com/socialmedia/2011/09/22/social-media-women-do-it-longer-but-men-do-the-talking/.

MacDonald, K. (2012) 'Are Gamers Really Sexist?', *The Guardian*, 6 March, accessed August 2014, http://www.theguardian.com/technology/gamesblog/2012/mar/06/are-gamers-really-sexist.

Mackay, F. (2011) 'A Movement of Their Own: Voices of Young Feminist Activists in the London Feminist Network', *Interface: A Journal for and About Social Movements*, 3(2): 152–79.

MacNab, G. (2014) '"I Don't Want to be Liked": Inna Shevchenko, Leader of Women's Rights Group Femen, Talks Dictators, Documentaries and Death Threats', *The Independent*, 17 January, accessed April 2014, http://www.independent.co.uk/news/people/profiles/i-dont-want-to-be-liked-inna-shevchenko-leader-of-womens-rights-group-femen-talks-dictators-documentaries-and-death-threats-9062734.html.

Maddison, S. (2004) 'Young Women in the Australian Women's Movement', *International Feminist Journal of Politics*, 6(2): 234–56.

Malkin, M. (2004) 'A Message for Ashley Judd', *Townhall.com*, 28 April, http://townhall.com/columnists/michellemalkin/2004/04/28/a_message_for_ashley_judd/page/full.

Martinez, V. (2013) 'On "Sleepy Hollow" and Nicole Beharie's "Abbie Mills" Saving the World', *Indiewire*, 7 October, accessed February 2014, http://blogs.indiewire.com/shadowandact/on-sleepy-hollow-and-nicole-beharies-abbie-mills-saving-the-world.

Mascia-Lees, F.E. and Sharpe, P. (2000) *Taking a Stand in a Postfeminist World: Toward an Engaged Cultural Criticism*, New York: State University of New York Press.

MasculistFeminist (2013) 'The Transformation of Feminism Into a Hate Movement and Their Censorship of Free Speech', *MasculistFeminist*, 27 May, accessed 26 October 2014, http://masculistfeminist.hubpages.com/hub/The-Transformation-Feminism-Into-A-Hate-Movement-And-Censorship-Of-Free-Speech.

McCann, J. and Wilson, J. (2012) 'Representation of Women in Australian Parliaments', 7 March, accessed February 2014, http://www.aph.gov.au/About_Parliament/Parliamentary_Departments/Parliamentary_Library/pubs/BN/2011-2012/Womenin parliament#_Toc318895766.

McDougall, S. (2013) 'I Hate Strong Female Characters', *New Statesman*, 15 August, accessed November 2013, http://www.newstatesman.com/culture/2013/08/i-hate-strong-female-characters.

McDowell, L. (1997) *Capital Culture: Gender at Work in the City*, Oxford: Blackwell.

McKay, J. (2005) 'Enlightened Racism and Celebrity Feminism in Contemporary Sports Advertising Discourse', in S.J. Jackson and D.L. Andrews (eds) *Sport, Culture and Advertising: Identities, Commodities and the Politics of Representation*, London: Routledge, pp. 81–99.

McRobbie, A. (2009) *The Aftermath of Feminism: Gender, Culture and Social Change*, London: Sage.

Meanwhile in Australia (n.d.) image, accessed April 2012, https://www.facebook.com/MeanwhileInAustralia.

Medical News Today (2014) 'Multitasking with Media Devices Linked to Brain Changes', *Medical News Today*, 26 September, accessed September 2014, http://www.medicalnewstoday.com/articles/283059.php.

Merskin, D. (2005) 'Where are the Clothes? The Pornographic Gaze in Mainstream American Fashion Advertising', in T. Riechert and J. Lambiase (eds) *Sex in Consumer Culture: The Erotic Content of Media and Marketing*. London: Lawrence Erlbaum Associates, pp. 199–218.

Meyer, S (2011) 'How to Combine Two Wrongs to Make a Profit', *Cracked*, 25 February, accessed July 2013, http://www.cracked.com/article_19059_how-to-combine-two-wrongs-to-make-profit-5Bcomic5D.html.

Mirzoeff, N. (2002) (ed.) *The Visual Culture Reader*, 2nd edn, London: Routledge.

Misciagno, P. (1997) *Rethinking Feminist Identification: The Case for De Facto Feminism*, Westport, CT: Praeger.

Milestone, K. and Meyer, A. (2012) *Gender and Popular Culture*, Cambridge: Polity.

Miller, D. (2012) *Consumption and Its Consequences*, Cambridge: Polity.

Mirk, S. (2014) 'Blockbuster Films Featuring Actual Female Characters Made Serious Money in 2013', *Bitch* magazine, 6 January, http://bitchmagazine.org/post/blockbuster-films-featuring-actual-female-characters-made-serious-money-in-2013.

Miss Representation (2011). Documentary. Dir.: J. Siebel Newsom, K. Acquaro. USA.

Moran, A. (1998) *Copycat TV: Globalization, Program Formats, and Cultural Identity*, Luton, UK: University of Luton Press.

Moran, C. (2012) *How To Be a Woman*, London: Ebury.

Morris, L. (2010) 'Feminism Turns Capitalist', *Sydney Morning Herald*, October 23, accessed July 2013, http://www.smh.com.au/executive-style/executive-women/feminism-turns-capitalist-20101022-16xxn.html.

Mosco, V. (2009) *The Political Economy of Communication*, 2nd edn, London: Sage.

Moss, C. (2007) 'D&G Launch Racy New Ad Campaign', *Female First*, 30 August, accessed April 2013, http://www.femalefirst.co.uk/lifestyle-fashion/stylenews/Dolce+Gabbana-3836.html.

224 Bibliography

MRW (2012) 'Industry Statistics', *Media Report to Women*, March, accessed November 2013, http://www.mediareporttowomen.com/statistics.htm.

Ms. Magazine (2009) Special Inaugural Issue Cover, Winter 2009, accessed July 2013, http://www.msmagazine.com/winter2009/index.asp.

Mulkerrins, J. (2013) 'Girls' Lena Dunham: Women Saying "I'm Not a Feminist" is My Greatest Pet Peeve', *Metro (UK)*, 14 January, http://metro.co.uk/2013/01/14/lena-dunham-the-fact-my-girls-character-is-not-a-size-4-is-meaningful-3348636/.

Mullinger, J. (2012) '100 Best Funny Jokes in the World', Milton Jones 16/28, *GQ Magazine*, 13 April, accessed May 2013, http://www.gq-magazine.co.uk/entertainment/articles/2012-04/19/100-best-funny-jokes-in-the-world/viewgallery/15.

Navi Dean (2010) 'MY Feminism', accessed October 2012, http://navi-dean.tumblr.com/post/33669618879/my-feminism.

Nessman, R. (2013) 'India Passes Strict New Sexual Violence Laws After Gang Rape Outrage', *News.com.au*, 22 March, accessed March 2014, http://www.news.com.au/world-news/india-passes-strict-new-sexual-violence-laws-after-gang-rape-outrage/story-fndir2ev-1226603057289

Newemotion (2007) 'Dolce and Gabbana Women's Fall/Winter 2007–2008', accessed July 2009, http://www.newemotion.com/fashion.php?ProdID=333.

News.com.au (2014) 'Women Earn Less Than Men as Gender Gap Grows', 15 August, accessed September 2014, http://www.news.com.au/finance/women-earn-less-than-men-as-gender-gap-grows/story-e6frfm1i-1227024676703.

Nielsen (2011) 'Australian Media Consumption', *The Australian Online Consumer Landscape*, March.

Nielsen (2012) 'Global Report: Multi-Screen Media Usage', 15 May, accessed September 2013, http://www.nielsen.com/us/en/newswire/2012/global-report-multi-screen-media-usage.html.

Not Another Wave (2012) 'A Feminist Review: *The Dark Knight Rises*', *Not Another Wave*, 22 July, accessed September 2013, http://notanotherwave.blogspot.com.au/2012/07/a-feminist-review-dark-knight-rises.html.

O'Brien, R. (2000) 'Labour and IPE,' in R. Palan (ed.) *Global Political Economy: Contemporary Theories*, London: Routledge, pp. 89–99.

O'Leary, S. and Reilly, J. (2012) 'The Big Feminst BUT', *Kickstarter*, accessed July 2013, https://www.kickstarter.com/projects/832892268/the-big-feminist-but/posts/364072.

O'Sullivan, T. (2007) 'Advertising Goes to the Cinema', *Open Learn*, 26 July, accessed July 2013, http://www.open.edu/openlearn/history-the-arts/culture/media-studies/advertising-goes-the-cinema.

Odell, A (2011) '*The Economist* Asks: "Why Should Women Read *The Economist*?"', 10 November, accessed July 2013, http://nymag.com/thecut/2011/11/economist-asks-why-women-should-read-them.html.

Oliver, M.B. and Kalyanaraman, S. (2005) 'Using Sex to Sell Movies: A Content Analysis of Movie Trailers', in T. Riechert and J. Lambiase (eds) *Sex in Consumer Culture: The Erotic Content of Media and Marketing*, London: Lawrence Erlbaum Associates, pp. 13–30.

Open University (2006) 'How do Adverts Get Made?', *OpenLearn*, 7 July, accessed February 2014, http://www.open.edu/openlearn/money-management/management/business-studies/how-do-adverts-get-made.

Osgerby, B. (2003) 'A Pedigree of the Consuming Male: Masculinity Consumption and the American "Leisure Class"', in B. Benwell (ed.) *Masculinity and Men's Lifestyle Magazines*, Oxford: Blackwell, pp. 57–86.

Overbeek, H. (2000) 'Transnational Historical Materialism: Theories of Transnational Class Formation and World Order', in R. Palan (ed.) *Global Political Economy: Contemporary Theories*, London and New York: Routledge, pp. 168–83.

Pahle, R. (2013) 'Legendary Pictures Turned Down a Movie Because Its Main Character is a Female Action Hero', *The Mary Sue*, 21 August, accessed November 2013, http://www.themarysue.com/legendary-pictures-legend-of-the-red-reaper/.

Palan, R. (ed.) (2000) *Global Political Economy: Contemporary Theories*, London: Routledge.

Passey, K. (2012) 'I Think I'm Addicted to Feminist Media Criticism', image, accessed June 2013, http://karapassey.tumblr.com/post/17857832011/everything-makes-me-grumpy.

Peirce, C. (1931–58) 'The Icon, Index and Symbol', in C. Hartshorne and P. Weiss (eds) *Collected Papers*, Cambridge, MA: Harvard University Press, pp. 156–73.

People Against Sexist Advertising (2010) 'Airbag by Porsche', image, accessed November 2013, https://www.facebook.com/photo.php?fbid=390085213993&set=a.390085208993.167645.246436803993&type=1&theater.

Pérez-Peña, R. (2008) 'Amid Market Turmoil, Some Journalists Try to Tone Down Emotion', *New York Times*, 22 September, accessed January 2014, http://www.nytimes.com/2008/09/22/business/media/22press.html?scp=1&sq=emotion%20market&st=cse.

Phillips, K.M. and Reay, B. (2011) *Sex Before Sexuality: A Premodern History*, Cambridge: Polity.

Piascik, C. (2012) 'Rush Limbaugh, It Was the Feminism' image, accessed July 2013, http://chrispiascik.com/2012/10/

Pistelli, J. (2008) '*The Dark Knight*: Hollywood's Terror Dream', *Dissident Voice*, 26 July, accessed June 2013, http://dissidentvoice.org/2008/07/the-dark-knight-hollywood's-terror-dream/.

Poniewozik, J. (2012) 'Dead Tree Alert: Brave New Girls', *Time*, 5 April, accessed July 2013, http://entertainment.time.com/2012/04/05/dead-tree-alert-brave-new-girls/.

Pozner, J.L. (2004) 'The Unreal World', *Ms.*, Fall, accessed July 2013, http://www.msmagazine.com/fall2004/unrealworld.asp.

Pozner, J.L. (2010) 'Why Does Reality TV Present Women as Marriage-Obsessed Bimbos', accessed April 2013, http://www.alternet.org/story/149206/why_does_reality_tv_present_women_as_marriage_obsessed_bimbos.

Pozner, J.L. (2011) 'Reality TV (Re)Rewrites Gender Roles', *On The Issues* Magazine, Winter, accessed July 2013, http://www.ontheissuesmagazine.com/2011winter/2011_winter_Pozner.php.

Prügl, E. (2011) 'Diversity Management and Gender Mainstreaming as Technologies of Government', *Politics and Gender*, 7: 71–89.

Prügl, E. (2012) 'If Lehman Brothers had been Lehman Sisters', *International Political Sociology*, 6: 21–35.

Prügl, E. and Marcus, T. (eds) (2009) *Diversity in the European Union*, Basingstoke: Palgrave Macmillan.

Pua Wiki (2014) 'Sensitive New Age Guy', accessed September 2014, http://puamore.com/wiki/snag-sensitive-new-age-guy/.

Pulver, A. (2005) '"He's Not a God, He's Human', *The Guardian*, 15 June, accessed November 2013, http://www.theguardian.com/film/2005/jun/15/features.features11.

Pulver, A. (2013) 'Tina Fey and Amy Poehler to Host 2014 and 2015 Golden Globes', *The Guardian*, 16 October, accessed November 2013, http://www.theguardian.com/film/2013/oct/15/tina-fey-amy-poehler-host-2014-2015-golden-globes.

Purcell, C. (2001) 'To Import or to Format? That is the Question', *Electronic Media*, 15 January, 64.

226 Bibliography

Quigley, A. (2010) 'Christopher Nolan's Longstanding Practice of "Fridging" Female Characters', *Slash Film*, 31 August, accessed November 2013, http://www.slashfilm.com/christopher-nolans-longstanding-practice-of-fridging-female-characters/.

RainbowWish (2008) 'What is Feminism?', image, accessed June 2012, http://rainbowwish.deviantart.com/art/What-is-Feminism-67910228.

Ralph, T. (2013) 'Father of Delhi Gang Rape Victim: "Name My Daughter"', *Global Post*, 6 January, accessed November 2013, http://www.globalpost.com/dispatch/news/regions/asia-pacific/india/130106/father-delhi-gang-rape-victim-names-daughter.

Reichert, T. (2007) 'Dolce and Gabbana's Sexual Fantasy Ad Crosses the Line', 7 March, accessed July 2009, http://sexinadvertising.blogspot.com.au/2007/03/dolce-gabbanas-sexual-fantasy-ad.html.

Reisinger, D. (2008) 'Just Stop It Already: Women Do Play Video Games', *CNET*, 10 July, accessed November 2013, http://www.cnet.com/au/news/just-stop-it-already-women-do-play-video-games/.

Reuters (2007) 'Spain Behind the Rimes on Ad Says Dolce and Gabbana', 23 February, accessed July 2009, http://www.reuters.com/article/2007/02/23/idUSL2346398220070223.

Reynolds, J. (2013) 'Men's Upmarket Lifestyle Magazines are Leading the Digital Market', *The Guardian*, 16 August, accessed January 2014, http://www.theguardian.com/media/2013/aug/15/mens-magazines-digital-market-gq-economist-esquire.

Rich, E. (2005) 'Young Women, Feminist Identities and Neo-Liberalism', *Women's Studies International Forum*, 28: 495–508.

Ritchie, M. (2013) 'Revenue Flow and Making Money Out of Film', Creative Skill Set, accessed September 2013, http://www.creativeskillset.org/film/knowledge/article_5103_1.asp.

Roberts, C. (2012) 'Michigan State Rep. Lisa Brown Silenced After "Vagina" Comments', *Daily News*, 15 June, accessed November 2013, http://www.nydailynews.com/news/politics/michigan-state-rep-lisa-brown-silenced-vagina-comments-article-1.1096480.

Roberts, D. (2008) 'The Intellectual Perils of Broad Human Security: Deepening the Critique of International Relations', *Politics*, 28(2): 124–7.

Rodriguez, N. (2013) 'How to Triple Your Success Using Social Media Advertising Platforms', *Forbes*, 1 May, accessed October 2013, http://www.forbes.com/sites/groupthink/2013/05/01/how-to-triple-your-success-using-social-media-advertising-platforms/.

Rogers, V. (2009) 'Fangirl Invasion: Hollywood Takes Notice', *News-a-Rama*, 2 September, accessed November 2013, http://www.newsarama.com/3773-fangirl-invasion-hollywood-takes-notice.html.

Romano, T. (2013) 'Blurred Lines', Robin Thicke's Summer Anthem, is Kind of Rapey', *The Daily Beast*, 17 June, accessed November 2013, http://www.thedailybeast.com/articles/2013/06/17/blurred-lines-robin-thicke-s-summer-anthem-is-kind-of-rapey.html.

Rothman, N. (2012) 'Obama Overtakes Reagan as Most Televised President in History', *Mediaite*, 23 April, accessed July 2013, http://www.mediaite.com/online/obama-overtakes-reagan-as-most-televised-president-in-history/.

Rothwell, K. (2013) 'Think with Your Ovaries: A Defense of *The Walking Dead's* Andrea', *Heroes and Heartbreakers*, 17 March, accessed November 2013, http://www.heroesandheartbreakers.com/blogs/2013/03/think-with-your-ovaries-a-defense-of-the-walking-deads-andrea.

Rourke, A. (2012) 'Julia Gillard's Attack on Sexism Hailed as Turning Point for Australian Women', *The Guardian*, 13 October, accessed March 2014, http://www.theguardian.com/world/2012/oct/12/julia-gillard-sexism-australian-women.

Rowley, C. (2009) 'Popular Culture and the Politics of the Visual', in L. Shepherd (ed.) *Gender Matters in Global Politics: A Feminist Introduction to International Relations*, London and New York: Routledge.

Ruiz, M. (2013) 'A Handy Guide to Celebrity Feminists', *Cosmopolitan Magazine*, March, http://www.cosmopolitan.com/entertainment/celebs/news/g2956/celebrity-feminists/?slide=10.

Ruskin, G. and Schor, J. (2009) 'Every Nook and Cranny: The Dangerous Spread of Commercialized Culture', in J. Turow and M. Mcallister (eds) *The Advertising and Consumer Culture Reader*, London and New York: Routledge.

Salmons, L. and Crosbie, R. (2012) 'The Female of the Species is More Digital than the Male', *The Guardian*, 22 March, accessed on 18 October 2014, http://www.theguardian.com/media-network/media-network-blog/2012/mar/02/female-species-more-digital-male.

Salvation Army (n.d.) *Sexualisation of Children: What You Need to Know*, accessed June 2013, http://www.sarmy.org.au/Global/SArmy/Social/justsalvos/Documents/Women and Children/infoBook.pdf.

Sánchez, E.L. (2012) 'The Perpetual Dumb Girl', *The Feminist Wire*, 6 December, accessed November 2013, http://thefeministwire.com/2012/12/the-perpetual-dumb-girl/.

Sarah Palin Facebook Page, https://www.facebook.com/sarahpalin.

Sargent, J. (2011) '5 Old-Timey Prejudices That Still Show Up in Every Movie', *Cracked*, 15 November, accessed June 2013, http://www.cracked.com/article_19549_5-old-timey-prejudices-that-still-show-up-in-every-movie.html.

Sargent, J. (2012) '6 Insane Stereotypes That Movies Can't Seem to Get Over', *Cracked*, 15 October, accessed June 2013, http://www.likemotion.com/show/9006/6-insane-stereotypes-that-movies-cant-seem-to-get-over.

Sarkeesian, A. (2012) 'Tropes Vs. Women in Video Games', *Kickstarter* project, accessed June 2013, http://www.kickstarter.com/projects/566429325/tropes-vs-women-in-video-games.

SavvyRed (2010) 'Don't Call Me "Sweetie"', *Deviant Art*, 6 June, accessed June 2013, http://savvyred.deviantart.com/journal/Don-t-Call-Me-quot-Sweetie-quot-Feminist-Feat-214227325.

Schlafly, P. (2012) 'Obama's War on Women', 18 April, accessed April 2014, http://www.eagleforum.org/column/2012/apr12/12-04-18.html.

Schlafly, P. (2014) 'Who Killed the American Family?', 24 September, accessed September 2014, http://www.eagleforum.org/publications/column/who-killed-the-american-family.html.

Scoop Marketing (2012) 'The Nielsen Company and Billboard 2012 Mid-Year US Music Industry Report', Scoop Marketing, 5 July, accessed January 2013, http://www.scoopmarketing.com/2012/07/the-nielsen-company-billboard-2012-mid-year-u-s-music-industry-report/.

Seddon, G. (2014) '50 Greatest Films That Pass the Bechdel Test', *Total Film*, accessed February 2014, http://www.totalfilm.com/features/50-greatest-films-that-pass-the-bechdel-test.

Seibert, A. and Roslaniec, D. (1998) 'Women, Power and the Public Sphere', *ABC*, accessed November 2013, http://www.abc.net.au/ola/citizen/women/women-power.htm.

Selinger-Morris, S. (2010) 'Look What They've Done to My Son, Ma', *Sydney Morning Herald*, 23–24 October.

Seximus Soup (n.d.) 'Guerilla – Various', images, accessed November 2013, http://seximus.soup.io/post/237218694/If-your-product-was-any-good-you.

Shapiro, M.J. (1986) 'Metaphor in the Philosophy of the Social Sciences', *Cultural Critique*, 2: 191–214.

Shapiro, M.J. (1992) *Reading the Postmodern Polity: Political Theory as Textual Practice*, Minneapolis: University of Minnesota Press.

228 Bibliography

Sharman, J. (2009) 'Neither Asia nor America: International Political Economy in Australia', in M. Blyth (ed.) *The Handbook of International Political Economy*, Baltimore, MD: Johns Hopkins University Press.

Shepherd, L.J. (2008) *Gender, Violence, Security*, London: Zed Books.

Shepherd, L.J. (ed.) (2009) *Gender Matters in Global Politics: A Feminist Introduction to International Relations*, London and New York: Routledge.

Shepherd, L.J. (2013) *Gender, Violence and Popular Culture: Telling Stories*, London and New York: Routledge.

Silverstein, M. (2011) 'Who Goes to the Movies? Moviegoers Stats from 2010', *Indiewire*, 25 February, accessed June 2013, http://blogs.indiewire.com/womenandhollywood/who_goes_to_the_movies_moviegoers_stats_from_2010.

Silverstein, M. and Kang, I. (2013) 'Goodbye to Strong Female Characters', *Indiewire*, 30 December, accessed June 2013, http://blogs.indiewire.com/womenandhollywood/goodbye-to-strong-female-characters.

Skrzydlewska, J.K. (2012) *Draft Report on the Sexualisation of Girls*, Committee on Women's Rights and Gender Equality, European Parliament, accessed June 2013, http://www.europarl.europa.eu/sides/getDoc.do?pubRef=-//EP//NONSGML+COMPARL+PE-491.090+01+DOC+PDF+V0//EN&language=EN.

Skyy Vodka (n.d.) advertising image, accessed July 2009, http://www.skyy.com/.

Small, C. (2011) Online Comments on Noah Berlatsky's '"Twilight" vs. "Hunger Games": Why Do So Many Grown-Ups Hate Bella?', *The Atlantic*, 15 November, accessed June 2013, http://www.theatlantic.com/entertainment/archive/2011/11/twilight-vs-hunger-games-why-do-so-many-grown-ups-hate-bella/248439/.

Smallwood, K., Hall, J. and Ohlms, S. (2012) 'The 7 Sneakiest Ways Corporations Manipulated Human Behavior', *Cracked*, 20 August, accessed November 2013, http://www.cracked.com/article_19833_the-7-sneakiest-ways-corporations-manipulated-human-behavior.html.

Smith, C. (2014) 'By the Numbers: 170 Amazing Facebook User and Demographic Statistics', *DMR: Digital Market Ramblings*, accessed April 2014, http://expandedramblings.com/index.php/by-the-numbers-17-amazing-facebook-stats/#.Ux5QOdwihFw.

Smith, K. (2014) 'Kyle Smith's Take on Globes: Too Much Estrogen!', *New York Post*, 13 January, accessed March 2014, http://nypost.com/2014/01/13/my-take-on-the-globes-too-much-estrogen/.

Smith, S.L., Choueiti, M., Scofield, E. and Pieper, K. (2013) 'Gender Inequality in 500 Popular Films: Examining On-Screen Portrayals and Behind-the-Scenes Employment Patterns in Motion Pictures Released Between 2007–2012', Annenberg School for Communication & Journalism, University of Southern California, accessed November 2013, http://annenberg.usc.edu/News%20and%20Events/News/~/media/PDFs/Smith_GenderInequality500Films.ashx.

Smith, S.L., Pieper, K. and Choueiti, M. (2014) 'Exploring the Barriers and Opportunities for Independent Women Filmmakers Phase I and II', *Sundance Institute and Women in Film Los Angeles Women Filmmakers Initiative*, 20 January, accessed April 2014, http://www.sundance.org/pdf/press-releases/Exploring-The-Barriers.pdf.

Sontag, S. (1999) 'The Visual World', in J. Evans and S. Hall (eds) *Visual Culture: The Reader*, London: Sage.

Souter, F. (2010) 'The Only Way is Up', *Sydney Morning Herald*, 1 May.

Springer, S.D. (2009) 'Neoliberalizing Violence: (Post)Marxian Political Economy, Poststructuralism and the Production of Space in "Postconflict" Cambodia', Ph.D. Thesis submitted to the Faculty of Geography, University of British Colombia, June 2012, http://profile.nus.edu.sg/fass/geosds/Springer, S. 2009. Neoliberalizing Violence. Final Version.pdf.

Squire, C. (1997) 'Empowering Women? The Oprah Winfrey Show', in C. Brunsdon, J. D'Acci and L. Spigel (eds) *Feminist Television Criticism: A Reader*, Oxford: Oxford University Press.

Squires, J. and Weldes, J. (2007) 'Beyond Being Marginal: Gender and International Relations in Britain', *British Journal of Politics and International Relations*, 9(2): 185–203.

Stacey, J. (1987) 'Sexism by a Subtler Name: Postindustrial Conditions and Postfeminist Consciousness in the Silicon Valley', *Socialist Review*, 17(6): 7–28.

Steele, M., Spencer, S.J. and Aronson, J. (2002) 'Contending with Group Image: The Psychology of Stereotype and Social Identity Threat', *Advances in Experimental Social Psychology*, 34: 379–440.

Stern, B.B. (2003) 'Masculinism(s) and the Male Image: What Does It Mean to be a Man? Sex in Advertising', in T. Reichert and J. Lambiase (eds) *Sex in Advertising: Perspectives on the Erotic Appeal*, Mahwah, NJ: Lawrence Erlbaum Associates, pp. 215–28.

Storey, J. (2003) *Inventing Popular Culture: From Folklore to Globalization*, Oxford: Wiley-Blackwell.

Storey, J. (2006) *Cultural Theory and Popular Culture: A Reader*, 4th edn, Harlow: Pearson.

Storey, J. (2012) *Cultural Theory and Popular Culture: An Introduction*, 6th edn, Harlow: Pearson.

Strickland, J. (2009) 'How Do Social Networking Sites Make Money?', *How Stuff Works*, 10 July, accessed September 2013, http://computer.howstuffworks.com/internet/social-networking/information/how-social-networking-sites-make-money1.htm.

Strinati, D. (2004) *An Introduction to Theories of Popular Culture*, 2nd edn, London: Routledge.

Stuever, H. (2012) 'HBO's "Girls": Smartly Cracking Gen Y's Morose Code', *The Washington Post*, 13 April, accessed November 2013, http://www.washingtonpost.com/entertainment/tv/hbos-girls-smartly-cracking-gen-ys-morose-code/2012/04/13/gIQAkaX5ET_story.html.

Sundance Institute (2013) 'Sundance Institute and Women in Film Los Angeles Study Examines Gender Disparity in Independent Film', Press Release, 21 January, accessed September 2013, http://www.sundance.org/press-center/release/sundance-institute-and-women-in-film-los-angeles-study-examines-gender-disp/.

Sundaram, V. (2012) 'Indian Rape Protests Foretell Feminist Spring', *New America Media*, 31 December, accessed October 2013, http://newamericamedia.org/2012/12/indian-rape-protests-foretell-feminist-spring.php.

Sweeney, M. (2009) 'Internet Overtakes Television to Become Biggest Advertising Sector in the UK', *The Guardian*, 30 September, accessed June 2013, http://www.theguardian.com/media/2009/sep/30/internet-biggest-uk-advertising-sector.

Sydney Morning Herald (2012) 'Transcript of Julia Gillard's Speech', 10 October 2012, accessed April 2014, http://www.smh.com.au/federal-politics/political-news/transcript-of-julia-gillards-speech-20121010-27c36.html.

Sydney Morning Herald (2013) *Sydney Morning Herald Good Weekend Magazine*, 5 October.

Sydney Riders (2013) Sydney Rider's Facebook Page, screenshot image, created 17 July, author's file.

Symon, E.V. (2011) 'The 6 Most Wildly Irresponsible Publicity Stunts in History', *Cracked*, 26 June, accessed June 2013, http://www.cracked.com/article_19275_the-6-most-wildly-irresponsible-publicity-stunts-in-history_p2.html.

Taylor, C.P. (2007) 'D&G's Knife-Wielding Models in Bad Taste?', *Adweek*, 11 January, accessed July 2009, http://www.adweek.com/adfreak/dgs-knife-wielding-models-bad-taste-17892.

The Telegraph (2009) 'Pictures of the Day: 19 November 2009', accessed February 2014, http://www.telegraph.co.uk/news/picturegalleries/picturesoftheday/6604998/Pictures-of-the-day-19-November-2009.html?image=25.

230 Bibliography

Thornton, B. (2013) 'Margaret Thatcher and the Death of Feminism', *Front Page Mag*, 9 April, accessed January 2014, http://www.frontpagemag.com/2013/bruce-thornton/margaret-thatcher-and-the-death-of-feminism/.

Time (1998) 'Is Feminism Dead?', *Time Magazine*, Cover Image, 29 June, accessed July 2009, http://content.time.com/time/specials/2007/article/0,28804,1704183_1704257_1704514,00.html.

True, J. (2005) 'Feminism', in S. Burchill, A. Linklater, R. Devetak, J. Donnelly, M. Paterson, C. Reus-Smit and J. True (eds) *Theories of International Relations*, 3rd edn, Basingstoke: Palgrave Macmillan, pp. 213–34.

Tulloch, L. (2013) 'Ben Stiller in the Moment', *The Sydney Morning Herald*, 16 November.

Turner, J. (2014) 'Hands Up Who's a Feminist?', *The Sunday Telegraph Sunday Style Magazine*, 19 January.

Turow, J. and Mcallister, M. (eds) (2009) *The Advertising and Consumer Culture Reader*, London: Routledge.

TV Tropes (2013a) 'Stuffed into the Fridge', *TV Tropes*, accessed June 2013, http://tvtropes.org/pmwiki/pmwiki.php/Main/StuffedIntoTheFridge.

TV Tropes (2013b) 'Men are the Expendable Gender', *TV Tropes*, accessed June 2013, http://tvtropes.org/pmwiki/pmwiki.php/Main/MenAreTheExpendableGender.

UN-Habitat (2013) *State of Women in Cities 2012–2013: Gender and the Prosperity of Cities*, Nairobi: United Nations Human Settlements Programme.

USA Today (2011) 'Letters: Young Feminists Keeping Movement Alive', 31 October, accessed June 2013, http://usatoday30.usatoday.com/news/opinion/letters/story/2011-10-31/feminism-young-feminists/51019404/1.

uzerfriendly (2014) 'Controversies in Geek Culture: The Big Bang Theory', 14 July, accessed August 2014, http://uzerfriendly.com/controversies-in-geek-culture-the-big-bang-theory/.

Valenti, J. (2007) *Full Frontal Feminism: A Young Woman's Guide to Why Feminism Matters*, Emeryville, CA: Avalon.

Valenzuela, A. (1993) 'Liberal Gender Role Attitudes and Academic Achievement Among Mexican-Origin Adolescents in Two Houston Inner-City Catholic Schools', *Hispanic Journal of Behavioral Sciences*, 15: 310–23.

Vinjamuri, D. (2012) 'Bic for Her: What They Were Actually Thinking (as Told by a Man Who Worked on Tampons)', *Forbes*, 30 August, accessed November 2013, http://www.forbes.com/sites/davidvinjamuri/2012/08/30/bic-for-her-what-they-were-actually-thinking-as-told-by-a-man-who-worked-on-tampons/.

Vitchers, T. (2012) 'What is FEMEN? Post-Soviet "Sextremism," Not American Feminism', *Identities.Mic*, 12 April, accessed January 2014, http://mic.com/articles/34599/what-is-femen-post-soviet-sextremism-not-american-feminism.

Wagner, C. (2007) 'Dolce and Gabbana Win the Macho Prize for Most Sexist Advertising and Le Mouvement du Nid for Least Sexist Ad', *The Scented Salamander*, 10 March, accessed July 2009, http://www.mimifroufrou.com/scentedsalamander/2008/03/dolce_gabbana_wins_the_macho_p.html#more.

Waisbord, S. (2004) 'McTV: Understanding the Global Popularity of Television Formats', *Television New Media*, 5(4): 359–83.

Walby, S. (2011) *The Future of Feminism*, Cambridge: Polity.

Walker, R.B.J. (2010) 'Conclusion: Cultural, Political, Economy', in J. Best and M. Paterson (eds) *Cultural Political Economy*, London and New York: Routledge, pp. 225–33.

Walter, N. (1999) *The New Feminism*, London: Little, Brown.

Walter, N. (2010) *Living Dolls: The Return of Sexism*, London: Virago.

Weber, C. (2008) 'Popular Visual Language as Global Communication: The Remediation of United Airlines Flight 93', *Review of International Studies*, 34: 137–53.

Weldes, J. (2003) *To Seek Out New Worlds: Science Fiction and World Politics*, Basingstoke: Palgrave Macmillan.

Weldes, J. (2006) 'High Politics and Low Data: Globalization Discourses and Popular Culture', in D. Yanow and P. Schwartz-Shea (eds) *Interpretation and Method: Empirical Research Methods and the Interpretive Turn*, New York: M.E. Sharpe.

Wemple, E. (2011) 'The Economist Does Gender Edgy', *The Washington Post*, 11 November, accessed May 2013, http://www.washingtonpost.com/blogs/erik-wemple/post/the-economist-goes-gender-edgy/2011/11/11/gIQA45piCN_blog.html.

Westbury, M. (2009) 'Niche Cultures: Or Why Opera is Like Comic Books', *Marcus Westbury*, 15 September, accessed June 2013, http://www.marcuswestbury.net/2009/09/15/niche-cultures-or-why-opera-is-like-comic-books/.

What's the Run Dude (2012) '20 Quotes from Tony Abbott', *What's the Run Dude*, 23 August, accessed April 2014, http://whatistherundude.wordpress.com/2012/08/23/20-quotes-from-tony-abbott-to-remind-you-why-he-shouldnt-be-prime-minister/

Whelehan, I. (2000) *Overloaded: Popular Culture and the Future of Feminism*, London: The Women's Press.

Who Needs Feminism? (2013) *Who Needs Feminism?*, Facebook Page, accessed November 2013, https://www.facebook.com/WhoNeedsFeminism.

Wicke, J. (1994) 'Celebrity Material: Materialist Feminism and the Culture of Celebrity', *The South Atlantic Quarterly*, 93(4): 751–78.

Williams, R. (1958) 'Culture is Ordinary', in N. McKenzie (ed.) *Convictions*, London: MacGibbon and Kee, pp. 74–92.

Williamson, D. A. (2008), 'Men, You're Outnumbered Online', *eMarketer*, 24 March, http://www.emarketer.com/Article/Men-Youre-Outnumbered-Online/1006082.

Willis, P. (1990) *Common Culture*, Buckingham, UK: Open University Press.

Wolf, N. (1991) *The Beauty Myth: How Images of Beauty are used Against Women*, London: Vintage.

Women in Refrigerators (2013) *Women in Refrigerators*, accessed June 2013, http://lby3.com/wir/.

Wong, D. (2012) '5 Ways Modern Men are Trained to Hate Women', *Cracked*, 27 March, accessed November 2013, http://www.cracked.com/article_19785_5-ways-modern-men-are-trained-to-hate-women.html.

Words Over Pixels (n.d.) 'Guerrilla 6 – Reflections', image, accessed February 2014, http://www.wordsoverpixels.com/warning-reflections-in-this-mirror-may-be-distorte/17226193f6cedc90e1bb046a369a0004.html.

Wray, R. (2010) 'Media Consumption on the Increase', *The Guardian*, 19 April, accessed July 2013, http://www.theguardian.com/business/2010/apr/19/media-consumption-survey.

WWD (2007) 'Memo Pad: It's Raining Men…New Recipe…Bra Banter…', *Women's Wear Daily*, 30 August, accessed July 2009, http://www.wwd.com/media-news/fashion-memopad/memo-pad-it-s-raining-men-new-recipe-bra-banter-485621?full=true.

Yare, B. (2012) 'Gaming Booth Expo Babe', image, taken from 'Why I'm Sick of Seeing Booth Babes at Gaming Expos', *Feminspire*, accessed April 2014, http://feminspire.com/why-im-sick-of-seeing-booth-babes-at-gaming-expos/.

YouTube (2013a) 'All New Sportage: Grow Up, Not Old', Kia advertisement, accessed March 2013, http://www.youtube.com/watch?v=kFFz_MVSq5s&list=PLe7uIs4bKQzcjbhQdUMpYZet3iZ7Bdu0E.

232 Bibliography

YouTube (2013b) 'All New Sportage: Grow Up, Not Old', online comment on Kia advertisement, accessed March 2013, http://www.youtube.com/watch?v=kFFz_MVSq5s&list=PLe7uIs4bKQzcjbhQdUMpYZet3iZ7Bdu0E.

YouTube (2013c) 'Man of Now', Kia advertisement, accessed March 2013, http://www.youtube.com/watch?v=9UB68ryn35s.

YouTube (2013d) 'Woman of Now', Kia advertisement, accessed March 2013, http://www.youtube.com/watch?v=0hudxmmo-uM.

Zalewski, M. (2007) 'Do We Understand Each Other Yet? Troubling Feminist Encounters With(in) International Relations', *British Journal of Politics and International Relations*, 9(2): 302–12.

Zalewski, M. (2013) *Feminist International Relations: Exquisite Corpse*, London and New York: Routledge.

Zehfuss, M. (2009) 'Jacques Derrida', in J. Edkins and N. Vaughan-Williams, *Critical Theorists and International Relations*, London and New York: Routledge, pp. 137–49.

Zucker, A.N. and Stewart, A.J. (2007) 'Growing Up and Growing Older: Feminism as a Context for Women's Lives', *Psychology of Women Quarterly*, 31: 137–45.

INDEX

Note: *italic* page numbers indicate tables; **bold** indicate figures.

Abbott, T. 106, 108–9, 197
abuse and threats 162
academia: attitude to visual form 61–2;
   attitudes to popular culture 4
access costs 78
access, to spaces of consumption 82–3
accessibility, of feminism *158–9*
acquisition 68
activism 3, 158, 159, 162, 197
Adorno, T. 9, 31–2, 36–7
advertising: Airbag by Porsche **51**; Cif **86**;
   derogatory and violent 13; Dolce and
   Gabbana 189–95; Facebook 49–50,
   50; importance of 84–8; influence 85;
   making adverts 86–8; means of harm 68;
   public space 84–5; representations 85–6;
   visual signage 26–7
aesthetics, and gender violence 1
Aftermath of Feminism, The (McRobbie)
   11–12
age, and attitudes to feminism 100
agency 70, 99, 112, 143, 144
Airbag by Porsche **51**
Aitken, R. 40
Alexander, V. 135
Alien tetralogy 124
alienation of labour 72
Alvarez, S. 90
Americanization 37
analysis of popular culture: commercial
   viability and popularity 44–53; consumer
   culture, consumerism and popular

culture 41–4; context and overview
21–2; cultural studies and political
economy 32–6; culture and IPE 36–41;
global/local success 45–8; high/low
binaries of culture 27–31; political
economy 31–2; social media 48–53;
visual language and global politics
22–4; visual language and social
practice 25–7
anchorage 63–4
Andersen, N.A. 7
Annenberg study 56–7
anonymity 149
antifeminism: in commodity form 73;
   consumption 71; cultural sites of 44;
   growth of 99–100; hate speech 13; overt
   see overt antifeminism; power of 101;
   tacit *see* tacit antifeminism; viability 2
Aronowitz, N.W. 174
Aronson, P. 17, 99, 100, 104, 106
articulation 41
attendance at events 30–1, **30**
attitudes to feminism, complexity 103
audiences: cinema 121–3; difficulties of
   research 71; *The Economist* 148, 150;
   gay men 153; meaning making 81–2;
   reception and interpretation 80–2; video
   games 130–1
Aune, K. 159–60
Australia: locating feminism 106–9; politics
   and feminism 161; women from
   non-English speaking backgrounds 109

234 Index

Australian Human Rights Commission 107
author: experiences of feminism 3–4;
    starting point 2
Avengers, The 146
Ayers, M. 110–11

backlash 101–2, 104, 136, 180
Bagnato, D. 170
Bailey, J. 57
Bakhtin, M. 1
Barthes, R. 63–4, 81
Bechdel Test 123, 124, 198
behaviour, gendered hierarchies 11
Being Feminist 103
Bella, *Twilight* series 168–9
Benjamin, W. 22, 62, 70
Berlatsky, N. 168
Best, J. 37–9
Beyoncé 161
BIC pens 166–7
'Big Feminist But, The' cartoon **105**
Bigelow, K. 58
bimbo feminism 113
Blair, T. 9
Bleiker, R. 4, 23, 62, 65
blogosphere 198–9
blogs, antifeminism 13
Blurred Lines (Thicke) 110–11
bodies: as objects of discourse 8;
    as saleable 73
body image 115
book: aims 4, 11, 178; approaches taken 6;
    background 3–5; focus of 41; overview 1;
    starting point 2; summary and
    conclusions 177–83
boundaries 4, 9
boys and young men, as cinema audience
    121–3
boys, effects of sexualization 114–15
BRIC countries, video consumption 77–8
Bricken, R. 125–6
Britpop 199
Brittain, M. 74, 76
broadcast news reporting 59
Bruni-Sarkozy, C. 100
brutality 134
Buffy 168
Butler, J. 10

cable networks, local language
    programming 47
Cagney and Lacey 73, 139, 173
campaigning 91, 162
capitalism: as context of culture 29; as
    contradictory 38

capitalist culture, commodities in 72–4
cartoons: 'The Big Feminist But' **105**;
    feminist criticism **20**; How to Synergize
    85; Rush Vs Feminism **141**
Carver, T. 7, 24, 55, 61–2, 65
Castor, A. 161
Catwoman/ Selena Kyle 128–9
celebrities, feminism 174
celebrity feminism 165–9
Center for the Study of Women in Film in
    Television 58
Chant, S. 83–4
Chemaly, S. 60, 147
Chenowith, Brenda, *Six Feet Under*
    141–2, 144
child protection 113
children: effects of sexualization 114–15;
    self-identification 70; television 137–8
choice, enlightened sexism 156
choices 92
Christopherson, S. 83
Cif, advertising **86**
cinema: attendance and gender 79–80;
    audiences 121–3; barriers to women's
    participation 58–9; female characters
    120–5; gender inequality 56;
    independent film 124; mass production
    28; product quality 123–4; profit-making
    47–8, 57; women in 'superhero' films
    126–9; women's presence 58
cities, wealth generation 83–4
Clarkson, K. 173
class: and feminism 109; as focus of IPE 177
class power 36–7, 83
class relations 40
Cochrane, K. 156–7, 160
coded messages 63, 64
codes 25–6, 61, 69
coding 65
commercial interests 42
commercial viability: antifeminism vs
    feminism 180–3; of feminism 44; and
    popularity 44–53; sexism 110
commercialism 101, 102, 166
commercialization 28, 101, 112
commodification 29, 74
commodities: in capitalist culture 72–4;
    role of 71
common sense 21
communication: power and influence 25;
    shared language 55
communication industry, ownership and
    control 35
complexity 41, 103, 181
conditions of existence 40–1

Connor, Sarah, *Terminator* 139
conservativism 9–10
consumer culture, and consumerism 41–4
consumption 70–88; advertising 84–8;
  commodities in capitalist culture
  72–4; digital 74–5; exclusion from 178;
  feminism/antifeminism 71; and gender
  151; of media **75**; nature of 42–3;
  private/public 71; and production 33–4,
  37; and self-worth 166; spaces of 72;
  spaces of and power 82–4; ways of
  understanding 71; women and men
  74–80; see *also* production,
  representation and consumption
content monitoring 49, 51
contradiction 41
control: of media 46; through images 70
Cool Britannia 9
corporate interests 42
costs of media 35–6
Crane, Ichabod 142, 144
crime dramas 1
critical facilities 70
Crowther, G. 149, 150
cult classics 44
cult status 44–5
cultural bias 61
cultural economy 37–8
cultural effects 91
cultural gendering 168–9
cultural homogenization 46
cultural political economy (CPE)
  38, 39–40
cultural products, determination of 38
cultural rules 8
cultural specificity 96
cultural studies, and political economy 32–6
cultural turn 23, 39
culture: dynamism 31; and economy 40;
  high/low binaries 27–31; immaterial 71;
  and International Political Economy
  (IPE) 36–41; production 56
cyber cafes 77
cycles, in attitudes to feminism 181
Cyrus, M. 161

D'Acci, J. 173–4
Damsel in Distress trope 132
Dark Knight trilogy 126–9, *127*
data analysis 13, 17–18
dating 137
Davidson, N. 47–8
Davies, G. 121–2
Dawes, Rachel 128
De Brito, S. 107

death of feminism 96–8, 181
decodings, positions of 65–7
deconstruction 6–7, 65
decorum 132
Degeneres, E. 166–7
dehumanization 195
Deloitte 76, 79
Democratic Corporatist Model 46
depoliticization 37, 106
Derrida, J. 6–7, 65
desirability 73
developer fees 48
difference 41
digital consumption 74–5
digital technology, proliferation 78–9
Dini, P. 137
direct-effects model 81
discourse: power and popular culture 6–10;
  use of term 8
discourse analysis 7, 8
discourses, functions and effects 8
dispossession 35, 178
Ditto, B. 170
Dockterman, E. 138–9
Dolce and Gabbana 189–95; *Esquire*
  campaign 190–1, **191**; knives campaign
  191–3, **192**; objectifying men campaign
  193–5, **194**
dominant-hegemonic position 65–6
double bind 115
Douglas, S.J. 98, 155–6
Draper, J. 151, 152–3, 154
dualism, conceptual and methodological 39
Dumb Girl 136–7
Dunham, L. 161, 164, 165, 167
During, S. 25, 31
DVD sales 135
dynamism, of culture 31

Eagle Forum, The 91, 199–200
economic reductionism 40
economics, application of 5
Economist, The 148–50; slip cover **149**
economy, and culture 40
Eisenstein, H. 91, 92
Elias, J. 92–3, 165
elites 24, 35, 83
elitism 29
embedded feminism 155
embodiment, of feminism 181
emotion, representations of 62
empowerment 112
Enerson, C. 100–1
enlightened sexism 154–6
Eowyn, *Lord of the Rings* 145

236 Index

Esquire 151–2; Dolce and Gabbana 190–1, **191**
ethics of consent 115
European Parliament report on sexualization 113–14
European Parliament's Committee on Women's Rights and Gender Equality (CWRGE) 113–14
Evans, J. 22–3, 32
events, attendance at 30–1, **30**
exclusion 9, 35–6, 83, 178
expenditure 30
'Exploring the Barriers and Opportunities for Independent Women Filmmakers' 58–9

Facebook 48, 77; advertising platform 49–50, **50**; Sydney Riders motorbike group 51–3, **52**; *Zoo Weekly* 49
Faludi, S. 101
Family Guy 141
fantasy 10
female characters: gaming 129–31; killing off 126; strong to boring 141–4
Female Eunuch, The (Greer) 162
female movie characters 120–5
Femen 170
feminazis 139
Feminine Mystique, The (Friedan) 162
feminism: accessibility *158–9*; ambivalence towards 13; appropriations of 12; in commodity form 73–4; as complete 101; consumption 71; cultural effects 91; death of 96–8; embedded 155; as focus of book 41; geek 83; influence of popular culture 2; institutionalization of 12; locating *see* locating feminism; and male anxiety 153; as personal 4; second-wave 90, 97, 99, 109, 139, 152–3, 168; surveys of 17; tropes 139–40; utilization of 179; *see also* overt feminism
feminist activities 90
feminist criticism, cartoon **20**
Feminist Project, The 94–7
Feminist Sex Wars 112
feminists are. Google searches **140**
Fernandes, R. 136–7
Fey, T. 147
film: audiences 121–3; female characters 120–5; independent film 124; product quality 123–4; women in 'superhero' films 126–9
Final Girl trope 133
Fine, C. 103, 104
Firefly 146–7

flexibilized production systems 72
format shows, adaptability 47
founding antagonism 32
fragmentation 181, 183
Fraser, N. 93, 165
freedom: sexual 113; urban vs. rural women 84
Freeman, N. 169
fridging 126
Friedan, B. 156

Galifianakis, Z. 9, 200
Gamble, C. 84
gaming: culture 200–1; female characters 129–31; sexualization 116
gaming consoles, gender and use 79
gaming industry, sexism 131
Garnham, N. 32–5
gay men 153
gay villages 83
geek culture 123, 201
geek feminism 83, 115–16
GeekFeminismWiki 115
gender: and cinema attendance 79–80; as cohesive 11; and consumption 151; and popular culture 10–11; representation and participation 108; taking seriously 10
gender analysis, as disconnected 93
gender codes 69, 179
gender disparities, in media 58–60
gender gaps 84
gender inequality, cinema 56–7
'Gender Inequality in 500 Popular Films' 56–7
gender mainstreaming 90–1
gender pay gap 13, 201
gender roles 68
gender stereotypes 26–7
gender tropes 119
gendered identities, construction 80
gendered representations 67–70
geopolitical realisms 24
Germain, R.D. 36–7, 38, 39
Gibson, Stella, *The Fall* 161
Gill, R. 5, 21, 151, 153
Gillard, J. 106–7, 108–9, 157–8, 180–1, 202; *see also* Misogyny Speech
Gingrich, A. 152
girl power 144–7, 170
girls: as cinema audience 122–3; effects of sexualization 114
Girls 73–4, 161, 167–8
global financial crisis 94
global gender gap 207

Index 237

global/local, contexts for
    success 45–8
Global Media Habits 2010
    (Lindsay) 76, 78
Global Media Monitoring Day 59
global politics, and visual language 22–4
Golden Globes 147
goods, as meaningful 73
Gordon-Levitt, J. 161, 165
Gosling, R. 168
governance, and liberal feminism 164–5
governance feminism 12–13, 91–7, 165
governmental programmes 90–1
GQ 154
Gramsci, A. 36, 40, 72
Gravity 124, 144
Green Lantern 126
Griffin, P. 7, 8, 10, 65
Grossberg, L. 33–5, 36, 37, 38, 41, 56, 61
GTFO 207
guerrilla feminisms 169–72; photos **171**

Hall, E.J. 99–100, 101, 104, 106
Hall, S. 10, 22–3, 25–7, 32, 65–7
Halley, J. 11–13, 91, 92, 94–7, 113,
    162–3, 164–5
Halliwell, G. 106
Hann, M. 199
Harding, C. 79
Harris, A. 92, 99, 101, 103
Harvey, D. 83
hate speech 13
Hathaway, A. 128
Hawkesworth, M. 90, 96, 97–9
Hefner, H. 152
hegemony 36–7, 65–6
Heldman, C. 193–4
Henderson, D. 168
Hess, A. 148, 149, 150
high/low binaries of culture 27–31
high/low politics 9
Hollows, J. 5, 67, 71, 74, 166, 179
Hollywood: Golden Age 121; market
    position 46–7; production 56; sexism
    57–8; use of female talent 147
Holmes, L. 121, 134
Holmes, Sherlock 144
homophobia 154
Hooper, C. 148, 149–50
Horkheimer, M. 9, 31–2, 36–7
How to be a Woman (Moran) 161
How to Synergize, cartoon **85**
humour 167
Hunter, R. 57–8, 59
Hutchison, E. 62

iconic messages 63, 64
identities: construction 80; emergent 41;
    multiplication of 43; as performance 36
identity, questions of 41
ideologies, nature of 6
I'm not a feminist, but . . .' 13, 103–6, 158,
    174, 181
imagery: 'sexy' 115; use of 1; violent and
    sexually explicit 13
images: and control 70; effects of 8;
    learning to read 68–9; political reading
    65; reading 63–7; of reality 64–5; as
    representations 177
immaterial culture 71
independent cinema, women in 58
independent film 124
indigenous peoples 109, 172–3
individualism 92, 102, 106
inferiority, of popular culture 28
inner slut 112–16
innuendo 13
institutionalization, of feminism 12
international feminism 98
International Political Economy (IPE) 4–5;
    approaches to culture 32; attitude to
    popular culture 23–4; and culture 36–41;
    problems of 177–8
International Relations (IR) 4–5, 23–4
internet sites: antifeminism 13; and media
    consumption 47
interpretation 41, 80–2
interpretive methodologies 7
interpretive resistance 81–2

Jessop, B. 38
journalism 59–60
Joyner, S. 134–5

Kalb, J. 139, 181
Kang, I. 137, 139, 142, 143
Katniss, *The Hunger Games* 168–9
Kerwin, A.M. 47, 76–9
Kesler, J. 120–2, 125, 133–4, 139
Kessler, A. 126
Kia cars, advertising 26–7
Kinchen, R. 97
knives campaign 191–3, **192**
knowledge of the world 1–2
Knox, S. 159
KPMG 77, 207
Kuchera, B. 130, 131

labelling 103, 106
labour, alienation of 72
lads' magazines 153–4

238 Index

Lady Gaga 89
language: local 47; as mediator 25; as medium 7; shared 55
Legally Blonde 73
Levy, A. 102, 166, 180
Lewis, P. 108, 109
Liang, J. 145–7
liberal feminism 162–5
Liggett, R. 68, 84–5
Limbaugh, R. 140
Lindsay, G. 76, 77–8
linguistic messages 63
linguistic turn 23
linking, text and image 63
Lipschutz, R.D. 38
literal messages 63
literature, expenditure 30
local language programming 47
locating feminism 181–2, 183; Australia 106–9; context and overview 89–90; death of feminism 96–8; international feminism 98; Janet Halley 94–7; neoliberalism 91–4; new feminism 100–3; postfeminism 98–100; sexualization 109–16; stereotype threat 103–6; successes 90–6
Lorde 162
Love, C. 172
Lunden, I. 79
Lury, C. 35–6, 42–3, 70, 178
Lyttelton, O. 122, 123

MacFarlane, S. 147
Mackay, F. 109–10, 159
magazines 151–5
male domination, as structure 112–13
male roles 107
male violence, understandings of 109–10
Mancini, P. 46
marginalization 96–7
marketability 73
marketing, video games 131
marketization 83
Martel, D. 110–11
Marx, K. 72, 73
Marxist critique 31–2
masculinity 151
mass culture 28
material culture 42–4
material objects 1
matrices of power 10
McDougall, S. 143, 144, 145
McDowell, L. 37–8
McIlwaine, C. 83–4

McRobbie, A. 2, 11–12, 43, 101, 102–3, 104, 166, 180, 181
meaning: bestowal of 7; creation of 2; determination of 35; regulation of 23
meaning creation 65
meaning-making 24, 40, 44, 67–8, 81–2, 177–8
meaningfulness 41, 73
media 113; costs of 35–6; feminism in 160–1; feminist analyses 5–6; gender disparities 58–60; ideological impact 6; increasing demand 79; influence 106; internet sites 47; misogyny 109; ownership and control 35; paying for 77; portrayal of feminism 100, 104; production outlets 46; profit-making 47; state control 46; stereotyping 104; as symbolic institutions 41; system models 46
media consumption **75**, 76
Media Report to Women (MRW) 59, 79
men: consumption of popular culture 74–80; discussion sites 140–1; entitlement to sex 132–4; gay 153; magazines for 151–5; objectification 193–5, **194**
Men are the Expendable Gender trope 129
messages 63–4
metrosexuality 154
Meyer, A. 9, 10, 11, 28, 29, 32, 55, 56, 66–7, 71–2, 80, 81–2, 83, 178
Milestone, K. 9, 10, 11, 21, 28, 29, 32, 55, 56, 66–7, 71–2, 80, 81–3, 178
militarization, and popular culture 23–4
military terms 197–8
Miller, D. 42, 73
Mills, Lieut. Abbie, *Sleepy Hollow* 142, 143–4
mimesis, dangers of 70
misogyny 107, 109, 138, 152
Misogyny Speech 107, 157, 161, 180–1, 202–7; *see also* Gillard, J.
Mison, T. 142
Miss Representation 21–2
mobile phones, video consumption 78
moments of production 25–6
Moran, C. 161
Moseley, R. 5, 67, 71, 74, 179
'Motion for a European Parliament Resolution on the Sexualisation of Girls' (2012/2047(INI)) 113–14
Motion Picture Association of America (MPAA) 79–80
mouse pad, photo **116**
multitasking 207
myths 43, 97, 100

narratives 10; of dissolution 97–8
negative characterization 139–41
negotiated codes 66
neogramscians 37
neoliberalism 37, 83, 91–4, 207
neoliberalization, dangers of 165
new age man 207
new feminism 100–3
New Lads 153
New Man 152–3
new Marxists 37
new media 32, 208
new screens 78–9
news directors 59
news media 59–60
newspapers, circulation 77
Newsweek **69**
niche cultures, attendance at events 31
niche status 44
Nickelodeon 22
Nielsen, 76, 78, 79, 199
'No, but…' feminism 106
Nolan, C. 126–8
non-coded messages 63
non-governmental programmes 90–1
norms 82–3, 179
Not Another Wave 128–9
nudity 110–12

Obama, B. 9
objectification 101, 112; Dolce and
    Gabbana 193–5, **194**
old feminism 102, 104
old media 208–9
online dating 48
online media consumption 74–5
Oosterlynck, S. 38
oppositional codes 66
Oprah 166
othering 83
overt antifeminism 120–41; female movie
    characters 120–5; games 129–31;
    negative characterization 139–41;
    profitability of female stupidity 134–9;
    sex and sexuality 132–4; women in
    refrigerators 125–9
overt feminism: celebrity feminism 165–9;
    liberal feminism 162–5; riot grrrl
    169–72; young women 156–62
ownership 42, 164

Padme, *Star Wars* 145–6
Palin, S. 69, **69**
participation, and representation 108
participation costs 35–6

Paterson, M. 37–9
people with disabilities 109
Perry, K. 104
photographs 64–5, 70
pink collar work 60, 208
Plato 64, 65
Playboy 152
Poehler, Amy 147
political economy: context and overview
    31–2; and cultural studies 32–6;
    defining 40
'Political Economy and Cultural Studies'
    (Garnham) 32–3
*Political Economy, Capitalism and Popular
    Culture* (Lipschutz) 38
politicians, use of popular culture 9
politics: and feminism 161; high/low 9;
    sexism 107
polysemy 63, 81
popular culture: academic attitudes to 4;
    and complexity of feminism 110; as
    invented category 29; scope 11
popular culture form, context and overview
    119–20
popularity, and commercial viability 44–53
popularity gap 89–90
post-Fordism 72–3
post-Marxist hegemony theory 37, 39
postfeminism 3, 12, 89, 98–100, 101, 180
poststructuralism 65
poverty, and participation 35–6
power: class power 36–7; communication
    and influence 25; elites 83; explanations
    of 36; of meaning-making 24; or popular
    culture 2; and popular culture 6–10;
    representations as 23; social relations 40
power relations: research sensitivity 8;
    understanding 178
Pozner, J.L. 135, 136, 138
pregnancy 145–6
prejudice, and stereotypes 68
pressures on women *108*
priorities, of young people 92
privatization, of public space 83
product placement 135
production: and consumption 33–4,
    37; consumption as 43; as culturally
    produced 56; of message 25–6
production of consent 24
production, representation and
    consumption: audience reception and
    interpretation 80–2; commodity in
    capitalist culture 72–4; consumption
    70–88; context and overview 55; gender
    and consumption 74–80; gendered

240 Index

representations 67–70; importance of advertising 84–8; production 56–60; representations 60–70; spaces of consumption and power 82–4

profit-making 47

profitability 73; antifeminism vs feminism 180–3; children's television 137; of female stupidity 134–9; of male/female movie leads 121, 125; popular culture for women 124–5; video games 129–31

programmes, governmental/non-governmental 90–1

promiscuity 132

Prügl, E. 94, 165

psychographic content 49

public radio, women's presence 59

public space: advertising 84–5; privatization 83

Pulver, A. 127, 147

punk rock 169–70

Pussy Riot 170

questions of articulation 41

Ratajkowski, E. 110–12

raunch culture 99, 102, 180

reading the image 63–7

reality: and images 64–5; mediated through language 25

reality television 134–6, 138

reception, and interpretation 80–2

Redfern, C. 157, 159–60

Reeve, C. 127–8

regulation, spaces of consumption 82–3

relay 64

representation, and participation 108

representations 60–70; in advertising 85–6; contradictions of 181; gendered 67–70; images and text 177; importance of 1, 21; as interpretation 62; negative 104; as power 23; reading the image 63–7; and sense of self 70; *see also* production, representation and consumption

research: audience participation and observation 80; data analysis 13; disciplinary base 4; findings 103–4; focus of 41, 179; lessons of 181; questions and concerns 16–17; respondents 14, **14–16**; sensitivity of 8; sources 11–18; statistically viable relationships 17–18; survey 13–17; survey questions 185–7; survey responses 80–1, 110, 112, 157, 158–60, *158–9*, 172–3; theoretical framework 5

research strategies 5–6

researcher effects 7–8

resistance 9–10, 34, 81–2, 90, 110

respondents 14; descriptive statistics **14–16**

Return of the King, Lord of the Rings 145

riot grrrl 169–72

Ripley, Ellen, *Alien* 124, 139

Rise of Enlightened Sexism, The (Douglas) 155

Robinow, J. 124

Robinson, H. 37

Rodriguez, M.S. 99–100, 101, 104, 106

role models 138

Rourke, A. 107, 108

Rowley, C. 4, 21, 55, 65, 68, 71, 80

rural women 84

Rush vs Feminism, cartoon **141**

sales, and cultural levels 29–30

Salvation Army 114–15

Sánchez, E.L. 22, 134, 136–7, 138

Sandberg, S. 165

Sarandon, S. 89

Sargent, J. 124, 132–4

Sarkeesian, A. 129–31, 139–40

sassy black women 144

SavvyRed 141

Schlafly, P. 91, 199–200

second-wave feminism, *see* feminism

self-description 95

self-help ideology 102

self-identification 42, 70, 100, 103–4

self-objectification 113

self-production 41

self-representation 96–7

sense-making, regulation of 8

sense of self 70, 179

sensitivity, of research 8

Serenity 146–7

Sex and the City 74, 166

sexiness, as rewarded 138

sexism: commercial viability 110; enlightened 154–6; gaming 129–31; in gaming industry 131; Hollywood 57–8; means of harm 68; in politics 107; prevalence 107; as routine 154; worsening 108–9

sexist content, monitoring 49, 51

Sexist Jerk Who Scores trope 133

sextremism 169–72

sexual abuse scandals 161

sexual freedom 113

sexual harassment 107, 108, 114–15

sexual marketplace 166

sexual objectification 101

sexuality: conflicting attitudes to 115, 132–4; male 151–2

sexualization 2, 70, 109–16

sexualized environments 83, 115–16
Shakespeare, W. 29–30
shame 161
Shapiro, M.J. 7, 9
sharing, of culture 28
Shepherd, L.J. 3
'shock and awe' 9
Silly Me Syndrome (SMS) 136–7
Silverstein, M. 80, 122, 142, 143
Simone, G. 126, 209
Singh, Jyoti 161
Six Feet Under 141–2, 144
Skrzydlewska, J.K. 70, 113–14
Sleepy Hollow 142, 143–4
slums 84
sluttishness 133
Small, C. 168, 169
Smith, C. 56, 58, 77
Smith, K. 77, 147
social democratic politics 94
social media 77, 181, 208; advertising **50**; campaigning 162; charges 48–9; content monitoring 49, 51; gender and use 79; importance of 48–53
social power, and representation 61
social practice, and visual language 25–7
social relations 32–4, 92, 181
Sontag, S. 64–5, 68, 70, 179
sources 11–18
Souter, F. 154–5
spaces of consumption 72, 82–3
spectacle 62
Split Decisions: How and Why to Take a Break from Feminism (Halley) 11–13, 94–6
sports reporting 59
Stacey, J. 92, 99
Star Wars prequels 145–6
state failure 94
stereotype threat 103–6, 159–60
stereotypes 26–7, 68, 110, 180
stigma 161
Storey, J. 6, 27–8, 29, 34, 35, 36, 37, 38, 39, 40–1, 43, 61
stories 10
Straw Feminists 140
Strickland, J. 48–9
Strinati, D. 28, 43, 73
Strong Female Character (SFC) trope 141–4, 174
students, and feminism 13, 156–8, 181
stupidity 134–9
subordination 33–5
success: of feminism 44, 90–6; social media 48
successful women 108–9

Sundance report 58–9
Superman 127–8
survey: findings 103–4; overview 13–17; questions 185–7; responses 80–1, 89, 110, 112, 157, 158–60, *158–9*, 172–3; statistically viable relationships 17–18
surveys, of feminism 17
Sydney Riders, Facebook page 51–3, **52**

tacit antifeminism 141–56; *The Economist* 148–50; enlightened sexism 154–6; female characters – strong to boring 141–4; gender and consumption 151–5; girl power 144–7
tacit feminism 172–4
technology: access to 79; and availability of culture 28; cultural effects 4
teenagers, television 137–8
television: for children and teenagers 137–8; decoding positions 65–7; definition of women 10; DVD sales 135; female-male relations 138–9; gender and use 79; gendered employment 60; global and national 45; growth forecast 48; housewife reality shows 135–6; increased consumption 76; as international 45–6; as leisure activity 21–2; market dominance 46–7; as necessity 76; power of 22; production expenditure 134; programming popularity 76–7; reality television 134–6; research sources 11; viewing figures 30; wedding shows 135–6
texts, as representations 177
textual essentialism 40
textuality 41
Thicke, R. 110–11
third-wave feminism 99, 170–2
Thornton, B. 97–8
threats and abuse 162
tomboys 168–9
Tower Prep 137
trademark applications 9
tropes 178–80; Damsel in Distress 132; Dumb Girl 136–7; feminists 139–40; Final Girl 133; of liberal feminism 164; Men are the Expendable Gender 129; Sexist Jerk Who Scores 133; Strong Female Character (SFC) 141–4; video games 129–31; women in refrigerators 125–9; young women 137–8
Tropes vs. Women in Video Games project 129–31; responses to project 130
Turner, J. 160, 161–2, 180
Twitter 48, 49, 79
Twilight series 168

242 Index

Ukraine is Not a Brothel 170
UN-Habitat 84
Underwood, C. 103
United Nations Convention to Eliminate
   Discrimination Against Women
   (CEDAW) 68, 90
urban women 84
USA: cultural specificity 96; popular culture
   and militarization 23–4

value 73
Veronica Mars 73, 140
video consumption 74–5, 77–8
video games 129–31
violence 180
virtual spaces 83
visual form, vs. textual 61–2
visual language: discomfort with 61–2; and
   global politics 22–4; power of 177; and
   social practice 25–7
visual signage, advertising 26–7

Waisbord, S. 45, 46–7
Walby, S. 90, 92, 93–4, 99, 101, 102
Walker, R.B.J. 39–40
Walking Dead 132–3
Walter, N. 173
Warner Bros. 124
wealth generation, opportunities for 83–4
Weber, C. 23
Weldes, J. 2, 4, 9, 23, 24
What is Feminism? photo **162**
Whedon, Joss 146–7
Whelehan, I. 101, 102, 120, 151, 153, 180
WikiLeaks 66
women: barriers to participation 58–9;
   as cinema audience 123; consumption

of popular culture 74–80; cultural
definition 10; in independent cinema 58;
independent sexuality 132–4; from
non-English speaking backgrounds 109;
objectification 112; perceptions 181;
portrayed as stupid 134–9; presence in
cinema 58; pressures on *108*; on public
radio 59; reality television 134–6; in
refrigerators 125–9, 209; representation
and participation 108; representations
in cinema 56; representations of 1;
successful 108–9; urban vs. rural 84;
video games audience/players 122–3
'Women for Gillard' campaign 106
women's sexuality, conflicting attitudes
   to 115
Wong, D. 133, 140–1
Woods, J. 108, 109
World Bank 96
World Economic Forum (WEF) 93
writing styles, *The Economist* 150

young people: priorities 92; television
   137–8
young women: activism 158; characteristics
   106; feminist perspective 100; overt
   feminism 156–62; perspectives on
   feminism 103–4, 106; portrayal 137–8;
   postfeminism 102; self-identification
   103–4; tropes 137–8
Yousafzai, Malala 161

Zalewski, M. 4
Zehfuss, M. 65
Zero Dark Thirty 124–5
Zoo Weekly **182**
Zuckerberg, M. 49